2020 SUPPLEMENT TO
AMERICAN CRIMINAL PROCEDURE
CASES AND COMMENTARY

Eleventh Edition

■   ■   ■

Stephen A. Saltzburg
Wallace and Beverley Woodbury University Professor,
The George Washington University School of Law

Daniel J. Capra
Philip D. Reed Professor of Law,
Fordham University School of Law

David C. Gray
Jacob A France Professor of Law,
University of Maryland, Carey School of Law

AMERICAN CASEBOOK SI

D1318698

WEST ACADEMIC PUBLISHING

American Casebook Series is a trademark registered in the U.S. Patent and Trademark Office.

© 2018–2019 LEG, Inc. d/b/a West Academic
© 2020 LEG, Inc. d/b/a West Academic
    444 Cedar Street, Suite 700
    St. Paul, MN 55101
    1-877-888-1330

West, West Academic Publishing, and West Academic are trademarks of West Publishing Corporation, used under license.

Printed in the United States of America

ISBN: 978-1-68467-893-8

TABLE OF CONTENTS

TABLE OF CASES

The principal cases are in bold type.

TABLE OF AUTHORITIES

2020 SUPPLEMENT TO

AMERICAN CRIMINAL PROCEDURE

CASES AND COMMENTARY

Eleventh Edition

CHAPTER 1

BASIC PRINCIPLES

■ ■ ■

II. TWO SPECIAL ASPECTS OF CONSTITUTIONAL LAW: THE INCORPORATION DOCTRINE AND RETROACTIVE APPLICATION OF CONSTITUTIONAL DECISIONS

A. INCORPORATION

Page 15. Add the following after the Note on *McDonald*:

Incorporation of the Eighth Amendment Right to Be Free from Excessive Fines: Timbs v. Indiana

In the following case, the Court holds that the Eighth Amendment right to be free from excessive fines is an incorporated protection applicable to the States under the Fourteenth Amendment's Due Process Clause. Note that Justice Thomas, in his concurrence, asserts a different source for incorporation: the Privileges and Immunities Clause.

TIMBS V. INDIANA
Supreme Court of the United States, 2019.
139 S.Ct. 682.

JUSTICE GINSBURG delivered the opinion of the Court.

Tyson Timbs pleaded guilty in Indiana state court to dealing in a controlled substance and conspiracy to commit theft. The trial court sentenced him to one year of home detention and five years of probation * * * . At the time of Timbs's arrest, the police seized his vehicle, a Land Rover SUV Timbs had purchased for about $42,000. Timbs paid for the vehicle with money he received from an insurance policy when his father died.

The State engaged a private law firm to bring a civil suit for forfeiture of Timbs's Land Rover, charging that the vehicle had been used to transport heroin. After Timbs's guilty plea in the criminal case, the trial court held a hearing on the forfeiture demand. Although finding that Timbs's vehicle had been used to facilitate violation of a criminal statute, the court denied the requested forfeiture, observing that Timbs had recently purchased the vehicle for $42,000, more than four times the maximum $10,000 monetary fine assessable against him for his drug conviction. Forfeiture of the Land Rover, the court determined, would be grossly disproportionate to the gravity of Timbs's offense, hence unconstitutional under the Eighth Amendment's Excessive Fines Clause. The Court of Appeals of Indiana affirmed that determination, but the Indiana Supreme Court reversed. The Indiana Supreme Court did not decide whether the forfeiture would be excessive. Instead, it held that the Excessive Fines Clause constrains only federal action and is inapplicable to state impositions.

The question presented: Is the Eighth Amendment's Excessive Fines Clause an "incorporated" protection applicable to the States under the Fourteenth Amendment's Due Process Clause? Like the Eighth Amendment's proscriptions of "cruel and unusual punishment" and "[e]xcessive bail," the protection against excessive fines guards against abuses of government's punitive or criminal-law-enforcement authority. This safeguard, we hold, is "fundamental to our scheme of ordered liberty," with "dee[p] root[s] in [our] history and tradition." *McDonald v. Chicago*, 561 U. S. 742, 767 (2010) (internal quotation marks omitted; emphasis deleted). The Excessive Fines Clause is therefore incorporated by the Due Process Clause of the Fourteenth Amendment.

I

A

When ratified in 1791, the Bill of Rights applied only to the Federal Government. Barron ex rel. Tiernan v. Mayor of Baltimore, 32 U.S. 243 (1833). "The constitutional Amendments adopted in the aftermath of the Civil War," however, "fundamentally altered our country's federal system." McDonald, 561 U. S., at 754. With only "a handful" of exceptions, this Court has held that the Fourteenth Amendment's Due Process Clause incorporates the protections contained in the Bill of Rights, rendering them applicable to the States. A Bill of Rights protection is incorporated, we have explained, if it is "fundamental to our scheme of ordered liberty," or "deeply rooted in this Nation's history and tradition."

Incorporated Bill of Rights guarantees are "enforced against the States under the Fourteenth Amendment according to the same standards that protect those personal rights against federal encroachment." Thus, if a Bill of Rights protection is incorporated, there is no daylight between the federal and state conduct it prohibits or requires.[a]

---

[a] The sole exception is our holding that the Sixth Amendment requires jury unanimity in federal, but not state, criminal proceedings. *Apodaca v. Oregon*, 406 U. S. 404 (1972). As we have explained, that "exception to th[e] general rule . . . was the result of an unusual division among the Justices," and it "does not undermine the well-established rule that incorporated Bill of Rights protections apply identically to the States and the Federal Government." *McDonald*, 561 U. S., at 766, n. 14. [Author Note: The Court overruled *Apodaca* in *Ramos v. Louisiana*, 140 S.Ct. 139

B

Under the Eighth Amendment, "[e]xcessive bail shall not be required, nor excessive fines imposed, nor cruel and unusual punishments inflicted." Taken together, these Clauses place "parallel limitations" on "the power of those entrusted with the criminal-law function of government." *Browning-Ferris Industries of Vt., Inc. v. Kelco Disposal, Inc.*, 492 U. S. 257, 263 (1989) (quoting *Ingraham v. Wright*, 430 U. S. 651, 664 (1977)). Directly at issue here is the phrase "nor excessive fines imposed," which "limits the government's power to extract payments, whether in cash or in kind, 'as punishment for some offense.'" *United States v. Bajakajian*, 524 U. S. 321 (1998) (quoting *Austin v. United States*, 509 U. S. 602, 609–610 (1993)). The Fourteenth Amendment, we hold, incorporates this protection.

The Excessive Fines Clause traces its venerable lineage back to at least 1215, when Magna Carta guaranteed that "[a] Free-man shall not be amerced for a small fault, but after the manner of the fault; and for a great fault after the greatness thereof, saving to him his contenement . . . ." § 20, 9 Hen. III, ch. 14, in 1 Eng. Stat. at Large 5 (1225). As relevant here, Magna Carta required that economic sanctions "be proportioned to the wrong" and "not be so large as to deprive [an offender] of his livelihood." *Browning-Ferris*, 492 U. S., at 271. * * *

Despite Magna Carta, imposition of excessive fines persisted. The 17th century Stuart kings, in particular, were criticized for using large fines to raise revenue, harass their political foes, and indefinitely detain those unable to pay. When James II was overthrown in the Glorious Revolution, the attendant English Bill of Rights reaffirmed Magna Carta's guarantee by providing that "excessive Bail ought not to be required, nor excessive Fines imposed; nor cruel and unusual Punishments inflicted." 1 Wm. & Mary, ch. 2, § 10, in 3 Eng. Stat. at Large 441 (1689).

Across the Atlantic, this familiar language was adopted almost verbatim, first in the Virginia Declaration of Rights, then in the Eighth Amendment, which states: "Excessive bail shall not be required, nor excessive fines imposed, nor cruel and unusual punishments inflicted."

Adoption of the Excessive Fines Clause was in tune not only with English law; the Clause resonated as well with similar colonial-era provisions. See, *e.g.*, Pa. Frame of Govt., Laws Agreed Upon in England, Art. XVIII (1682), in 5 Federal and State Constitutions 3061 (F. Thorpe ed. 1909) ("[A]ll fines shall be moderate, and saving men's contenements, merchandize, or wainage."). In 1787, the constitutions of eight States— accounting for 70% of the U. S. population—forbade excessive fines.

(2020), holding that, the Sixth Amendment unanimity requirement applies in both state and federal proceedings. *Ramos* is excerpted in Chapter 10 of this Supplement].

Calabresi, Agudo, & Dore, State Bills of Rights in 1787 and 1791, 85 S. Cal. L. Rev. 1451, 1517 (2012).

An even broader consensus obtained in 1868 upon ratification of the Fourteenth Amendment. By then, the constitutions of 35 of the 37 States—accounting for over 90% of the U. S. population—expressly prohibited excessive fines. Calabresi & Agudo, Individual Rights Under State Constitutions When the Fourteenth Amendment Was Ratified in 1868, 87 Texas L. Rev. 7, 82 (2008).

Notwithstanding the States' apparent agreement that the right guaranteed by the Excessive Fines Clause was fundamental, abuses continued. Following the Civil War, Southern States enacted Black Codes to subjugate newly freed slaves and maintain the prewar racial hierarchy. Among these laws' provisions were draconian fines for violating broad proscriptions on "vagrancy" and other dubious offenses. When newly freed slaves were unable to pay imposed fines, States often demanded involuntary labor instead. Congressional debates over the Civil Rights Act of 1866, the joint resolution that became the Fourteenth Amendment, and similar measures repeatedly mentioned the use of fines to coerce involuntary labor. See, *e.g.*, Cong. Globe, 39th Cong., 1st Sess., 443 (1866); *id.*, at 1123–1124.

Today, acknowledgment of the right's fundamental nature remains widespread. As Indiana itself reports, all 50 States have a constitutional provision prohibiting the imposition of excessive fines either directly or by requiring proportionality. * * *

For good reason, the protection against excessive fines has been a constant shield throughout Anglo-American history: Exorbitant tolls undermine other constitutional liberties. Excessive fines can be used, for example, to retaliate against or chill the speech of political enemies, as the Stuarts' critics learned several centuries ago. Even absent a political motive, fines may be employed "in a measure out of accord with the penal goals of retribution and deterrence," for "fines are a source of revenue," while other forms of punishment "cost a State money." *Harmelin* v. *Michigan*, 501 U.S. 957, 979 (1991) (opinion of Scalia, J.) ("it makes sense to scrutinize governmental action more closely when the State stands to benefit"). This concern is scarcely hypothetical. See Brief for American Civil Liberties Union et al. as *Amici Curiae* 7 ("Perhaps because they are politically easier to impose than generally applicable taxes, state and local governments nationwide increasingly depend heavily on fines and fees as a source of general revenue.").

In short, the historical and logical case for concluding that the Fourteenth Amendment incorporates the Excessive Fines Clause is overwhelming. Protection against excessive punitive economic sanctions secured by the Clause is, to repeat, both "fundamental to our scheme of ordered liberty" and "deeply rooted in this Nation's history and tradition."

II

The State of Indiana does not meaningfully challenge the case for incorporating the Excessive Fines Clause as a general matter. Instead, the State argues that the Clause does not apply to its use of civil *in rem* forfeitures because, the State says, the Clause's specific application to such forfeitures is neither fundamental nor deeply rooted.

In *Austin v. United States*, 509 U. S. 602 (1993), however, this Court held that civil *in rem* forfeitures fall within the Clause's protection when they are at least partially punitive. *Austin* arose in the federal context. But when a Bill of Rights protection is incorporated, the protection applies identically to both the Federal Government and the States. Accordingly, to prevail, Indiana must persuade us either to overrule our decision in *Austin* or to hold that, in light of *Austin*, the Excessive Fines Clause is not incorporated because the Clause's application to civil *in rem* forfeitures is neither fundamental nor deeply rooted. The first argument is not properly before us, and the second misapprehends the nature of our incorporation inquiry.

A

In the Indiana Supreme Court, the State argued that forfeiture of Timbs's SUV would not be excessive. It never argued, however, that civil *in rem* forfeitures were categorically beyond the reach of the Excessive Fines Clause. * * * We thus decline the State's invitation to reconsider our unanimous judgment in *Austin* that civil *in rem* forfeitures are fines for purposes of the Eighth Amendment when they are at least partially punitive.

B

As a fallback, Indiana argues that the Excessive Fines Clause cannot be incorporated if it applies to civil *in rem* forfeitures. We disagree. In considering whether the Fourteenth Amendment incorporates a protection contained in the Bill of Rights, we ask whether the right guaranteed—not each and every particular application of that right—is fundamental or deeply rooted. * * * See * * * *e.g.*, *Riley v. California*, 573 U. S. 373 (2014) (holding, without separately considering incorporation, that States' warrantless search of digital information stored on cell phones ordinarily violates the Fourth Amendment). Similarly here, regardless of whether application of the Excessive Fines *Clause* to civil *in rem* forfeitures is itself fundamental or deeply rooted, our conclusion that the Clause is incorporated remains unchanged.

* * *

For the reasons stated, the judgment of the Indiana Supreme Court is vacated, and the case is remanded for further proceedings not inconsistent with this opinion.

JUSTICE GORSUCH, concurring.

The majority faithfully applies our precedent and, based on a wealth of historical evidence, concludes that the Fourteenth Amendment incorporates the Eighth Amendment's Excessive Fines Clause against the States. I agree with that conclusion. As an original matter, I acknowledge, the appropriate vehicle for incorporation may well be the Fourteenth Amendment's Privileges or Immunities Clause, rather than, as this Court has long assumed, the Due Process Clause. But nothing in this case turns on that question, and, regardless of the precise vehicle, there can be no serious doubt that the Fourteenth Amendment requires the States to respect the freedom from excessive fines enshrined in the Eighth Amendment.

JUSTICE THOMAS, concurring in the judgment.

I agree with the Court that the Fourteenth Amendment makes the Eighth Amendment's prohibition on excessive fines fully applicable to the States. But I cannot agree with the route the Court takes to reach this conclusion. Instead of reading the Fourteenth Amendment's Due Process Clause to encompass a substantive right that has nothing to do with "process," I would hold that the right to be free from excessive fines is one of the "privileges or immunities of citizens of the United States" protected by the Fourteenth Amendment.

I

The Fourteenth Amendment provides that "[n]o State shall make or enforce any law which shall abridge the privileges or immunities of citizens of the United States." "On its face, this appears to grant . . . United States citizens a certain collection of rights—i.e., privileges or immunities— attributable to that status." *McDonald v. Chicago*, 561 U. S. 742 (2010) (THOMAS, J., concurring in part and concurring in judgment). But as I have previously explained, this Court "marginaliz[ed]" the Privileges or Immunities Clause in the late 19th century by defining the collection of rights covered by the Clause "quite narrowly." *Id.* Litigants seeking federal protection of substantive rights against the States thus needed "an alternative fount of such rights," and this Court "found one in a most curious place," *id.*, at 809—the Fourteenth Amendment's Due Process Clause, which prohibits "any State" from "depriv[ing] any person of life, liberty, or property, without due process of law."

Because this Clause speaks only to "process," the Court has "long struggled to define" what substantive rights it protects. *McDonald, supra*, at 810, (opinion of THOMAS, J.). The Court ordinarily says, as it does today, that the Clause protects rights that are "fundamental." Sometimes that means rights that are "deeply rooted in this Nation's history and tradition." Other times, when that formulation proves too restrictive, the Court defines the universe of "fundamental" rights so broadly as to border on meaningless. Because the oxymoronic "substantive" "due process" doctrine has no basis in the Constitution, it is unsurprising that the Court has been unable to adhere to any "guiding principle to distinguish 'fundamental' rights that warrant protection from nonfundamental rights that do not." *McDonald, supra*, at 811 (opinion of THOMAS, J.). * * *

The present case illustrates the incongruity of the Court's due process approach to incorporating fundamental rights against the States. Petitioner argues that the forfeiture of his vehicle is an excessive punishment. He does not argue that the Indiana courts failed to "proceed according to the law of the land" * * * or that the State failed to provide "some baseline procedures." His claim has nothing to do with any "process" "due" him. I therefore decline to apply the "legal fiction" of substantive due process.

II

When the Fourteenth Amendment was ratified, "the terms 'privileges' and 'immunities' had an established meaning as synonyms for 'rights.'" *Id.*, at 813. Those "rights" were the "inalienable rights" of citizens that had been "long recognized," and "the ratifying public understood the Privileges or Immunities Clause to protect constitutionally enumerated rights" against interference by the States. Many of these rights had been adopted from English law into colonial charters, then state constitutions and bills of rights, and finally the Constitution. "Consistent with their English heritage, the founding generation generally did not consider many of the rights identified in [the Bill of Rights] as new entitlements, but as inalienable rights of all men, given legal effect by their codification in the Constitution's text." *Id.*, at 818.

The question here is whether the Eighth Amendment's prohibition on excessive fines was considered such a right. The historical record overwhelmingly demonstrates that it was.

A

[Justice Thomas sets forth the English history and concludes: "In sum, at the time of the founding, the prohibition on excessive fines was a longstanding right of Englishmen."]

B

As English subjects, the colonists considered themselves to be vested with the same fundamental rights as other Englishmen, including the prohibition on excessive fines. * * *

When the States were considering whether to ratify the Constitution, advocates for a separate bill of rights emphasized the need for an explicit prohibition on excessive fines mirroring the English prohibition. In colonial times, fines were "the drudge-horse of criminal justice," "probably the most common form of punishment." L. Friedman, Crime and Punishment in American History 38 (1993). To some, this fact made a constitutional prohibition on excessive fines all the more important. * * *

* * *

For all the debate about whether an explicit prohibition on excessive fines was necessary in the Federal Constitution, all agreed that the prohibition on excessive fines was a well-established and fundamental right of citizenship. When the Excessive Fines Clause was eventually considered by Congress, it received hardly any discussion before "it was agreed to by a considerable majority." 1 Annals of Cong. 754 (1789). And when the Bill of Rights was ratified, most of the States had a prohibition on excessive fines in their constitutions.

[Justice Thomas relies on early American commentary confirming "the widespread agreement about the fundamental nature of the prohibition on excessive fines."]

C

The prohibition on excessive fines remained fundamental at the time of the Fourteenth Amendment. In 1868, 35 of 37 state constitutions expressly prohibited excessive fines. Nonetheless, as the Court notes, abuses of fines continued, especially through the Black Codes adopted in several States. The "centerpiece" of the Codes was their "attempt to stabilize the black work force and limit its economic options apart from plantation labor." E. Foner, Reconstruction: America's Unfinished Revolution 1863–1877, p. 199 (1988). Under the Codes, "the state would enforce labor agreements and plantation discipline, punish those who refused to contract, and prevent whites from competing among themselves for black workers." *Ibid.* The Codes also included " 'antienticement' measures punishing anyone offering higher wages to an employee already under contract." *Id.*, at 200.

The 39th Congress focused on these abuses during its debates over the Fourteenth Amendment, the Civil Rights Act of 1866, and the Freedmen's Bureau Act. During those well-publicized debates, Members of Congress consistently highlighted and lamented the "severe penalties" inflicted by the Black Codes and similar measures, suggesting that the prohibition on excessive fines was understood to be a basic right of citizenship.

* * *

Similar examples abound. One congressman noted that Alabama's "aristocratic and anti-republican laws, almost reenacting slavery, among other harsh inflictions impose . . . a fine of fifty dollars and six months' imprisonment on any servant or laborer (white or black) who loiters away his time or is stubborn or refractory." *Id.*, at 1621 (Rep. Myers). He also noted that Florida punished vagrants with "a fine not exceeding $500 and imprison[ment] for a term not exceeding twelve months, or by being sold for a term not exceeding twelve months, at the discretion of the court." *Ibid.* At the time, such fines would have been ruinous for laborers. Cf. *id.*, at 443 (Sen. Howe) ("A thousand dollars! That sells a negro for his life").

These and other examples of excessive fines from the historical record informed the Nation's consideration of the Fourteenth Amendment. * * * The attention given to abusive fines at the time of the Fourteenth Amendment, along with the ubiquity of state excessive-fines provisions, demonstrates that the public continued to understand the prohibition on excessive fines to be a fundamental right of American citizenship.

* * *

The right against excessive fines traces its lineage back in English law nearly a millennium, and from the founding of our country, it has been consistently recognized as a core right worthy of constitutional protection. As a constitutionally enumerated right understood to be a privilege of American citizenship, the Eighth Amendment's prohibition on excessive fines applies in full to the States.

CHAPTER 2

SEARCHES AND SEIZURES OF PERSONS AND THINGS

■ ■ ■

I. AN INTRODUCTION TO THE FOURTH AMENDMENT

B. THE BASICS OF THE FOURTH AMENDMENT

"The People" as a Limiting Term:
United States v. Verdugo-Urquidez

Page 36. Add at the end of the section on *Verdugo-Urquidez*:

In *Hernandez v. Mesa*, 140 S.Ct. 735 (2020), the Court maintained its reluctance to give extraterritorial effect to the Fourth Amendment. Mesa, a border patrol agent, shot and killed Sergio Adrián Hernández Güereca, a 15-year-old a Mexican-national. At the time of the shooting, Mesa was standing in the United States and Hernàndez was across the border in Mexico. Hernández parents filed a civil action under *Bivens v. Six Unknown Fed. Narcotics Agents*, 403 U.S. 388 (1971), alleging violations of their son's Fourth and Fifth Amendment rights. In an opinion written by Justice Alito, the Court declined to expand *Bivens* to encompass claims based on cross-border shootings. Although the Court's holding in *Hernandez* was limited to *Bivens* actions, its opinion was based in part on respect for executive authority at the border—where interests in national security and foreign relations predominate—suggesting that the Court would be equally reluctant to apply the Fourth Amendment in other litigation contexts involving cross-border actions.

II. THRESHOLD REQUIREMENTS FOR FOURTH AMENDMENT PROTECTIONS: WHAT IS A "SEARCH?" WHAT IS A "SEIZURE?"

B. THE RETURN OF THE TRESPASS ANALYSIS

Pervasive, Prolonged Surveillance After Jones

Page 55. This section replaces the section with the same title:

The concurring opinions in *Jones* constitute what some analysts described as a "shadow majority" of five justices who appeared willing to expand the scope of Fourth Amendment protections against modern tracking technologies. Although she did not join Justice Alito's concurring opinion in *Jones*, Justice Sotomayor specifically agreed with his proposed holding "that, at the very least, 'longer term GPS monitoring in investigations of most offenses impinges on expectations of privacy.' "

In addition to the duration of surveillance, Justice Sotomayor identified in her concurring opinion some features of GPS tracking technologies that might raise Fourth Amendment concerns, even in "cases involving . . . short-term monitoring." Among these were:

1. the capacity to generate "a precise, comprehensive record of a person's public movements";

2. that comprehensive records of a person's movements may "reflect a wealth of detail about . . . familial, political, professional, religious, and sexual associations;"

3. that location records can be "store[d] and efficiently mine[d] for information years into the future";

4. that the technology is "cheap in comparison to conventional surveillance techniques";

5. that the technology "by design, proceeds surreptitiously"; and

6. that deployment and use of the technology "evades the ordinary checks that constrain abusive law enforcement practices: 'limited police resources and community hostility.' "

In Justice Sotomayor's view, these features of GPS tracking technology, when deployed by law enforcement, raise the specter of pervasive surveillance. She therefore worried about granting "unfettered discretion . . . to the Executive, in the absence of any oversight from a coordinate branch, a tool so amenable to misuse, especially in light of the Fourth Amendment's goal to curb arbitrary exercises of police power [and to] prevent 'a too permeating police surveillance,' " a result that "may 'alter the relationship between citizen and government in a way that is inimical to democratic society.' "

Two years after *Jones*, the Court expressed broad sympathy for Justice Sotomayor's concern that new technologies could be exploited to intrude upon reasonable expectations of privacy. In *Riley v. California*, 573 U.S. 373 (2014), which is excerpted on page 343 of the main text, the Court highlighted the unique features of cellular phones, the quantity and nature of the data they store, and what that data can reveal about private associations as grounds for excluding cellular phones from the search incident to arrest doctrine.

The majority opinion in *Riley* was written by Chief Justice Roberts, who was joined by all the remaining members of the Court save Justice Alito, who concurred in a separate opinion. Given that near unanimity, it seemed that a stable majority had emerged in support of the proposition that technologies capable of facilitating what Professor Christopher Slobogin has dubbed "panvasive" surveillance should be subject to Fourth Amendment regulation. Christopher Slobogin, *Panvasive Surveillance, Political Process Theory and the Nondelegation Doctrine*, 102 Geo. L. Rev. 1721 (2014). Because *Jones* was decided on narrow grounds, however, questions remained. In particular, law enforcement, courts, and commentators were left to wonder whether "enlisting factory- or owner-installed vehicle tracking devices or GPS-enabled smart-phones" to conduct surveillance impinges upon reasonable expectations of privacy. The Court provided some clarity in *Carpenter v. United States*.

CARPENTER V. UNITED STATES
Supreme Court of the United States, 2018.
138 S.Ct. 2206.

CHIEF JUSTICE ROBERTS delivered the opinion of the Court.

This case presents the question whether the Government conducts a search under the Fourth Amendment when it accesses historical cell phone records that provide a comprehensive chronicle of the user's past movements.

I

A

There are 396 million cell phone service accounts in the United States—for a Nation of 326 million people. Cell phones perform their wide and growing variety of functions by connecting to a set of radio antennas called "cell sites." Although cell sites are usually mounted on a tower, they can also be found on light posts, flagpoles, church steeples, or the sides of buildings. Cell sites have several directional antennas that divide the covered area into sectors.

Cell phones continuously scan their environment looking for the best signal, which generally comes from the closest cell site. Most modern devices, such as smartphones, tap into the wireless network several times a minute whenever their signal is on, even if the owner is not using one of the phone's features. Each time the phone connects to a cell site, it generates a time-stamped record known as cell-site location information (CSLI). The precision of this information depends on the size of the geographic area covered by the cell site. The greater the concentration of cell sites, the smaller the coverage area. As data usage from cell phones has increased, wireless carriers have installed more cell sites to handle the traffic. That has led to increasingly compact coverage areas, especially in urban areas.

Wireless carriers collect and store CSLI for their own business purposes, including finding weak spots in their network and applying "roaming" charges when another carrier routes data through their cell sites. In addition, wireless carriers often sell aggregated location records to data brokers, without individual identifying information of the sort at issue here. While carriers have long retained CSLI for the start and end of incoming calls, in recent years phone companies have also collected location information from the transmission of text messages and routine data connections. Accordingly, modern cell phones generate increasingly vast amounts of increasingly precise CSLI.

B

In 2011, police officers arrested four men suspected of robbing a series of Radio Shack and (ironically enough) T-Mobile stores in Detroit. One of the men confessed that, over the previous four months, the group (along with a rotating cast of getaway drivers and lookouts) had robbed nine different stores in Michigan and Ohio. The suspect identified 15 accomplices who had participated in the heists and gave the FBI some of their cell phone numbers; the FBI then reviewed his call records to identify additional numbers that he had called around the time of the robberies.

Based on that information, the prosecutors applied for court orders under the Stored Communications Act to obtain cell phone records for petitioner Timothy Carpenter and several other suspects. That statute, as amended in 1994, permits the Government to compel the disclosure of certain telecommunications records when it "offers specific and articulable facts showing that there are reasonable grounds to believe" that the records sought "are relevant and material to an ongoing criminal investigation." 18 U. S. C. § 2703(d). Federal Magistrate Judges issued two orders directing Carpenter's wireless carriers—MetroPCS and Sprint—to disclose "cellsite sector [information] for [Carpenter's] telephone[ ] at call origination and at call termination for incoming and outgoing calls" during the four-month period when the string of robberies occurred. The first order sought 152 days of cell-site records from MetroPCS, which produced records spanning 127 days. The second order requested seven days of CSLI from Sprint, which produced two days of records covering the period when Carpenter's phone was "roaming" in northeastern Ohio. Altogether the Government obtained 12,898 location points cataloging Carpenter's movements—an average of 101 data points per day.

Carpenter was charged with six counts of robbery and an additional six counts of carrying a firearm during a federal crime of violence. See 18 U. S. C. §§ 924(c), 1951(a). Prior to trial, Carpenter moved to suppress the cell-site data provided by the wireless carriers. He argued that the Government's seizure of the records violated the Fourth Amendment because they had been obtained without a warrant supported by probable cause. The District Court denied the motion.

At trial, seven of Carpenter's confederates pegged him as the leader of the operation. In addition, FBI agent Christopher Hess offered expert testimony about the cell-site data. Hess explained that each time a cell phone taps into the wireless network, the carrier logs a time-stamped record of the cell site and particular sector that were used. With this information, Hess produced maps that placed Carpenter's phone near four of the charged robberies. In the Government's view, the location records clinched the case: They confirmed that Carpenter was "right where the . . . robbery was at the exact time of the robbery." Carpenter was convicted on all but one of the firearm counts and sentenced to more than 100 years in prison.

The Court of Appeals for the Sixth Circuit affirmed. The court held that Carpenter lacked a reasonable expectation of privacy in the location information collected by the FBI because he had shared that information with his wireless carriers. Given that cell phone users voluntarily convey cell-site data to their carriers as "a means of establishing communication," the court concluded that the resulting business records are not entitled to Fourth Amendment protection. (quoting Smith v. Maryland, 442 U. S. 735, 741 (1979)).

We granted certiorari.

II

A

The Fourth Amendment protects "[t]he right of the people to be secure in their persons, houses, papers, and effects, against unreasonable searches and seizures." The "basic purpose of this Amendment," our cases have recognized, "is to safeguard the privacy and security of individuals against arbitrary invasions by governmental officials." The Founding generation crafted the Fourth Amendment as a "response to the reviled 'general warrants' and 'writs of assistance' of the colonial era, which allowed British officers to rummage through homes in an unrestrained search for evidence of criminal activity." In fact, as John Adams recalled, the patriot James Otis's 1761 speech condemning writs of assistance was "the first act of opposition to the arbitrary claims of Great Britain" and helped spark the Revolution itself.

For much of our history, Fourth Amendment search doctrine was "tied to common-law trespass" and focused on whether the Government "obtains information by physically intruding on a constitutionally protected area." More recently, the Court has recognized that "property rights are not the sole measure of Fourth Amendment violations." In *Katz v. United States*, we established that "the Fourth Amendment protects people, not places," and expanded our conception of the Amendment to protect certain expectations of privacy as well. When an individual "seeks to preserve something as private," and his expectation of privacy is "one that society is prepared to recognize as reasonable," we have held that official intrusion into that private sphere generally qualifies as a search and requires a warrant supported by probable cause.

Although no single rubric definitively resolves which expectations of privacy are entitled to protection,[a] the analysis is informed by historical understandings "of what was deemed an unreasonable search and seizure when [the Fourth Amendment] was adopted." Carroll v. United States, 267 U. S. 132, 149 (1925). On this score, our cases have recognized some basic guideposts. First, that the Amendment seeks to secure "the privacies of life" against "arbitrary power." Boyd v. United States, 116 U. S. 616, 630 (1886). Second, and relatedly, that a central aim of the Framers was "to place obstacles in the way of a too permeating police surveillance." United States v. Di Re, 332 U. S. 581, 595 (1948).

We have kept this attention to Founding-era understandings in mind when applying the Fourth Amendment to innovations in surveillance tools. As technology has enhanced the Government's capacity to encroach upon areas normally guarded from inquisitive eyes, this Court has sought to "assure[ ] preservation of that degree of privacy against government that existed when the Fourth Amendment was adopted." Kyllo v. United States, 533 U. S. 27, 34 (2001). For that reason, we rejected in *Kyllo* a "mechanical interpretation" of the Fourth Amendment and held that use of a thermal

---

[a]   JUSTICE KENNEDY believes that there is such a rubric—the "property-based concepts" that *Katz* purported to move beyond. But while property rights are often informative, our cases by no means suggest that such an interest is "fundamental" or "dispositive" in determining which expectations of privacy are legitimate. JUSTICE THOMAS (and to a large extent JUSTICE GORSUCH) would have us abandon *Katz* and return to an exclusively property-based approach. *Katz* of course "discredited" the "premise that property interests control," 389 U. S., at 353, and we have repeatedly emphasized that privacy interests do not rise or fall with property rights, see, *e.g., United States* v. *Jones*, 565 U. S. 400, 411 (2012) (refusing to "make trespass the exclusive test"); *Kyllo* v. *United States*, 533 U. S. 27, 32 (2001) ("We have since decoupled violation of a person's Fourth Amendment rights from trespassory violation of his property."). Neither party has asked the Court to reconsider *Katz* in this case.

imager to detect heat radiating from the side of the defendant's home was a search. Because any other conclusion would leave homeowners "at the mercy of advancing technology," we determined that the Government—absent a warrant—could not capitalize on such new sense-enhancing technology to explore what was happening within the home.

Likewise in *Riley*, the Court recognized the "immense storage capacity" of modern cell phones in holding that police officers must generally obtain a warrant before searching the contents of a phone. We explained that while the general rule allowing warrantless searches incident to arrest "strikes the appropriate balance in the context of physical objects, neither of its rationales has much force with respect to" the vast store of sensitive information on a cell phone. * * *

III

The question we confront today is how to apply the Fourth Amendment to a new phenomenon: the ability to chronicle a person's past movements through the record of his cell phone signals. Such tracking partakes of many of the qualities of the GPS monitoring we considered in *Jones*. Much like GPS tracking of a vehicle, cell phone location information is detailed, encyclopedic, and effortlessly compiled. * * *

A

A person does not surrender all Fourth Amendment protection by venturing into the public sphere. To the contrary, "what [one] seeks to preserve as private, even in an area accessible to the public, may be constitutionally protected." *Katz*, 389 U. S., at 351–352. A majority of this Court has already recognized that individuals have a reasonable expectation of privacy in the whole of their physical movements. *Jones*, 565 U. S., at 430 (ALITO, J., concurring in judgment); *id.*, at 415 (SOTOMAYOR, J., concurring). Prior to the digital age, law enforcement might have pursued a suspect for a brief stretch, but doing so "for any extended period of time was difficult and costly and therefore rarely undertaken." *Id.*, at 429 (opinion of ALITO, J.). For that reason, "society's expectation has been that law enforcement agents and others would not—and indeed, in the main, simply could not—secretly monitor and catalogue every single movement of an individual's car for a very long period."

Allowing government access to cell-site records contravenes that expectation. Although such records are generated for commercial purposes, that distinction does not negate Carpenter's anticipation of privacy in his physical location. Mapping a cell phone's location over the course of 127 days provides an all-encompassing record of the holder's whereabouts. As with GPS information, the time-stamped data provides an intimate window into a person's life, revealing not only his particular movements, but through them his "familial, political, professional, religious, and sexual associations." *Id.*, at 415 (opinion of SOTOMAYOR, J.). These location records "hold for many Americans the 'privacies of life.' " *Riley*, 573 U. S., at ___ (slip op., at 28). And like GPS monitoring, cell phone tracking is remarkably easy, cheap, and efficient compared to traditional investigative tools. With just the click of a button, the Government can access each carrier's deep repository of historical location information at practically no expense.

In fact, historical cell-site records present even greater privacy concerns than the GPS monitoring of a vehicle we considered in *Jones*. Unlike the bugged container in *Knotts* or the car in *Jones*, a cell phone— almost a "feature of human anatomy," *Riley*, 573 U. S., at ___ (slip op., at 9)—tracks nearly exactly the movements of its owner. While individuals regularly leave their vehicles, they compulsively carry cell phones with them all the time. A cell phone faithfully follows its owner beyond public thoroughfares and into private residences, doctor's offices, political headquarters, and other potentially revealing locales. See *id.*, at ___ (slip op., at 19) (noting that "nearly three-quarters of smartphone users report being within five feet of their phones most of the time, with 12% admitting that they even use their phones in the shower"); contrast Cardwell v. Lewis, 417 U. S. 583, 590 (1974) (plurality opinion) ("A car has little capacity for escaping public scrutiny."). Accordingly, when the Government tracks the location of a cell phone it achieves near perfect surveillance, as if it had attached an ankle monitor to the phone's user.

Moreover, the retrospective quality of the data here gives police access to a category of information otherwise unknowable. In the past, attempts to reconstruct a person's movements were limited by a dearth of records and the frailties of recollection. With access to CSLI, the Government can now travel back in time to retrace a person's whereabouts, subject only to the retention polices of the wireless carriers, which currently maintain records for up to five years. Critically, because location information is continually logged for all of the 400 million devices in the United States— not just those belonging to persons who might happen to come under investigation—this newfound tracking capacity runs against everyone. Unlike with the GPS device in *Jones*, police need not even know in advance whether they want to follow a particular individual, or when.

Whoever the suspect turns out to be, he has effectively been tailed every moment of every day for five years, and the police may—in the Government's view—call upon the results of that surveillance without regard to the constraints of the Fourth Amendment. Only the few without cell phones could escape this tireless and absolute surveillance.

The Government and JUSTICE KENNEDY contend, however, that the collection of CSLI should be permitted because the data is less precise than GPS information. Not to worry, they maintain, because the location records did "not on their own suffice to place [Carpenter] at the crime scene"; they placed him within a wedge-shaped sector ranging from one-eighth to four square miles. Yet the Court has already rejected the proposition that "inference insulates a search." *Kyllo*, 533 U. S., at 36. From the 127 days of location data it received, the Government could, in combination with other information, deduce a detailed log of Carpenter's movements, including when he was at the site of the robberies. And the Government thought the CSLI accurate enough to highlight it during the closing argument of his trial.

At any rate, the rule the Court adopts "must take account of more sophisticated systems that are already in use or in development." *Kyllo*, 533 U. S., at 36. While the records in this case reflect the state of technology at the start of the decade, the accuracy of CSLI is rapidly approaching GPS-level precision. As the number of cell sites has proliferated, the geographic area covered by each cell sector has shrunk, particularly in urban areas. In addition, with new technology measuring the time and angle of signals hitting their towers, wireless carriers already have the capability to pinpoint a phone's location within 50 meters.

Accordingly, when the Government accessed CSLI from the wireless carriers, it invaded Carpenter's reasonable expectation of privacy in the whole of his physical movements. * * *

Our decision today is a narrow one. We do not express a view on matters not before us: real-time CSLI or "tower dumps" (a download of information on all the devices that connected to a particular cell site during a particular interval). We do not disturb the application of *Smith* and *Miller* or call into question conventional surveillance techniques and tools, such as security cameras. Nor do we address other business records that might incidentally reveal location information. Further, our opinion does not consider other collection techniques involving foreign affairs or national security. As Justice Frankfurter noted when considering new innovations in airplanes and radios, the Court must tread carefully in such cases, to ensure that we do not "embarrass the future." Northwest Airlines, Inc. v. Minnesota, 322 U. S. 292, 300 (1944).[d]

IV

Having found that the acquisition of Carpenter's CSLI was a search, we also conclude that the Government must generally obtain a warrant supported by probable cause before acquiring such records. * * * Thus, "[i]n the absence of a warrant, a search is reasonable only if it falls within a specific exception to the warrant requirement."

---

[d]   JUSTICE GORSUCH faults us for not promulgating a complete code addressing the manifold situations that may be presented by this new technology—under a constitutional provision turning on what is "reasonable," no less. Like JUSTICE GORSUCH, we "do not begin to claim all the answers today," and therefore decide no more than the case before us.

As Justice Brandeis explained in his famous dissent, the Court is obligated—as "[s]ubtler and more far-reaching means of invading privacy have become available to the Government"—to ensure that the "progress of science" does not erode Fourth Amendment protections. Olmstead v. United States, 277 U. S. 438, 473–474 (1928). Here the progress of science has afforded law enforcement a powerful new tool to carry out its important responsibilities. At the same time, this tool risks Government encroachment of the sort the Framers, "after consulting the lessons of history," drafted the Fourth Amendment to prevent.

We decline to grant the state unrestricted access to a wireless carrier's database of physical location information. In light of the deeply revealing nature of CSLI, its depth, breadth, and comprehensive reach, and the inescapable and automatic nature of its collection, the fact that such information is gathered by a third party does not make it any less deserving of Fourth Amendment protection. The Government's acquisition of the cell-site records here was a search under that Amendment.

JUSTICE KENNEDY, with whom JUSTICE THOMAS and JUSTICE ALITO join, dissenting.

This case involves new technology, but the Court's stark departure from relevant Fourth Amendment precedents and principles is, in my submission, unnecessary and incorrect, requiring this respectful dissent.

In concluding that the Government engaged in a search, the Court unhinges Fourth Amendment doctrine from the property-based concepts that have long grounded the analytic framework that pertains in these cases. In doing so it draws an unprincipled and unworkable line between cell-site records on the one hand and financial and telephonic records on the other. According to today's majority opinion, the Government can acquire a record of every credit card purchase and phone call a person makes over months or years without upsetting a legitimate expectation of privacy. But, in the Court's view, the Government crosses a constitutional line when it obtains a court's approval to issue a subpoena for more than six days of cell-site records in order to determine whether a person was within several hundred city blocks of a crime scene. That distinction is illogical and will frustrate principled application of the Fourth Amendment in many routine yet vital law enforcement operations. * * *

In general, the Court "risks error by elaborating too fully on the Fourth Amendment implications of emerging technology before its role in society has become clear." That judicial caution, prudent in most cases, is imperative in this one.

Technological changes involving cell phones have complex effects on crime and law enforcement. Cell phones make crimes easier to coordinate and conceal, while also providing the Government with new investigative tools that may have the potential to upset traditional privacy expectations. How those competing effects balance against each other, and how property norms and expectations of privacy form around new technology, often will be difficult to determine during periods of rapid technological change. In those instances, and where the governing legal standard is one of reasonableness, it is wise to defer to legislative judgments like the one embodied in § 2703(d) of the Stored Communications Act. In § 2703(d) Congress weighed the privacy interests at stake and imposed a judicial check to prevent executive overreach. The Court should be wary of upsetting that legislative balance and erecting constitutional barriers that foreclose further legislative instructions. The last thing the Court should do is incorporate an arbitrary and outside limit—in this case six days' worth of cell-site records—and use it as the foundation for a new constitutional framework. The Court's decision runs roughshod over the mechanism Congress put in place to govern the acquisition of cell-site records and closes off further legislative debate on these issues.

* * *

This case should be resolved by interpreting accepted property principles as the baseline for reasonable expectations of privacy. Here the Government did not search anything over which Carpenter could assert ownership or control. Instead, it issued a court-authorized subpoena to a third party to disclose information it alone owned and controlled. That should suffice to resolve this case.

Having concluded, however, that the Government searched Carpenter when it obtained cell-site records from his cell phone service providers, the proper resolution of this case should have been to remand for the Court of Appeals to determine in the first instance whether the search was reasonable. Most courts of appeals, believing themselves bound by *Miller* and *Smith*, have not grappled with this question. And the Court's reflexive imposition of the warrant requirement obscures important and difficult issues, such as the scope of Congress' power to authorize the Government to collect new forms of information using processes that deviate from traditional warrant procedures, and how the Fourth Amendment's reasonableness requirement should apply when the Government uses compulsory process instead of engaging in an actual, physical search.

* * *

JUSTICE THOMAS, dissenting.

This case should not turn on "whether" a search occurred. It should turn, instead, on *whose* property was searched. * * * By obtaining the cell-site records of MetroPCS and Sprint, the Government did not search

Carpenter's property. He did not create the records, he does not maintain them, he cannot control them, and he cannot destroy them. Neither the terms of his contracts nor any provision of law makes the records his. The records belong to MetroPCS and Sprint.

The Court concludes that, although the records are not Carpenter's, the Government must get a warrant because Carpenter had a reasonable "expectation of privacy" in the location information that they reveal. I agree with JUSTICE KENNEDY, JUSTICE ALITO, JUSTICE GORSUCH, and every Court of Appeals to consider the question that this is not the best reading of our precedents.

The more fundamental problem with the Court's opinion, however, is its use of the "reasonable expectation of privacy" test, which was first articulated by Justice Harlan in *Katz* v. *United States*, 389 U. S. 347, 360–361 (1967) (concurring opinion). The *Katz* test has no basis in the text or history of the Fourth Amendment. And, it invites courts to make judgments about policy, not law. Until we confront the problems with this test, *Katz* will continue to distort Fourth Amendment jurisprudence.

I respectfully dissent.

* * *

JUSTICE ALITO, with whom JUSTICE THOMAS joins, dissenting.

I share the Court's concern about the effect of new technology on personal privacy, but I fear that today's decision will do far more harm than good. The Court's reasoning fractures two fundamental pillars of Fourth Amendment law, and in doing so, it guarantees a blizzard of litigation while threatening many legitimate and valuable investigative practices upon which law enforcement has rightfully come to rely.

First, the Court ignores the basic distinction between an actual search (dispatching law enforcement officers to enter private premises and root through private papers and effects) and an order merely requiring a party to look through its own records and produce specified documents. The former, which intrudes on personal privacy far more deeply, requires probable cause; the latter does not. Treating an order to produce like an actual search, as today's decision does, is revolutionary. It violates both the original understanding of the Fourth Amendment and more than a century of Supreme Court precedent. Unless it is somehow restricted to the particular situation in the present case, the Court's move will cause upheaval. Must every grand jury subpoena *duces tecum* be supported by probable cause? If so, investigations of terrorism, political corruption, white-collar crime, and many other offenses will be stymied. And what about subpoenas and other document-production orders issued by administrative agencies?

Second, the Court allows a defendant to object to the search of a third party's property. This also is revolutionary. The Fourth Amendment protects "[t]he right of the people to be secure in *their* persons, houses, papers, and effects" (emphasis added), not the persons, houses, papers, and effects of others. Until today, we have been careful to heed this fundamental feature of the Amendment's text. This was true when the Fourth Amendment was tied to property law, and it remained true after *Katz* v. *United States*, 389 U. S. 347 (1967), broadened the Amendment's reach.

By departing dramatically from these fundamental principles, the Court destabilizes long-established Fourth Amendment doctrine. We will be making repairs—or picking up the pieces—for a long time to come. * * *

Although the majority professes a desire not to "embarrass the future," we can guess where today's decision will lead.

One possibility is that the broad principles that the Court seems to embrace will be applied across the board. All subpoenas *duces tecum* and all other orders compelling the production of documents will require a demonstration of probable cause, and individuals will be able to claim a protected Fourth Amendment interest in any sensitive personal information about them that is collected and owned by third parties. Those would be revolutionary developments indeed.

The other possibility is that this Court will face the embarrassment of explaining in case after case that the principles on which today's decision rests are subject to all sorts of qualifications and limitations that have not yet been discovered. If we take this latter course, we will inevitably end up "making a crazy quilt of the Fourth Amendment."

All of this is unnecessary. In the Stored Communications Act, Congress addressed the specific problem at issue in this case. The Act restricts the misuse of cell-site records by cell service providers, something that the Fourth Amendment cannot do. The Act also goes beyond current Fourth Amendment case law in restricting access by law enforcement. It permits law enforcement officers to acquire cell-site records only if they meet a heightened standard and obtain a court order. If the American people now think that the Act is inadequate or needs updating, they can turn to their elected representatives to adopt more protective provisions. Because the collection and storage of cell-site records affects nearly every American, it is unlikely that the question whether the current law requires strengthening will escape Congress's notice.

Legislation is much preferable to the development of an entirely new body of Fourth Amendment caselaw for many reasons, including the enormous complexity of the subject, the need to respond to rapidly changing technology, and the Fourth Amendment's limited scope. The Fourth Amendment restricts the conduct of the Federal Government and the States; it does not apply to private actors. But today, some of the greatest threats to individual privacy may come from powerful private companies that collect and sometimes misuse vast quantities of data about the lives of ordinary Americans. If today's decision encourages the public to think that this Court can protect them from this looming threat to their privacy, the decision will mislead as well as disrupt. And if holding a provision of the Stored Communications Act to be unconstitutional dissuades Congress from further legislation in this field, the goal of protecting privacy will be greatly disserved.

The desire to make a statement about privacy in the digital age does not justify the consequences that today's decision is likely to produce.

JUSTICE GORSUCH, dissenting.

In the late 1960s this Court suggested for the first time that a search triggering the Fourth Amendment occurs when the government violates an "expectation of privacy" that "society is prepared to recognize as 'reasonable.'" Then, in a pair of decisions in the 1970s applying the *Katz* test, the Court held that a "reasonable expectation of privacy" doesn't attach to information shared with "third parties." See Smith v. Maryland, 442 U. S. 735, 743–744 (1979); United States v. Miller, 425 U. S. 435, 443 (1976). By these steps, the Court came to conclude, the Constitution does nothing to limit investigators from searching records you've entrusted to your bank, accountant, and maybe even your doctor.

What's left of the Fourth Amendment? Today we use the Internet to do most everything. Smartphones make it easy to keep a calendar, correspond with friends, make calls, conduct banking, and even watch the game. Countless Internet companies maintain records about us and, increasingly, *for* us. Even our most private documents—those that, in other eras, we would have locked safely in a desk drawer or destroyed—now reside on third party servers. *Smith* and *Miller* teach that the police can review all of this material, on the theory that no one reasonably expects any of it will be kept private. But no one believes that, if they ever did. * * *

Katz's problems start with the text and original understanding of the Fourth Amendment, as JUSTICE THOMAS thoughtfully explains today. The Amendment's protections do not depend on the breach of some abstract "expectation of privacy" whose contours are left to the judicial imagination. Much more concretely, it protects your "person," and your "houses, papers, and effects." Nor does your right to bring a Fourth Amendment claim depend on whether a judge happens to agree that your subjective expectation to privacy is a "reasonable" one. Under its plain terms, the Amendment grants you the right to invoke its guarantees whenever one of your protected things (your person, your house, your papers, or your effects) is unreasonably searched or seized. Period.

History too holds problems for *Katz*. Little like it can be found in the law that led to the adoption of the Fourth Amendment or in this Court's jurisprudence until the late 1960s. The Fourth Amendment came about in response to a trio of 18th century cases "well known to the men who wrote and ratified the Bill of Rights, [and] famous throughout the colonial population." The first two were English cases invalidating the Crown's use of general warrants to enter homes and search papers. Entick v. Carrington, 19 How. St. Tr. 1029 (K. B. 1765); Wilkes v. Wood, 19 How. St. Tr. 1153 (K. B. 1763). The third was American: the Boston Writs of Assistance Case, which sparked colonial outrage at the use of writs permitting government agents to enter houses and business, breaking open doors and chests along the way, to conduct searches and seizures—and to force third parties to help them. No doubt the colonial outrage engendered by these cases rested in part on the government's intrusion upon privacy. But the framers chose not to protect privacy in some ethereal way dependent on judicial intuitions. They chose instead to protect privacy in particular places and things—"persons, houses, papers, and effects"—and against particular threats—"unreasonable" governmental "searches and seizures."

Even taken on its own terms, *Katz* has never been sufficiently justified. In fact, we still don't even know what its "reasonable expectation of privacy" test *is*. Is it supposed to pose an empirical question (what privacy expectations do people *actually* have) or a normative one (what expectations *should* they have)? Either way brings problems. If the test is supposed to be an empirical one, it's unclear why judges rather than legislators should conduct it. Legislators are responsive to their constituents and have institutional resources designed to help them discern and enact majoritarian preferences. Politically insulated judges come armed with only the attorneys' briefs, a few law clerks, and their own idiosyncratic experiences. They are hardly the representative group you'd expect (or want) to be making empirical judgments for hundreds of millions of people. Unsurprisingly, too, judicial judgments often fail to reflect public views. * * *

Maybe, then, the *Katz* test should be conceived as a normative question. But if that's the case, why (again) do judges, rather than legislators, get to determine whether society *should be* prepared to recognize an expectation of privacy as legitimate? Deciding what privacy interests *should be* recognized often calls for a pure policy choice, many times between incommensurable goods—between the value of privacy in a particular setting and society's interest in combating crime. Answering questions like that calls for the exercise of raw political will belonging to legislatures, not the legal judgment proper to courts. When judges abandon legal judgment for political will we not only risk decisions where "reasonable expectations of privacy" come to bear "an uncanny resemblance to those expectations of privacy" shared by Members of this Court. Minnesota v. Carter, 525 U. S. 83, 97 (1998) (Scalia, J., concurring). We also risk undermining public confidence in the courts themselves. * * * As a result, *Katz* has yielded an often unpredictable—and sometimes unbelievable—jurisprudence. *Smith* and *Miller* are only two examples; there are many others. Take Florida v. Riley, 488 U. S. 445 (1989), which says that a police helicopter hovering 400 feet above a person's property invades no reasonable expectation of privacy. Try that one out on your neighbors. Or California v. Greenwood, 486 U. S. 35 (1988), which holds that a person has no reasonable expectation of privacy in the garbage he puts out for collection. In that case, the Court said that the homeowners forfeited their privacy interests because "[i]t is common knowledge that plastic garbage bags left on or at the side of a public street are readily accessible to animals, children, scavengers, snoops, and other members of the public." But the habits of raccoons don't prove much about the habits of the country. I doubt, too, that most people spotting a neighbor rummaging through their garbage would think they lacked reasonable grounds to confront the rummager. Making the decision all the stranger, California state law expressly *protected* a homeowner's property rights in discarded trash. Yet rather than defer to that as evidence of the people's habits and reasonable expectations of privacy, the Court substituted its own curious judgment.

Resorting to *Katz* in data privacy cases threatens more of the same. Just consider. The Court today says that judges should use *Katz*'s reasonable expectation of privacy test to decide what Fourth Amendment rights people have in cell-site location information, explaining that "no single rubric definitively resolves which expectations of privacy are entitled to protection." But then it offers a twist. Lower courts should be sure to add two special principles to their *Katz* calculus: the need to avoid "arbitrary power" and the importance of "plac[ing] obstacles in the way of a too permeating police surveillance." While surely laudable, these principles don't offer lower courts much guidance. The Court does not tell us, for example, how far to carry either principle or how to weigh them against the legitimate needs of law enforcement. At what point does access to electronic data amount to "arbitrary" authority? When does police surveillance become "too permeating"? And what sort of "obstacles" should judges "place" in law enforcement's path when it does? We simply do not know.

The Court's application of these principles supplies little more direction. The Court declines to say whether there is any sufficiently limited period of time "for which the Government may obtain an individual's historical [location information] free from Fourth Amendment scrutiny." But then it tells us that access to seven days' worth of information *does* trigger Fourth Amendment scrutiny—even though here the carrier "produced only two days of records." Why is the relevant fact the seven days of information the government *asked for* instead of the two days of information the government *actually saw*? Why seven days instead of ten or three or one? And in what possible sense did the government "search" five days' worth of location information it was never even sent? We do not know.

Later still, the Court adds that it can't say whether the Fourth Amendment is triggered when the government collects "real-time CSLI or 'tower dumps' (a download of information on all the devices that connected to a particular cell site during a particular interval)." But what distinguishes historical data from real-time data, or seven days of a single person's data from a download of *everyone*'s data over some indefinite period of time? Why isn't a tower dump the *paradigmatic* example of "too permeating police surveillance" and a dangerous tool of "arbitrary" authority—the touchstones of the majority's modified *Katz* analysis? On what possible basis could such mass data collection survive the Court's test while collecting a single person's data does not? Here again we are left to guess. At the same time, though, the Court offers some firm assurances. It tells us its decision does *not* "call into question conventional surveillance techniques and tools, such as security cameras." That, however, just raises more questions for lower courts to sort out about what techniques qualify as "conventional" and why those techniques would be okay *even if* they lead to "permeating police surveillance" or "arbitrary police power."

Nor is this the end of it. After finding a reasonable expectation of privacy, the Court says there's still more work to do. Courts must determine whether to "extend" *Smith* and *Miller* to the circumstances before them. So apparently *Smith* and *Miller* aren't quite left for dead; they just no longer have the clear reach they once did. How do we measure their new reach? The Court says courts now must conduct a *second Katz*-like balancing inquiry, asking whether the fact of disclosure to a third party outweighs privacy interests in the "category of information" so disclosed. But how are lower courts supposed to weigh these radically different interests? Or assign values to different categories of information? All we know is that historical cell-site location information (for seven days, anyway) escapes *Smith* and *Miller*'s shorn grasp, while a lifetime of bank or phone records does not. As to any other kind of information, lower courts will have to stay tuned.

In the end, our lower court colleagues are left with two amorphous balancing tests, a series of weighty and incommensurable principles to consider in them, and a few illustrative examples that seem little more than the product of judicial intuition. In the Court's defense, though, we have arrived at this strange place not because the Court has misunderstood *Katz*. Far from it. We have arrived here because this is where *Katz* inevitably leads.

* * *

There is another way. From the founding until the 1960s, the right to assert a Fourth Amendment claim didn't depend on your ability to appeal to a judge's personal sensibilities about the "reasonableness" of your expectations or privacy. It was tied to the law. The Fourth Amendment protects "the right of the people to be secure in their persons, houses, papers and effects, against unreasonable searches and seizures." True to those words and their original understanding, the traditional approach asked if a house, paper or effect was *yours* under law. No more was needed to trigger the Fourth Amendment. Though now often lost in *Katz*'s shadow, this traditional understanding persists. *Katz* only "supplements, rather than displaces the traditional property-based understanding of the Fourth Amendment."

Beyond its provenance in the text and original understanding of the Amendment, this traditional approach comes with other advantages. Judges are supposed to decide cases based on "democratically legitimate sources of law"—like positive law or analogies to items protected by the enacted Constitution—rather than "their own biases or personal policy preferences." Pettys, Judicial Discretion in Constitutional Cases, 26 J. L. & Pol. 123, 127 (2011). A Fourth Amendment model based on positive legal rights carves out significant room for legislative participation in the Fourth Amendment context, too, by asking judges to consult what the people's representatives have to say about their rights. Nor is this approach hobbled by *Smith* and *Miller*, for those cases are just *limitations* on *Katz*, addressing only the question whether individuals have a reasonable expectation of privacy in materials they share with third parties. Under this more traditional approach, Fourth Amendment protections for your papers and effects do not automatically disappear just because you share them with third parties.

Given the prominence *Katz* has claimed in our doctrine, American courts are pretty rusty at applying the traditional approach to the Fourth Amendment. We know that if a house, paper, or effect is yours, you have a Fourth Amendment interest in its protection. But what kind of legal interest is sufficient to make something *yours*? And what source of law determines that? Current positive law? The common law at 1791, extended by analogy to modern times? Both? Much work is needed to revitalize this area and answer these questions. I do not begin to claim all the answers today, but (unlike with *Katz*) at least I have a pretty good idea what the questions *are*. And it seems to me a few things can be said.

First, the fact that a third party has access to or possession of your papers and effects does not necessarily eliminate your interest in them. Ever hand a private document to a friend to be returned? Toss your keys to a valet at a restaurant? Ask your neighbor to look after your dog while you travel? You would not expect the friend to share the document with others; the valet to lend your car to his buddy; or the neighbor to put Fido up for adoption. Entrusting your stuff to others is a *bailment*. A bailment is the "delivery of personal property by one person (the *bailor*) to another (the *bailee*) who holds the property for a certain purpose." * * * A bailee normally owes a legal duty to keep the item safe, according to the terms of the parties' contract if they have one, and according to the "implication[s] from their conduct" if they don't. A bailee who uses the item in a different way than he's supposed to, or against the bailor's instructions, is liable for conversion. This approach is quite different from *Smith* and *Miller's* (counter-)intuitive approach to reasonable expectations of privacy; where those cases extinguish Fourth Amendment interests once records are given to a third party, property law may preserve them.

Our Fourth Amendment jurisprudence already reflects this truth. In Ex parte Jackson, 96 U. S. 727 (1878), this Court held that sealed letters placed in the mail are "as fully guarded from examination and inspection, except as to their outward form and weight, as if they were retained by the parties forwarding them in their own domiciles." The reason, drawn from the Fourth Amendment's text, was that "[t]he constitutional guaranty of the right of the people to be secure in their papers against unreasonable searches and seizures extends to *their papers*, thus closed against inspection, *wherever they may be*." It did not matter that letters were bailed to a third party (the government, no less). The sender enjoyed the same Fourth Amendment protection as he does "when papers are subjected to search in one's own household."

These ancient principles may help us address modern data cases too. Just because you entrust your data—in some cases, your modern-day papers and effects—to a third party may not mean you lose any Fourth Amendment interest in its contents. Whatever may be left of *Smith* and *Miller*, few doubt that e-mail should be treated much like the traditional mail it has largely supplanted—as a bailment in which the owner retains a vital and protected legal interest. * * *

Second, I doubt that complete ownership or exclusive control of property is always a necessary condition to the assertion of a Fourth Amendment right. Where houses are concerned, for example, individuals can enjoy Fourth Amendment protection without fee simple title. Both the text of the Amendment and the common law rule support that conclusion. * * * That is why tenants and resident family members—though they have no legal title—have standing to complain about searches of the houses in which they live.

Another point seems equally true: just because you *have* to entrust a third party with your data doesn't necessarily mean you should lose all Fourth Amendment protections in it. Not infrequently one person comes into possession of someone else's property without the owner's consent. Think of the finder of lost goods or the policeman who impounds a car. The law recognizes that the goods and the car still belong to their true owners, for "where a person comes into lawful possession of the personal property of another, even though there is no formal agreement between the property's owner and its possessor, the possessor will become a constructive bailee when justice so requires." At least some of this Court's decisions have already suggested that use of technology is functionally compelled by the demands of modern life, and in that way the fact that we store data with third parties may amount to a sort of involuntary bailment too. See *Riley v. California*, 573 U. S. ___, ___ (2014) (slip op., at 9).

Third, positive law may help provide detailed guidance on evolving technologies without resort to judicial intuition. State (or sometimes federal) law often creates rights in both tangible and intangible things. In the context of the Takings Clause we often ask whether those state-created rights are sufficient to make something someone's property for constitutional purposes. A similar inquiry may be appropriate for the Fourth Amendment. Both the States and federal government are actively legislating in the area of third party data storage and the rights users enjoy. See, *e.g.*, Stored Communications Act, 18 U. S. C. § 2701 *et seq.*; Tex. Prop. Code Ann. § 111.004(12) (West 2017) (defining "[p]roperty" to include "property held in any digital or electronic medium"). State courts are busy expounding common law property principles in this area as well. *E.g.*, Ajemian v. Yahoo!, Inc., 478 Mass. 169, 170, 84 N. E. 3d 766, 768 (2017) (e-mail account is a "form of property often referred to as a 'digital asset'"); Eysoldt v. ProScan Imaging, 194 Ohio App. 3d 630, 638, 2011-Ohio-2359, 957 N. E. 2d 780, 786 (2011) (permitting action for conversion of web account as intangible property). If state legislators or state courts say that a digital record has the attributes that normally make something property, that may supply a sounder basis for judicial decision making than judicial guesswork about societal expectations.

Fourth, while positive law may help establish a person's Fourth Amendment interest there may be some circumstances where positive law cannot be used to defeat it. *Ex parte Jackson* reflects that understanding. There this Court said that "[n]o law of Congress" could authorize letter carriers "to invade the secrecy of letters." So the post office couldn't impose a regulation dictating that those mailing letters surrender all legal interests in them once they're deposited in a mailbox. If that is right, *Jackson* suggests the existence of a constitutional floor below which Fourth Amendment rights may not descend. Legislatures cannot pass laws declaring your house or papers to be your property except to the extent the police wish to search them without cause. As the Court has previously explained, "we must assur[e] preservation of that degree of privacy against government that existed when the Fourth Amendment was adopted."

Jones, 565 U. S., at 406). Nor does this mean protecting only the specific rights known at the founding; it means protecting their modern analogues too. So, for example, while thermal imaging was unknown in 1791, this Court has recognized that using that technology to look inside a home constitutes a Fourth Amendment "search" of that "home" no less than a physical inspection might.

Fifth, this constitutional floor may, in some instances, bar efforts to circumvent the Fourth Amendment's protection through the use of subpoenas. No one thinks the government can evade *Jackson*'s prohibition on opening sealed letters without a warrant simply by issuing a subpoena to a postmaster for "all letters sent by John Smith" or, worse, "all letters sent by John Smith concerning a particular transaction." So the question courts will confront will be this: What other kinds of records are sufficiently similar to letters in the mail that the same rule should apply?

It may be that, as an original matter, a subpoena requiring the recipient to produce records wasn't thought of as a "search or seizure" by the government implicating the Fourth Amendment, but instead as an act of compelled self-incrimination implicating the Fifth Amendment. But the common law of searches and seizures does not appear to have confronted a case where private documents equivalent to a mailed letter were entrusted to a bailee and then subpoenaed. As a result, "[t]he common-law rule regarding subpoenas for documents held by third parties entrusted with information from the target is . . . unknown and perhaps unknowable." Given that (perhaps insoluble) uncertainty, I am content to adhere to *Jackson* and its implications for now.

* * *

What does all this mean for the case before us? To start, I cannot fault the Sixth Circuit for holding that *Smith* and *Miller* extinguish any *Katz*-based Fourth Amendment interest in third party cell-site data. That is the plain effect of their categorical holdings. Nor can I fault the Court today for its implicit but unmistakable conclusion that the rationale of *Smith* and *Miller* is wrong; indeed, I agree with that. The Sixth Circuit was powerless to say so, but this Court can and should. At the same time, I do not agree with the Court's decision today to keep *Smith* and *Miller* on life support and supplement them with a new and multilayered inquiry that seems to be only *Katz*-squared. Returning there, I worry, promises more trouble than help. Instead, I would look to a more traditional Fourth Amendment approach. * * * Neglecting more traditional approaches may mean failing to vindicate the full protections of the Fourth Amendment.

Our case offers a cautionary example. It seems to me entirely possible a person's cell-site data could qualify as *his* papers or effects under existing law. Yes, the telephone carrier holds the information. But 47 U. S. C. § 222 designates a customer's cell-site location information as "customer proprietary network information" (CPNI), § 222(h)(1)(A), and gives customers certain rights to control use of and access to CPNI about themselves. The statute generally forbids a carrier to "use, disclose, or permit access to individually identifiable" CPNI without the customer's consent, except as needed to provide the customer's telecommunications services. § 222(c)(1). It also requires the carrier to disclose CPNI "upon affirmative written request by the customer, to any person designated by the customer." § 222(c)(2). Congress even afforded customers a private cause of action for damages against carriers who violate the Act's terms. § 207. Plainly, customers have substantial legal interests in this information, including at least some right to include, exclude, and control its use. Those interests might even rise to the level of a property right.

The problem is that we do not know anything more. Before the district court and court of appeals, Mr. Carpenter pursued only a *Katz* "reasonable expectations" argument. He did not invoke the law of property or any analogies to the common law, either there or in his petition for certiorari. Even in his merits brief before this Court, Mr. Carpenter's discussion of his positive law rights in cell-site data was cursory. He offered no analysis, for example, of what rights state law might provide him in addition to those supplied by § 222. In these circumstances, I cannot help but conclude— reluctantly—that Mr. Carpenter forfeited perhaps his most promising line of argument.

Unfortunately, too, this case marks the second time this Term that individuals have forfeited Fourth Amendment arguments based on positive law by failing to preserve them. See *Byrd*, 584 U. S., at ___ (slip op., at 7). Litigants have had fair notice since at least *United States v. Jones* (2012) and *Florida v. Jardines* (2013) that arguments like these may vindicate Fourth Amendment interests even where *Katz* arguments do not. Yet the arguments have gone unmade, leaving courts to the usual *Katz* handwaving. These omissions do not serve the development of a sound or fully protective Fourth Amendment jurisprudence.

QUESTIONS AFTER CARPENTER

Carpenter answered one critical question: whether law enforcement officers need a warrant to access cell-site location information. It specifically declined to address the Fourth Amendment status of other records and other technologies. This has left lower courts to wonder whether *Carpenter* marks a watershed along the lines of *Katz* or is, instead, an application of *Katz* to a specific circumstance. Part of the challenge is that Chief Justice Roberts's majority opinion does not set forth a clear test for determining what kinds of data should be subject to Fourth Amendment protections and what kinds of surveillance technologies should be subject to Fourth Amendment restraints. Some courts and scholars have attempted to distill from that opinion a set of factors relevant to making those determinations, including the duration of surveillance, what kinds of personal and intimate information surveillance can reveal, the scope of threat to the right of "the people to be secure . . . against unreasonable searches and seizures," and whether people meaningfully consent to or can reasonably avoid surveillance. *See, e.g.*, Paul Ohm, *The Many Revolutions of* Carpenter, 32 Harv. J. L & Tech. 357 (2019); David Gray, *Collective Rights and the Fourth Amendment after* Carpenter, 79 Md. L. Rev. 66 (2019); Susan Freiwald & Stephen W. Smith, *The Carpenter Chronicle: A Near Perfect Surveillance*, 132 Harv. L. Rev. 205 (2018). Advocates have cited some of these factors to challenge the warrantless deployment and use of a variety of surveillance technologies. Few of these efforts have succeeded, however. In the two years since *Carpenter* was decided, lower courts largely declined to extend *Carpenter* beyond its facts. *See* Tyler Jones, *Examining Lower Courts' Treatments of Cell Phone Data After* Carpenter v. United States (Jan. 20, 2020) (https://papers.ssrn.com/sol3/papers.cfm?abstract_id=3596579). *But see* State v. Andrews, 227 Md. App. 350 (2016) (holding that a warrant is required to deploy and use a cell-site simulator ("stingray")).

In his concurring opinion, Justice Gorsuch wonders about what some scholars have called the "positive law" theory of the Fourth Amendment. *See* William Baude & James Stern, *The Positive Law Model of the Fourth Amendment*, 129 Harv. L. Rev. 1821 (2016). On this account, legislation can control the scope of Fourth Amendment protections by either grounding or withdrawing grounds for privacy expectations or by creating or denying claims based on trespass. This proposal has been subject to considerable criticism. *See, e.g.*, Richard Re, *The Positive Law Floor*, 129 Harv. L. Rev. F. 313 (2016). It also in tension with cases where the Court has declined to bind Fourth Amendment protections to state law. *See, e.g.*, Virginia v. Moore, 553 U.S. 164 (2008); Atwater v. Lago Vista, 532 U.S. 318 (2001). Nevertheless, with one potential advocate on the Court, and increasing public pressure for privacy legislation, the positive law may well become a significant factor for evaluating the reasonable expectations of privacy and property rights that ground Fourth Amendment rights.

Another important question left unanswered by the majority opinion in *Carpenter* implicates the state action requirement. The Fourth Amendment governs state actors but does not regulate private actors unless they are agents of the state. This requirement highlights a remarkable omission on the part of the Court to identify, precisely, when the "search" occurred in *Carpenter* and who did it. Was Carpenter's service provider conducting a "search" when it gathered and stored records of his location ("The location information obtained from Carpenter's wireless carriers was the product of a search.")? If so, then on what analysis was it acting as an agent of the state? Did the investigating agents conduct a search when they requested and accessed cell site location records ("The Government's acquisition of the cell-site records was a search within the meaning of the Fourth Amendment.")? Was the service provider conducting a "search" when it looked through its records in response to the government's request? Or did the "search" occur when the FBI agent analyzed the records to determine the location of Carpenter's phone on dates and times associated with the robberies ("From the 127 days of location data it received, the Government could, in combination with other information, deduce a detailed log of Carpenter's movements.")? The answers to these questions may matter quite a bit as courts wrestle with the Fourth Amendment status of other surveillance methods. For example, would it be a search if the government requested information about a suspect from a commercial data aggregator or used its own "Big Data" technologies to paint a detailed picture of an individual's activities and associations using third-party data?

D. APPLICATIONS OF THE REASONABLE EXPECTATION OF PRIVACY ANALYSIS (WITH THE TRESPASS SUPPLEMENT)

3. Access by Members of the Public—the Third-Party Doctrine

d. *Cellphone Location, Subscriber Information, etc.*

Page 74. The following replaces the note titled *Cellphone Location, Subscriber Information, etc.***:**

In *Carpenter v. United States*, 138 S.Ct. 2206 (2018) (excerpted above), the Court held that law enforcement must get a warrant to access historical cell-site location data. In a forceful dissent joined by Justices Thomas and Alito, Justice Kennedy contended that this holding runs contrary to the Court's precedents involving third-party business records, including *Miller* and *Smith*, both of which involved "records contain[ing] personal and sensitive information." In Justice Kennedy's view, cell-site location information, which is gathered and stored by cellular service providers in the normal course of their business, is "no different from the many other kinds of business records the Government has a lawful right to obtain by compulsory process."

Writing for the majority in *Carpenter*, Chief Justice Roberts responded, arguing that Justice Kennedy's

> position fails to contend with the seismic shifts in digital technology that made possible the tracking of not only Carpenter's location but also everyone else's, not for a short period but for years and years. Sprint Corporation and its competitors are not your typical witnesses. Unlike the nosy neighbor who keeps an eye on comings and goings, they are ever alert, and their memory is nearly infallible. There is a world of difference between the limited types of personal information addressed in *Smith* and *Miller* and the exhaustive chronicle of location information casually collected by wireless carriers today. The Government thus is not asking for a straightforward application of the third-party doctrine, but instead a significant extension of it to a distinct category of information.

The third-party doctrine partly stems from the notion that an individual has a reduced expectation of privacy in information knowingly shared with another. But the fact of "diminished privacy interests does not mean that the Fourth Amendment falls out of the picture entirely." *Smith* and *Miller*, after all, did not rely solely on the act of sharing. Instead, they considered "the nature of the particular documents sought" to determine whether "there is a legitimate 'expectation of privacy' concerning their contents." *Smith* pointed out the limited capabilities of a pen register; as explained in *Riley*, telephone call logs reveal little in the way of "identifying information." *Miller* likewise noted that checks were "not confidential communications but negotiable instruments to be used in commercial transactions." * * *

Neither does the second rationale underlying the third-party doctrine—voluntary exposure—hold up when it comes to CSLI. Cell phone location information is not truly "shared" as one normally understands the term. In the first place, cell phones and the services they provide are "such a pervasive and insistent part of daily life" that carrying one is indispensable to participation in modern society. Second, a cell phone logs a cell-site record by dint of its operation, without any affirmative act on the part of the user beyond powering up. Virtually any activity on the phone generates CSLI, including incoming calls, texts, or e-mails and countless other data connections that a phone automatically makes when checking for news, weather, or social media updates. Apart from disconnecting the phone from the network, there is no way to avoid leaving behind a trail of location data. As a result, in no meaningful sense does the user voluntarily "assume the risk" of turning over a comprehensive dossier of his physical movements.

In this passage, Chief Justice Roberts argues that contemporary digital technologies are different from analog technologies not just in degree, but also in kind. In his *Carpenter* dissent, Justice Kennedy recognized that it "is true that the Cyber Age has vast potential both to expand and restrict individual freedoms in dimensions not contemplated in earlier times." He nevertheless maintained that Carpenter could not assert Fourth Amendment rights in cell-site location records because those records do not belong *to him*. "*Miller* and *Smith*," he writes "hold that individuals lack any protected Fourth Amendment interests in records that are possessed, owned, and controlled only by a third party."

They rest upon the commonsense principle that the absence of property law analogues can be dispositive of privacy expectations. The defendants in those cases could expect that the third-party businesses could use the records the companies collected, stored, and classified as their own for any number of business and commercial purposes. The businesses were not bailees or custodians of the records, with a duty to hold the records for the defendants' use. The defendants could make no argument that the records were their own papers or effects. . . .

Persons with no meaningful interests in the records sought by a subpoena, like the defendants in *Miller* and *Smith*, have no rights to object to the records' disclosure—much less to assert that the Government must obtain a warrant to compel disclosure of the records.

In addition to his concerns about the substance of the Court's holding in *Carpenter*, Justice Kennedy worried that it "will have dramatic consequences for law enforcement, courts, and society as a whole . . . that extend beyond cell-site records to other kinds of information held by third parties." For example, should law enforcement be required to secure a warrant before accessing metadata associated with internet usage or other forms of electronic communication, such as texts and social media posts, which often contain revealing information, including location data?

Before *Carpenter*, courts confronting these questions frequently drew on a distinction between the contents of communications and the information necessary to convey them. That distinction traces to *Ex Parte Jackson*, 96 U.S. 727 (1878), which involved postal workers opening sealed mail in an effort to enforce a congressional prohibition on the mailing of lottery circulars. Writing for the Court in that case, Justice Field made clear that:

Letters and sealed packages of this kind in the mail are as fully guarded from examination and inspection, except as to their outward form and weight, as if they were retained by the parties forwarding them in their own domiciles. The constitutional guaranty of the right of the people to be secure in their papers against unreasonable searches and seizures extends to their papers, thus closed against inspection, wherever they may be. Whilst in the mail, they can only be opened and examined under like warrant, issued upon similar oath or affirmation, particularly describing the thing to be seized, as is required when papers are subjected to search in one's own household.

Drawing on this content/non-content distinction, courts have held that accessing the routing information associated with electronic communications is not a "search" but intercepting and accessing the contents of those communications is. *See, e.g.*, United States v. Forrester, 512 F.3d 500 (9th Cir. 2008) ("E-mail, like physical mail, has an outside address "visible" to the third-party carriers that transmit it to its intended location, and also a package of content that the sender presumes will be read only by the intended recipient. The privacy interests in these two forms of communication are identical. The contents may deserve Fourth Amendment protection, but the address and size of the package do not."); Warshak v. United States, 490 F.3d 455 (6th Cir. 2007) ("The content of e-mail is something that the user 'seeks to preserve as private,' and therefore 'may be constitutionally protected.' ").

The content/non-content distinction may not provide such a clear Fourth Amendment dividing line in the wake of the Court's decision in *Carpenter*. Prior to *Carpenter*, courts—including the Sixth Circuit in its opinion overturned by the Supreme Court—had cited *Jackson* to hold that cellphone users do not have a reasonable expectation of privacy in historical cell-site location information. United States v. Carpenter, 819 F.3d 880 (6th Cir. 2016); see *also* United States v. Graham, 824 F.3d 421 (2016) ("Defendants rely on cases that afford Fourth Amendment protection to the content of communications to suggest that CSLI warrants the same protection. What Defendants fail to recognize is that for each medium of communication these cases address, there is also a case expressly withholding Fourth Amendment protection from non-content information, i.e., information involving addresses and routing." (internal citations omitted)). Citing concerns about the nature of cell-site location information and the intimate details it can reveal about the privacies of life, the Court declined to embrace the content/non-content distinction in *Carpenter*. Might lower court cases declining to protect non-content information associated with other forms of electronic communication be next? What factors should a court consider when determining whether accessing the non-content information associated with electronic mail, texts, social media, or other forms of electronic communication constitutes a "search"?

There is another form of computer surveillance that has been used in cases involving child pornography: the network investigative technique (NIT), which sends computer code to users' computers, instructing the computers to send back information to the government that assists the investigators in finding the computer. The technique allows the government to determine the IP address of the computer, operating system information, and the Media Access Control address, which is a unique number assigned to the network interface card of internet devices. The government has argued that the use of NIT is not a search because a defendant has no expectation of privacy in this information, which is accessible by a third party. But courts have found that the use of NIT is a search, reasoning that "the government is not permitted to conduct a warrantless search of a place in which a defendant has a reasonable expectation of privacy." United States v. Horton, 863 F.3d 1041 (8th Cir. 2017). The *Horton* court distinguished NIT from traditional third-party doctrine cases on the ground that NIT intrudes into a constitutionally protected effect to obtain information directly from a target's computer.

5. Use of Technology to Enhance Inspection

b. Electronic Tracking Devices

Knotts, Karo, and Public Tracking After Jones

Page 96. Add at the end of the note titled *Knotts, Karo, and Public Tracking After Jones*:

In *Carpenter v. United States*, 138 S.Ct. 2206 (2018) (excerpted above), the Court leaned on the "shadow majority" in *United States v. Jones* when analyzing the Fourth Amendment status of cell-site location information. Writing for the majority in *Carpenter*, Chief Justice Roberts pointed out that the "Court in *Knotts*, however, was careful to distinguish between the rudimentary tracking facilitated by the beeper and more sweeping modes of surveillance," and reserved the question whether " 'different constitutional principles may be applicable' if 'twenty-four hour surveillance of any citizen of this country [were] possible.' " Noting the ubiquity of cellular phones, the fact that users routinely carry their phones everywhere they go, the intimate details that location data can reveal, and the capacity for cellular tracking to facilitate long-term surveillance, the *Carpenter* Court found that the moment foretold in *Knotts* had arrived. It therefore declined to extend the public observation doctrine in that case, holding that government agents' accessing cell-site location information constitutes a "search" for purposes of the Fourth Amendment, requiring a warrant.

The *Carpenter* Court left unanswered how its new constitutional principles might or might not apply to other technologies and declined to address the Fourth Amendment status of surveillance methods such as "real-time" cell-site tracking, "tower dumps" (accessing "information on all the devices that connected to a particular cell-site during a particular interval"), and "conventional surveillance techniques and tools, such as security cameras." In a dissenting opinion joined by Justices Thomas and Alito, Justice Kennedy wondered how the Court could set limits on its new principles. In a separate opinion, Justice Gorsuch echoed those concerns, worrying that "our lower court colleagues are left with two amorphous balancing tests, a series of weighty and incommensurable principles to consider in them, and a few illustrative examples that seem little more than the product of judicial intuition." Cases decided in the two years after *Carpenter* indicate that lower courts have taken a very conservative approach, largely preserving the public observation doctrine. *See, e.g., Pressley v. United States*, 895 F.3d 1284 (11th Cir. 2019) (declining to extend *Carpenter* to cover Facebook data); *United States v. Adkinson*, 916 F.3d 605 (7th Cir. 2019) (declining to extend *Carpenter* to cover a tower dump); United States v. Kay, 17-CR-16, 2018 WL 3995902 (E.D. Wis., Aug.

21, 2018) (declining to extend *Carpenter* to cover the use of a pole camera to monitor the curtilage of a home for 87 days).

IV. OBTAINING A SEARCH WARRANT: CONSTITUTIONAL PREREQUISITES

A. DEMONSTRATING PROBABLE CAUSE

5. Quantity of Information Required for Probable Cause

Probable Cause to Arrest

Page 141. Add at the end of the section on Probable Cause to Arrest:

In *District of Columbia v. Wesby*, 138 S.Ct. 577 (2018), Justice Thomas wrote for the Court as it held that police officers had probable cause to arrest 21 individuals who were partying in a house with the permission of a woman with whom the owner of the house had been trying to negotiate a lease. The police arrived at the house in response to a complaint about loud music and illegal activities. They found the house to be in disarray, smelled marijuana and saw beer bottles and liquor cups on the floor, discovered a "makeshift strip club" in the living room and "more debauchery upstairs." An officer was told by two "women working the party" that a woman named "Peaches" or "Tasty" was renting the house and had given them permission to be there. One of the woman called Peaches at the officer's request, and Peaches said she had just gone to the store. A sergeant spoke with her, and she claimed to be renting the house from the owner who was fixing it up for her. In a subsequent call, she admitted she did not have permission to use the house. After the officers contacted the owner and he confirmed that he had not given Peaches or anyone else permission to be in house, the officers made the arrests.

16 of the 21 partygoers sued the District. The district court awarded them partial summary judgment and held that the officers lacked probable cause to arrest because nothing they learned suggested that the partygoers knew or should have known that they were in the house against the owner's will. A jury awarded damages. A divided panel of the court of appeals affirmed, and the court denied rehearing en banc over four dissents.

Justice Thomas's opinion found that the officers reasonably could have concluded that they had probable cause to arrest and, even assuming that there was no probable cause, they had qualified immunity.

B. PROBABLE CAUSE, SPECIFICITY AND REASONABLENESS

Page 173. Add the following section at the end of the material on obtaining a search warrant:

11. Warrants for Information Stored Abroad

In *United States v. Microsoft Corp.*, 138 S.Ct. 1186 (2018) (per curiam), the Court dismissed as moot a case in which the government obtained a warrant pursuant to 18 U.S.C. § 2703 (the Stored Communications Act) compelling Microsoft to disclose all e-mails and other information associated with the account of one of its customers. Microsoft determined that all of the e-mail contents were stored in a data center in Dublin and moved to quash the warrant as beyond the territorial coverage of the Stored Communications Act. The district court denied Microsoft's motion and, acting on a stipulation jointly submitted by the parties, held Microsoft in civil contempt. The Second Circuit reversed the decision, vacated the civil contempt finding, and held that requiring Microsoft to disclose the electronic communications in question would be an unauthorized extraterritorial application of § 2703. While the case was pending before the Supreme Court, Congress enacted and the President signed into law the Clarifying Lawful Overseas Use of Data Act (CLOUD Act), as part of the Consolidated Appropriations Act, 2018, Pub. L. 115–141. The Court held that the enactment of the CLOUD Act mooted the case.

The CLOUD Act amends the Stored Communications Act, 18 U. S. C. § 2701 et seq., by adding the following provision:

> A [service provider] shall comply with the obligations of this chapter to preserve, backup, or disclose the contents of a wire or electronic communication and any record or other information pertaining to a customer or subscriber within such provider's possession, custody, or control, regardless of whether such communication, record, or other information is located within or outside of the United States.

Litigation over the accessibility of records stored in foreign countries is not likely to end because the CLOUD Act is now law. The Act permits companies to challenge law enforcement data requests if an order would pose international conflict of law issues. Companies can challenge warrants for data if there is a bilateral law enforcement pact between the United States and a "qualifying foreign government," and also if the warrant would cause a conflict of law issue with other countries absent a law enforcement sharing agreement.

V.   TO APPLY OR NOT APPLY THE WARRANT CLAUSE

A.   ARRESTS IN PUBLIC AND IN THE HOME

3.   The Constitutional Rule: Arrests in Public

Page 199. Add after the second full paragraph:

Qualified Immunity: Kisela v. Hughes

In *Kisela v. Hughes*, 138 S.Ct. 1148 (2018) (per curiam), the Court summarily reversed the Ninth Circuit's holding that a police officer who shot a knife-wielding suspect was not entitled to qualified immunity. The Court did not decide whether the officer violated the Fourth Amendment, and held only that this was far from an obvious case in which any competent officer would have known that the shooting constituted excessive force under the Fourth Amendment.

Justice Sotomayor, joined by Justice Ginsburg, dissented, and argued that the Ninth Circuit was correct and the case should not have been summarily decided. She ended her opinion by pointing out the Court's willingness to intervene when lower courts deny officers qualified immunity and its unwillingness to intervene when the courts grant officers qualified immunity. She wrote that the Court's signal to law enforcement officers was "they can shoot first and think later."

On June 15, 2020, the Court declined an opportunity to restrict or abolish the doctrine of qualified immunity when it denied certiorari in *Baxter v. Bracey*, which involved the use of a police dog against a burglary suspect who had already surrendered to law enforcement. Dissenting from that denial, Justice Thomas reiterated his "strong doubts about our § 1983 qualified immunity doctrine."

B. STOP AND FRISK

3. Grounds for a Stop: Reasonable Suspicion

b. *Quantum of Suspicion*

Page 268. The following note replaces *"Assessment of Probabilities: United States v. Arvizu and California v. Navarette"*:

Probability, Alternative Explanations, and Common Sense: Assessing Reasonable Suspicion

In *United States v. Arvizu*, 534 U.S. 266 (2002), the Supreme Court rejected as contrary to its teachings a rigid, formalistic, and almost quantitative approach to assessing reasonable suspicion. In that case, the Ninth Circuit identified ten facts in the record that might have provided grounds for a border patrol officer to stop a minivan traveling unmarked dirt roads near the border with Mexico, analyzed each of them individually, found that seven were ambiguous, because susceptible to innocent explanation, and then concluded that the remaining three were insufficient to provide the officer with reason to suspect that the occupants of the minivan might be engaged in illegal activity. Writing for the Court, Chief Justice Rehnquist held that this approach to assessing reasonable suspicion "departs sharply from" the Court's teachings, which instead counsel assessing the "totality of the circumstances" to determine whether "the detaining officer has a 'particularized and objective basis' for suspecting legal wrongdoing." In making that assessment, the Court licensed officers to "make inferences and deductions about the cumulative information available to them that 'might elude an untrained person.'" Conceding that "the concept of reasonable suspicion is somewhat abstract," the *Arvizu* Court steadfastly refused to "reduc[e] it to a neat set of legal rules," echoing Chief Justice Rehnquist's elaboration of probable cause in *Illinois v. Gates*, 462 U.S. 213 1983) (see main text at 116) ("[P]robable cause is a fluid concept—turning on the assessment of probabilities in particular factual contexts—not readily, or even usefully, reduced to a neat set of legal rules.").

The *Arvizu* Court roundly rejected the Ninth Circuit's rigid, atomistic approach to analyzing individual facts giving rise to reasonable suspicion. While clarifying that reasonable suspicion requires much less than 50% certainty, the Court also declined to specify a probabilistic threshold for reasonable suspicion. Nevertheless, the Court allowed that innocent explanations and probabilities are both relevant when assessing the totality of circumstances potentially giving rise to reasonable suspicion. This left lower courts and commentators to wonder about the analytic role these considerations can and should play when determining whether a set of facts provides reason to suspect that a person is engaged in criminal wrongdoing. The Court provided useful guidance last term in *Kansas v. Glover*.

KANSAS V. GLOVER
Supreme Court of the United States, 2020.
140 S.Ct. 1183.

JUSTICE THOMAS delivered the opinion of the Court.

This case presents the question whether a police officer violates the Fourth Amendment by initiating an investigative traffic stop after running a vehicle's license plate and learning that the registered owner has a revoked driver's license. We hold that when the officer lacks information negating an inference that the owner is the driver of the vehicle, the stop is reasonable.

I

Kansas charged respondent Charles Glover, Jr., with driving as a habitual violator after a traffic stop revealed that he was driving with a revoked license. Glover filed a motion to suppress all evidence seized during the stop, claiming that the officer lacked reasonable suspicion. Neither Glover nor the police officer testified at the suppression hearing. Instead, the parties stipulated to the following facts:

1. Deputy Mark Mehrer is a certified law enforcement officer employed by the Douglas County Kansas Sheriff's Office.

2. On April 28, 2016, Deputy Mehrer was on routine patrol in Douglas County when he observed a 1995 Chevrolet 1500 pickup truck with Kansas plate 295ATJ.

3. Deputy Mehrer ran Kansas plate 295ATJ through the Kansas Department of Revenue's file service. The registration came back to a 1995 Chevrolet 1500 pickup truck.

4. Kansas Department of Revenue files indicated the truck was registered to Charles Glover Jr. The files also indicated that Mr. Glover had a revoked driver's license in the State of Kansas.

5. Deputy Mehrer assumed the registered owner of the truck was also the driver, Charles Glover Jr.

6. Deputy Mehrer did not observe any traffic infractions, and did not attempt to identify the driver [of] the truck. Based solely on the information that the registered owner of the truck was revoked, Deputy Mehrer initiated a traffic stop.

7.   The driver of the truck was identified as the defendant, Charles Glover Jr.

The District Court granted Glover's motion to suppress. The Court of Appeals reversed, holding that "it was reasonable for [Deputy] Mehrer to infer that the driver was the owner of the vehicle" because "there were specific and articulable facts from which the officer's common-sense inference gave rise to a reasonable suspicion." The Kansas Supreme Court reversed. According to the court, Deputy Mehrer did not have reasonable suspicion because his inference that Glover was behind the wheel amounted to "only a hunch" that Glover was engaging in criminal activity. The court further explained that Deputy Mehrer's "hunch" involved "applying and stacking unstated assumptions that are unreasonable without further factual basis," namely, that "the registered owner was likely the primary driver of the vehicle" and that "the owner will likely disregard the suspension or revocation order and continue to drive." We granted Kansas' petition for a writ of certiorari and now reverse.

II

Under this Court's precedents, the Fourth Amendment permits an officer to initiate a brief investigative traffic stop when he has "a particularized and objective basis for suspecting the particular person stopped of criminal activity." "Although a mere 'hunch' does not create reasonable suspicion, the level of suspicion the standard requires is considerably less than proof of wrongdoing by a preponderance of the evidence, and obviously less than is necessary for probable cause." Because it is a "less demanding" standard, "reasonable suspicion can be established with information that is different in quantity or content than that required to establish probable cause." The standard "depends on the factual and practical considerations of everyday life on which reasonable and prudent men, not legal technicians, act." Courts "cannot reasonably demand scientific certainty . . . where none exists." Rather, they must permit officers to make "commonsense judgments and inferences about human behavior."

III

We have previously recognized that States have a "vital interest in ensuring that only those qualified to do so are permitted to operate motor vehicles [and] that licensing, registration, and vehicle inspection requirements are being observed." With this in mind, we turn to whether the facts known to Deputy Mehrer at the time of the stop gave rise to reasonable suspicion. We conclude that they did.

Before initiating the stop, Deputy Mehrer observed an individual operating a 1995 Chevrolet 1500 pickup truck with Kansas plate 295ATJ. He also knew that the registered owner of the truck had a revoked license and that the model of the truck matched the observed vehicle. From these three facts, Deputy Mehrer drew the commonsense inference that Glover was likely the driver of the vehicle, which provided more than reasonable suspicion to initiate the stop.

The fact that the registered owner of a vehicle is not always the driver of the vehicle does not negate the reasonableness of Deputy Mehrer's inference. Such is the case with all reasonable inferences. The reasonable suspicion inquiry "falls considerably short" of 51% accuracy, for, as we have explained, "[t]o be reasonable is not to be perfect." Glover's revoked license does not render Deputy Mehrer's inference unreasonable either. Empirical studies demonstrate what common experience readily reveals: Drivers with revoked licenses frequently continue to drive and therefore to pose safety risks to other motorists and pedestrians. *See, e.g.,* 2 T. Neuman et al., National Coop. Hwy. Research Program Report 500: A Guide for Addressing Collisions Involving Unlicensed Drivers and Drivers With Suspended or Revoked Licenses, p. III–1 (2003) (noting that 75% of drivers with suspended or revoked licenses continue to drive); National Hwy. and Traffic Safety Admin., Research Note: Driver License Compliance Status in Fatal Crashes 2 (Oct. 2014) (noting that approximately 19% of motor vehicle fatalities from 2008–2012 "involved drivers with invalid licenses").

Although common sense suffices to justify this inference, Kansas law reinforces that it is reasonable to infer that an individual with a revoked license may continue driving. The State's license-revocation scheme covers drivers who have already demonstrated a disregard for the law or are categorically unfit to drive. The Division of Vehicles of the Kansas Department of Revenue (Division) "shall" revoke a driver's license upon certain convictions for involuntary manslaughter, vehicular homicide, battery, reckless driving, fleeing or attempting to elude a police officer, or conviction of a felony in which a motor vehicle is used. Reckless driving is defined as "driv[ing] any vehicle in willful or wanton disregard for the safety of persons or property." The Division also has discretion to revoke a license if a driver "[h]as been convicted with such frequency of serious offenses against traffic regulations governing the movement of vehicles as to indicate a disrespect for traffic laws and a disregard for the safety of other persons on the highways," "has been convicted of three or more moving traffic violations committed on separate occasions within a 12-month period," "is incompetent to drive a motor vehicle," or "has been convicted of a moving traffic violation, committed at a time when the person's driving privileges were restricted, suspended[,] or revoked." Other reasons include violating license restrictions, being under house arrest, and being a habitual violator, which Kansas defines as a resident or nonresident who has been convicted three or more times within the past five years of certain enumerated driving offenses. The concerns motivating the State's various grounds for revocation lend further credence to the inference that a registered owner with a revoked Kansas driver's license might be the one driving the vehicle.

IV

Glover and the dissent respond with two arguments as to why Deputy Mehrer lacked reasonable suspicion. Neither is persuasive.

A

First, Glover and the dissent argue that Deputy Mehrer's inference was unreasonable because it was not grounded in his law enforcement training or experience. Nothing in our Fourth Amendment precedent supports the notion that, in determining whether reasonable suspicion exists, an officer can draw inferences based on knowledge gained only through law enforcement training and experience. We have repeatedly recognized the opposite. In *Navarette*, we noted a number of behaviors— including driving in the median, crossing the center line on a highway, and swerving—that as a matter of common sense provide "sound indicia of drunk driving." In *Wardlow*, we made the unremarkable observation that "[h]eadlong flight—wherever it occurs—is the consummate act of evasion" and therefore could factor into a police officer's reasonable suspicion determination. And in *Sokolow*, we recognized that the defendant's method of payment for an airplane ticket contributed to the agents' reasonable suspicion of drug trafficking because we "fe[lt] confident" that "[m]ost business travelers . . . purchase airline tickets by credit card or check" rather than cash. So too here. The inference that the driver of a car is its registered owner does not require any specialized training; rather, it is a reasonable inference made by ordinary people on a daily basis.

The dissent reads our cases differently, contending that they permit an officer to use only the common sense derived from his "experiences in law enforcement." Such a standard defies the "common sense" understanding of common sense, i.e., information that is accessible to people generally, not just some specialized subset of society. More importantly, this standard appears nowhere in our precedents. In fact, we have stated that reasonable suspicion is an "abstract" concept that cannot be reduced to "a neat set of legal rules," and we have repeatedly rejected courts' efforts to impose a rigid structure on the concept of reasonableness. This is precisely what the dissent's rule would do by insisting that officers must be treated as bifurcated persons, completely precluded from drawing factual inferences based on the commonly held knowledge they have acquired in their everyday lives.

The dissent's rule would also impose on police the burden of pointing to specific training materials or field experiences justifying reasonable suspicion for the myriad infractions in municipal criminal codes. And by removing common sense as a source of evidence, the dissent would considerably narrow the daylight between the showing required for probable cause and the "less stringent" showing required for reasonable suspicion. Such requirements are inconsistent with our Fourth Amendment jurisprudence, and we decline to adopt them here.

In reaching this conclusion, we in no way minimize the significant role that specialized training and experience routinely play in law enforcement investigations. We simply hold that such experience is not required in every instance.

B

Glover and the dissent also contend that adopting Kansas' view would eviscerate the need for officers to base reasonable suspicion on "specific and articulable facts" particularized to the individual, because police could instead rely exclusively on probabilities. Their argument carries little force. As an initial matter, we have previously stated that officers, like jurors, may rely on probabilities in the reasonable suspicion context. Moreover, as explained above, Deputy Mehrer did not rely exclusively on probabilities. He knew that the license plate was linked to a truck matching the observed vehicle and that the registered owner of the vehicle had a revoked license. Based on these minimal facts, he used common sense to form a reasonable suspicion that a specific individual was potentially engaged in specific criminal activity—driving with a revoked license. Traffic stops of this nature do not delegate to officers "broad and unlimited discretion" to stop drivers at random. Nor do they allow officers to stop drivers whose conduct is no different from any other driver's. Accordingly, combining database information and commonsense judgments in this context is fully consonant with this Court's Fourth Amendment precedents.

V

This Court's precedents have repeatedly affirmed that "the ultimate touchstone of the Fourth Amendment is reasonableness." Under the totality of the circumstances of this case, Deputy Mehrer drew an entirely reasonable inference that Glover was driving while his license was revoked.

We emphasize the narrow scope of our holding. Like all seizures, "[t]he officer's action must be 'justified at its inception.' " "The standard takes into account the totality of the circumstances—the whole picture." As a result, the presence of additional facts might dispel reasonable suspicion. For example, if an officer knows that the registered owner of the vehicle is in his mid-sixties but observes that the driver is in her mid-twenties, then the totality of the circumstances would not "raise a suspicion that the particular individual being stopped is engaged in wrongdoing." Here, Deputy Mehrer possessed no exculpatory information—let alone sufficient information to rebut the reasonable inference that Glover was driving his own truck—and thus the stop was justified.

* * *

For the foregoing reasons, we reverse the judgment of the Kansas Supreme Court, and we remand the case for further proceedings not inconsistent with this opinion.

It is so ordered.

JUSTICE KAGAN, with whom JUSTICE GINSBURG joins, concurring.

When you see a car coming down the street, your common sense tells you that the registered owner may well be behind the wheel. Not always, of course. Families share cars; friends borrow them. Still, a person often buys a vehicle to drive it himself. So your suspicion that the owner is driving would be perfectly reasonable.

Now, though, consider a wrinkle: Suppose you knew that the registered owner of the vehicle no longer had a valid driver's license. That added fact raises a new question. What are the odds that someone who has lost his license would continue to drive? The answer is by no means obvious. You might think that a person told not to drive on pain of criminal penalty would obey the order—so that if his car was on the road, someone else (a family member, a friend) must be doing the driving. Or you might have the opposite intuition—that a person's reasons for driving would overcome his worries about violating the law, no matter the possible punishment. But most likely (let's be honest), you just wouldn't know. Especially if you've not had your own license taken away, your everyday experience has given you little basis to assess the probabilities. Your common sense can therefore no longer guide you.

Even so, Deputy Mark Mehrer had reasonable suspicion to stop the truck in this case, and I join the Court's opinion holding as much. Crucially for me, Mehrer knew yet one more thing about the vehicle's registered owner, and it related to his proclivity for breaking driving laws. As the Court recounts, Mehrer learned from a state database that Charles Glover, the truck's owner, had had his license revoked under Kansas law. And Kansas almost never revokes a license except for serious or repeated driving offenses. Crimes like vehicular homicide and manslaughter, or vehicular flight from a police officer, provoke a license revocation; so too do multiple convictions for moving traffic violations within a short time. In other words, a person with a revoked license has already shown a willingness to flout driving restrictions. That fact, as the Court states, provides a "reason[ ] to infer" that such a person will drive without a license—at least often enough to warrant an investigatory stop. And there is nothing else here to call that inference into question. That is because the parties' unusually austere stipulation confined the case to the facts stated above—i.e., that Mehrer stopped Glover's truck because he knew that Kansas had revoked Glover's license.

But as already suggested, I would find this a different case if Kansas had barred Glover from driving on a ground that provided no similar evidence of his penchant for ignoring driving laws. Consider, for example, if Kansas had suspended rather than revoked Glover's license. Along with many other States, Kansas suspends licenses for matters having nothing to do with road safety, such as failing to pay parking tickets, court fees, or child support. Indeed, several studies have found that most license suspensions do not relate to driving at all; what they most relate to is being poor. So the good reason the Court gives for thinking that someone with a revoked license will keep driving—that he has a history of disregarding driving rules—would no longer apply. And without that, the case for assuming that an unlicensed driver is at the wheel is hardly self-evident. It would have to rest on an idea about the frequency with which even those who had previously complied with driving laws would defy a State's penalty-backed command to stay off the roads. But where would that idea come from? As discussed above, I doubt whether our collective common sense could do the necessary work. Or otherwise said, I suspect that any common sense invoked in this altered context would not much differ from a "mere 'hunch' "—and so "not create reasonable suspicion."

And even when, as under the revocation scheme here, a starting presumption of reasonable suspicion makes sense, the defendant may show that in his case additional information dictates the opposite result. The Court is clear on this point, emphasizing that under the applicable totality-of-the-circumstances test, "the presence of additional facts might dispel reasonable suspicion" even though an officer knows that a car on the road belongs to a person with a revoked license. Just as the Court once said of a trained drug-detection dog's "alert," the license-revocation signal is always subject to a defendant's challenge, whether through cross-examination of the officer or introduction of his own fact or expert witnesses. That challenge may take any number of forms. The Court offers a clear example of observational evidence dispelling reasonable suspicion: if the officer knows the registered owner of a vehicle is an elderly man, but can see the driver is a young woman. Similarly (if not as cut-and-dry), when the officer learns a car has two or more registered owners, the balance of circumstances may tip away from reasonable suspicion that the one with the revoked license is driving. And so too, the attributes of the car may be relevant. Consider if a car bears the markings of a peer-to-peer carsharing service; or compare the likelihoods that someone other than the registered owner is driving (1) a family minivan and (2) a Ferrari. The officer himself may have a wealth of accumulated information about such matters, and the defendant may probe what that knowledge suggests about the stop at issue.

Such a challenge may also use statistical evidence, which is almost daily expanding in sophistication and scope. States or municipalities often keep information about "hit rates" in stops like this one—in other words, the frequency with which those stops discover unlicensed drivers behind the wheel. Somewhat less direct but also useful are state and local data (collected by governments, insurance companies, and academics alike) about the average number of drivers for each registered automobile and the extent to which unlicensed persons continue to drive. (If, to use an extreme example, every car had 10 associated drivers, and losing a license reduced driving time by 90%, an officer would not have reasonable suspicion for a stop.) Here too, defendants may question testifying officers about such information. Indeed, an officer may have his own hit rate, which if low enough could itself negate reasonable suspicion.

In this strange case, contested on a barebones stipulation, the record contains no evidence of these kinds. There is but a single, simple fact: A police officer learned from a state database that a car on the road belonged to a person with a revoked license. Given that revocations in Kansas nearly always stem from serious or repeated driving violations, I agree with the Court about the reasonableness of the officer's inference that the owner, "Glover[,] was driving while his license was revoked." And because Glover offered no rebuttal, there the matter stands. But that does not mean cases with more complete records will all wind up in the same place. A defendant like Glover may still be able to show that his case is different—that the "presence of additional facts" and circumstances "dispel[s] reasonable suspicion." Which is to say that in more fully litigated cases, the license-revocation alert does not (as it did here) end the inquiry. It is but the first, though no doubt an important, step in assessing the reasonableness of the officer's suspicion.

JUSTICE SOTOMAYOR, dissenting.

In upholding routine stops of vehicles whose owners have revoked licenses, the Court ignores key foundations of our reasonable-suspicion jurisprudence and impermissibly and unnecessarily reduces the State's burden of proof. I therefore dissent.

I

I begin with common ground. The Fourth Amendment permits "brief investigatory" vehicle stops, on "facts that do not constitute probable cause," To assess whether an officer had the requisite suspicion to seize a driver, past cases have considered the "totality of the circumstances—the whole picture," and analyzed whether the officer assembled "fact on fact and clue on clue."

The stop at issue here, however, rests on just one key fact: that the vehicle was owned by someone with a revoked license. The majority concludes—erroneously, in my view—that seizing this vehicle was constitutional on the record below because drivers with revoked licenses (as opposed to suspended licenses) in Kansas "have already demonstrated a disregard for the law or are categorically unfit to drive." This analysis breaks from settled doctrine and dramatically alters both the quantum and nature of evidence a State may rely on to prove suspicion.

A

The State bears the burden of justifying a seizure. This requires the government to articulate factors supporting its reasonable suspicion, usually through a trained agent. While the Court has not dictated precisely what evidence a government must produce, it has stressed that an officer must at least "articulate more than an 'inchoate and unparticularized suspicion or "hunch" ' of criminal activity." That articulation must include both facts and an officer's "rational inferences from those facts." A logical "gap as to any one matter" in this analysis may be overcome by " 'a strong showing' " regarding " 'other indicia of reliability.' " But gaps may not go unfilled.

Additionally, reasonable suspicion eschews judicial common sense in favor of the perspectives and inferences of a reasonable officer viewing "the facts through the lens of his police experience and expertise." It is the reasonable officer's assessment, not the ordinary person's—or judge's—judgment, that matters.

Finally, a stop must be individualized—that is, based on "a suspicion that the particular [subject] being stopped is engaged in wrongdoing." This does not mean that the officer must know the driver's identity. But a seizure must rest on more than the "likelihood that [a] given person" or particular vehicle is engaged in wrongdoing. The inquiry ordinarily involves some observation or report about the target's behavior—not merely the class to which he belongs.

B

Faithful adherence to these precepts would yield a significantly different analysis and outcome than that offered by the majority.

For starters, the majority flips the burden of proof. It permits Kansas police officers to effectuate roadside stops whenever they lack "information negating an inference" that a vehicle's unlicensed owner is its driver. This has it backwards: The State shoulders the burden to supply the key inference that tethers observation to suspicion. The majority repeatedly attributes such an inference to Deputy Mehrer. But that is an after-the fact gloss on a seven-paragraph stipulation. Nowhere in his terse submission did Deputy Mehrer indicate that he had any informed belief about the propensity of unlicensed drivers to operate motor vehicles in the area—let alone that he relied on such a belief in seizing Glover.

The consequence of the majority's approach is to absolve officers from any responsibility to investigate the identity of a driver where feasible. But that is precisely what officers ought to do—and are more than capable of doing. Of course, some circumstances may not warrant an officer approaching a car to take a closer look at its occupants. But there are countless other instances where officers have been able to ascertain the identity of a driver from a distance and make out their approximate age and gender. Indeed, our cases are rife with examples of officers who have perceived more than just basic driver demographics. The majority underestimates officers' capabilities and instead gives them free rein to stop a vehicle involved in no suspicious activity simply because it is registered to an unlicensed person. That stop is based merely on a guess or a "hunch" about the driver's identity.

With no basis in the record to presume that unlicensed drivers routinely continue driving, the majority endeavors to fill the gap with its own "common sense." But simply labeling an inference "common sense" does not make it so, no matter how many times the majority repeats it. Whether the driver of a vehicle is likely to be its unlicensed owner is "by no means obvious." And like the concurrence, I "doubt" that our collective judicial common sense could answer that question, even if our Fourth Amendment jurisprudence allowed us to do so.

Contrary to the majority's claims, the reasonable-suspicion inquiry does not accommodate the average person's intuition. Rather, it permits reliance on a particular type of common sense—that of the reasonable officer, developed through her experiences in law enforcement. This approach acknowledges that what may be "common sense" to a layperson may not be relevant (or correct) in a law enforcement context. Indeed, this case presents the type of geographically localized inquiry where an officer's "inferences and deductions that might well elude an untrained person" would come in handy. By relying on judicial inferences instead, the majority promotes broad, inflexible rules that overlook regional differences.

Allowing judges to offer their own brand of common sense where the State's proffered justifications for a search come up short also shifts police work to the judiciary. Our cases—including those the majority cites—have looked to officer sensibility to establish inferences about human behavior, even though they just as easily could have relied on the inferences "made by ordinary people on a daily basis." There is no reason to depart from that practice here.

Finally, to bolster its conclusion as grounded in "common experience," the majority cites "empirical studies." But its use of statistics illustrates the danger of relying on large-scale data to carry out what is supposed to be a particularized exercise. Neither of the referenced reports tells us the percentage of vehicle owners with revoked licenses in Kansas who continue to drive their cars. Neither report even offers a useful denominator: One lumps drivers with suspended and revoked licenses together, while the other examines the license status of only motorists involved in fatal collisions. The figures say nothing about how the behavior of revoked drivers measures up relative to their licensed counterparts—whether one group is more likely to be involved in accidents, or whether the incidences are comparable—which would inform a trooper's inferences about driver identity.

As the concurrence recognizes, while statistics may help a defendant challenge the reasonableness of an officer's actions, they "cannot substitute for the individualized suspicion that the Fourth Amendment requires." If courts do not scrutinize officer observation or expertise in the reasonable-suspicion analysis, then seizures may be made on large-scale data alone— data that say nothing about the individual save for the class to which he belongs. That analytical approach strays far from "acting upon observed violations" of law—which this Court has said is the "foremost method of enforcing traffic and vehicle safety regulations."

The majority today has paved the road to finding reasonable suspicion based on nothing more than a demographic profile. Its logic has thus made the State's task all but automatic. That has never been the law, and it never should be.

II

The majority's justifications for this new approach have no foundation in fact or logic. It supposes that requiring officers to point to "training materials or field experiences" would demand " 'scientific certainty.' " But that is no truer in this case than in other circumstances where the reasonable-suspicion inquiry applies. Indeed, the State here was invited to stipulate to the evidence it relied on to make the stop. It could have easily described the individual or "accumulated experience" of officers in the jurisdiction.

In fact, it is the majority's approach that makes scant policy sense. If the State need not set forth all the information its officers considered before forming suspicion, what conceivable evidence could be used to mount an effective challenge to a vehicle stop, as the concurrence imagines? Who could meaningfully interrogate an officer's action when all the officer has to say is that the vehicle was registered to an unlicensed driver? How would a driver counter that evidence—by stating that they were of a different age or gender than the owner and insisting that the officer could have easily discerned that? And where would a defendant bring his arguments if the trial judge makes the key inference, or by the same token, fails to make an inference that "might well elude" the untrained?

Moreover, the majority's distinction between revocation and suspension may not hold up in other jurisdictions. For one, whether drivers with suspended licenses have "demonstrated a disregard for the law or are categorically unfit to drive" is completely unknown. And in several States, the grounds for revocation include offenses unrelated to driving fitness, such as using a license to unlawfully buy alcohol. In yet other jurisdictions, "revocation" is the label assigned to a temporary sanction, which may be imposed for such infractions as the failure to comply with child support payments. Whether the majority's "common sense" assumptions apply outside of Kansas is thus open to challenge.

* * *

Vehicle stops "interfere with freedom of movement, are inconvenient, and consume time." Worse still, they "may create substantial anxiety" through an "unsettling show of authority." Before subjecting motorists to this type of investigation, the State must possess articulable facts and officer inferences to form suspicion. The State below left unexplained key components of the reasonable-suspicion inquiry. In an effort to uphold the conviction, the Court destroys Fourth Amendment jurisprudence that requires individualized suspicion. I respectfully dissent.

QUESTIONS AFTER KANSAS V. GLOVER

There are a number of important takeaways from the Court's opinion in *Kansas v. Glover*. Foremost is that reasonable suspicion is fundamentally indeterminate. It is neither quantifiable nor amenable to assessments based on abstract rules. It is, instead, a context-sensitive, qualitative, commonsense assessment. This does not mean that reasonable suspicion is a free-flying balloon, immune from rational constraint. Rather, as Justice Thomas and Justice Kagan describe it, common sense is grounded in logic. In this case, for example, Justice Thomas posits a simple syllogism:

1. If a car is registered in a person's name, then it is likely that he is driving it.

2. The pickup truck was registered to Charles Glover, Jr.

3. Therefore, it is likely that Charles Glover, Jr., was driving the pickup truck.

The Court divides on to the validity of the major premise. For Justice Thomas and the majority, the major premise is obviously true, so an officer would only be denied the conclusion if she stumbled on evidence defeating the inference (e.g. that the car is registered to a middle aged man, but the driver is a young woman). Statistical data and details about state law provide helpful, but unnecessary, support for the obvious. By contrast, Justice Kagan appears unwilling to rely solely on the intuitive appeal of the major premise, and is only persuaded that it holds in this case because of the substantive law in Kansas. Justice Sotomayor appears to reject the major premise entirely. She would instead require that officers' decisions to effect stops be grounded in reliable data and experience applied to each particular circumstance rather than common intuition. Who do you think has the better part of the argument?

The Court also appears to divide on whether officers confronted with circumstances that might support reasonable suspicion have a duty to engage in less intrusive investigative measures to confirm or dispel that suspicion before resorting to a stop. The majority does not seem to believe that is necessary at all. If an officer has reasonable suspicion, then she may engage in a stop and has no obligation to choose less intrusive alternatives first. By contrast, Justice Sotomayor seems to favor a rule requiring that officers conduct additional, non-intrusive, investigative measures such as gaining visual confirmation that the driver of a car roughly matches the profile of the registered owner. Which view best reflects the text of the Fourth Amendment? The Court's jurisprudence? For some additional thoughts on the potential impact of *Glover*, see Stephen A. Saltzburg, Response, Kansas v. Glover: Just Common Sense?, Geo. Wash. L. Rev. On the Docket (Apr. 13, 2020), https://www.gwlr.org/kansas-v-glover-just-common-sense/.

The force of Justice Sotomayor's arguments notwithstanding, *Glover* seems to virtually cast aside quantitative analysis when assessing reasonable suspicion. So long as an officer can cite specific facts and a plausible logical narrative explaining their suspicions, her decision to conduct a stop in order to confirm or dispel her suspicions is likely to clear the low hurdle erected by *Terry*. In a world where data and sophisticated means of data analysis are increasingly available, do you agree with the majority that common intuitions are sufficient to ground decisions to stop, or should we instead require quantitative, data-driven decisions? *See* Kiel Brennan Marquez, *Plausible Cause: Explanatory Standards in the Age of Powerful Machines*, 70 Vand. L. Rev., Vol. 1249 (2017). Relatedly, Justice Kagan suggests that law enforcement agents and agencies should subject their stated grounds for stops to review, discarding those that too often yield negative results. Is this constitutionally required, or may officers rely on intuitively appealing, but empirically unreliable grounds for their suspicions? *See* Shima Baradaran Baughman, *Rebalancing the Fourth Amendment*, 102 Geo. L. Rev. 1 (2013).

D. PRETEXTUAL STOPS AND ARRESTS

Page 381. Add after second full paragraph:

First Amendment Issues

In *Nieves v. Bartlett*, 139 S.Ct. 1715 (2019), the Court held that the existence of probable cause provided a defense to a claim of retaliation against the exercise of First Amendment rights. Russell Bartlett was arrested by Officer Luis Nieves for disorderly conduct and resisting arrest during "Arctic Man," a raucous winter sports festival held in a remote part of Alaska. Nieves was speaking with a group of attendees when a seemingly intoxicated Bartlett started shouting at them not to talk to the police. When Nieves approached him, Bartlett began yelling at the officer to leave. Rather than escalate the situation, Nieves left. Minutes later, Bartlett approached Officer Bryce Weight in an aggressive manner while he was questioning a minor, stood between Weight and the teenager, and yelled with slurred speech that Weight should not speak with the minor. When Bartlett stepped toward Weight, the officer pushed him back. Nieves saw the confrontation and initiated an arrest. When Bartlett was slow to comply, the officers forced him to the ground. After he was handcuffed, Nieves said "bet you wish you would have talked to me now." Bartlett sued under 42 U.S.C. § 1983, claiming that the officers violated his First Amendment rights by arresting him in retaliation for his speech—i.e., his initial refusal to speak with Nieves and his intervention in Weight's discussion with the minor.

Chief Justice Roberts wrote for the Court and concluded that the existence of probable cause to arrest provided a defense to any First Amendment claim for retaliatory arrest. He reasoned that the plaintiff is required to show that the arrest was caused by an intent to retaliate for exercise of First Amendment rights, and when there is probable cause to make the arrest anyway, such causation cannot be shown. The Chief Justice rejected Bartlett's argument that the primary focus should be on the officer's intent. He explained as follows:

> Bartlett's approach dismisses the need for any threshold showing, moving directly to consideration of the subjective intent of the officers. In the Fourth Amendment context, however, we have almost uniformly rejected invitations to probe subjective intent. See *Kentucky v. King*, 563 U.S. 452, 464 (2011) ("Legal tests based on reasonableness are generally objective, and this Court has long taken the view that evenhanded law enforcement is best achieved by the application of objective standards of conduct, rather than standards that depend upon the subjective state of mind of the officer."). Police officers conduct approximately 29,000 arrests every day—a dangerous task that requires making quick decisions in circumstances that are tense, uncertain, and rapidly evolving. To ensure that officers may go about their work without undue apprehension of being sued, we generally review their conduct under objective standards of reasonableness. Thus, when reviewing an arrest, we ask "whether the circumstances, viewed objectively, justify [the challenged] action," and if so, conclude "that action was reasonable *whatever* the subjective intent motivating the relevant officials." *al-Kidd*, 563 U.S. at 736. A particular officer's state of mind is simply "irrelevant," and it provides "no basis for invalidating an arrest." *Devenpeck v. Alford*, 543 U.S. 146, 153, 155 (2004).

Bartlett's purely subjective approach would undermine that precedent by allowing even doubtful retaliatory arrest suits to proceed based solely on allegations about an arresting officer's mental state. Because a state of mind is easy to allege and hard to disprove, a subjective inquiry would threaten to set off broad-ranging discovery in which there often is no clear end to the relevant evidence. As a result, policing certain events like an unruly protest would pose overwhelming litigation risks. Any inartful turn of phrase or perceived slight during a legitimate arrest could land an officer in years of litigation. Bartlett's standard would thus dampen the ardor of all but the most resolute, or the most irresponsible, in the unflinching discharge of their duties. It would also compromise evenhanded application of the law by making the constitutionality of an arrest "vary from place to place and from time to time" depending on the personal motives of individual officers. *Devenpeck*, 543 U.S. at 154. Yet another "predictable consequence" of such a rule is that officers would simply minimize their communication during arrests to avoid having their words scrutinized for hints of improper motive—a result that would leave everyone worse off.

Chief Justice Roberts did recognize an exception to a "probable cause defense" against a First Amendment retaliation claim: the defense should not apply "where officers have probable cause to make arrests, but typically exercise their discretion not to do so." In such cases, "an unyielding requirement to show the absence of probable cause could pose a risk that some police officers may exploit the arrest power as a means of suppressing speech." The Chief Justice explained as follows:

For example, at many intersections, jaywalking is endemic but rarely results in arrest. If an individual who has been vocally complaining about police conduct is arrested for jaywalking at such an intersection, it would seem insufficiently protective of First Amendment rights to dismiss the individual's retaliatory arrest claim on the ground that there was undoubted probable cause for the arrest. In such a case, because probable cause does little to prove or disprove the causal connection between animus and injury, applying *Hartman*'s rule would come at the expense of *Hartman*'s logic.

For those reasons, we conclude that the no-probable-cause requirement should not apply when a plaintiff presents objective evidence that he was arrested when otherwise similarly situated individuals not engaged in the same sort of protected speech had not been. * * * Because this inquiry is objective, the statements and motivations of the particular arresting officer are irrelevant at this stage. After making the required showing, the plaintiff's claim may proceed in the same manner as claims where the plaintiff has met the threshold showing of the absence of probable cause.

Justice Thomas, concurring in part and concurring in the judgment, disagreed with the "narrow qualification." He emphasized that the existence of probable cause at common law generally excused an officer from liability for false imprisonment, malicious arrest, and malicious prosecution. He observed that, despite the fact that the Chief Justice illustrated the narrow qualification by using an example of jaywalking that results in few arrests, the narrow qualification applies to all offenses, including felonies. He warned that "[t]his overbroad exception thus is likely to encourage protracted litigation about which individuals are 'similarly situated.'"

Justice Gorsuch, concurring in part and dissenting in part, reasoned that simply because a practice passes muster under the Fourth Amendment does not mean that it does not violate another constitutional provision—e.g., racial discrimination in violation of the Fourteenth Amendment. He stated that "[l]ike a Fourteenth Amendment selective arrest claim, a First Amendment retaliatory arrest claim serves a different purpose than a Fourth Amendment unreasonable arrest claim, and that purpose does not depend on the presence or absence of probable cause." He concluded as follows:

> I would hold, as the majority does, that the absence of probable cause is not an absolute requirement of such a claim and its presence is not an absolute defense. * * * But rather than attempt to sort out precisely when and how probable cause plays a role in First Amendment claims, I would reserve decision on those questions until they are properly presented to this Court and we can address them with the benefit of full adversarial testing.

Justice Ginsburg, concurring in the judgment in part and dissenting in part, argued that "[t]he plaintiff bears the burden of demonstrating that unconstitutional animus was a motivating factor for an adverse action; the burden then shifts to the defendant to demonstrate that, even without any impetus to retaliate, the defendant would have taken the action complained of."

Justice Sotomayor, dissenting, argued that "[t]here is no basis in § 1983 or in the Constitution to withhold a remedy for an arrest that violated the First Amendment solely because an officer could point to probable cause that some offense, no matter how trivial or obviously pretextual, has occurred."

F. AUTOMOBILES AND OTHER MOVABLE OBJECTS

2. The Progeny of *Carroll*

Page 398. Add at the end of the section:

Vehicles on Private Property: Collins v. Virginia

COLLINS V. VIRGINIA
Supreme Court of the United States, 2018.
138 S.Ct. 1663.

JUSTICE SOTOMAYOR delivered the opinion of the Court.

This case presents the question whether the automobile exception to the Fourth Amendment permits a police officer, uninvited and without a warrant, to enter the curtilage of a home in order to search a vehicle parked therein. It does not.

I

Officer Matthew McCall of the Albemarle County Police Department in Virginia saw the driver of an orange and black motorcycle with an extended frame commit a traffic infraction. The driver eluded Officer McCall's attempt to stop the motorcycle. A few weeks later, Officer David Rhodes of the same department saw an orange and black motorcycle traveling well over the speed limit, but the driver got away from him, too. The officers compared notes and concluded that the two incidents involved the same motorcyclist.

Upon further investigation, the officers learned that the motorcycle likely was stolen and in the possession of petitioner Ryan Collins. After discovering photographs on Collins' Facebook profile that featured an orange and black motorcycle parked at the top of the driveway of a house, Officer Rhodes tracked down the address of the house, drove there, and parked on the street. It was later established that Collins' girlfriend lived in the house and that Collins stayed there a few nights per week.

From his parked position on the street, Officer Rhodes saw what appeared to be a motorcycle with an extended frame covered with a white tarp, parked at the same angle and in the same location on the driveway as in the Facebook photograph. Officer Rhodes, who did not have a warrant, exited his car and walked toward the house. He stopped to take a photograph of the covered motorcycle from the sidewalk, and then walked onto the residential property and up to the top of the driveway to where the motorcycle was parked. In order "to investigate further," Officer Rhodes pulled off the tarp, revealing a motorcycle that looked like the one from the speeding incident. He then ran a search of the license plate and vehicle identification numbers, which confirmed that the motorcycle was stolen.

After gathering this information, Officer Rhodes took a photograph of the uncovered motorcycle, put the tarp back on, left the property, and returned to his car to wait for Collins.

Shortly thereafter, Collins returned home. Officer Rhodes walked up to the front door of the house and knocked. Collins answered, agreed to speak with Officer Rhodes, and admitted that the motorcycle was his and that he had bought it without title. Officer Rhodes then arrested Collins.

Collins was indicted by a Virginia grand jury for receiving stolen property. He filed a pretrial motion to suppress the evidence that Officer Rhodes had obtained as a result of the warrantless search of the motorcycle. Collins argued that Officer Rhodes had trespassed on the curtilage of the house to conduct an investigation in violation of the Fourth Amendment. The trial court denied the motion and Collins was convicted.

The Court of Appeals of Virginia affirmed. It assumed that the motorcycle was parked in the curtilage of the home and held that Officer Rhodes had probable cause to believe that the motorcycle under the tarp was the same motorcycle that had evaded him in the past. It further concluded that Officer Rhodes' actions were lawful under the Fourth Amendment even absent a warrant because "numerous exigencies justified both his entry onto the property and his moving the tarp to view the motorcycle and record its identification number."

The Supreme Court of Virginia affirmed on different reasoning. It explained that the case was most properly resolved with reference to the Fourth Amendment's automobile exception. Under that framework, it held that Officer Rhodes had probable cause to believe that the motorcycle was contraband, and that the warrantless search therefore was justified.

We granted certiorari, and now reverse.

II

The Fourth Amendment provides in relevant part that the "right of the people to be secure in their persons, houses, papers, and effects, against unreasonable searches and seizures, shall not be violated." This case arises at the intersection of two components of the Court's Fourth Amendment jurisprudence: the automobile exception to the warrant requirement and the protection extended to the curtilage of a home.

A

1

The Court has held that the search of an automobile can be reasonable without a warrant. The Court first articulated the so-called automobile exception in Carroll v. United States, 267 U. S. 132 (1925). In that case, law enforcement officers had probable cause to believe that a car they observed traveling on the road contained illegal liquor. They stopped and searched the car, discovered and seized the illegal liquor, and arrested the occupants. The Court upheld the warrantless search and seizure, explaining that a "necessary difference" exists between searching "a store, dwelling house or other structure" and searching "a ship, motor boat, wagon or automobile" because a "vehicle can be quickly moved out of the locality or jurisdiction in which the warrant must be sought."

The "ready mobility" of vehicles served as the core justification for the automobile exception for many years. California v. Carney, 471 U. S. 386, 390 (1985) (citing, e.g., Cooper v. California, 386 U. S. 58, 59 (1967); Chambers v. Maroney, 399 U. S. 42, 51–52 (1970)). Later cases then introduced an additional rationale based on "the pervasive regulation of vehicles capable of traveling on the public highways." *Carney,* 471 U. S., at 392.

In announcing each of these two justifications, the Court took care to emphasize that the rationales applied only to automobiles and not to houses, and therefore supported "treating automobiles differently from houses" as a constitutional matter. Cady v. Dombrowski, 413 U. S. 433, 441 (1973).

When these justifications for the automobile exception "come into play," officers may search an automobile without having obtained a warrant so long as they have probable cause to do so. *Carney,* 471 U. S., at 392–393.

2

Like the automobile exception, the Fourth Amendment's protection of curtilage has long been black letter law. "[W]hen it comes to the Fourth Amendment, the home is first among equals." Florida v. Jardines, 569 U. S. 1, 6 (2013). "At the Amendment's 'very core' stands 'the right of a man to retreat into his own home and there be free from unreasonable governmental intrusion.'" *Ibid.* To give full practical effect to that right, the Court considers curtilage—"the area immediately surrounding and associated with the home"—to be "part of the home itself for Fourth Amendment purposes." *Jardines,* 569 U. S., at 6. "The protection afforded the curtilage is essentially a protection of families and personal privacy in an area intimately linked to the home, both physically and psychologically, where privacy expectations are most heightened." California v. Ciraolo, 476 U. S. 207, 212–213 (1986).

When a law enforcement officer physically intrudes on the curtilage to gather evidence, a search within the meaning of the Fourth Amendment has occurred. *Jardines,* 569 U. S., at 11. Such conduct thus is presumptively unreasonable absent a warrant.

B

1

With this background in mind, we turn to the application of these doctrines in the instant case. As an initial matter, we decide whether the part of the driveway where Collins' motorcycle was parked and subsequently searched is curtilage.

According to photographs in the record, the driveway runs alongside the front lawn and up a few yards past the front perimeter of the house. The top portion of the driveway that sits behind the front perimeter of the house is enclosed on two sides by a brick wall about the height of a car and on a third side by the house. A side door provides direct access between this partially enclosed section of the driveway and the house. A visitor endeavoring to reach the front door of the house would have to walk partway up the driveway, but would turn off before entering the enclosure and instead proceed up a set of steps leading to the front porch. When Officer Rhodes searched the motorcycle, it was parked inside this partially enclosed top portion of the driveway that abuts the house.

The "conception defining the curtilage is . . . familiar enough that it is 'easily understood from our daily experience." *Jardines*, 569 U. S., at 7 . Just like the front porch, side garden, or area "outside the front window," *Jardines,* 569 U. S., at 6, the driveway enclosure where Officer Rhodes searched the motorcycle constitutes "an area adjacent to the home and to which the activity of home life extends," and so is properly considered curtilage, *id.,* at 7.

2

In physically intruding on the curtilage of Collins' home to search the motorcycle, Officer Rhodes not only invaded Collins' Fourth Amendment interest in the item searched, *i.e.,* the motorcycle, but also invaded Collins' Fourth Amendment interest in the curtilage of his home. The question before the Court is whether the automobile exception justifies the invasion of the curtilage. The answer is no.

Applying the relevant legal principles to a slightly different factual scenario confirms that this is an easy case. Imagine a motorcycle parked inside the living room of a house, visible through a window to a passerby on the street. Imagine further that an officer has probable cause to believe that the motorcycle was involved in a traffic infraction. Can the officer, acting without a warrant, enter the house to search the motorcycle and confirm whether it is the right one? Surely not.

The reason is that the scope of the automobile exception extends no further than the automobile itself. See, e.g., Pennsylvania v. Labron, 518 U. S. 938, 940 (1996) (*per curiam*) (explaining that the automobile exception "permits police to search the vehicle"); Wyoming v. Houghton,

526 U. S. 295, 300 (1999) ("[T]he Framers would have regarded as reasonable (if there was probable cause) the warrantless search of containers *within* an automobile"). Virginia asks the Court to expand the scope of the automobile exception to permit police to invade any space outside an automobile even if the Fourth Amendment protects that space. Nothing in our case law, however, suggests that the automobile exception gives an officer the right to enter a home or its curtilage to access a vehicle without a warrant. Expanding the scope of the automobile exception in this way would both undervalue the core Fourth Amendment protection afforded to the home and its curtilage and untether the automobile exception from the justifications underlying it.

The Court already has declined to expand the scope of other exceptions to the warrant requirement to permit warrantless entry into the home. The reasoning behind those decisions applies equally well in this context. For instance, under the plain-view doctrine, "any valid warrantless seizure of incriminating evidence" requires that the officer "have a lawful right of access to the object itself." Horton v. California, 496 U. S. 128, 136–137 (1990); see also id., at 137, n. 7 ("[E]ven where the object is contraband, this Court has repeatedly stated and enforced the basic rule that the police may not enter and make a warrantless seizure"); G. M. Leasing Corp. v. United States, 429 U. S. 338, 354 (1977) ("It is one thing to seize without a warrant property resting in an open area . . . , and it is quite another thing to effect a warrantless seizure of property . . . situated on private premises to which access is not otherwise available for the seizing officer"). A plain-view seizure thus cannot be justified if it is effectuated by unlawful trespass. Soldal v. Cook County, 506 U. S. 56, 66 (1992). Had Officer Rhodes seen illegal drugs through the window of Collins' house, for example, assuming no other warrant exception applied, he could not have entered the house to seize them without first obtaining a warrant.

Similarly, it is a settled rule that warrantless arrests in public places are valid, but, absent another exception such as exigent circumstances, officers may not enter a home to make an arrest without a warrant, even when they have probable cause. Payton v. New York, 445 U. S. 573, 587–590 (1980). That is because being "arrested in the home involves not only the invasion attendant to all arrests but also an invasion of the sanctity of the home." *Id.*, at 588–589. Likewise, searching a vehicle parked in the curtilage involves not only the invasion of the Fourth Amendment interest in the vehicle but also an invasion of the sanctity of the curtilage.

Just as an officer must have a lawful right of access to any contraband he discovers in plain view in order to seize it without a warrant, and just as an officer must have a lawful right of access in order to arrest a person in his home, so, too, an officer must have a lawful right of access to a vehicle in order to search it pursuant to the automobile exception. The automobile exception does not afford the necessary lawful right of access to search a vehicle parked within a home or its curtilage because it does not justify an intrusion on a person's separate and substantial Fourth Amendment interest in his home and curtilage.

As noted, the rationales underlying the automobile exception are specific to the nature of a vehicle and the ways in which it is distinct from a house. The rationales thus take account only of the balance between the intrusion on an individual's Fourth Amendment interest in his vehicle and the governmental interests in an expedient search of that vehicle; they do not account for the distinct privacy interest in one's home or curtilage. To allow an officer to rely on the automobile exception to gain entry into a house or its curtilage for the purpose of conducting a vehicle search would unmoor the exception from its justifications, render hollow the core Fourth Amendment protection the Constitution extends to the house and its curtilage, and transform what was meant to be an exception into a tool with far broader application. Indeed, its name alone should make all this clear enough: It is, after all, an exception for automobiles.[a]

Given the centrality of the Fourth Amendment interest in the home and its curtilage and the disconnect between that interest and the justifications behind the automobile exception, we decline Virginia's invitation to extend the automobile exception to permit a warrantless intrusion on a home or its curtilage.

---

[a]   The dissent concedes that "the degree of the intrusion on privacy" is relevant in determining whether a warrant is required to search a motor vehicle "located on private property." *Post*, at 5–6 (opinion of ALITO, J.). Yet it puzzlingly asserts that the "privacy interests at stake" here are no greater than when a motor vehicle is searched "on public streets." "An ordinary person of common sense," however, clearly would understand that the privacy interests at stake in one's private residential property are far greater than on a public street. Contrary to the dissent's suggestion, it is of no significance that the motorcycle was parked just a "short walk up the driveway." The driveway was private, not public, property, and the motorcycle was parked in the portion of the driveway beyond where a neighbor would venture, in an area "intimately linked to the home, . . . where privacy expectations are most heightened." California v. Ciraolo, 476 U. S. 207, 213 (1986). Nor does it matter that Officer Rhodes "did not damage any property," for an officer's care in conducting a search does not change the character of the place being searched. And, as we explain, it is not dispositive that Officer Rhodes did not "observe anything along the way" to the motorcycle "that he could not have seen from the street." Law enforcement officers need not "shield their eyes when passing by a home on public thoroughfares," *Ciraolo*, 476 U. S., at 213, but the ability visually to observe an area protected by the Fourth Amendment does not give officers the green light physically to intrude on it. It certainly does not permit an officer physically to intrude on curtilage, remove a tarp to reveal license plate and vehicle identification numbers, and use those numbers to confirm that the defendant committed a crime.

The dissent also mistakenly relies on a law enacted by the First Congress and mentioned in Carroll v. United States, 267 U. S. 32, 150–151 (1925), that authorized the warrantless search of vessels. The dissent thinks it implicit in that statute that "officers could cross private property such as wharves in order to reach and board those vessels." Even if it were so that a police officer could have entered a private wharf to search a vessel, that would not prove he could enter the curtilage of a home to do so. To the contrary, whereas the statute relied upon in *Carroll* authorized warrantless searches of vessels, it expressly required warrants to search houses. See 267 U. S., at 150–157; Act of July 31, 1789, § 24, 1 Stat. 43. Here, Officer Rhodes did not invade a private wharf to undertake a search; he invaded the curtilage of a home.

III

* * *

B

* * * Virginia urges the Court to adopt a more limited rule regarding the intersection of the automobile exception and the protection afforded to curtilage. Virginia would prefer that the Court draw a bright line and hold that the automobile exception does not permit warrantless entry into "the physical threshold of a house or a similar fixed, enclosed structure inside the curtilage like a garage." Requiring officers to make "case-by-case curtilage determinations," Virginia reasons, unnecessarily complicates matters and "raises the potential for confusion and . . . error."

The Court, though, has long been clear that curtilage is afforded constitutional protection. See *Oliver*, 466 U. S., at 180. As a result, officers regularly assess whether an area is curtilage before executing a search. Virginia provides no reason to conclude that this practice has proved to be unadministrable, either generally or in this context. Moreover, creating a carveout to the general rule that curtilage receives Fourth Amendment protection, such that certain types of curtilage would receive Fourth Amendment protection only for some purposes but not for others, seems far more likely to create confusion than does uniform application of the Court's doctrine.

In addition, Virginia's proposed rule rests on a mistaken premise about the constitutional significance of visibility. The ability to observe inside curtilage from a lawful vantage point is not the same as the right to enter curtilage without a warrant for the purpose of conducting a search to obtain information not otherwise accessible. Cf. *Ciraolo*, 476 U. S., at 213–214 (holding that "physically nonintrusive" warrantless aerial observation of the curtilage of a home did not violate the Fourth Amendment, and could form the basis for probable cause to support a warrant to search the curtilage). So long as it is curtilage, a parking patio or carport into which an officer can see from the street is no less entitled to protection from trespass and a warrantless search than a fully enclosed garage.

Finally, Virginia's proposed bright-line rule automatically would grant constitutional rights to those persons with the financial means to afford residences with garages in which to store their vehicles but deprive those persons without such resources of any individualized consideration as to whether the areas in which they store their vehicles qualify as curtilage. See *United States* v. *Ross*, 456 U. S. 798, 822 (1982) ("[T]he most frail cottage in the kingdom is absolutely entitled to the same guarantees of privacy as the most majestic mansion").

IV

For the foregoing reasons, we conclude that the automobile exception does not permit an officer without a warrant to enter a home or its curtilage in order to search a vehicle therein. We leave for resolution on remand whether Officer Rhodes' warrantless intrusion on the curtilage of Collins' house may have been reasonable on a different basis, such as the exigent circumstances exception to the warrant requirement. The judgment of the Supreme Court of Virginia is therefore reversed, and the case is remanded for further proceedings not inconsistent with this opinion.

JUSTICE THOMAS, concurring.

I join the Court's opinion because it correctly resolves the Fourth Amendment question in this case. Notably, the only reason that Collins asked us to review this question is because, if he can prove a violation of the Fourth Amendment, our precedents require the Virginia courts to apply the exclusionary rule and potentially suppress the incriminating evidence against him. I write separately because I have serious doubts about this Court's authority to impose that rule on the States. * * *

[Justice Thomas goes on to explain his doubts about the Court's authority to incorporate the exclusionary rule to the states. Those portions of his opinion are excerpted *infra* in Part VII, Section B of this Supplement.]

JUSTICE ALITO, dissenting.

The Fourth Amendment prohibits "unreasonable" searches. What the police did in this case was entirely reasonable. The Court's decision is not.

On the day in question, Officer David Rhodes was standing at the curb of a house where petitioner, Ryan Austin Collins, stayed a couple of nights a week with his girlfriend. From his vantage point on the street, Rhodes saw an object covered with a tarp in the driveway, just a car's length or two from the curb. It is undisputed that Rhodes had probable cause to believe that the object under the tarp was a motorcycle that had been involved a few months earlier in a dangerous highway chase, eluding the police at speeds in excess of 140 mph. Rhodes also had probable cause to believe that petitioner had been operating the motorcycle and that a search of the motorcycle would provide evidence that the motorcycle had been stolen.

If the motorcycle had been parked at the curb, instead of in the driveway, it is undisputed that Rhodes could have searched it without obtaining a warrant. Nearly a century ago, this Court held that officers with probable cause may search a motor vehicle without obtaining a warrant. Carroll v. United States, 267 U. S. 132, 153, 155–156 (1925). The principal rationale for this so-called automobile or motor-vehicle exception to the warrant requirement is the risk that the vehicle will be moved during the time it takes to obtain a warrant. *Id.*, at 153; California v. Carney, 471 U. S. 386, 390–391 (1985). We have also observed that the owner of an automobile has a diminished expectation of privacy in its contents.

So why does the Court come to the conclusion that Officer Rhodes needed a warrant in this case? Because, in order to reach the motorcycle, he had to walk 30 feet or so up the driveway of the house rented by petitioner's girlfriend, and by doing that, Rhodes invaded the home's "curtilage." The Court does not dispute that the motorcycle, when parked in the driveway, was just as mobile as it would have been had it been parked at the curb. Nor does the Court claim that Officer Rhodes's short walk up the driveway did petitioner or his girlfriend any harm. Rhodes did not damage any property or observe anything along the way that he could not have seen from the street. But, the Court insists, Rhodes could not enter the driveway without a warrant, and therefore his search of the motorcycle was unreasonable and the evidence obtained in that search must be suppressed.

An ordinary person of common sense would react to the Court's decision the way Mr. Bumble famously responded when told about a legal rule that did not comport with the reality of everyday life. If that is the law, he exclaimed, "the law is an ass—an idiot." C. Dickens, Oliver Twist 277 (1867).

The Fourth Amendment is neither an "ass" nor an "idiot." Its hallmark is reasonableness, and the Court's strikingly unreasonable decision is based on a misunderstanding of Fourth Amendment basics.

* * * Ascertaining the boundaries of the curtilage thus determines only whether a search is governed by the Fourth Amendment. The concept plays no other role in Fourth Amendment analysis.

In this case, there is no dispute that the search of the motorcycle was governed by the Fourth Amendment, and therefore whether or not it occurred within the curtilage is not of any direct importance. The question before us is not whether there was a Fourth Amendment search but whether the search was reasonable. And the only possible argument as to why it might not be reasonable concerns the need for a warrant. For nearly a century, however, it has been well established that officers do not need a warrant to search a motor vehicle on public streets so long as they have probable cause. * * * Thus, the issue here is whether there is any good reason why this same rule should not apply when the vehicle is parked in plain view in a driveway just a few feet from the street.

In considering that question, we should ask whether the reasons for the "automobile exception" are any less valid in this new situation. Is the vehicle parked in the driveway any less mobile? Are any greater privacy interests at stake? If the answer to those questions is "no," then the automobile exception should apply. And here, the answer to each question is emphatically "no." The tarp-covered motorcycle parked in the driveway could have been uncovered and ridden away in a matter of seconds. And Officer Rhodes's brief walk up the driveway impaired no real privacy interests.

In this case, the Court uses the curtilage concept in a way that is contrary to our decisions regarding other, exigency-based exceptions to the warrant requirement. Take, for example, the "emergency aid" exception. See Brigham City v. Stuart, 547 U. S. 398 (2006). When officers reasonably believe that a person inside a dwelling has urgent need of assistance, they may cross the curtilage and enter the building without first obtaining a warrant. The same is true when officers reasonably believe that a person in a dwelling is destroying evidence. See Kentucky v. King, 563 U. S. 452, 460 (2011). In both of those situations, we ask whether "the exigencies of the situation make the needs of law enforcement so compelling that the warrantless search is objectively reasonable." *Brigham City, supra,* at 403. We have not held that the need to cross the curtilage independently necessitates a warrant, and there is no good reason to apply a different rule here.[c]

It is no answer to this argument that the emergency-aid and destruction-of-evidence exceptions require an inquiry into the practicality of obtaining a warrant in the particular circumstances of the case. Our precedents firmly establish that the motor-vehicle exception, unlike these other exceptions, "has no separate exigency requirement." Maryland v. Dyson, 527 U. S. 465, 466–467 (1999) *(per curiam)*. It is settled that the mobility of a motor vehicle categorically obviates any need to engage in such a case-specific inquiry. Requiring such an inquiry here would mark a substantial alteration of settled Fourth Amendment law.

This does not mean, however, that a warrant is never needed when officers have probable cause to search a motor vehicle, no matter where the vehicle is located. While a case-specific inquiry regarding *exigency* would be inconsistent with the rationale of the motor-vehicle exception, a case-specific inquiry regarding *the degree of intrusion on privacy* is entirely appropriate when the motor vehicle to be searched is located on private property. After all, the ultimate inquiry under the Fourth Amendment is

---

[c]   Indeed, I believe that the First Congress implicitly made the same judgment in enacting the statute on which *Carroll* v. *United States,* 267 U. S. 132 (1925), relied when the motor-vehicle exception was first recognized. Since the First Congress sent the Bill of Rights to the States for ratification, we have often looked to laws enacted by that Congress as evidence of the original understanding of the meaning of those Amendments. * * * *Carroll* itself noted that the First Congress enacted a law authorizing officers to search vessels without a warrant. Although this statute did not expressly state that these officers could cross private property such as wharves in order to reach and board those vessels, I think that was implicit. Otherwise, the statute would very often have been ineffective. And when Congress later enacted similar laws, it made this authorization express. See, *e.g.,* An Act Further to Prevent Smuggling and for Other Purposes, § 5, 14 Stat. 179. For this reason, Officer Rhodes's conduct in this case is consistent with the original understanding of the Fourth Amendment, as explicated in *Carroll.*

whether a search is reasonable, and that inquiry often turns on the degree of the intrusion on privacy. Thus, contrary to the opinion of the Court, an affirmance in this case would not mean that officers could perform a warrantless search if a motorcycle were located inside a house. In that situation, the intrusion on privacy would be far greater than in the present case, where the real effect, if any, is negligible.

I would affirm the decision below.

G. EXIGENT CIRCUMSTANCES

4. The Risk of Destruction of Evidence

Page 425. Add at the end of the section:

DUI Tests on Unconscious Persons: Mitchell v. Wisconsin

MITCHELL V. WISCONSIN
Supreme Court of the United States, 2019.
139 S.Ct. 2525.

JUSTICE ALITO announced the judgment of the Court and delivered an opinion, in which THE CHIEF JUSTICE, JUSTICE BREYER, and JUSTICE KAVANAUGH join.

In this case, we return to a topic that we have addressed twice in recent years: the circumstances under which a police officer may administer a warrantless blood alcohol concentration (BAC) test to a motorist who appears to have been driving under the influence of alcohol. We have previously addressed what officers may do in two broad categories of cases. First, an officer may conduct a BAC test if the facts of a particular case bring it within the exigent-circumstances exception to the Fourth Amendment's general requirement of a warrant. Second, if an officer has probable cause to arrest a motorist for drunk driving, the officer may conduct a breath test (but not a blood test) under the rule allowing warrantless searches of a person incident to arrest.

Today, we consider what police officers may do in a narrow but important category of cases: those in which the driver is unconscious and therefore cannot be given a breath test. In such cases, we hold, the exigent-circumstances rule almost always permits a blood test without a warrant. When a breath test is impossible, enforcement of the drunk-driving laws depends upon the administration of a blood test. And when a police officer encounters an unconscious driver, it is very likely that the driver would be taken to an emergency room and that his blood would be drawn for diagnostic purposes even if the police were not seeking BAC information. In addition, police officers most frequently come upon unconscious drivers when they report to the scene of an accident, and under those circumstances, the officers' many responsibilities—such as attending to other injured drivers or passengers and preventing further accidents—may be incompatible with the procedures that would be required to obtain a warrant. Thus, when a driver is unconscious, the general rule is that a warrant is not needed.

I

A

In *Birchfield* v. *North Dakota*, 579 U. S. ___ (2016), we recounted the country's efforts over the years to address the terrible problem of drunk driving. Today, "all States have laws that prohibit motorists from driving with a [BAC] that exceeds a specified level." And to help enforce BAC limits, every State has passed what are popularly called implied-consent laws. As "a condition of the privilege of" using the public roads, these laws require that drivers submit to BAC testing "when there is sufficient reason to believe they are violating the State's drunk-driving laws."

Wisconsin's implied-consent law is much like those of the other 49 States and the District of Columbia. It deems drivers to have consented to breath or blood tests if an officer has reason to believe they have committed one of several drug- or alcohol-related offenses. Officers seeking to conduct a BAC test must read aloud a statement declaring their intent to administer the test and advising drivers of their options and the implications of their choice. If a driver's BAC level proves too high, his license will be suspended; but if he refuses testing, his license will be *revoked* and his refusal may be used against him in court. No test will be administered if a driver refuses—or, as the State would put it, "withdraws" his statutorily presumed consent. But "[a] person who is unconscious or otherwise not capable of withdrawing consent is presumed not to have" withdrawn it. More than half the States have provisions like this one regarding unconscious drivers.

B

The sequence of events that gave rise to this case began when Officer Alexander Jaeger of the Sheboygan Police Department received a report that petitioner Gerald Mitchell, appearing to be very drunk, had climbed into a van and driven off. Jaeger soon found Mitchell wandering near a lake. Stumbling and slurring his words, Mitchell could hardly stand without the support of two officers. Jaeger judged a field sobriety test hopeless, if not dangerous, and gave Mitchell a preliminary breath test. It registered a BAC level of 0.24%, triple the legal limit for driving in Wisconsin. Jaeger arrested Mitchell for operating a vehicle while intoxicated and, as is standard practice, drove him to a police station for a more reliable breath test using better equipment.

On the way, Mitchell's condition continued to deteriorate—so much so that by the time the squad car had reached the station, he was too lethargic even for a breath test. Jaeger therefore drove Mitchell to a nearby hospital for a blood test; Mitchell lost consciousness on the ride over and had to be wheeled in. Even so, Jaeger read aloud to a slumped Mitchell the standard statement giving drivers a chance to refuse BAC testing. Hearing no response, Jaeger asked hospital staff to draw a blood sample. Mitchell remained unconscious while the sample was taken, and analysis of his blood showed that his BAC, about 90 minutes after his arrest, was 0.222%.

Mitchell was charged with violating two related drunk-driving provisions. He moved to suppress the results of the blood test on the ground that it violated his Fourth Amendment right * * * because it was conducted without a warrant. Wisconsin chose to rest its response on the notion that its implied-consent law (together with Mitchell's free choice to drive on its highways) rendered the blood test a consensual one, thus curing any Fourth Amendment problem. In the end, the trial court denied Mitchell's motion to suppress, and a jury found him guilty of the charged offenses. * * * [W]e granted certiorari, to decide whether a statute authorizing a blood draw from an unconscious motorist provides an exception to the Fourth Amendment warrant requirement.

II

In considering Wisconsin's implied-consent law, we do not write on a blank slate. "Our prior opinions have referred approvingly to the general concept of implied-consent laws that impose civil penalties and evidentiary consequences on motorists who refuse to comply." *Birchfield*, 579 U. S., at ___. But our decisions have not rested on the idea that these laws do what their popular name might seem to suggest—that is, create actual consent to all the searches they authorize. Instead, we have based our decisions on the precedent regarding the specific constitutional claims in each case, while keeping in mind the wider regulatory scheme developed over the years to combat drunk driving. That scheme is centered on legally specified BAC limits for drivers—limits enforced by the BAC tests promoted by implied-consent laws.

Over the last 50 years, we have approved many of the defining elements of this scheme. We have held that forcing drunk-driving suspects to undergo a blood test does not violate their constitutional right against self-incrimination. See *Schmerber v. California*, 384 U. S. 757, 765 (1966). Nor does using their refusal against them in court. See *South Dakota v. Neville*, 459 U. S. 553, 563 (1983). And punishing that refusal with automatic license revocation does not violate drivers' due process rights if they have been arrested upon probable cause, *Mackey v. Montrym*, 443 U. S. 1 (1979); on the contrary, this kind of summary penalty is "unquestionably legitimate." *Neville*, *supra*, at 560.

These cases generally concerned the Fifth and Fourteenth Amendments, but motorists charged with drunk driving have also invoked the Fourth Amendment's ban on "unreasonable searches" since BAC tests are "searches." Though our precedent normally requires a warrant for a lawful search, there are well-defined exceptions to this rule. In *Birchfield*, we applied precedent on the "search-incident-to-arrest" exception to BAC testing of conscious drunk-driving suspects. We held that their drunk-driving arrests, taken alone, justify warrantless breath tests but not blood tests, since breath tests are less intrusive, just as informative, and (in the case of conscious suspects) readily available.

We have also reviewed BAC tests under the "exigent circumstances" exception—which, as noted, allows warrantless searches "to prevent the imminent destruction of evidence." *Missouri v. McNeely*, 569 U. S. 141, 149 (2013). In *McNeely*, we were asked if this exception covers BAC testing of drunk-driving suspects in light of the fact that blood-alcohol evidence is always dissipating due to "natural metabolic processes." We answered that the fleeting quality of BAC evidence alone is not enough. But in *Schmerber* it *did* justify a blood test of a drunk driver who had gotten into a car accident that gave police other pressing duties, for then the "*further* delay" caused by a warrant application really "*would* have threatened the destruction of evidence."

Like *Schmerber*, this case sits much higher than *McNeely* on the exigency spectrum. *McNeely* was about the minimum degree of urgency common to all drunk-driving cases. In *Schmerber*, a car accident heightened that urgency. And here Mitchell's medical condition did just the same.

Mitchell's stupor and eventual unconsciousness also deprived officials of a reasonable opportunity to administer a breath test. To be sure, Officer Jaeger managed to conduct "a preliminary breath test" using a portable machine when he first encountered Mitchell at the lake. But he had no reasonable opportunity to give Mitchell a breath test using evidence-grade breath testing machinery. As a result, it was reasonable for Jaeger to seek a better breath test at the station; he acted with reasonable dispatch to procure one; and when Mitchell's condition got in the way, it was reasonable for Jaeger to pursue a blood test. * * *

Because the standard evidentiary breath test is conducted after a motorist is arrested and transported to a police station or another appropriate facility, the important question here is what officers may do when a driver's unconsciousness (or stupor) eliminates any reasonable opportunity for *that* kind of breath test.

III

* * * In *McNeely*, we considered how the exigent-circumstances exception applies to the broad category of cases in which a police officer has

probable cause to believe that a motorist was driving under the influence of alcohol, and we do not revisit that question. Nor do we settle whether the exigent-circumstances exception covers the specific facts of this case. Instead, we address how the exception bears on the category of cases encompassed by the question on which we granted certiorari—those involving unconscious drivers. In those cases, the need for a blood test is compelling, and an officer's duty to attend to more pressing needs may leave no time to seek a warrant.

A

The importance of the needs served by BAC testing is hard to overstate. The bottom line is that BAC tests are needed for enforcing laws that save lives. The specifics, in short, are these: Highway safety is critical; it is served by laws that criminalize driving with a certain BAC level; and enforcing these legal BAC limits requires efficient testing to obtain BAC evidence, which naturally dissipates. So BAC tests are crucial links in a chain on which vital interests hang. And when a breath test is unavailable to advance those aims, a blood test becomes essential.

* * *

For these reasons, there clearly is a "compelling need" for a blood test of drunk-driving suspects whose condition deprives officials of a reasonable opportunity to conduct a breath test. The only question left, under our exigency doctrine, is whether this compelling need justifies a warrantless search because there is, furthermore, " 'no time to secure a warrant.' "

B

We held that there was no time to secure a warrant before a blood test of a drunk-driving suspect in *Schmerber* because the officer there could "reasonably have believed that he was confronted with an emergency, in which the delay necessary to obtain a warrant, under the circumstances, threatened the destruction of evidence." So even if the constant dissipation of BAC evidence *alone* does not create an exigency, *Schmerber* shows that it does so when combined with other pressing needs:

> "We are told that [1] the percentage of alcohol in the blood begins to diminish shortly after drinking stops, as the body functions to eliminate it from the system. Particularly in a case such as this, where [2] time had to be taken to bring the accused to a hospital and to investigate the scene of the accident, there was no time to seek out a magistrate and secure a warrant. Given these special facts, we conclude that the attempt to secure evidence of blood-alcohol content in this case [without a warrant] was . . . appropriate . . . ." 384 U. S., at 770–771.

Thus, exigency exists when (1) BAC evidence is dissipating and (2) some other factor creates pressing health, safety, or law enforcement needs that would take priority over a warrant application. Both conditions are met when a drunk-driving suspect is unconscious, so *Schmerber* controls: With such suspects, too, a warrantless blood draw is lawful.

1

In *Schmerber*, the extra factor giving rise to urgent needs that would only add to the delay caused by a warrant application was a car accident; here it is the driver's unconsciousness. Indeed, unconsciousness does not just create pressing needs; it is *itself* a medical emergency. It means that the suspect will have to be rushed to the hospital or similar facility not just for the blood test itself but for urgent medical care. Police can reasonably anticipate that such a driver might require monitoring, positioning, and support on the way to the hospital; that his blood may be drawn anyway, for diagnostic purposes, immediately on arrival; and that immediate medical treatment could delay (or otherwise distort the results of) a blood draw conducted later, upon receipt of a warrant, thus reducing its evidentiary value. All of that sets this case apart from the uncomplicated drunk-driving scenarios addressed in *McNeely*. Just as the ramifications of a car accident pushed *Schmerber* over the line into exigency, so does the condition of an unconscious driver bring his blood draw under the exception. * * *

Indeed, in many unconscious-driver cases, the exigency will be *more* acute, as elaborated in the briefing and argument in this case. A driver so drunk as to lose consciousness is quite likely to crash, especially if he passes out before managing to park. And then the accident might give officers a slew of urgent tasks beyond that of securing (and working around) medical care for the suspect. Police may have to ensure that others who are injured receive prompt medical attention; they may have to provide first aid themselves until medical personnel arrive at the scene. In some cases, they may have to deal with fatalities. They may have to preserve evidence at the scene and block or redirect traffic to prevent further accidents. These pressing matters, too, would require responsible officers to put off applying for a warrant, and that would only exacerbate the delay—and imprecision—of any subsequent BAC test.

In sum, all these rival priorities would put officers, who must often engage in a form of triage, to a dilemma. It would force them to choose between prioritizing a warrant application, to the detriment of critical health and safety needs, and delaying the warrant application, and thus the BAC test, to the detriment of its evidentiary value and all the compelling interests served by BAC limits. This is just the kind of scenario for which the exigency rule was born—just the kind of grim dilemma it lives to dissolve.

2

Mitchell objects that a warrantless search is unnecessary in cases involving unconscious drivers because warrants these days can be obtained faster and more easily. But even in our age of rapid communication,

> "[w]arrants inevitably take some time for police officers or prosecutors to complete and for magistrate judges to review. Telephonic and electronic warrants may still require officers to follow time-consuming formalities designed to create an adequate record, such as preparing a duplicate warrant before calling the magistrate judge.... And improvements in communications technology do not guarantee that a magistrate judge will be available when an officer needs a warrant after making a late-night arrest." *McNeely*, 569 U. S., at 155.

In other words, with better technology, the time required has shrunk, but it has not disappeared. In the emergency scenarios created by unconscious drivers, forcing police to put off other tasks for even a relatively short period of time may have terrible collateral costs. That is just what it means for these situations to *be* emergencies.

IV

When police have probable cause to believe a person has committed a drunk-driving offense and the driver's unconsciousness or stupor requires him to be taken to the hospital or similar facility before police have a reasonable opportunity to administer a standard evidentiary breath test, they may almost always order a warrantless blood test to measure the driver's BAC without offending the Fourth Amendment. We do not rule out the possibility that in an unusual case a defendant would be able to show that his blood would not have been drawn if police had not been seeking BAC information, and that police could not have reasonably judged that a warrant application would interfere with other pressing needs or duties. Because Mitchell did not have a chance to attempt to make that showing, a remand for that purpose is necessary.

The judgment of the Supreme Court of Wisconsin is vacated, and the case is remanded for further proceedings.

JUSTICE THOMAS, concurring in the judgment.

Today, the plurality adopts a difficult-to-administer rule: Exigent circumstances are generally present when police encounter a person suspected of drunk driving—except when they aren't. The plurality's presumption will rarely be rebutted, but it will nevertheless burden both officers and courts who must attempt to apply it. The better (and far simpler) way to resolve this case is to apply "the *per se* rule" I proposed in *Missouri* v. *McNeely*. Under that rule, the natural metabolization of alcohol in the blood stream "creates an exigency once police have probable cause to believe the driver is drunk," regardless of whether the driver is conscious. Because I am of the view that the Wisconsin Supreme Court should apply that rule on remand, I concur only in the judgment.

* * *

[T]he plurality makes a flawed distinction between ordinary drunk-driving cases in which blood alcohol concentration evidence "is dissipating" and those that also include "some other [pressing] factor." But whether "some other factor creates pressing health, safety, or law-enforcement needs that would take priority over a warrant application" is irrelevant. When police have probable cause to conclude that an individual was driving drunk, probative evidence is dissipating by the minute. And that evidence dissipates regardless of whether police had another reason to draw the driver's blood or whether "a warrant application would interfere with other pressing needs or duties." The destruction of evidence alone is sufficient to justify a warrantless search based on exigent circumstances.

Presumably, the plurality draws these lines to avoid overturning *McNeely*. But *McNeely* was wrongly decided, and our decision in *Birchfield* has already undermined its rationale. Specifically, the Court determined in *McNeely* that "[t]he context of blood testing is different in critical respects from other destruction-of-evidence cases in which the police are truly confronted with a now or never situation." But the Court stated in *Birchfield* that a distinction between "an arrestee's active destruction of evidence and the loss of evidence due to a natural process makes little sense." Moreover, to the extent *McNeely* was grounded in the belief that a *per se* rule was inconsistent with the "case by case," "totality of the circumstances" analysis ordinarily applied in exigent-circumstances cases, that rationale was suspect from the start. That the exigent-circumstances exception might ordinarily require an evaluation of the particular facts of each case does not foreclose us from recognizing that a certain, dispositive fact is always present in some categories of cases. In other words, acknowledging that destruction of evidence is at issue in every drunk-driving case does not undermine the general totality-of-the-circumstances approach that *McNeely* and *Birchfield* endorsed.

* * *

The Court has consistently held that police officers may perform searches without a warrant when destruction of evidence is a risk. The rule should be no different in drunk-driving cases. Because the plurality instead adopts a rule more likely to confuse than clarify, I concur only in the judgment.

JUSTICE SOTOMAYOR, with whom JUSTICE GINSBURG and JUSTICE KAGAN join, dissenting.

The plurality's decision rests on the false premise that today's holding is necessary to spare law enforcement from a choice between attending to emergency situations and securing evidence used to enforce state drunk-driving laws. Not so. To be sure, drunk driving poses significant dangers that Wisconsin and other States must be able to curb. But the question here is narrow: What must police do before ordering a blood draw of a person suspected of drunk driving who has become unconscious? Under the Fourth Amendment, the answer is clear: If there is time, get a warrant.

The State of Wisconsin conceded in the state courts that it had time to get a warrant to draw Gerald Mitchell's blood, and that should be the end of the matter. Because the plurality needlessly casts aside the established protections of the warrant requirement in favor of a brand new presumption of exigent circumstances that Wisconsin does not urge, that the state courts did not consider, and that contravenes this Court's precedent, I respectfully dissent.

For decades, this Court has stayed true to the Fourth Amendment's warrant requirement and the narrowness of its exceptions, even in the face of attempts categorically to exempt blood testing from its protections. * * *

Those cases resolve this one. *Schmerber* and *McNeely* establish that there is no categorical exigency exception for blood draws, although exigent circumstances might justify a warrantless blood draw on the facts of a particular case. And from *Birchfield*, we know that warrantless blood draws cannot be justified as searches incident to arrest. The lesson is straightforward: Unless there is too little time to do so, police officers must get a warrant before ordering a blood draw.

Against this precedential backdrop, Wisconsin's primary argument has always been that Mitchell consented to the blood draw through the State's "implied-consent law." Under that statute, a motorist who drives on the State's roads is "deemed" to have consented to a blood draw, breath test, and urine test, and that supposed consent allows a warrantless blood draw from an unconscious motorist as long as the police have probable cause to believe that the motorist has violated one of the State's impaired driving statutes.

The plurality does not rely on the consent exception here. With that sliver of the plurality's reasoning I agree. I would go further and hold that the state statute, however phrased, cannot itself create the actual and informed consent that the Fourth Amendment requires. That should be the end of this case.

* * *

According to the plurality, when the police attempt to obtain a blood sample from a person suspected of drunk driving, there will "almost always" be exigent circumstances if the person falls unconscious. As this case demonstrates, however, the fact that a suspect fell unconscious at some point before the blood draw does not mean that there was insufficient time to get a warrant. And if the police have time to secure a warrant before the blood draw, "the Fourth Amendment mandates that they do so." *McNeely*, 569 U. S., at 152. In discarding that rule for its own, the plurality may not "revisit" *McNeely,* but the plurality does ignore it.

* * *

The reasons the Court gave for rejecting a categorical exigency exception in *McNeely* apply with full force when the suspected drunk driver is (or becomes) unconscious. In these cases, there is still a period of delay during which a police officer might take steps to secure a warrant. Indeed, as the plurality observes, that delay is guaranteed because an unconscious person will need to be transported to the hospital for medical attention. * * *

Likewise, an unconscious person's BAC dissipates just as gradually and predictably as a conscious person's does. Furthermore, because unconsciousness is more likely to occur at higher BACs, the BACs of suspected drunk drivers who are unconscious will presumably be higher above the legal limit—and thus remain above the legal limit for longer—than is true for suspects who are conscious and close to sobering up. And, of course, the process for getting a warrant remains the same.

All told, the mere fact that a person is unconscious does not materially change the calculation that the Court made in *McNeely* when it rejected a categorical exigency exception for blood draws. In many cases, even when the suspect falls unconscious, police officers will have sufficient time to secure a warrant—meaning that the Fourth Amendment requires that they do so.

The plurality distinguishes unconscious drunk-driving suspects from others based on the fact that their unconsciousness means that they will, invariably, need urgent medical attention due to their loss of consciousness. But the need for medical care is not unique to unconscious suspects. Drunk drivers often end up in an emergency room, whether or not they are unconscious when the police encounter them. The defendant in *Schmerber* was hospitalized, yet the Court did not, in that case or in *McNeely* decades later, promulgate a categorical exception for every warrantless blood draw. That Mitchell was hospitalized is likewise insufficient here. * * *

Because the precedent is so squarely against it, the plurality devotes much of its opinion instead to painting a dire picture: the scene of a drunk-driving-related accident, where police officers must tend to the unconscious person, others who need medical attention, oncoming traffic, and investigatory needs. There is no indication, however, in the record or elsewhere that the tableau of horribles the plurality depicts materializes in most cases. Such circumstances are certainly not present in this case, in which the police encountered Mitchell alone, after he had parked and left his car; indeed, Mitchell lost consciousness over an hour after he was found walking along the lake. The potential variation in circumstances is a good reason to decide each case on its own facts, as *McNeely* instructs and as the Court did in *Schmerber*.

* * *

The Fourth Amendment, as interpreted by our precedents, requires police officers seeking to draw blood from a person suspected of drunk driving to get a warrant if possible. That rule should resolve this case.

The plurality misguidedly departs from this rule, setting forth its own convoluted counterpresumption instead. But the Fourth Amendment is not as pliable as the plurality suggests. * * * Acting entirely on its own freewheeling instincts—with no briefing or decision below on the question—the plurality permits officers to order a blood draw of an unconscious person in all but the rarest cases, even when there is ample time to obtain a warrant. The plurality may believe it is helping to ameliorate the scourge of drunk driving, but what it really does is to strike another needless blow at the protections guaranteed by the Fourth Amendment. With respect, I dissent.

JUSTICE GORSUCH, dissenting.

We took this case to decide whether Wisconsin drivers impliedly consent to blood alcohol tests thanks to a state statute. That law says that anyone driving in Wisconsin agrees—by the very act of driving—to testing under certain circumstances. But the Court today declines to answer the question presented. Instead, it upholds Wisconsin's law on an entirely different ground—citing the exigent circumstances doctrine. While I do not doubt that the Court may affirm for any reason supported by the record, the application of the exigent circumstances doctrine in this area poses complex and difficult questions that neither the parties nor the courts below discussed. Rather than proceeding solely by self-direction, I would have dismissed this case as improvidently granted and waited for a case presenting the exigent circumstances question.

H. ADMINISTRATIVE SEARCHES AND OTHER SEARCHES AND SEIZURES BASED ON "SPECIAL NEEDS"

Page 526. Add at the end of the material on border searches:

8. Public Health Surveillance

In the midst of the global pandemic of SARS-CoV-2, which is the contagion that causes COVID-19, public health officials have proposed a range of interventions that may implicate the Fourth Amendment. Based on the material we have covered in this chapter, which, if any, of the following programs do you think would constitute a "search" or a "seizure" under the Fourth Amendment. For programs effecting searches or seizures, how would you evaluate their constitutionality? How would you advise officials considering these measures?

1. Mandatory weekly testing of all public school children for active SARS-CoV-2 infections.

2. Mandatory testing for active SARS-CoV-2 infections of all individuals exhibiting two or more of the symptoms characterizing COVID-19 (loss of sense of smell, loss of sense of taste, fatigue, fever, shortness of breath, and dry cough).

3. Mandatory testing for active SARS-CoV-2 infections of all individuals entering the United States at an international border, including ports and airports.

4. Mandatory home quarantine of individuals who have been exposed to SARS-CoV-2.

5. Mandatory quarantine in a public facility of individuals who have been exposed to SARS-CoV-2.

6. Mandatory home quarantine of individuals who test positive for SARS-CoV-2.

7. Mandatory quarantine in a public facility of individuals who test positive for SARS-CoV-2.

8. Accessing the cell-site location history of all individuals testing positive for SARS-CoV-2 for purposes of contact tracing (identifying potential contacts between individuals who have tested positive for SARS-CoV-2 and others).

9. Accessing the contact lists on phones belonging to individuals testing positive for SARS-CoV-2 for purposes of contact tracing.

10. Accessing the social media sites associated with individuals testing positive for SARS-CoV-2.

11. "Dumping" cell phone towers in proximity to known locations of SARS-CoV-2 exposure for purposes of contact tracing.

12. Requiring individuals to download an app on their phone that will gather, store, and report data relevant to assessing public health risks associated with SARS-CoV-2, to communicate information about exposure risks, and to conduct contact tracing.

13. "Scraping" data from social media platforms for purposes of assessing public health risks associated with SARS-CoV-2, including information about group gatherings.

14. Accessing databases of location information aggregated by cellphone providers and technology companies for purposes of assessing public health risks associated with SARS-CoV-2, including information about public gatherings and population flows.

For some early thoughts on these emerging issues, see Natalie Ram & David Gray, *Mass Surveillance in the Age of COVID-19*, ___ J.L. & Biosci. ___ (2020) (available at https://doi.org/10.1093/jlb/lsaa023).

9. Public Health Seizures

Authority to enforce quarantines under U.S. law traces to at least 1796, when officials sought to stem the spread of yellow fever. *See* James Misrahi, *The CDC's Communicable Disease Regulations: Striking the Balance Between Public Health & Individual Rights*, 67 Emory L.J. 463, 464–72 (2018) (providing historical and statutory overview of federal quarantine authority). Federal authority to develop plans for quarantine resides with the Secretary of Health and Human Services and the Center for Disease Control. *See* 42 U.S.C. §§ 243, 264–272 (2012); 42 C.F.R. pts. 70 & 71. Authority to impose quarantines at the state level is governed by state law, which varies widely between jurisdictions, and often implicates thorny administrative law issues. *See, e.g.*, Wisconsin Legislature v. Palm, 391 Wis.2d 497 (Wis. 2020) (overturning executive stay-at-home order due to failure to follow administrative rule-making procedures).

Quarantines may affect a variety of constitutional rights, including First Amendment rights of free association and exercise of religion, due process rights under the Fifth and Fourteenth Amendments, Fourteenth Amendment guarantees of equal protection, and Fourth Amendment protections from unreasonable seizures. For purposes of the Fourth Amendment, quarantines likely fall within the broad compass of the special needs doctrine, and therefore require striking a reasonable balance between the governmental and liberty interests at stake. There is little doubt that controlling the spread of a deadly contagion represents a compelling government interest. *See* People ex rel. Barmore v. Robertson,

134 N.E. 815, 817 (1922) ("Among all the objects sought to be secured by governmental laws none is more important than the preservation of public health."). On the other hand, quarantines can have dramatic impact on liberty interests, sometimes amounting to civil commitment or home arrest.

Due in part to the level of medical and epidemiological expertise necessary to determine the merits of a quarantine, courts have been reluctant to interfere with public efforts to combat dangerous contagions. As one court put the point in the midst of an early twentieth century typhoid epidemic:

> The exercise of the police power is a matter resting in the discretion of the Legislature or the board or tribunal to which the power is delegated, and the courts will not interfere with the exercise of this power except where the regulations adopted for the protection of the public health are arbitrary, oppressive and unreasonable. The court has nothing to do with the wisdom or expediency of the measures adopted.

People ex rel. Barmore v. Robertson, 134 N.E. 815, 817 (1922). That authority is not unlimited, however.

> Health authorities cannot promulgate and enforce rules which merely have a tendency to prevent the spread of contagious and infectious diseases, which are not founded upon an existing condition or upon a well-founded belief that a condition is threatened which will endanger the public health. The health authorities cannot interfere with the liberties of a citizen until the emergency actually exists. . . .

Id. at 819. And "when the necessity ceases the right to enforce the regulations ceases." *Id.*

There are relatively few modern cases dealing with authority to enforce quarantines, but the issue is likely to arise more frequently in the near future as federal and state authorities confront threats posed by dangerous contagions such as Ebola and SARS-CoV-2. The following case provides some insight into how courts asked to review quarantines and similar measures might evaluate the Fourth Amendment issues at stake.

HICKOX V. CHRISTIE

United States District Court, District of New Jersey, 2016.
205 F.Supp.3d 579.

MCNULTY, J.

This is a civil rights action brought pursuant to 42 U.S.C. § 1983 ("Section 1983"). The plaintiff, Kaci Hickox, is a nurse who cared for individuals affected by the 2014–16 Ebola epidemic in West Africa, specifically in Sierra Leone. Upon her return to the United States, Ms.

Hickox was stopped at Newark Liberty International Airport while her health was monitored. Hickox alleges that this quarantine, which lasted approximately 80 hours, violated her rights under the Fourth and Fourteenth Amendments to the U.S. Constitution. * * *

The federal government possesses the power to declare and enforce a quarantine. That power, based on the commerce clause, would appear to be at its zenith with respect to preventive measures at the border. Section 361 of the Public Health Service Act provides that "[t]he Surgeon General, with the approval of the Secretary [of Health and Human Services], is authorized to make and enforce such regulations as in his [sic] judgment are necessary to prevent the introduction, transmission, or spread of communicable diseases from foreign countries into the States or possessions, or from one State or possession into any other State or possession." 42 U.S.C. § 264. Authority to carry out these functions has been delegated to the Centers for Disease Control and Prevention (CDC). "Under 42 Code of Federal Regulations parts 70 and 71, CDC is authorized to detain, medically examine, and release persons arriving into the United States and traveling between states who are suspected of carrying these communicable diseases.

In response to the Ebola outbreak, the CDC promulgated interim guidelines for screening. The CDC's Interim Guidance recognizes the unfortunate risk of infection, even among trained healthcare workers:

> The high toll of Ebola virus infections among healthcare workers providing direct care to Ebola patients in countries with widespread transmission suggests that there are multiple potential sources of exposure to Ebola virus in these countries, including unrecognized breaches in PPE, inadequate decontamination procedures, and exposure in patient triage areas. Due to this higher risk, these healthcare workers are classified in the "some risk" category, for which additional precautions may be recommended upon their arrival in the United States.

Federal quarantine orders, as such, have been comparatively rare. Since as long ago as 1799, however, federal legislation has mandated federal noninterference and cooperation with the states' execution of their quarantine laws. In the modern era, the CDC has most commonly played a supportive role, with the States taking the lead in quarantine matters. That is what happened here. After an initial screening at the CDC Quarantine Station, the State of New Jersey took over, in accordance with the [State's Ebola Preparedness Plan]. Ms. Hickox was detained by the Department of Health (DOH), pursuant to state law. By statute, the DOH or a local board of health has the power to:

> Maintain and enforce proper and sufficient quarantine, wherever deemed necessary ... [and] Remove any person infected with a

communicable disease to a suitable place, if in its judgment removal is necessary and can be accomplished without any undue risk to the person infected

The administrative rule cited by the State to justify Ms. Hickox's quarantine reads as follows:

> The Department or health officer may, by written order, isolate or quarantine any person who has been exposed to a communicable disease as medically or epidemiologically necessary to prevent the spread of the disease, provided such period of restriction shall not exceed the period of incubation of the disease.

More than a century ago, the United States Supreme Court upheld such exercises of the states' general police powers to protect public health through quarantines and other measures. *See Jacobson v. Commonwealth of Massachusetts*, 197 U.S. 11, 25 (1905) (recognizing the "authority of a state to enact quarantine laws and health laws of every description") (internal quotations and citations omitted); *see also Compagnie Francaise de Navigation a Vapeur v. La. State Bd. of Health*, 186 U.S. 380, 387 (1902)("[T]he power of States to enact and enforce quarantine laws for the safety and the protection of the health of their inhabitants . . . is beyond question."); *Ogden v. Gibbons*, 22 U.S. (9 Wheat.) 1, 203, 6 L. Ed. 23 (1824) (*dicta* that a state has the power "to provide for the health of its citizens" by quarantine laws).

In *Jacobson*, for example, the Court upheld a Massachusetts law requiring vaccination against smallpox. The Court held that such a measure, enacted to protect public health, will not be struck down unless it "has no real or substantial relation to [that goal], or is, beyond all question, a plain, palpable invasion of rights" secured by the Constitution. To uphold that law, the Court analogized to the unquestioned power to quarantine even an outwardly healthy individual entering the United States:

> An American citizen arriving at an American port on a vessel in which, during the voyage, there had been cases of yellow fever or Asiatic cholera, he, although apparently free from disease himself, may yet, in some circumstances, be held in quarantine against his will on board of such vessel or in a quarantine station, until it be ascertained by inspection, conducted with due diligence, that the danger of the spread of the disease among the community at large has disappeared.

Courts facing similar public health issues have recognized that the authorities possess similarly broad discretion.

Thus *Reynolds v. McNichols*, 488 F.2d 1378 (10th Cir.1973), relying in part on *Jacobson*, upheld an ordinance "authorizing limited detention in jail without bond for the purpose of examination and treatment for a venereal disease of one reasonably suspected of having a venereal disease" as a valid exercise of the police power.

In *U.S. ex rel. Siegel v. Shinnick*, 219 F. Supp. 789 (E.D.N.Y. 1963), the court permitted the quarantine of a woman who had arrived in the U.S. from Stockholm (deemed "a smallpox infected area") without presenting a certificate of vaccination. The court upheld an administrative order that she be quarantined for 14 days, the length of the smallpox incubation period. It acknowledged that public health officials "deal in a terrible context [where] the consequences of mistaken indulgence can be irretrievably tragic." A better-safe-than-sorry determination was therefore entitled to deference, absent a "reliable showing of error":

> Their conclusion, reached in obvious good faith, cannot be challenged on the ground that they had no evidence of the exposure . . . to the disease; they, simply, were not free and certainly not bound to ignore the facts that opportunity for exposure existed during four days in Stockholm, that no one on earth could know for fourteen days whether or not there had been exposure . . .

Courts have sometimes struck down quarantine orders, however, when they were found to be arbitrary and unreasonable in relation to their goal of protecting the public health. In *Jew Ho v. Williamson*, 103 F. 10 (C.C.D. Cal. 1900), the court found that sealing off an entire section of San Francisco to prevent the spread of the bubonic plague was "unreasonable, unjust, and oppressive." Such an overbroad order, the court declared, was "not in harmony with the declared purpose" of preventing the spread of the disease.

Overbreadth was of similar concern in *In re Smith*, 101 Sickels 68, 76, 146 N.Y. 68, 40 N.E. 497 (1895). There, the New York Court of Appeals rejected the blanket quarantine of individuals who refused vaccination, when there was no reason to believe they had been infected or even exposed to that disease.

Building on the principles of such cases, Hickox argues that the initial decision to quarantine her did not bear a "real or substantial relation" to protection of the public health, but instead was "arbitrary and oppressive." At a minimum, she says, her quarantine became arbitrary and oppressive in the early hours of October 25, 2014, when her first blood test results came back negative for Ebola. She argues that the DOH epidemiologist's subsequent recommendation that she be held for 72 hours for further observation was "entirely arbitrary, related neither to the incubation period nor to any symptoms displayed by Hickox at the time."

I sympathize with Hickox's plight, but I cannot find that her isolation violated any clearly established constitutional principle embodied in quarantine case law. Of course, even as to a dread disease, it is possible to overreact; as it was with cholera and yellow fever, so it is with Ebola today.

A restriction can be so arbitrary or overbroad as to be impermissible. The parties cite no case striking down a quarantine order, however, that is even close to Hickox's factual scenario, or that would have clearly indicated to any of these defendants that their actions violated established law.

Hickox was returning from treating patients in a country then ravaged by an Ebola epidemic, thankfully now under control. The disease is a very serious one, and there is no vaccine or medicine to prevent or cure it. The State could reasonably have thought that prevention and containment were therefore paramount.

True, Ms. Hickox was not a patient, but a health care worker, and she was trained in the avoidance of infection. She alleges that she wore protective gear and took other appropriate measures to prevent the spread of the disease to herself or others. The authorities were not required, however, to take it on faith that Ms. Hickox had been 100% compliant, or the measures 100% effective. Exposure, or at least the risk of exposure, was conceded; she worked in close proximity to Ebola patients and other health care workers. Hickox returned to the United States just two days after having left Sierra Leone; if she had contracted an infection close to the end of her stay, she would have been in the very early, asymptomatic days of the incubation period. At the CDC quarantine station, Hickox was questioned regarding the nature and timing of her work in Sierra Leone. Based on her answers, DOH officials decided to detain her for further evaluation. Very early in her detention, certain thermometer readings reflected that she had an elevated temperature, and some continued to reflect a fever for a relatively short time thereafter. Other readings, however, did not; the main divergence seems to have been between the temporal and oral thermometer measurements. The allegations do not indicate that any other cause for the elevated temperature readings was identified.

On such facts, I cannot find that the decision to quarantine Hickox for a limited additional period of observation violated clearly established law of which a reasonable officer would have been aware. The facts do not suggest arbitrariness or unreasonableness as recognized in the prior cases—i.e., application of the quarantine laws to a person (or, more commonly, vast numbers of persons) who had no exposure to the disease at all. Indeed, her quarantine fits well within the Supreme Court's dicta in *Jacobson*, as well as the holdings in *Reynolds* and *Shinnick*. In *Reynolds*, the court authorized a short detention for the purpose of assessing whether an at risk individual had the disease at issue. In *Shinnick*, the individual was held for the incubation period of the disease (14 days) to rule out her infection with smallpox during her travel in an infected area. In short, given the important public interests at stake, the cases give the authorities a great deal of leeway to detain persons who may turn out not to have been sick at all. Here, Hickox was quarantined, in total, for approximately 80 hours, and released well before the expiration of even the shortest estimate of the incubation period (8 days). Hickox's argument, that a 72 or 80 hour quarantine is "unrelated" to the incubation period would seem to support a longer, not a shorter, quarantine period. It tends to suggest that the response of the authorities was measured and reasonable, not arbitrary. * * *

Plaintiff also argues that civil commitment case law put defendants on notice that their conduct violated clearly established law. * * * Civil commitment is subject to the Fourth Amendment, which guards against "unreasonable searches and seizures." "[T]he ultimate touchstone of the Fourth Amendment is reasonableness." In the civil commitment context, "it is not unreasonable to temporarily detain an individual who is dangerous to himself or others." The standard is one of probable cause. Probable cause for emergency civil commitment exists where "there are reasonable grounds for believing that the person seized is subject to the governing legal standard." Shorter detentions require "less compelling" evidence of dangerousness. Similarly, the larger "the magnitude of the harm the person may do if left at large, the stronger is the case for commitment."

For the "governing legal standard" the parties look to the New Jersey administrative code provision cited above (and in Hickox's quarantine order):

> The Department or health officer may, by written order, isolate or quarantine any person who has been exposed to a communicable disease as medically or epidemiologically necessary to prevent the spread of the disease, provided such period of restriction shall not exceed the period of incubation of the disease.

This provision is relevant to Ms. Hickox's detention, whether viewed through the lens of quarantine or civil commitment. The question here, as presented by the parties, is whether the authorities had probable cause to believe that standard was met.

I fail to see a lack of probable cause so clear as to overcome the officials' qualified immunity. As discussed *supra*, plaintiff was returning from a country experiencing a severe Ebola epidemic, and she was consistently engaged in Ebola-related care while in Sierra Leone. It would not have been unreasonable for a public health official to believe that she had been "exposed" to Ebola. Exposure does not necessarily equate to infection, but temporary quarantine is authorized based on a risk, or potential, for infection, not proof of infection itself. Nor was it unreasonable that health officials remained concerned, even following Hickox's favorable blood work, because she had repeatedly registered a fever, for which no other explanation has been given.

Other factors found relevant to civil commitment support a finding of probable cause. Ms. Hickox was not institutionalized on an ongoing basis; she was detained for approximately 80 hours. The fever appeared very early on, a few hours into the detention period. The magnitude of the harm that could have occurred had she been released, weighed against the relatively short period of detention, also weighs in favor of finding that the detention was supported by probable cause.

Ms. Hickox argues that her compliance with anti-infection protocols in Sierra Leone should have indicated to any reasonable officer that she was not infected, and defeated probable cause. As noted above, this argument presupposes that the health officials were required to take at face value her statements, as well as to assume that such measures were fail-safe. The CDC's Interim Guidance recognizes the unfortunate risk of infection, even among trained healthcare workers. Indeed, the CDC suggested direct active monitoring for such healthcare workers, even if asymptomatic, while noting that "[t]he public health authority, based on a specific assessment of the individual's situation, will determine whether additional restrictions are appropriate." For healthcare workers showing symptoms, "rapid isolation" is recommended. The risk of such infection only underscores the admirability of what Nurse Hickox did; it also, however, provides justification for the actions of the authorities.

Applying analogous civil commitment case law, I do not find that plaintiff's border quarantine constituted a clear violation of her Fourth Amendment rights that would have been apparent to any reasonable officer, exposing that officer to a claim for damages under § 1983.

CONSTITUTIONAL QUESTIONS IN A PANDEMIC

Under Executive Order 13295, as amended on July 31, 2014, by Executive Order 13674, federal agencies have authority to effect quarantines for "severe acute respiratory syndromes," which likely encompasses SARS-CoV-2. But that does not mean that a specific exercise of this authority is necessarily constitutional. In the spring of 2020, state and local officials in most American jurisdictions issued stay-at-home orders, mandated the closure of many businesses open to the public, closed public spaces, and required that individuals exposed to SARS-CoV-2 or traveling from areas with high rates of SARS-CoV-2 infections self-quarantine for 14 days. Based on Judge McNulty's analysis in *Hickox*, do you think these measures are constitutional under the Fourth Amendment? Consider *Benner v. Wolf*, 2020 WL 2564920 (M.D. Pa. May 21, 2020); *Henry v. DeSantis*, 2020 WL 2479447 (S.D. Fla. May 14, 2020); *Givens v. Newsom*, 2020 WL 2307224 (E.D. Cal. May 8, 2020); *Lawrence v. Colorado*, 2020 WL 2737811 (D. Colo. Apr. 19, 2020). If you were advising a governor, mayor, or chief-of-police, where would you suggest that she draw the line on her powers to impose and enforce these and similar measures under the Fourth Amendment? If you were advising a legislator considering a law authorizing these and similar measures, what powers, limits, and safeguards would you suggest?

VI. ELECTRONIC SURVEILLANCE AND UNDERCOVER ACTIVITY

C. STATUTORY REGULATION OF DOMESTIC ELECTRONIC SURVEILLANCE

The Federal Statutory Response: Title III and Its Amendments

Page 555. Add after Factor 12:

13. *Territorial Reach:* In *Dahda v. United States*, 138 S.Ct. 1491 (2018), the Court addressed the scope of a federal judge's power to order an interception of communications. Under federal law, a judge normally may issue a wiretap order permitting the interception of communications only "within the territorial jurisdiction of the court in which the judge is sitting." 18 U. S. C. § 2518(3). But, in this case a Kansas federal judge authorized nine wiretap orders as part of a Government investigation of a suspected drug distribution ring in that state. The Government intercepted most of the communications from a listening post within Kansas, but also relied on a sentence in each order purporting to authorize interceptions outside Kansas to intercept communications from a listening post in Missouri. Two defendants indicted as drug conspirators moved to suppress the evidence because the judge had no authority to authorize interceptions outside Kansas, and this meant the orders were insufficient on their face so that suppression of all intercepted communications was required. The government agreed it would not use evidence obtained from the Missouri listening post, but the defendants argued that this did not cure the facial defect in the orders.

The statute, § 2518(10)(a), provides for the suppression of "the contents of any wire or oral communication" that a wiretap "intercept[s]" along with any "evidence derived therefrom" if

(i) the communication was unlawfully intercepted;

(ii) the order of . . . approval under which it was intercepted is insufficient on its face; or

(iii) the interception was not made in conformity with the order of authorization or approval.

Justice Breyer wrote for the Court as it rejected the defendant's argument that the orders were "insufficient" on their face. He described what a federal judge must find pursuant to § 2518(4)(a)–(e) before issuing an interception order:

[T]he Government must submit an application that describes the particular offense being investigated as well as the type of communications it seeks to intercept; that sets forth the basis for an appropriate finding of "probable cause"; that explains why other less intrusive methods are inadequate, have failed, or are too dangerous to try; and that meets other requirements, showing, for example, authorization by a specified governmental official. § 2518(1). If the judge accepts the application, finds probable cause, and issues an authorizing order, that order must itself contain specified information, including, for example, the identity of the "person" whose "communications are to be intercepted"; the "nature and location of the [relevant] communications facilities"; a "particular description of the type of communication sought to be intercepted"; a statement of the "particular offense" to which the intercept "relates"; the "identity of the agency authorized to intercept"; the identity of the "person authorizing the application"; and "the period of time during which" the "interception is authorized." §§ 2518(4)(a)–(e).

The Tenth Circuit had agreed with the government's position that subdivision (ii) focused on the core concerns of the statute which were "protecting the privacy of wire and oral communications, and delineating on a uniform basis the circumstances and conditions under which the interception of wire and oral communications may be authorized"—and concluded that neither applies to the statute's territorial limitation. Justice Breyer found that this approach was too narrow.

Instead, Justice Breyer concluded that

subparagraph (ii) does not cover each and every error that appears in an otherwise sufficient order. It is clear that subparagraph (ii) covers at least an order's failure to include information that § 2518(4) specifically requires the order to contain. See §§ 2518(4)(a)–(e) * * *. An order lacking that information would deviate from the uniform authorizing requirements that Congress explicitly set forth, while also falling literally within the phrase "insufficient on its face."

He explicitly rejected the Dahdas' argument that any defect that may appear on an order's face would render it insufficient and recognized that the nine orders contained a defect:

The Orders do contain a defect, namely, the sentence authorizing interception outside Kansas, which we set forth above. But not every defect results in an insufficiency. In that sentence, the District Court "further" ordered that interception may take place "outside the territorial jurisdiction of the court." The sentence is without legal effect because, as the parties agree, the Orders could not legally authorize a wiretap outside the District Court's "territorial jurisdiction." But, more importantly, the sentence itself is surplus. Its presence is not connected to any other relevant part of the Orders. Were we to remove the sentence from the Orders, they would then properly authorize wiretaps within the authorizing court's territorial jurisdiction. As we discussed above, a listening post within the court's territorial jurisdiction could lawfully intercept communications to or from telephones located within Kansas or outside Kansas. Consequently, every wiretap that produced evidence introduced at the Dahdas' trial was properly authorized under the statute.

Justice Gorsuch did not participate in the case.

VII. REMEDIES FOR FOURTH AMENDMENT VIOLATIONS

B. THE EXCLUSIONARY RULE AND THE STATES

Page 569. Add after the note on *Mapp*:

Justice Thomas, in his opinion concurring in the judgment in *Collins v. Virginia*, 138 S.Ct. 1663 (2018), launched into an attack on the exclusionary rule, and, in particular, criticized the Court's rulings requiring the exclusionary rule to be applied in *state* criminal cases like *Collins*. Justice Thomas proceeded as follows:

I have serious doubts about this Court's authority to impose that rule on the States. The assumption that state courts must apply the federal exclusionary rule is legally dubious, and many jurists have complained that it encourages "distort[ions]" in substantive Fourth Amendment law. *Rakas v. Illinois*, 439 U. S. 128, 157 (1978) (White, J., dissenting); see also *Coolidge v. New Hampshire*, 403 U. S. 443, 490 (1971) (Harlan, J., concurring); Calabresi, The Exclusionary Rule, 26 Harv. J. L. & Pub. Pol'y 111, 112 (2003).

While those who ratified the Fourth and Fourteenth Amendments would agree that a constitutional violation occurred here, they would be deeply confused about the posture of this case and the remedy that Collins is seeking. Historically, the only remedies for unconstitutional searches and seizures were "tort suits" and "self-help."

The exclusionary rule—the practice of deterring illegal searches and seizures by suppressing evidence at criminal trials—did not exist. No such rule existed in "Roman Law, Napoleonic Law or even the Common Law of England." Burger, Who Will Watch the Watchman? 14 Am. U. L. Rev. 1 (1964). And this Court did not adopt the federal exclusionary rule until the 20th century. See *Weeks v. United States*, 232 U. S. 383 (1914). As late as 1949, nearly two-thirds of the States did not have an exclusionary rule. See *Wolf v. Colorado*, 338 U. S. 25, 29 (1949). Those States, as then-Judge Cardozo famously explained, did not understand the logic of a rule that allowed "[t]he criminal . . . to go free because the constable has blundered." *People v. Defore*, 242 N. Y. 13, 21, 150 N. E. 585, 587 (1926).

The Founders would not have understood the logic of the exclusionary rule either. Historically, if evidence was relevant and reliable, its admissibility did not "depend upon the lawfulness or unlawfulness of the mode, by which it [was] obtained." * * * And the common law sometimes reflected the inverse of the exclusionary rule: The fact that someone turned out to be guilty could *justify* an illegal seizure. See *Gelston v. Hoyt*, 3 Wheat. 246, 310 (1818) (Story, J.) ("At common law, any person may at his peril, seize for a forfeiture to the government; and if the government adopt his seizure, and the property is condemned, he will be completely justified"); 2 W. Hawkins, Pleas of the Crown 77 (1721) ("And where a Man arrests another, who is actually guilty of the Crime for which he is arrested, . . . he needs not in justifying it, set forth any special Cause of his Suspicion").

Despite this history, the Court concluded in *Mapp v. Ohio*, 367 U. S. 643 (1961), that the States must apply the federal exclusionary rule in their own courts. *Mapp* suggested that the exclusionary rule was required by the Constitution itself. * * * But that suggestion could not withstand even the slightest scrutiny. The exclusionary rule appears nowhere in the Constitution, postdates the founding by more than a century, and contradicts several longstanding principles of the common law. * * *

Recognizing this, the Court has since rejected *Mapp*'s "[e]xpansive dicta" and clarified that the exclusionary rule is not required by the Constitution. *Davis v. United States*, 564 U. S. 229, 237 (2011) (quoting *Hudson v. Michigan*, 547 U. S. 586, 591 (2006)). Suppression, this Court has explained, is not "a personal constitutional right." *United States v. Calandra*, 414 U. S. 338, 348 (1974); accord, *Stone v. Powell*, 428 U. S. 465, 486 (1976). The Fourth Amendment "says nothing about suppressing evidence," *Davis, supra*, at 236, and a prosecutor's "use of fruits of a past unlawful search or seizure works no new Fourth Amendment wrong," *United States v. Leon*, 468 U. S. 897, 906 (1984). Instead, the exclusionary rule is a "judicially created" doctrine that is "prudential rather than constitutionally mandated." *Pennsylvania Bd. of Probation and Parole v. Scott*, 524 U. S. 357, 363 (1998); accord, *Herring v. United* States, 555 U. S. 135, 139 (2009); *Arizona v. Evans*, 514 U. S. 1, 10 (1995); *United States v. Janis*, 428 U. S. 433, 459–460 (1976).

Although the exclusionary rule is not part of the Constitution, this Court has continued to describe it as "federal law" and assume that it applies to the States. Yet the Court has never attempted to justify this assumption. If the exclusionary rule is federal law, but is not grounded in the Constitution or a federal statute, then it must be federal common law. As federal common law, however, the exclusionary rule cannot bind the States.

* * *

In sum, I am skeptical of this Court's authority to impose the exclusionary rule on the States. We have not yet revisited that question in light of our modern precedents, which reject *Mapp*'s essential premise that the exclusionary rule is required by the Constitution. We should do so.

E. LIMITATIONS ON EXCLUSION

3. Establishing a Violation of a Personal Fourth Amendment Right

Page 616. Add the following at the end of "*NOTE ON RAKAS*":

The picture was complicated further by the Court's decision in *Carpenter v. United States*, 138 S.Ct. 2206 (2018), which is excerpted above in the materials on search. There, the Court held that law enforcement's accessing cell-site location records is a "search" for purposes of the Fourth Amendment requiring a warrant. In a spirited dissenting opinion joined by Justices Thomas and Alito, Justice Kennedy wonders how a cellular phone customer like Carpenter could possibly have "standing" to challenge a government's request for business records belonging to a cellular service provider given that "Fourth Amendment rights . . . are personal" and that the "Amendment protects '[t]he right of the people to be secure in their . . . persons, houses, papers, and effects'—not the persons, houses, papers, and effects of others."

Writing separately, Justice Thomas presses this point further:

It bears repeating that the Fourth Amendment guarantees "[t]he right of the people to be secure in *their* persons, houses, papers, and effects." (Emphasis added.) The Fourth Amendment does not confer rights with respect to the persons, houses, papers, and effects of others. Its language makes clear that "Fourth Amendment rights are personal," and as a result, this Court has long insisted that they "may not be asserted vicariously." It follows that a "person who is aggrieved only through the introduction of damaging evidence secured by a search of a third person's premises or property has not had any of his Fourth Amendment rights infringed."

In this case, as Justice KENNEDY cogently explains, the cell-site records obtained by the Government belong to Carpenter's cell service providers, not to Carpenter.

By way of response on behalf of the majority, Chief Justice Roberts claims that this "position fails to contend with the seismic shifts in digital technology that made possible the tracking of not only Carpenter's location but also everyone else's, not for a short period but for years and years." Later, he chides the dissenters for failing to "recognize that CSLI is an entirely different species of business record—something that implicates basic Fourth Amendment concerns about arbitrary government power much more directly than corporate tax or payroll ledgers."

How, if at all, does the argument that digital records are different resolve Justices Kennedy, Thomas, and Alito's concerns about standing? If it does not, then is Justice Thomas right in suggesting that the majority opinion rides implicitly on a different theory of Fourth Amendment "standing" that allows some litigants to assert Fourth Amendment rights in the "persons, houses, papers, and effects" of others? If so, then what is that theory? How might it apply in other cases?

Rental Cars

Page 621. In the section on Rental Cars, add the following case:

BYRD V. UNITED STATES
Supreme Court of the United States, 2018.
138 S.Ct. 1518.

JUSTICE KENNEDY delivered the opinion of the Court.

In September 2014, Pennsylvania State Troopers pulled over a car driven by petitioner Terrence Byrd. Byrd was the only person in the car. In the course of the traffic stop the troopers learned that the car was rented and that Byrd was not listed on the rental agreement as an authorized driver. For this reason, the troopers told Byrd they did not need his consent to search the car, including its trunk where he had stored personal effects. A search of the trunk uncovered body armor and 49 bricks of heroin.

The evidence was turned over to federal authorities, who charged Byrd with distribution and possession of heroin with the intent to distribute * * * and possession of body armor by a prohibited person * * *. Byrd moved to suppress the evidence as the fruit of an unlawful search. The United States District Court * * * denied the motion, and the Court of Appeals for the Third Circuit affirmed. Both courts concluded that, because Byrd was not listed on the rental agreement, he lacked a reasonable expectation of privacy in the car. Based on this conclusion, it appears that both the District Court and Court of Appeals deemed it unnecessary to consider whether the troopers had probable cause to search the car.

This Court granted certiorari to address the question whether a driver has a reasonable expectation of privacy in a rental car when he or she is not listed as an authorized driver on the rental agreement. The Court now holds that, as a general rule, someone in otherwise lawful possession and control of a rental car has a reasonable expectation of privacy in it even if the rental agreement does not list him or her as an authorized driver.

The Court concludes a remand is necessary to address in the first instance the Government's argument that this general rule is inapplicable because, in the circumstances here, Byrd had no greater expectation of privacy than a car thief. If that is so, our cases make clear he would lack a legitimate expectation of privacy. It is necessary to remand as well to determine whether, even if Byrd had a right to object to the search, probable cause justified it in any event.

I

On September 17, 2014, petitioner Terrence Byrd and Latasha Reed drove in Byrd's Honda Accord to a Budget car-rental facility in Wayne, New Jersey. Byrd stayed in the parking lot in the Honda while Reed went to the Budget desk and rented a Ford Fusion. The agreement Reed signed required her to certify that she had a valid driver's license and had not committed certain vehicle-related offenses within the previous three years. An addendum to the agreement, which Reed initialed, provides the following restriction on who may drive the rental car:

> "I understand that the only ones permitted to drive the vehicle other than the renter are the renter's spouse, the renter's co-employee (with the renter's permission, while on company business), or a person who appears at the time of the rental and signs an Additional Driver Form. These other drivers must also be at least 25 years old and validly licensed.

> "PERMITTING AN UNAUTHORIZED DRIVER TO OPERATE THE VEHICLE IS A VIOLATION OF THE RENTAL AGREEMENT. THIS MAY RESULT IN ANY AND ALL COVERAGE OTHERWISE PROVIDED BY THE RENTAL AGREEMENT BEING VOID AND MY BEING FULLY RESPONSIBLE FOR ALL LOSS OR DAMAGE, INCLUDING LIABILITY TO THIRD PARTIES."

In filling out the paperwork for the rental agreement, Reed did not list an additional driver.

With the rental keys in hand, Reed returned to the parking lot and gave them to Byrd. The two then left the facility in separate cars—she in his Honda, he in the rental car. Byrd returned to his home in Patterson, New Jersey, and put his personal belongings in the trunk of the rental car. Later that afternoon, he departed in the car alone and headed toward Pittsburgh, Pennsylvania.

After driving nearly three hours, or roughly half the distance to Pittsburgh, Byrd passed State Trooper David Long, who was parked in the median of Interstate 81 near Harrisburg, Pennsylvania. Long was suspicious of Byrd because he was driving with his hands at the "10 and 2" position on the steering wheel, sitting far back from the steering wheel, and driving a rental car. Long knew the Ford Fusion was a rental car because one of its windows contained a barcode. Based on these observations, he decided to follow Byrd and, a short time later, stopped him for a possible traffic infraction.

When Long approached the passenger window of Byrd's car to explain the basis for the stop and to ask for identification, Byrd was "visibly nervous" and "was shaking and had a hard time obtaining his driver's license." He handed an interim license and the rental agreement to Long, stating that a friend had rented the car. Long returned to his vehicle to verify Byrd's license and noticed Byrd was not listed as an additional driver on the rental agreement. Around this time another trooper, Travis Martin, arrived at the scene. While Long processed Byrd's license, Martin conversed with Byrd, who again stated that a friend had rented the vehicle. After Martin walked back to Long's patrol car, Long commented to Martin that Byrd was "not on the renter agreement," to which Martin replied, "yeah, he has no expectation of privacy."

A computer search based on Byrd's identification returned two different names. Further inquiry suggested the other name might be an alias and also revealed that Byrd had prior convictions for weapons and drug charges as well as an outstanding warrant in New Jersey for a probation violation. After learning that New Jersey did not want Byrd arrested for extradition, the troopers asked Byrd to step out of the vehicle and patted him down.

Long asked Byrd if he had anything illegal in the car. When Byrd said he did not, the troopers asked for his consent to search the car. At that point Byrd said he had a "blunt" in the car and offered to retrieve it for them. The officers understood "blunt" to mean a marijuana cigarette. They declined to let him retrieve it and continued to seek his consent to search the car, though they stated they did not need consent because he was not listed on the rental agreement. The troopers then opened the passenger and driver doors and began a thorough search of the passenger compartment.

Martin proceeded from there to search the car's trunk, including by opening up and taking things out of a large cardboard box, where he found a laundry bag containing body armor. At this point, the troopers decided to detain Byrd. As Martin walked toward Byrd and said he would be placing him in handcuffs, Byrd began to run away. A third trooper who had arrived on the scene joined Long and Martin in pursuit. When the troopers caught up to Byrd, he surrendered and admitted there was heroin in the car. Back at the car, the troopers resumed their search of the laundry bag and found 49 bricks of heroin.

In pretrial proceedings Byrd moved to suppress the evidence found in the trunk of the rental car, arguing that the search violated his Fourth Amendment rights. Although Long contended at a suppression hearing that the troopers had probable cause to search the car after Byrd stated it contained marijuana, the District Court denied Byrd's motion on the ground that Byrd lacked "standing" to contest the search as an initial matter. Byrd later entered a conditional guilty plea, reserving the right to appeal the suppression ruling.

The Court of Appeals affirmed in a brief summary opinion. As relevant here, the Court of Appeals recognized that a "circuit split exists as to whether the sole occupant of a rental vehicle has a Fourth Amendment expectation of privacy when that occupant is not named in the rental agreement"; but it noted that Circuit precedent already had "spoken as to this issue . . . and determined such a person has no expectation of privacy and therefore no standing to challenge a search of the vehicle." The Court of Appeals did not reach the probable-cause question.

This Court granted Byrd's petition for a writ of certiorari to address the conflict among the Courts of Appeals over whether an unauthorized driver has a reasonable expectation of privacy in a rental car. * * *

II

Few protections are as essential to individual liberty as the right to be free from unreasonable searches and seizures. The Framers made that right explicit in the Bill of Rights following their experience with the indignities and invasions of privacy wrought by "general warrants and warrantless searches that had so alienated the colonists and had helped speed the movement for independence." Chimel v. California, 395 U. S. 752, 761 (1969). Ever mindful of the Fourth Amendment and its history, the Court has viewed with disfavor practices that permit "police officers unbridled discretion to rummage at will among a person's private effects." Arizona v. Gant, 556 U. S. 332, 345 (2009).

This concern attends the search of an automobile. See Delaware v. Prouse, 440 U. S. 648, 662 (1979). The Court has acknowledged, however, that there is a diminished expectation of privacy in automobiles, which often permits officers to dispense with obtaining a warrant before conducting a lawful search. See, e.g., California v. Acevedo, 500 U. S. 565, 579 (1991).

Whether a warrant is required is a separate question from the one the Court addresses here, which is whether the person claiming a constitutional violation "has had his own Fourth Amendment rights infringed by the search and seizure which he seeks to challenge." Rakas v.

Illinois, 439 U. S. 128, 133 (1978). Answering that question requires examination of whether the person claiming the constitutional violation had a "legitimate expectation of privacy in the premises" searched. "Expectations of privacy protected by the Fourth Amendment, of course, need not be based on a common-law interest in real or personal property, or on the invasion of such an interest." Still, "property concepts" are instructive in "determining the presence or absence of the privacy interests protected by that Amendment."

Indeed, more recent Fourth Amendment cases have clarified that the test most often associated with legitimate expectations of privacy, which was derived from the second Justice Harlan's concurrence in Katz v. United States, 389 U. S. 347 (1967), supplements, rather than displaces, "the traditional property-based understanding of the Fourth Amendment." Florida v. Jardines, 569 U. S. 1, 11 (2013). Perhaps in light of this clarification, Byrd now argues in the alternative that he had a common-law property interest in the rental car as a second bailee that would have provided him with a cognizable Fourth Amendment interest in the vehicle. But he did not raise this argument before the District Court or Court of Appeals, and those courts did not have occasion to address whether Byrd was a second bailee or what consequences might follow from that determination. In those courts he framed the question solely in terms of the *Katz* test noted above. Because this is "a court of review, not of first view," it is generally unwise to consider arguments in the first instance, and the Court declines to reach Byrd's contention that he was a second bailee.

Reference to property concepts, however, aids the Court in assessing the precise question here: Does a driver of a rental car have a reasonable expectation of privacy in the car when he or she is not listed as an authorized driver on the rental agreement?

III

A

One who owns and possesses a car, like one who owns and possesses a house, almost always has a reasonable expectation of privacy in it. More difficult to define and delineate are the legitimate expectations of privacy of others.

On the one hand, as noted above, it is by now well established that a person need not always have a recognized common-law property interest in the place searched to be able to claim a reasonable expectation of privacy in it. *See* Jones v. United States, 362 U. S. 257, 259 (1960); *Katz*, supra, at 352; Minnesota v. Olson, 495 U. S. 91, 98 (1990).

On the other hand, it is also clear that legitimate presence on the premises of the place searched, standing alone, is not enough to accord a reasonable expectation of privacy, because it "creates too broad a gauge for measurement of Fourth Amendment rights." *Rakas*, 439 U.S. at 142; see also *id.*, at 148 ("We would not wish to be understood as saying that legitimate presence on the premises is irrelevant to one's expectation of privacy, but it cannot be deemed controlling").

Although the Court has not set forth a single metric or exhaustive list of considerations to resolve the circumstances in which a person can be said to have a reasonable expectation of privacy, it has explained that "[l]egitimation of expectations of privacy by law must have a source outside of the Fourth Amendment, either by reference to concepts of real or personal property law or to understandings that are recognized and permitted by society." *Rakas*, 439 U. S., at 144, n. 12. The two concepts in cases like this one are often linked. "One of the main rights attaching to property is the right to exclude others," and, in the main, "one who owns or lawfully possesses or controls property will in all likelihood have a legitimate expectation of privacy by virtue of the right to exclude." This general property-based concept guides resolution of this case.

B

Here, the Government contends that drivers who are not listed on rental agreements always lack an expectation of privacy in the automobile based on the rental company's lack of authorization alone. This per se rule rests on too restrictive a view of the Fourth Amendment's protections. Byrd, by contrast, contends that the sole occupant of a rental car always has an expectation of privacy in it based on mere possession and control. There is more to recommend Byrd's proposed rule than the Government's; but, without qualification, it would include within its ambit thieves and others who, not least because of their lack of any property-based justification, would not have a reasonable expectation of privacy.

1

Stripped to its essentials, the Government's position is that only authorized drivers of rental cars have expectations of privacy in those vehicles. This position is based on the following syllogism: Under *Rakas*, passengers do not have an expectation of privacy in an automobile glove compartment or like places; an unauthorized driver like Byrd would have been the passenger had the renter been driving; and the unauthorized driver cannot obtain greater protection when he takes the wheel and leaves the renter behind. The flaw in this syllogism is its major premise, for it is a misreading of *Rakas*.

The Court in *Rakas* did not hold that passengers cannot have an expectation of privacy in automobiles. To the contrary, the Court disclaimed any intent to hold "that a passenger lawfully in an automobile may not invoke the exclusionary rule and challenge a search of that vehicle unless he happens to own or have a possessory interest in it." The Court instead rejected the argument that legitimate presence alone was sufficient to assert a Fourth Amendment interest, which was fatal to the petitioners' case there because they had "claimed only that they were 'legitimately on [the] premises' and did not claim that they had any legitimate expectation of privacy in the areas of the car which were searched."

What is more, the Government's syllogism is beside the point, because this case does not involve a passenger at all but instead the driver and sole occupant of a rental car. As Justice Powell observed in his concurring opinion in *Rakas*, a "distinction . . . may be made in some circumstances between the Fourth Amendment rights of passengers and the rights of an individual who has exclusive control of an automobile or of its locked compartments." This situation would be similar to the defendant in *Jones*, *supra*, who, as *Rakas* notes, had a reasonable expectation of privacy in his friend's apartment because he "had complete dominion and control over the apartment and could exclude others from it." Justice Powell's observation was also consistent with the majority's explanation that "one who owns or lawfully possesses or controls property will in all likelihood have a legitimate expectation of privacy by virtue of [the] right to exclude," an explanation tied to the majority's discussion of Jones.

The Court sees no reason why the expectation of privacy that comes from lawful possession and control and the attendant right to exclude would differ depending on whether the car in question is rented or privately owned by someone other than the person in current possession of it, much as it did not seem to matter whether the friend of the defendant in Jones owned or leased the apartment he permitted the defendant to use in his absence. Both would have the expectation of privacy that comes with the right to exclude. Indeed, the Government conceded at oral argument that an unauthorized driver in sole possession of a rental car would be permitted to exclude third parties from it, such as a carjacker.

2

The Government further stresses that Byrd's driving the rental car violated the rental agreement that Reed signed, and it contends this violation meant Byrd could not have had any basis for claiming an expectation of privacy in the rental car at the time of the search. As anyone who has rented a car knows, car-rental agreements are filled with long lists of restrictions. Examples include prohibitions on driving the car on unpaved roads or driving while using a handheld cellphone. Few would contend that violating provisions like these has anything to do with a driver's reasonable expectation of privacy in the rental car—as even the Government agrees.

Despite this concession, the Government argues that permitting an unauthorized driver to take the wheel of a rental car is a breach different in kind from these others, so serious that the rental company would consider the agreement "void" the moment an unauthorized driver takes the wheel. To begin with, that is not what the contract says. It states: "Permitting an unauthorized driver to operate the vehicle is a violation of the rental agreement. This may result in any and all coverage otherwise provided by the rental agreement being void and my being fully responsible for all loss or damage, including liability to third parties."

Putting the Government's misreading of the contract aside, there may be countless innocuous reasons why an unauthorized driver might get behind the wheel of a rental car and drive it—perhaps the renter is drowsy or inebriated and the two think it safer for the friend to drive them to their destination. True, this constitutes a breach of the rental agreement, and perhaps a serious one, but the Government fails to explain what bearing this breach of contract, standing alone, has on expectations of privacy in the car. Stated in different terms, for Fourth Amendment purposes there is no meaningful difference between the authorized-driver provision and the other provisions the Government agrees do not eliminate an expectation of privacy, all of which concern risk allocation between private parties—violators might pay additional fees, lose insurance coverage, or assume liability for damage resulting from the breach. But that risk allocation has little to do with whether one would have a reasonable expectation of privacy in the rental car if, for example, he or she otherwise has lawful possession of and control over the car.

3

The central inquiry at this point turns on the concept of lawful possession, and this is where an important qualification of Byrd's proposed rule comes into play. *Rakas* makes clear that "wrongful presence at the scene of a search would not enable a defendant to object to the legality of the search." "A burglar plying his trade in a summer cabin during the off season," for example, "may have a thoroughly justified subjective expectation of privacy, but it is not one which the law recognizes as legitimate." Likewise, "a person present in a stolen automobile at the time of the search may [not] object to the lawfulness of the search of the automobile." No matter the degree of possession and control, the car thief would not have a reasonable expectation of privacy in a stolen car.

On this point, in its merits brief, the Government asserts that, on the facts here, Byrd should have no greater expectation of privacy than a car thief because he intentionally used a third party as a strawman in a calculated plan to mislead the rental company from the very outset, all to aid him in committing a crime. This argument is premised on the Government's inference that Byrd knew he would not have been able to rent the car on his own, because he would not have satisfied the rental company's requirements based on his criminal record, and that he used

Reed, who had no intention of using the car for her own purposes, to procure the car for him to transport heroin to Pittsburgh.

It is unclear whether the Government's allegations, if true, would constitute a criminal offense in the acquisition of the rental car under applicable law. And it may be that there is no reason that the law should distinguish between one who obtains a vehicle through subterfuge of the type the Government alleges occurred here and one who steals the car outright.

The Government did not raise this argument in the District Court or the Court of Appeals, however. It relied instead on the sole fact that Byrd lacked authorization to drive the car. And it is unclear from the record whether the Government's inferences paint an accurate picture of what occurred. Because it was not addressed in the District Court or Court of Appeals, the Court declines to reach this question. The proper course is to remand for the argument and potentially further factual development to be considered in the first instance by the Court of Appeals or by the District Court.

IV

The Government argued in its brief in opposition to certiorari that, even if Byrd had a Fourth Amendment interest in the rental car, the troopers had probable cause to believe it contained evidence of a crime when they initiated their search. If that were true, the troopers may have been permitted to conduct a warrantless search of the car in line with the Court's cases concerning the automobile exception to the warrant requirement. The Court of Appeals did not reach this question because it concluded, as an initial matter, that Byrd lacked a reasonable expectation of privacy in the rental car.

It is worth noting that most courts analyzing the question presented in this case, including the Court of Appeals here, have described it as one of Fourth Amendment "standing," a concept the Court has explained is not distinct from the merits and "is more properly subsumed under substantive Fourth Amendment doctrine."

The concept of standing in Fourth Amendment cases can be a useful shorthand for capturing the idea that a person must have a cognizable Fourth Amendment interest in the place searched before seeking relief for an unconstitutional search; but it should not be confused with Article III standing, which is jurisdictional and must be assessed before reaching the merits. * * * Because Fourth Amendment standing is subsumed under substantive Fourth Amendment doctrine, it is not a jurisdictional question and hence need not be addressed before addressing other aspects of the merits of a Fourth Amendment claim. On remand, then, the Court of Appeals is not required to assess Byrd's reasonable expectation of privacy in the rental car before, in its discretion, first addressing whether there was probable cause for the search, if it finds the latter argument has been preserved.

V

Though new, the fact pattern here continues a well-traveled path in this Court's Fourth Amendment jurisprudence. Those cases support the proposition, and the Court now holds, that the mere fact that a driver in lawful possession or control of a rental car is not listed on the rental agreement will not defeat his or her otherwise reasonable expectation of privacy. The Court leaves for remand two of the Government's arguments: that one who intentionally uses a third party to procure a rental car by a fraudulent scheme for the purpose of committing a crime is no better situated than a car thief; and that probable cause justified the search in any event. The Court of Appeals has discretion as to the order in which these questions are best addressed.

* * *

JUSTICE THOMAS, with whom JUSTICE GORSUCH joins, concurring.

Although I have serious doubts about the "reasonable expectation of privacy" test from *Katz v. United States*, 389 U. S. 347 (1967) (Harlan, J., concurring), I join the Court's opinion because it correctly navigates our precedents, which no party has asked us to reconsider. As the Court notes, Byrd also argued that he should prevail under the original meaning of the Fourth Amendment because the police interfered with a property interest that he had in the rental car. I agree with the Court's decision not to review this argument in the first instance. In my view, it would be especially "unwise" to reach that issue because the parties fail to adequately address several threshold questions.

* * *

That issue seems to turn on at least three threshold questions. First, what kind of property interest do individuals need before something can be considered "their ... effec[t]" under the original meaning of the Fourth Amendment? Second, what body of law determines whether that property interest is present—modern state law, the common law of 1791, or something else? Third, is the unauthorized use of a rental car illegal or otherwise wrongful under the relevant law, and, if so, does that illegality or wrongfulness affect the Fourth Amendment analysis?

The parties largely gloss over these questions, but the answers seem vitally important to assessing whether Byrd can claim that the rental car is his effect. In an appropriate case, I would welcome briefing and argument on these questions.

JUSTICE ALITO, concurring.

The Court holds that an unauthorized driver of a rental car is not always barred from contesting a search of the vehicle. Relevant questions bearing on the driver's ability to raise a Fourth Amendment claim may include: the terms of the particular rental agreement; the circumstances surrounding the rental; the reason why the driver took the wheel; any property right that the driver might have; and the legality of his conduct under the law of the State where the conduct occurred. On remand, the Court of Appeals is free to reexamine the question whether petitioner may assert a Fourth Amendment claim or to decide the appeal on another appropriate ground. On this understanding, I join the opinion of the Court.

CHAPTER 3

SELF-INCRIMINATION AND CONFESSIONS

■ ■ ■

I. THE PRIVILEGE AGAINST COMPELLED SELF-INCRIMINATION

B. SCOPE OF THE PRIVILEGE

Page 679. Add as new section 5:

5. Suppression Hearings

The Court in *City of Hays v. Vogt*, 138 S.Ct. 720 (2018), granted certiorari to decide whether the Fifth Amendment permitted compelled statements to be used in a probable cause hearing.

Vogt was employed as a police officer in city A and applied for a position with city B. During an interview with city B, he disclosed that he kept a knife obtained while working at city A. The city B police chief offered Vogt employment provided that he reported his acquisition of the knife to city A and returned it. Vogt did this, and city A's police chief ordered Vogt to issue a statement regarding the knife along with a letter of resignation. Vogt complied, and city A's police chief began an informal investigation of Vogt and required him to issue a more detailed statement which led to additional evidence and a criminal investigation by the state Bureau of Investigation. City B then withdrew its employment offer. State A charged Vogt with two counts relating to his possession of the knife, but the state district court found probable cause lacking and dismissed the charges. Vogt sued in federal court and alleged that the use of his compelled statements at the probable cause hearing violated his Fifth Amendment rights. The district court dismissed all claims, but the Tenth Circuit found that one claim—the state's use of Vogt's statements during the probable cause hearing—did violate the Fifth Amendment.

The Supreme Court dismissed the case as improvidently granted. 138 S.Ct. 1683 (2018).

IV. CONFESSIONS AND THE SIXTH AMENDMENT RIGHT TO COUNSEL

E. WAIVER OF SIXTH AMENDMENT PROTECTIONS

Waiving the Sixth Amendment Right to Counsel After Invoking It: Michigan v. Jackson and Montejo v. Louisiana

Page 892. Add at the end of the excerpt of *Montejo v. Louisiana*:

QUESTIONS AFTER PATTERSON AND MONTEJO

The Court's holding in *Patterson v. Illinois* has come under renewed scrutiny in recent years as courts and scholars have come to terms with *Montejo* and the effective merger of Fifth and Sixth Amendment rights in the context of warnings, invocation, and waiver. *See, e.g.,* Arnold H. Loewy, *Distinguishing Confessions Obtained in Violation of the Fifth Amendment from Those Obtained in Violation of the Sixth Amendment*, 50 Tex. Tech L. Rev. 145 (2017); Wayne A. Logan, *The Case for Greater Transparency in Sixth Amendment Right to Pretrial Counsel Warnings*, 52 Tex. Tech L. Rev. 23 (2019). Do you think that *Miranda* warnings are adequate to ensure that a defendant knowingly waives his Sixth Amendment right to counsel as well as his Fifth Amendment protection against self-incrimination?

CHAPTER 6

THE SCREENING AND CHARGING PROCESS

■ ■ ■

IV. THE GRAND JURY

G. THE GRAND JURY'S POWERS OF INVESTIGATION

Minimal Limits on Grand Jury Subpoenas: United States v. R. Enterprises, Inc.

Page 1023. Add at the end of the section:

The Supreme Court had occasion to revisit some of the rules and principles limiting the scope of a grand jury's investigative powers during the 2019 term when President Donald J. Trump sought broad immunity against subpoenas issued by the District Attorney for New York County on behalf of a grand jury conducting a criminal investigation. Although the Court was unanimous in rejecting President Trump's claim of absolute immunity, the Justices divided on the legal and constitutional standards that should apply when the President challenges a specific subpoena.

TRUMP V. VANCE
Supreme Court of the United States, 2020.
140 S. Ct. 2412.

CHIEF JUSTICE ROBERTS delivered the opinion of the Court.

In our judicial system, "the public has a right to every man's evidence." Since the earliest days of the Republic, "every man" has included the President of the United States. Beginning with Jefferson and carrying on through Clinton, Presidents have uniformly testified or produced documents in criminal proceedings when called upon by federal courts. This case involves—so far as we and the parties can tell—the first *state* criminal subpoena directed to a President. The President contends that the subpoena is unenforceable. We granted certiorari to decide whether Article II and the Supremacy Clause categorically preclude, or require a heightened standard for, the issuance of a state criminal subpoena to a sitting President.

I

In the summer of 2018, the New York County District Attorney's Office opened an investigation into what it opaquely describes as "business transactions involving multiple individuals whose conduct may have violated state law." A year later, the office—acting on behalf of a grand jury—served a subpoena *duces tecum* (essentially a request to produce evidence) on Mazars USA, LLP, the personal accounting firm of President Donald J. Trump. The subpoena directed Mazars to produce financial records relating to the President and business organizations affiliated with him, including "[t]ax returns and related schedules," from "2011 to the present."

The President, acting in his personal capacity, sued the district attorney and Mazars in Federal District Court to enjoin enforcement of the subpoena. He argued that, under Article II and the Supremacy Clause, a sitting President enjoys absolute immunity from state criminal process. He asked the court to issue a "declaratory judgment that the subpoena is invalid and unenforceable while the President is in office" and to permanently enjoin the district attorney "from taking any action to enforce the subpoena." Mazars, concluding that the dispute was between the President and the district attorney, took no position on the legal issues raised by the President.

The District Court abstained from exercising jurisdiction and dismissed the case based on *Younger* v. *Harris*, 401 U. S. 37 (1971), which generally precludes federal courts from intervening in ongoing state criminal prosecutions. In an alternative holding, the court ruled that the President was not entitled to injunctive relief.

The Second Circuit met the District Court halfway. As to the dismissal, the Court of Appeals held that *Younger* abstention was inappropriate because that doctrine's core justification—"preventing friction" between States and the Federal Government—is diminished when state and federal actors are already in conflict, as the district attorney and the President were.

On the merits, the Court of Appeals agreed with the District Court's denial of a preliminary injunction. Drawing on the 200-year history of Presidents being subject to federal judicial process, the Court of Appeals concluded that "presidential immunity does not bar the enforcement of a state grand jury subpoena directing a third party to produce non-privileged material, even when the subject matter under investigation pertains to the President." It also rejected the argument raised by the United States as *amicus curiae* that a state grand jury subpoena must satisfy a heightened showing of need. The court reasoned that the proposed test, derived from cases addressing privileged Executive Branch communications, "ha[d] little bearing on a subpoena" seeking "information relating solely to the

President in his private capacity and disconnected from the discharge of his constitutional obligations."

We granted certiorari.

II

In the summer of 1807, all eyes were on Richmond, Virginia. Aaron Burr, the former Vice President, was on trial for treason. Fallen from political grace after his fatal duel with Alexander Hamilton, and with a murder charge pending in New Jersey, Burr followed the path of many down-and-out Americans of his day—he headed West in search of new opportunity. But Burr was a man with outsized ambitions. Together with General James Wilkinson, the Governor of the Louisiana Territory, he hatched a plan to establish a new territory in Mexico, then controlled by Spain. Both men anticipated that war between the United States and Spain was imminent, and when it broke out they intended to invade Spanish territory at the head of a private army.

But while Burr was rallying allies to his cause, tensions with Spain eased and rumors began to swirl that Burr was conspiring to detach States by the Allegheny Mountains from the Union. Wary of being exposed as the principal coconspirator, Wilkinson took steps to ensure that any blame would fall on Burr. He sent a series of letters to President Jefferson accusing Burr of plotting to attack New Orleans and revolutionize the Louisiana Territory.

Jefferson, who despised his former running mate Burr for trying to steal the 1800 presidential election from him, was predisposed to credit Wilkinson's version of events. The President sent a special message to Congress identifying Burr as the "prime mover" in a plot "against the peace and safety of the Union." According to Jefferson, Burr contemplated either the "severance of the Union" or an attack on Spanish territory. Jefferson acknowledged that his sources contained a "mixture of rumors, conjectures, and suspicions" but, citing Wilkinson's letters, he assured Congress that Burr's guilt was "beyond question."

The trial that followed was "the greatest spectacle in the short history of the republic," complete with a Founder-studded cast. People flocked to Richmond to watch, massing in tents and covered wagons along the banks of the James River, nearly doubling the town's population of 5,000. Burr's defense team included Edmund Randolph and Luther Martin, both former delegates at the Constitutional Convention and renowned advocates. Chief Justice John Marshall, who had recently squared off with the Jefferson administration in *Marbury* v. *Madison*, presided as Circuit Justice for Virginia. Meanwhile Jefferson, intent on conviction, orchestrated the prosecution from afar, dedicating Cabinet meetings to the case, peppering the prosecutors with directions, and spending nearly $100,000 from the Treasury on the five-month proceedings.

In the lead-up to trial, Burr, taking aim at his accusers, moved for a subpoena *duces tecum* directed at Jefferson. The draft subpoena required the President to produce an October 21, 1806 letter from Wilkinson and accompanying documents, which Jefferson had referenced in his message to Congress. The prosecution opposed the request, arguing that a President could not be subjected to such a subpoena and that the letter might contain state secrets. Following four days of argument, Marshall announced his ruling to a packed chamber.

The President, Marshall declared, does not "stand exempt from the general provisions of the constitution" or, in particular, the Sixth Amendment's guarantee that those accused have compulsory process for obtaining witnesses for their defense. At common law the "single reservation" to the duty to testify in response to a subpoena was "the case of the king," whose "dignity" was seen as "incompatible" with appearing "under the process of the court." But, as Marshall explained, a king is born to power and can "do no wrong." The President, by contrast, is "of the people" and subject to the law. According to Marshall, the sole argument for exempting the President from testimonial obligations was that his "duties as chief magistrate demand his whole time for national objects." But, in Marshall's assessment, those demands were "not unremitting." And should the President's duties preclude his attendance at a particular time and place, a court could work that out upon return of the subpoena.

Marshall also rejected the prosecution's argument that the President was immune from a subpoena *duces tecum* because executive papers might contain state secrets. "A subpoena duces tecum," he said, "may issue to any person to whom an ordinary subpoena may issue." As he explained, no "fair construction" of the Constitution supported the conclusion that the right "to compel the attendance of witnesses[] does not extend" to requiring those witnesses to "bring[] with them such papers as may be material in the defence." And, as a matter of basic fairness, permitting such information to be withheld would "tarnish the reputation of the court." As for "the propriety of introducing any papers," that would "depend on the character of the paper, not on the character of the person who holds it." Marshall acknowledged that the papers sought by Burr could contain information "the disclosure of which would endanger the public safety," but stated that, again, such concerns would have "due consideration" upon the return of the subpoena.

While the arguments unfolded, Jefferson, who had received word of the motion, wrote to the prosecutor indicating that he would—subject to the prerogative to decide which executive communications should be withheld—"furnish on all occasions, whatever the purposes of justice may require." His "personal attendance," however, was out of the question, for it "would leave the nation without" the "sole branch which the constitution requires to be always in function."

Before Burr received the subpoenaed documents, Marshall rejected the prosecution's core legal theory for treason and Burr was accordingly acquitted. Jefferson, however, was not done. Committed to salvaging a conviction, he directed the prosecutors to proceed with a misdemeanor (yes, misdemeanor) charge for inciting war against Spain. Burr then renewed his request for Wilkinson's October 21 letter, which he later received a copy of, and subpoenaed a second letter, dated November 12, 1806, which the prosecutor claimed was privileged. Acknowledging that the President may withhold information to protect public safety, Marshall instructed that Jefferson should "state the particular reasons" for withholding the letter. The court, paying "all proper respect" to those reasons, would then decide whether to compel disclosure. But that decision was averted when the misdemeanor trial was cut short after it became clear that the prosecution lacked the evidence to convict.

In the two centuries since the Burr trial, successive Presidents have accepted Marshall's ruling that the Chief Executive is subject to subpoena. In 1818, President Monroe received a subpoena to testify in a court-martial against one of his appointees. His Attorney General, William Wirt—who had served as a prosecutor during Burr's trial—advised Monroe that, per Marshall's ruling, a subpoena to testify may "be properly awarded to the President." Monroe offered to sit for a deposition and ultimately submitted answers to written interrogatories.

Following Monroe's lead, his successors have uniformly agreed to testify when called in criminal proceedings, provided they could do so at a time and place of their choosing. In 1875, President Grant submitted to a three-hour deposition in the criminal prosecution of a political appointee embroiled in a network of tax-evading whiskey distillers. A century later, President Ford's attempted assassin subpoenaed him to testify in her defense. Ford obliged—from a safe distance—in the first videotaped deposition of a President. President Carter testified via the same means in the trial of two local officials who, while Carter was Governor of Georgia, had offered to contribute to his campaign in exchange for advance warning of any state gambling raids. Two years later, Carter gave videotaped testimony to a federal grand jury investigating whether a fugitive financier had entreated the White House to quash his extradition proceedings. President Clinton testified three times, twice via deposition pursuant to subpoenas in federal criminal trials of associates implicated during the Whitewater investigation, and once by video for a grand jury investigating possible perjury.

The bookend to Marshall's ruling came in 1974 when the question he never had to decide—whether to compel the disclosure of official communications over the objection of the President—came to a head. That spring, the Special Prosecutor appointed to investigate the break-in of the Democratic National Committee Headquarters at the Watergate complex filed an indictment charging seven defendants associated with President Nixon and naming Nixon as an unindicted co-conspirator. As the case moved toward trial, the Special Prosecutor secured a subpoena *duces tecum* directing Nixon to produce, among other things, tape recordings of Oval Office meetings. Nixon moved to quash the subpoena, claiming that the Constitution provides an absolute privilege of confidentiality to all presidential communications. This Court rejected that argument in *United States* v. *Nixon*, 418 U. S. 683 (1974), a decision we later described as "unequivocally and emphatically endors[ing] Marshall's" holding that Presidents are subject to subpoena. *Clinton* v. *Jones*, 520 U. S. 681, 704 (1997).

The *Nixon* Court readily acknowledged the importance of preserving the confidentiality of communications "between high Government officials and those who advise and assist them." "Human experience," the Court explained, "teaches that those who expect public dissemination of their remarks may well temper candor with a concern for appearances and for their own interests to the detriment of the decisionmaking process." Confidentiality thus promoted the "public interest in candid, objective, and even blunt or harsh opinions in Presidential decisionmaking."

But, like Marshall two centuries prior, the Court recognized the countervailing interests at stake. Invoking the common law maxim that "the public has a right to every man's evidence," the Court observed that the public interest in fair and accurate judicial proceedings is at its height in the criminal setting, where our common commitment to justice demands that "guilt shall not escape" nor "innocence suffer." Because these dual aims would be "defeated if judgments" were "founded on a partial or speculative presentation of the facts," the *Nixon* Court recognized that it was "imperative" that "compulsory process be available for the production of evidence needed either by the prosecution or the defense."

The Court thus concluded that the President's "generalized assertion of privilege must yield to the demonstrated, specific need for evidence in a pending criminal trial." Two weeks later, President Nixon dutifully released the tapes.

III

The history surveyed above all involved *federal* criminal proceedings. Here we are confronted for the first time with a subpoena issued to the President by a local grand jury operating under the supervision of a *state* court.[1]

In the President's view, that distinction makes all the difference. He argues that the Supremacy Clause gives a sitting President absolute

---

[1]   While the subpoena was directed to the President's accounting firm, the parties agree that the papers at issue belong to the President and that Mazars is merely the custodian. Thus, for purposes of immunity, it is functionally a subpoena issued to the President.

immunity from state criminal subpoenas because compliance with those subpoenas would categorically impair a President's performance of his Article II functions. The Solicitor General, arguing on behalf of the United States, agrees with much of the President's reasoning but does not commit to his bottom line. Instead, the Solicitor General urges us to resolve this case by holding that a state grand jury subpoena for a sitting President's personal records must, at the very least, "satisfy a heightened standard of need," which the Solicitor General contends was not met here.

A

We begin with the question of absolute immunity. No one doubts that Article II guarantees the independence of the Executive Branch. As the head of that branch, the President "occupies a unique position in the constitutional scheme." *Nixon* v. *Fitzgerald*, 457 U. S. 731, 749 (1982). His duties, which range from faithfully executing the laws to commanding the Armed Forces, are of unrivaled gravity and breadth. Quite appropriately, those duties come with protections that safeguard the President's ability to perform his vital functions. * * *

In addition, the Constitution guarantees "the entire independence of the General Government from any control by the respective States." * * *

Marshall's ruling in *Burr*, entrenched by 200 years of practice and our decision in *Nixon*, confirms that *federal* criminal subpoenas do not "rise to the level of constitutionally forbidden impairment of the Executive's ability to perform its constitutionally mandated functions." But the President, joined in part by the Solicitor General, argues that *state* criminal subpoenas pose a unique threat of impairment and thus demand greater protection. To be clear, the President does not contend here that *this* subpoena, in particular, is impermissibly burdensome. Instead he makes a *categorical* argument about the burdens generally associated with state criminal subpoenas, focusing on three: diversion, stigma, and harassment. We address each in turn.

1

The President's primary contention, which the Solicitor General supports, is that complying with state criminal subpoenas would necessarily divert the Chief Executive from his duties. He grounds that concern in *Nixon* v. *Fitzgerald*, which recognized a President's "absolute immunity from damages liability predicated on his official acts." In explaining the basis for that immunity, this Court observed that the prospect of such liability could "distract a President from his public duties, to the detriment of not only the President and his office but also the Nation that the Presidency was designed to serve." The President contends that the diversion occasioned by a state criminal subpoena imposes an equally intolerable burden on a President's ability to perform his Article II functions.

But *Fitzgerald* did not hold that distraction was sufficient to confer absolute immunity. We instead drew a careful analogy to the common law absolute immunity of judges and prosecutors, concluding that a President, like those officials, must "deal fearlessly and impartially with the duties of his office"—not be made "unduly cautious in the discharge of [those] duties" by the prospect of civil liability for official acts. Indeed, we expressly rejected immunity based on distraction alone 15 years later in *Clinton* v. *Jones*. There, President Clinton argued that the risk of being "distracted by the need to participate in litigation" entitled a sitting President to absolute immunity from civil liability, not just for official acts, as in *Fitzgerald*, but for private conduct as well. We disagreed with that rationale, explaining that the "dominant concern" in *Fitzgerald* was not mere distraction but the distortion of the Executive's "decisionmaking process" with respect to official acts that would stem from "worry as to the possibility of damages." The Court recognized that Presidents constantly face myriad demands on their attention, "some private, some political, and some as a result of official duty." But, the Court concluded, "[w]hile such distractions may be vexing to those subjected to them, they do not ordinarily implicate constitutional . . . concerns."

The same is true of criminal subpoenas. Just as a "properly managed" civil suit is generally "unlikely to occupy any substantial amount of" a President's time or attention, two centuries of experience confirm that a properly tailored criminal subpoena will not normally hamper the performance of the President's constitutional duties. If anything, we expect that in the mine run of cases, where a President is subpoenaed during a proceeding targeting someone else, as Jefferson was, the burden on a President will ordinarily be lighter than the burden of defending against a civil suit.

The President, however, believes the district attorney is investigating him and his businesses. In such a situation, he contends, the "toll that criminal process . . . exacts from the President is even heavier" than the distraction at issue in *Fitzgerald* and *Clinton*, because "criminal litigation" poses unique burdens on the President's time and will generate a "considerable if not overwhelming degree of mental preoccupation."

But the President is not seeking immunity from the diversion occasioned by the prospect of future criminal *liability*. Instead he concedes—consistent with the position of the Department of Justice—that state grand juries are free to investigate a sitting President with an eye toward charging him after the completion of his term. The President's objection therefore must be limited to the *additional* distraction caused by the subpoena itself. But that argument runs up against the 200 years of precedent establishing that Presidents, and their official communications, are subject to judicial process, even when the President is under investigation.

2

The President next claims that the stigma of being subpoenaed will undermine his leadership at home and abroad. Notably, the Solicitor General does not endorse this argument, perhaps because we have twice denied absolute immunity claims by Presidents in cases involving allegations of serious misconduct. But even if a tarnished reputation were a cognizable impairment, there is nothing inherently stigmatizing about a President performing "the citizen's normal duty of . . . furnishing information relevant" to a criminal investigation. Nor can we accept that the risk of association with persons or activities under criminal investigation can absolve a President of such an important public duty. Prior Presidents have weathered these associations in federal cases, and there is no reason to think any attendant notoriety is necessarily greater in state court proceedings.

To be sure, the consequences for a President's public standing will likely increase if he is the one under investigation. But, again, the President concedes that such investigations are permitted under Article II and the Supremacy Clause, and receipt of a subpoena would not seem to categorically magnify the harm to the President's reputation.

Additionally, while the current suit has cast the Mazars subpoena into the spotlight, longstanding rules of grand jury secrecy aim to prevent the very stigma the President anticipates. Of course, disclosure restrictions are not perfect. See *Nixon*, 418 U. S., at 687, n. 4 (observing that news media reporting made the protective order shielding the fact that the President had been named as an unindicted co-conspirator "no longer meaningful"). But those who make unauthorized disclosures regarding a grand jury subpoena do so at their peril. See, *e.g.*, N. Y. Penal Law Ann. § 215.70 (West 2010) (designating unlawful grand jury disclosure as a felony).

3

Finally, the President and the Solicitor General warn that subjecting Presidents to state criminal subpoenas will make them "easily identifiable target[s]" for harassment. But we rejected a nearly identical argument in *Clinton*, where then-President Clinton argued that permitting civil liability for unofficial acts would "generate a large volume of politically motivated harassing and frivolous litigation." The President and the Solicitor General nevertheless argue that state criminal subpoenas pose a heightened risk and could undermine the President's ability to "deal fearlessly and impartially" with the States. They caution that, while federal prosecutors are accountable to and removable by the President, the 2,300 district attorneys in this country are responsive to local constituencies, local interests, and local prejudices, and might "use criminal process to register their dissatisfaction with" the President. What is more, we are told, the state courts supervising local grand juries may not exhibit the same respect that federal courts show to the President as a coordinate branch of Government.

We recognize, as does the district attorney, that harassing subpoenas could, under certain circumstances, threaten the independence or effectiveness of the Executive. Even so, in *Clinton* we found that the risk of harassment was not "serious" because federal courts have the tools to deter and, where necessary, dismiss vexatious civil suits. And, while we cannot ignore the possibility that state prosecutors may have political motivations, here again the law already seeks to protect against the predicted abuse.

First, grand juries are prohibited from engaging in "arbitrary fishing expeditions" and initiating investigations "out of malice or an intent to harass." *United States* v. *R. Enterprises, Inc.*, 498 U. S. 292, 299 (1991). See also, *e.g.*, *Virag* v. *Hynes*, 54 N. Y. 2d 437, 442–443, 430 N. E. 2d 1249, 1252 (1981) (recognizing that grand jury subpoenas can be "challenged by an affirmative showing of impropriety," including "bad faith" (internal quotation marks omitted)). These protections, as the district attorney himself puts it, "apply with special force to a President, in light of the office's unique position as the head of the Executive Branch." And, in the event of such harassment, a President would be entitled to the protection of federal courts. The policy against federal interference in state criminal proceedings, while strong, allows "intervention in those cases where the District Court properly finds that the state proceeding is motivated by a desire to harass or is conducted in bad faith."

Second, contrary to JUSTICE ALITO's characterization, our holding does not allow States to "run roughshod over the functioning of [the Executive B]ranch." The Supremacy Clause prohibits state judges and prosecutors from interfering with a President's official duties. Any effort to manipulate a President's policy decisions or to "retaliat[e]" against a President for official acts through issuance of a subpoena, would thus be an unconstitutional attempt to "influence" a superior sovereign "exempt" from such obstacles. We generally "assume[ ] that state courts and prosecutors will observe constitutional limitations." Failing that, federal law allows a President to challenge any allegedly unconstitutional influence in a federal forum, as the President has done here. See 42 U. S. C. § 1983; *Ex parte Young*, 209 U. S. 123, 155–156 (1908) (holding that federal courts may enjoin state officials to conform their conduct to federal law).

Given these safeguards and the Court's precedents, we cannot conclude that absolute immunity is necessary or appropriate under Article II or the Supremacy Clause. Our dissenting colleagues agree. JUSTICE THOMAS reaches the same conclusion based on the original understanding of the Constitution reflected in Marshall's decision in *Burr*. And JUSTICE

ALITO, also persuaded by *Burr*, "agree[s]" that "not all" state criminal subpoenas for a President's records "should be barred." On that point the Court is unanimous.

B

We next consider whether a state grand jury subpoena seeking a President's private papers must satisfy a heightened need standard. The Solicitor General would require a threshold showing that the evidence sought is "critical" for "specific charging decisions" and that the subpoena is a "last resort," meaning the evidence is "not available from any other source" and is needed "now, rather than at the end of the President's term." JUSTICE ALITO, largely embracing those criteria, agrees that a state criminal subpoena to a President "should not be allowed unless a heightened standard is met."

We disagree, for three reasons. First, such a heightened standard would extend protection designed for official documents to the President's private papers. As the Solicitor General and JUSTICE ALITO acknowledge, their proposed test is derived from executive privilege cases that trace back to *Burr*. There, Marshall explained that if Jefferson invoked presidential privilege over executive communications, the court would not "proceed against the president as against an ordinary individual" but would instead require an affidavit from the defense that "would clearly show the paper to be essential to the justice of the case." The Solicitor General and JUSTICE ALITO would have us apply a similar standard to a President's personal papers. But this argument does not account for the relevant passage from *Burr*: "If there be a paper in the possession of the executive, which is *not of an official nature*, he must stand, as respects that paper, in nearly the same situation with any other individual." And it is only "nearly"—and not "entirely"—because the President retains the right to assert privilege over documents that, while ostensibly private, "partake of the character of an official paper."

Second, neither the Solicitor General nor JUSTICE ALITO has established that heightened protection against state subpoenas is necessary for the Executive to fulfill his Article II functions. Beyond the risk of harassment, which we addressed above, the only justification they offer for the heightened standard is protecting Presidents from "unwarranted burdens." In effect, they argue that even if federal subpoenas to a President are warranted whenever evidence is material, state subpoenas are warranted "only when [the] evidence is essential." But that double standard has no basis in law. For if the state subpoena is not issued to manipulate, the documents themselves are not protected, and the Executive is not impaired, then nothing in Article II or the Supremacy Clause supports holding state subpoenas to a higher standard than their federal counterparts.

Finally, in the absence of a need to protect the Executive, the public interest in fair and effective law enforcement cuts in favor of comprehensive access to evidence. Requiring a state grand jury to meet a heightened standard of need would hobble the grand jury's ability to acquire "all information that might possibly bear on its investigation." And, even assuming the evidence withheld under that standard were preserved until the conclusion of a President's term, in the interim the State would be deprived of investigative leads that the evidence might yield, allowing memories to fade and documents to disappear. This could frustrate the identification, investigation, and indictment of third parties (for whom applicable statutes of limitations might lapse). More troubling, it could prejudice the innocent by depriving the grand jury of *exculpatory* evidence.

Rejecting a heightened need standard does not leave Presidents with "no real protection." To start, a President may avail himself of the same protections available to every other citizen. These include the right to challenge the subpoena on any grounds permitted by state law, which usually include bad faith and undue burden or breadth. And, as in federal court, "[t]he high respect that is owed to the office of the Chief Executive . . . should inform the conduct of the entire proceeding, including the timing and scope of discovery." * * *

Furthermore, although the Constitution does not entitle the Executive to absolute immunity or a heightened standard, he is not "relegate[d]" only to the challenges available to private citizens. A President can raise subpoena-specific constitutional challenges, in either a state or federal forum. As previously noted, he can challenge the subpoena as an attempt to influence the performance of his official duties, in violation of the Supremacy Clause. This avenue protects against local political machinations "interposed as an obstacle to the effective operation of a federal constitutional power." In addition, the Executive can—as the district attorney concedes—argue that compliance with a particular subpoena would impede his constitutional duties. Incidental to the functions confided in Article II is "the power to perform them, without obstruction or impediment." As a result, "once the President sets forth and explains a conflict between judicial proceeding and public duties," or shows that an order or subpoena would "significantly interfere with his efforts to carry out" those duties, "the matter changes." *Clinton*, 520 U. S., at 710, 714 (opinion of BREYER, J.). At that point, a court should use its inherent authority to quash or modify the subpoena, if necessary to ensure that such "interference with the President's duties would not occur."

* * *

Two hundred years ago, a great jurist of our Court established that no citizen, not even the President, is categorically above the common duty to produce evidence when called upon in a criminal proceeding. We reaffirm that principle today and hold that the President is neither absolutely immune from state criminal subpoenas seeking his private papers nor entitled to a heightened standard of need. The "guard[ ] furnished to this high officer" lies where it always has—in "the conduct of a court" applying established legal and constitutional principles to individual subpoenas in a manner that preserves both the independence of the Executive and the integrity of the criminal justice system. *Burr*, 25 F. Cas., at 34.

The arguments presented here and in the Court of Appeals were limited to absolute immunity and heightened need. The Court of Appeals, however, has directed that the case be returned to the District Court, where the President may raise further arguments as appropriate.[2]

We affirm the judgment of the Court of Appeals and remand the case for further proceedings consistent with this opinion.

JUSTICE KAVANAUGH, with whom JUSTICE GORSUCH joins, concurring in the judgment.

The Court today unanimously concludes that a President does not possess absolute immunity from a state criminal subpoena, but also unanimously agrees that this case should be remanded to the District Court, where the President may raise constitutional and legal objections to the subpoena as appropriate. I agree with those two conclusions.

* * *

The dispute over this grand jury subpoena reflects a conflict between a State's interest in criminal investigation and a President's Article II interest in performing his or her duties without undue interference. Although this case involves personal information of the President and is therefore not an executive privilege case, the majority opinion correctly concludes based on precedent that Article II and the Supremacy Clause of the Constitution supply some protection for the Presidency against state criminal subpoenas of this sort.

In our system of government, as this Court has often stated, no one is above the law. That principle applies, of course, to a President. At the same time, in light of Article II of the Constitution, this Court has repeatedly declared—and the Court indicates again today—that a court

---

[2] The daylight between our opinion and JUSTICE THOMAS's "dissent" is not as great as that label might suggest. We agree that Presidents are neither absolutely immune from state criminal subpoenas nor insulated by a heightened need standard. We agree that Presidents may challenge specific subpoenas as impeding their Article II functions. And, although we affirm while JUSTICE THOMAS would vacate, we agree that this case will be remanded to the District Court.

may not proceed against a President as it would against an ordinary litigant. * * *

The question here, then, is how to balance the State's interests and the Article II interests. The longstanding precedent that has applied to federal criminal subpoenas for official, privileged Executive Branch information is *United States* v. *Nixon*, 418 U. S. 683 (1974). That landmark case requires that a prosecutor establish a "demonstrated, specific need" for the President's information. * * *

The *Nixon* "demonstrated, specific need" standard is a tried-and-true test that accommodates both the interests of the criminal process and the Article II interests of the Presidency. The *Nixon* standard ensures that a prosecutor's interest in subpoenaed information is sufficiently important to justify an intrusion on the Article II interests of the Presidency. The *Nixon* standard also reduces the risk of subjecting a President to unwarranted burdens, because it provides that a prosecutor may obtain a President's information only in certain defined circumstances.

Although the Court adopted the *Nixon* standard in a different Article II context—there, involving the confidentiality of official, privileged information—the majority opinion today recognizes that there are also important Article II (and Supremacy Clause) interests at stake here. A state criminal subpoena to a President raises Article II and Supremacy Clause issues because of the potential for a state prosecutor to use the criminal process and issue subpoenas in a way that interferes with the President's duties, through harassment or diversion.

Because this case again entails a clash between the interests of the criminal process and the Article II interests of the Presidency, I would apply the longstanding *Nixon* "demonstrated, specific need" standard to this case. The majority opinion does not apply the *Nixon* standard in this distinct Article II context, as I would have done. That said, the majority opinion appropriately takes account of some important concerns that also animate *Nixon* and the Constitution's balance of powers. The majority opinion explains that a state prosecutor may not issue a subpoena for a President's personal information out of bad faith, malice, or an intent to harass a President; as a result of prosecutorial impropriety; to seek information that is not relevant to an investigation; that is overly broad or unduly burdensome; to manipulate, influence, or retaliate against a President's official acts or policy decisions; or in a way that would impede, conflict with, or interfere with a President's official duties. All nine Members of the Court agree, moreover, that a President may raise objections to a state criminal subpoena not just in state court but also in federal court. And the majority opinion indicates that, in light of the "high respect that is owed to the office of the Chief Executive," courts "should be particularly meticulous" in assessing a subpoena for a President's personal records.

In the end, much may depend on how the majority opinion's various standards are applied in future years and decades. It will take future cases to determine precisely how much difference exists between (i) the various standards articulated by the majority opinion, (ii) the overarching *Nixon* "demonstrated, specific need" standard that I would adopt, and (iii) JUSTICE THOMAS's and JUSTICE ALITO's other proposed standards. In any event, in my view, lower courts in cases of this sort involving a President will almost invariably have to begin by delving into why the State wants the information; why and how much the State needs the information, including whether the State could obtain the information elsewhere; and whether compliance with the subpoena would unduly burden or interfere with a President's official duties.

* * *

I agree that the case should be remanded to the District Court for further proceedings, where the President may raise constitutional and legal objections to the state grand jury subpoena as appropriate.

JUSTICE THOMAS, dissenting.

Respondent Cyrus Vance, Jr., the district attorney for the County of New York, served a grand jury subpoena on the President's personal accounting firm. The subpoena, which is nearly identical to a subpoena issued by a congressional Committee, requests nearly 10 years of the President's personal financial records. In response to this troublingly broad request, the President, in his personal capacity, sought a declaration in federal court " 'that the subpoena is invalid and unenforceable' " and an injunction preventing respondent " 'from taking any action to enforce the subpoena.' " The District Court denied the President's motion for a preliminary injunction, and the Second Circuit affirmed in relevant part.

The President argues that he is absolutely immune from the issuance of any subpoena, but that if the Court disagrees, we should remand so that the District Court can develop a record about this particular subpoena. I agree with the majority that the President is not entitled to absolute immunity from *issuance* of the subpoena. But he may be entitled to relief against its *enforcement*. I therefore agree with the President that the proper course is to vacate and remand. If the President can show that "his duties as chief magistrate demand his whole time for national objects," *United States* v. *Burr*, 25 F. Cas. 30, 34 (No. 14,692d) (CC Va. 1807) (Marshall, C. J.), he is entitled to relief from enforcement of the subpoena.

I

* * *

I agree with the majority that the President does not have absolute immunity from the issuance of a grand jury subpoena. Unlike the majority, however, I do not reach this conclusion based on a primarily functionalist analysis. Instead, I reach it based on the text of the Constitution, which, as understood by the ratifying public and incorporated into an early circuit opinion by Chief Justice Marshall, does not support the President's claim of absolute immunity.

A

1

The text of the Constitution explicitly addresses the privileges of some federal officials, but it does not afford the President absolute immunity. Members of Congress are "privileged from Arrest during their Attendance at the Session of their respective Houses, and in going to and returning from the same," except for "Treason, Felony and Breach of the Peace." Art. I, § 6, cl. 1. The Constitution further specifies that, "for any Speech or Debate in either House, they shall not be questioned in any other Place." By contrast, the text of the Constitution contains no explicit grant of absolute immunity from legal process for the President. As a Federalist essayist noted during ratification, the President's "person is not so much protected as that of a member of the House of Representatives" because he is subject to the issuance of judicial process "like any other man in the ordinary course of law." An American Citizen I (Sept. 26, 1787), in 2 Documentary History of the Ratification of the Constitution 141 (M. Jansen ed. 1976) (emphasis deleted).

* * *

B

This original understanding is reflected in an early circuit decision by Chief Justice Marshall, on which the majority partially relies. In 1805, disgraced former Vice President Aaron Burr began a murky series of negotiations to raise a volunteer army in the Western Territories. One of his contacts, General James Wilkinson, was not only commander of the Army and Governor of Louisiana, but also a Spanish spy. After Burr set out with his army—perhaps to attack Spanish forces or perhaps to separate Western Territories from the United States—Wilkinson wrote to President Jefferson and accused Burr of the latter. Burr was arrested for treason and brought before a grand jury in Richmond, where Chief Justice Marshall presided.

During the grand jury proceedings, Burr moved for a *subpoena duces tecum* ordering President Jefferson to produce the correspondence concerning Burr. Chief Justice Marshall pre-emptively rejected any notion of absolute immunity, despite the fact that the Government did not so much as suggest it in court. He distinguished the President from the British monarch, who did have immunity, calling it an "essentia[l] . . . difference" in our system that the President "is elected from the mass of the people, and, on the expiration of the time for which he is elected, returns to the mass of the people again." Thus, the President was more like a state governor or a member of the British cabinet than a king. Chief Justice Marshall found no authority suggesting that these officials were immune from judicial process.

Based on the evidence of original meaning and Chief Justice Marshall's early interpretation in *Burr*, the better reading of the text of the Constitution is that the President has no absolute immunity from the issuance of a grand jury subpoena.

II

In addition to contesting the issuance of the subpoena, the President also seeks injunctive and declaratory relief against its enforcement. The majority recognizes that the President can seek relief from enforcement, but it does not vacate and remand for the lower courts to address this question. I would do so and instruct them to apply the standard articulated by Chief Justice Marshall in *Burr*: If the President is unable to comply because of his official duties, then he is entitled to injunctive and declaratory relief.

A

In *Burr*, after explaining that the President was not absolutely immune from issuance of a subpoena, Chief Justice Marshall proceeded to explain that the President might be excused from the enforcement of one. As he put it, "[t]he guard, furnished to this high officer, to protect him from being harassed by vexatious and unnecessary subpoenas, is to be looked for in the conduct of a court *after those subpoenas have issued*; not in any circumstance which is to precede their being issued." Chief Justice Marshall set out the pertinent standard: To avoid enforcement of the subpoena, the President must "sho[w]" that "his duties as chief magistrate demand his whole time for national objects."

Although *Burr* involved a federal subpoena, the same principle applies to a state subpoena. The ability of the President to discharge his duties until his term expires or he is removed from office by the Senate is "integral to the structure of the Constitution." The Constitution is the "supreme Law of the Land," Art. VI, cl. 2, so a state court can no more enforce a subpoena when national concerns demand the President's entire time than a federal court can. Accordingly, a federal court may provide injunctive and declaratory relief to stay enforcement of a state subpoena when the President meets the *Burr* standard.

B

The *Burr* standard places the burden on the President but also requires courts to take pains to respect the demands on the President's time. The Constitution vests the President with extensive powers and responsibilities, and courts are poorly situated to conduct a searching review of the President's assertion that he is unable to comply.

1

The President has vast responsibilities both abroad and at home. * * *

[JUSTICE THOMAS describes the powers and responsibilities of the President.]

* * *

The founding generation debated whether it was prudent to vest so many powers in a single person. Supporters of ratification responded that the design of the Presidency was necessary to the success of the Constitution. * * *

In sum, the demands on the President's time and the importance of his tasks are extraordinary, and the office of the President cannot be delegated to subordinates. A subpoena imposes both demands on the President's limited time and a mental burden, even when the President is not directly engaged in complying. This understanding of the Presidency should guide courts in deciding whether to enforce a subpoena for the President's documents.

2

Courts must also recognize their own limitations. When the President asserts that matters of foreign affairs or national defense preclude his compliance with a subpoena, the Judiciary will rarely have a basis for rejecting that assertion. Judges "simply lack the relevant information and expertise to second-guess determinations made by the President based on information properly withheld."[3]

---

[3]   The President and the Solicitor General argue that the grand jury must make a showing of heightened need. I agree with the majority's decision not to adopt this standard, but for different reasons. The constitutional question in this case is whether the President is able to perform the duties of his office, whereas a heightened need standard addresses a logically independent issue. Under a heightened-need standard, a grand jury with only the usual need for particular information would be refused it when the President is perfectly able to comply, while a grand jury with a heightened need would be entitled to it even if compliance would place undue obligations on the President. This result makes little sense and lacks any basis in the original understanding of the Constitution. I would leave questions of the grand jury's need to state law.

* * * Even with perfect information, courts lack the institutional competence to engage in a searching review of the President's reasons for not complying with a subpoena.

Here, too, Chief Justice Marshall was correct. A court should "fee[l] many, perhaps, peculiar motives for manifesting as guarded a respect for the chief magistrate of the Union as is compatible with its official duties." Courts should have the same "circumspection" as Chief Justice Marshall before "tak[ing] any step which would in any manner relate to that high personage."

* * *

I agree with the majority that the President has no absolute immunity from the issuance of this subpoena. The President also sought relief from enforcement of the subpoena, however, and he asked this Court to allow further proceedings on that question if we rejected his claim of absolute immunity. The Court inexplicably fails to address this request, although its decision leaves the President free to renew his request for an injunction against enforcement immediately on remand.

I would vacate and remand to allow the District Court to determine whether enforcement of this subpoena should be enjoined because the President's "duties as chief magistrate demand his whole time for national objects." Accordingly, I respectfully dissent.

JUSTICE ALITO, dissenting.

This case is almost certain to be portrayed as a case about the current President and the current political situation, but the case has a much deeper significance. While the decision will of course have a direct effect on President Trump, what the Court holds today will also affect all future Presidents—which is to say, it will affect the Presidency, and that is a matter of great and lasting importance to the Nation.

The event that precipitated this case is unprecedented. Respondent Vance, an elected state prosecutor, launched a criminal investigation of a sitting President and obtained a grand jury subpoena for his records. The specific question before us—whether the subpoena may be enforced—cannot be answered adequately without considering the broader question that frames it: whether the Constitution imposes restrictions on a State's deployment of its criminal law enforcement powers against a sitting President. If the Constitution sets no such limits, then a local prosecutor may prosecute a sitting President. And if that is allowed, it follows *a fortiori* that the subpoena at issue can be enforced. On the other hand, if the Constitution does not permit a State to prosecute a sitting President, the next logical question is whether the Constitution restrains any other prosecutorial or investigative weapons.

These are important questions that go to the very structure of the Government created by the Constitution. In evaluating these questions, two important structural features must be taken into account.

I

A

The first is the nature and role of the Presidency. The Presidency, like Congress and the Supreme Court, is a permanent institution created by the Constitution. All three of these institutions are distinct from the human beings who serve in them at any point in time. In the case of Congress or the Supreme Court, the distinction is easy to perceive, since they have multiple Members. But because "[t]he President is the only person who alone composes a branch of government . . . , there is not always a clear line between his personal and official affairs." As a result, the law's treatment of the person who serves as President can have an important effect on the institution, and the institution of the Presidency plays an indispensable role in our constitutional system.

The Constitution entrusts the President with responsibilities that are essential to the country's safety and well-being. * * *

"Constitutionally speaking, the President never sleeps. The President must be ready, at a moment's notice, to do whatever it takes to preserve, protect, and defend the Constitution and the American people." Without a President who is able at all times to carry out the responsibilities of the office, our constitutional system could not operate, and the country would be at risk. That is why the Twenty-fifth Amendment created a mechanism for temporarily transferring the responsibilities of the office to the Vice President if the President is incapacitated for even a brief time. The Amendment has been explicitly invoked on only two occasions, each time for a period of about two hours. This mechanism reflects an appreciation that the Nation cannot be safely left without a functioning President for even a brief time.

B

The second structural feature is the relationship between the Federal Government and the States. Just as our Constitution balances power against power among the branches of the Federal Government, it also divides power between the Federal Government and the States. The Constitution permitted the States to retain many of the sovereign powers that they previously possessed, but it gave the Federal Government powers that were deemed essential for the Nation's well-being and, indeed, its survival. And it provided for the Federal Government to be independent of and, within its allotted sphere, supreme over the States. Accordingly, a State may not block or interfere with the lawful work of the National Government.

[JUSTICE ALITO discusses McCulloch v. Maryland, 4 Wheat. 316 (1819).]

* * *

II

A

In *McCulloch*, Maryland's sovereign taxing power had to yield, and in a similar way, a State's sovereign power to enforce its criminal laws must accommodate the indispensable role that the Constitution assigns to the Presidency. This must be the rule with respect to a state prosecution of a sitting President. Both the structure of the Government established by the Constitution and the Constitution's provisions on the impeachment and removal of a President make it clear that the prosecution of a sitting President is out of the question. It has been aptly said that the President is the "sole indispensable man in government," and subjecting a sitting President to criminal prosecution would severely hamper his ability to carry out the vital responsibilities that the Constitution puts in his hands.

* * *

In the proceedings below, neither respondent, nor the District Court, nor the Second Circuit was willing to concede the fundamental point that a sitting President may not be prosecuted by a local district attorney. Respondent has said that he is investigating the President and, until oral argument in this Court, he never foreswore an intention to charge the President while he is still in office. The District Court conceded only that "perhaps" a sitting President could not be prosecuted for an offense punishable by "lengthy imprisonment" but that an offense requiring only a short trial would be another matter. And the Second Circuit was silent on the question.

The scenario apparently contemplated by the District Court is striking. If a sitting President were charged in New York County, would he be arrested and fingerprinted? He would presumably be required to appear for arraignment in criminal court, where the judge would set the conditions for his release. Could he be sent to Rikers Island or be required to post bail? Could the judge impose restrictions on his travel? If the President were scheduled to travel abroad—perhaps to attend a G–7 meeting—would he have to get judicial approval? If the President were charged with a complicated offense requiring a long trial, would he have to put his Presidential responsibilities aside for weeks on end while sitting in a Manhattan courtroom? While the trial was in progress, would aides be able to approach him and whisper in his ear about pressing matters? Would he be able to obtain a recess whenever he needed to speak with an aide at greater length or attend to an urgent matter, such as speaking with a foreign leader? Could he effectively carry out all his essential

Presidential responsibilities after the trial day ended and at the same time adequately confer with his trial attorneys regarding his defense? Or should he be expected to give up the right to attend his own trial and be tried in absentia? And if he were convicted, could he be imprisoned? Would aides be installed in a nearby cell?

This entire imagined scene is farcical. The "right of all the People to a functioning government" would be sacrificed. * * *

B

While the prosecution of a sitting President provides the most dramatic example of a clash between the indispensable work of the Presidency and a State's exercise of its criminal law enforcement powers, other examples are easy to imagine. Suppose state officers obtained and sought to execute a search warrant for a sitting President's private quarters in the White House. Suppose a state court authorized surveillance of a telephone that a sitting President was known to use. Or suppose that a sitting President was subpoenaed to testify before a state grand jury and, as is generally the rule, no Presidential aides, even those carrying the so-called "nuclear football," were permitted to enter the grand jury room. What these examples illustrate is a principle that this Court has recognized: legal proceedings involving a sitting President must take the responsibilities and demands of the office into account.

It is not enough to recite sayings like "no man is above the law" and "the public has a right to every man's evidence." These sayings are true—and important—but they beg the question. The law applies equally to all persons, including a person who happens for a period of time to occupy the Presidency. But there is no question that the nature of the office demands in some instances that the application of laws be adjusted at least until the person's term in office ends.

C

I now come to the specific investigative weapon at issue in the case before us—a subpoena for a sitting President's records. This weapon is less intrusive in an immediate sense than those mentioned above. Since the records are held by, and the subpoena was issued to, a third party, compliance would not require much work on the President's part. And after all, this is just one subpoena.

But we should heed the "great jurist," who rejected a similar argument in *McCulloch*. If we say that a subpoena to a third party is insufficient to undermine a President's performance of his duties, what about a subpoena served on the President himself? Surely in that case, the President could turn over the work of gathering the requested documents to attorneys or others recruited to perform the task. And if one subpoena is permitted, what about two? Or three? Or ten? Drawing a line based on such factors would involve the same sort of "perplexing inquiry, so unfit for the judicial department" that Marshall rejected in *McCulloch*.

The Court faced a similar issue when it considered whether a President can be sued for an allegedly unlawful act committed in the performance of official duties. See *Nixon* v. *Fitzgerald*, 457 U. S. 731 (1982). We did not ask whether the particular suit before us would have interfered with the carrying out of Presidential duties. (It could not have had that effect because President Nixon had already left office.)

Instead, we adopted a rule for all such suits, and we should take a similar approach here. The rule should take into account both the effect of subpoenas on the functioning of the Presidency and the risk that they will be used for harassment.

I turn first to the question of the effect of a state grand jury subpoena for a President's records. When the issuance of such a subpoena is part of an investigation that regards the President as a "target" or "subject," the subpoena can easily impair a President's "energetic performance of [his] constitutional duties." Few individuals will simply brush off an indication that they may be within a prosecutor's crosshairs. Few will put the matter out of their minds and go about their work unaffected. For many, the prospect of prosecution will be the first and last thing on their minds every day.

We have come to expect our Presidents to shoulder burdens that very few people could bear, but it is unrealistic to think that the prospect of possible criminal prosecution will not interfere with the performance of the duties of the office. * * *

As for the potential use of subpoenas to harass, we need not "'exhibit a naiveté from which ordinary citizens are free.'" As we have recognized, a President is "an easily identifiable target." There are more than 2,300 local prosecutors and district attorneys in the country. Many local prosecutors are elected, and many prosecutors have ambitions for higher elected office. * * * If a sitting President is intensely unpopular in a particular district—and that is a common condition—targeting the President may be an alluring and effective electoral strategy. But it is a strategy that would undermine our constitutional structure. * * *

D

In light of the above, a subpoena like the one now before us should not be enforced unless it meets a test that takes into account the need to prevent interference with a President's discharge of the responsibilities of the office. I agree with the Court that not all such subpoenas should be barred. There may be situations in which there is an urgent and critical need for the subpoenaed information. The situation in the Burr trial, where the documents at issue were sought by a criminal defendant to defend against a charge of treason, is a good example. But in a case like the one at hand, a subpoena should not be allowed unless a heightened standard is met.

Prior cases involving Presidential subpoenas have always applied special, heightened standards. In the Burr trial, Chief Justice Marshall was careful to note that "in no case of this kind would a court be required to proceed against the president as against an ordinary individual," and he held that the subpoena to President Jefferson was permissible only because the prosecutor had shown that the materials sought were "essential to the justice of the [pending criminal] case."

In *United States* v. *Nixon*, 418 U. S. 683 (1974), where the Watergate Special Prosecutor subpoenaed tape recordings and documents under the control of President Nixon, this Court refused to quash the subpoena because there was a "demonstrated, specific need for [the] evidence in a pending criminal trial." * * *

The important point is not that the subpoena in this case should necessarily be governed by the particular tests used in these cases, most of which involved official records that were claimed to be privileged. Rather, the point is that we should not treat this subpoena like an ordinary grand jury subpoena and should not relegate a President to the meager defenses that are available when an ordinary grand jury subpoena is challenged. But that, at bottom, is the effect of the Court's decision.

The Presidency deserves greater protection. Thus, in a case like this one, a prosecutor should be required (1) to provide at least a general description of the possible offenses that are under investigation, (2) to outline how the subpoenaed records relate to those offenses, and (3) to explain why it is important that the records be produced and why it is necessary for production to occur while the President is still in office.

In the present case, the district attorney made a brief proffer, but important questions were left hanging. It would not be unduly burdensome to insist on answers before enforcing the subpoena.

One obvious question concerns the scope of the subpoena. The subpoena issued by the grand jury is largely a copy of the subpoenas issued by Committees of the House of Representatives, and it would be quite a coincidence if the records relevant to an investigation of possible violations of New York criminal law just so happened to be almost identical to the records thought by congressional Committees to be useful in considering federal legislation. It is therefore appropriate to ask the district attorney to explain the need for the various items that the subpoena covers.

The district attorney should also explain why it is important that the information in question be obtained from the President's records rather than another source. And the district attorney should set out why he finds it necessary that the records be produced now as opposed to when the President leaves office. At argument, respondent's counsel told us that his office's concern is the expiration of the statute of limitations, but there are potential solutions to that problem. Even if New York law does not automatically suspend the statute of limitations for prosecuting a President until he leaves office, it may be possible to eliminate the problem by waiver. And if the prosecutor's statute-of-limitations concerns relate to parties other than the President, he should be required to spell that out.

There may be other good reasons why immediate enforcement is important, such as the risk that evidence or important leads will be lost, but if a prosecutor believes that immediate enforcement is needed for such a reason, the prosecutor should be required to provide a reasonably specific explanation why that is so and why alternative means, such as measures to preserve evidence and prevent spoliation, would not suffice.

E

Unlike this rule, which would not undermine any legitimate state interests, the opinion of the Court provides no real protection for the Presidency. The Court discounts the risk of harassment and assumes that state prosecutors will observe constitutional limitations, and I also assume that the great majority of state prosecutors will carry out their responsibilities responsibly. But for the reasons noted, there is a very real risk that some will not.

The Court emphasizes the protection afforded by "longstanding rules of grand jury secrecy," but that is no answer to the burdens that subpoenas may inflict, and in any event, grand jury secrecy rules are of limited value as safeguards against harassment. State laws on grand jury secrecy vary and often do not set out disclosure restrictions with the same specificity as federal law.

Under New York law, the decision whether to disclose grand jury evidence is committed to the discretion of the supervising judge under a test that simply balances the need for secrecy against "the public interest." * * * And even where grand jury information is not lawfully disclosed, confidential law enforcement information is avidly sought by the media in high-profile cases, leaks of such information are not uncommon, and those responsible are seldom called to account.

* * *

The Court says that a President can "*argue* that compliance with a particular subpoena would impede his constitutional duties," but under the Court's opinions in this case and *Mazars*, it is not easy to see how such an argument could prevail. The Court makes clear that any stigma or damage to a President's reputation does not count, and in *Mazars* [the Congressional subpoenas case decided the same day as this case], the Court states that "burdens on the President's time and attention" are generally not of constitutional concern. Elsewhere in its opinion in this case, the Court takes the position that when a President's non-official records are subpoenaed, his treatment should be little different from that of any other subpoena recipient. The most that the Court holds out is the possibility that there might be some unspecified extraordinary circumstances under which a President might obtain relief.

* * *

For all practical purposes, the Court's decision places a sitting President in the same unenviable position as any other person whose records are subpoenaed by a grand jury.

Attempting to justify this approach, the Court relies on Marshall's ruling in the Burr trial, but the Court ignores important differences between the situation in that case and the situation here. First, the subpoena in *Burr* was not issued by a grand jury at the behest of a prosecutor who was investigating the President. * * *

Second, it is significant that Burr, unlike the prosecutor in the present case, did not have the option of postponing his request for information until the President's term ended. * * *

The lesson we should take from Marshall's jurisprudence is the lesson of *McCulloch*—the importance of preventing a State from undermining the lawful exercise of authority conferred by the Constitution on the Federal Government. There is considerable irony in the Court's invocation of Marshall to defend a decision allowing a State's prosecutorial power to run roughshod over the functioning of a branch of the Federal Government.

* * *

The subpoena at issue here is unprecedented. Never before has a local prosecutor subpoenaed the records of a sitting President. The Court's decision threatens to impair the functioning of the Presidency and provides no real protection against the use of the subpoena power by the Nation's 2,300+ local prosecutors. Respect for the structure of Government created by the Constitution demands greater protection for an institution that is vital to the Nation's safety and well-being.

I therefore respectfully dissent.

CHAPTER 10

TRIAL AND TRIAL-RELATED RIGHTS

■ ■ ■

III. CONSTITUTIONALLY BASED PROOF REQUIREMENTS

C. THE SCOPE OF THE REASONABLE DOUBT REQUIREMENT: WHAT IS AN ELEMENT OF THE CRIME?

2. Element of the Crime or Sentencing Factor?

Application of Ring v. Arizona: Hurst v. Florida

Page 1250. Add at the end of the section:

In addition to aggravating factors, death penalty defendants have a constitutional right to present evidence of relevant mitigating factors. *See* Eddings v. Oklahoma, 455 U.S. 104 (1982); Lockett v. Ohio, 438 U.S. 586 (1978). Where trial courts err either in finding an aggravating factor or in failing to consider a relevant mitigating factor, it is not necessary to conduct a new sentencing hearing in front of a jury. Appellate courts may, instead, reweigh the sentence by disregarding any infirm aggravating factors and including any omitted mitigating factors. *See* McKinney v. Arizona, 140 S.Ct. 702 (2020); Clemons v. Mississippi, 494 U.S. 738 (1990).

Page 1259. Add at the end of the section:

Apprendi *Limitations as Applied to Supervised Release Revocation Proceedings: United States v. Haymond*

UNITED STATES V. HAYMOND
Supreme Court of the United States, 2019.
139 S.Ct. 2369.

JUSTICE GORSUCH announced the judgment of the Court and delivered an opinion, in which JUSTICE GINSBURG, JUSTICE SOTOMAYOR, and JUSTICE KAGAN joined.

Only a jury, acting on proof beyond a reasonable doubt, may take a person's liberty. That promise stands as one of the Constitution's most vital protections against arbitrary government. Yet in this case a congressional statute compelled a federal judge to send a man to prison for a minimum of five years without empaneling a jury of his peers or requiring the government to prove his guilt beyond a reasonable doubt. As applied here, we do not hesitate to hold that the statute violates the Fifth and Sixth Amendments.

I

After a jury found Andre Haymond guilty of possessing child pornography in violation of federal law, the question turned to sentencing. The law authorized the district judge to impose a prison term of between zero and 10 years, and a period of supervised release of between 5 years and life. Because Mr. Haymond had no criminal history and was working to help support his mother who had suffered a stroke, the judge concluded that Mr. Haymond was "not going to get much out of being in prison" and sentenced him to a prison term of 38 months, followed by 10 years of supervised release.

After completing his prison sentence, however, Mr. Haymond encountered trouble on supervised release. He sat for multiple polygraph tests in which he denied possessing or viewing child pornography, and each time the test indicated no deception. But when the government conducted an unannounced search of his computers and cellphone, it turned up 59 images that appeared to be child pornography. Based on that discovery, the government sought to revoke Mr. Haymond's supervised release and secure a new and additional prison sentence.

A hearing followed before a district judge acting without a jury, and under a preponderance of the evidence rather than a reasonable doubt standard. In light of expert testimony regarding the manner in which cellphones can "cache" images without the user's knowledge, the judge found insufficient evidence to show that Mr. Haymond knowingly possessed 46 of the images. At the same time, the judge found it more likely than not that Mr. Haymond knowingly downloaded and possessed the remaining 13 images.

With that, the question turned once more to sentencing. Under 18 U. S. C. § 3583(e)(3), enacted as part of the Sentencing Reform Act of 1984, a district judge who finds that a defendant has violated the conditions of his supervised release normally may (but is not required to) impose a new prison term up to the maximum period of supervised release authorized by statute for the defendant's original crime of conviction, subject to certain limits. Under that provision, the judge in this case would have been free to sentence Mr. Haymond to between zero and two additional years in prison.

But there was a complication. Under § 3583(k), added to the Act in 2003 and amended in 2006, if a judge finds by a preponderance of the evidence that a defendant on supervised release committed one of several enumerated offenses, including the possession of child pornography, the judge must impose an additional prison term of at least five years and up to life without regard to the length of the prison term authorized for the defendant's initial crime of conviction.

Because Mr. Haymond had committed an offense covered by § 3583(k), the judge felt bound to impose an additional prison term of at least five years. He did so, though, with reservations. It's one thing, Judge Terence Kern said, for a judge proceeding under a preponderance of the evidence standard to revoke a defendant's supervised release and order him to serve additional time in prison within the range already authorized by the defendant's original conviction; after all, the jury's verdict, reached under the reasonable doubt standard, permitted that much punishment. But the judge found it "repugnant" that a statute might impose a new and additional "mandatory five-year" punishment without those traditional protections. Were it not for § 3583(k)'s mandatory minimum, the judge added, he "probably would have sentenced in the range of two years or less."

On appeal to the Tenth Circuit, Mr. Haymond challenged both the factual support for his new punishment and its constitutionality. On the facts, the court of appeals held that the district court's findings against Mr. Haymond were clearly erroneous in certain respects. Even so, the court concluded, just enough evidence remained to sustain a finding that Mr. Haymond had knowingly possessed the 13 images at issue, in violation of § 3583(k). That left the question of the statute's constitutionality, and there the Tenth Circuit concluded that § 3583(k) violated the Fifth and Sixth Amendments. The court explained that a jury had convicted Mr. Haymond beyond a reasonable doubt of a crime carrying a prison term of zero to 10 years. Yet now Mr. Haymond faced a new potential prison term of five years to life. Because this new prison term included a new and higher mandatory minimum resting only on facts found by a judge by a preponderance of the evidence, the court held, the statute violated Mr. Haymond's right to trial by jury.

By way of remedy, the court held the last two sentences of § 3583(k), which mandate a 5-year minimum prison term, "unconstitutional and unenforceable." The court then vacated Mr. Haymond's revocation sentence and remanded the case to the district court for resentencing without regard to those provisions. In effect, the court of appeals left the district court free to issue a new sentence under the preexisting statute governing most every other supervised release violation, § 3583(e). Following the Tenth Circuit's directions, the district court proceeded to resentence Mr. Haymond to time served, as he had already been detained by that point for approximately 28 months. We granted review to consider the Tenth Circuit's constitutional holding.

II

[Justice Gorsuch discusses the history of the right to a jury trial.]

[J]uries in our constitutional order exercise supervisory authority over the judicial function by limiting the judge's power to punish. A judge's authority to issue a sentence derives from, and is limited by, the jury's factual findings of criminal conduct. * * *

For much of our history, the application of this rule of jury supervision proved pretty straightforward. At common law, crimes tended to carry with them specific sanctions, and "once the facts of the offense were determined by the jury, the judge was meant simply to impose the prescribed sentence." *Alleyne v. United States*, 570 U. S. 99, 108 (2013) (plurality opinion). Even when judges did enjoy discretion to adjust a sentence based on judge-found aggravating or mitigating facts, they could not "swell the penalty above what the law had provided for the acts charged" and found by the jury. *Apprendi*, 530 U. S., at 519 (THOMAS, J., concurring). In time, of course, legislatures adopted new laws allowing judges or parole boards to suspend part (parole) or all (probation) of a defendant's prescribed prison term and afford him a period of conditional liberty as an "act of grace," subject to revocation. But here, too, the prison sentence a judge or parole board could impose for a parole or probation violation normally could not exceed the remaining balance of the term of imprisonment already authorized by the jury's verdict. So even these developments did not usually implicate the historic concerns of the Fifth and Sixth Amendments.

More recent legislative innovations have raised harder questions. In *Apprendi*, for example, a jury convicted the defendant of a gun crime that carried a maximum prison sentence of 10 years. But then a judge sought to impose a longer sentence pursuant to a statute that authorized him to do so if he found, by a preponderance of the evidence, that the defendant had committed the crime with racial bias. *Apprendi* held this scheme unconstitutional. "[A]ny fact that increases the penalty for a crime beyond the prescribed statutory maximum," this Court explained, "must be submitted to a jury, and proved beyond a reasonable doubt" or admitted by the defendant. Nor may a State evade this traditional restraint on the judicial power by simply calling the process of finding new facts and imposing a new punishment a judicial "sentencing enhancement." "[T]he relevant inquiry is one not of form, but of effect—does the required [judicial] finding expose the defendant to a greater punishment than that authorized by the jury's guilty verdict?"

[I]n the years since *Apprendi* this Court has not hesitated to strike down other innovations that fail to respect the jury's supervisory function. See, e.g., *Ring v. Arizona*, 536 U. S. 584 (2002) (imposition of death penalty based on judicial factfinding); *Blakely*, 542 U. S., at 303 (mandatory state sentencing guidelines); *United States v. Booker*, 543 U. S. 220 (2005) (mandatory federal sentencing guidelines).

Still, these decisions left an important gap. In *Apprendi,* this Court recognized that "[i]t is unconstitutional for a legislature to remove from the jury the assessment of facts that increase the prescribed range of penalties." But by definition, a range of punishments includes not only a maximum but a minimum. And logically it would seem to follow that any facts necessary to increase a person's minimum punishment (the "floor") should be found by the jury no less than facts necessary to increase his maximum punishment (the "ceiling"). Before *Apprendi,* however, this Court had held that facts elevating the minimum punishment need not be proven to a jury beyond a reasonable doubt. *McMillan v. Pennsylvania,* 477 U. S. 79 (1986); see also *Harris v. United States,* 536 U. S. 545 (2002) (adhering to *McMillan*).

Eventually, the Court confronted this anomaly in *Alleyne.* There, a jury convicted the defendant of a crime that ordinarily carried a sentence of five years to life in prison. But a separate statutory "sentencing enhancement" increased the mandatory minimum to seven years if the defendant "brandished" the gun. At sentencing, a judge found by a preponderance of the evidence that the defendant had indeed brandished a gun and imposed the mandatory minimum 7-year prison term.

This Court reversed. Finding no basis in the original understanding of the Fifth and Sixth Amendments for *McMillan* and *Harris,* the Court expressly overruled those decisions and held that "the principle applied in *Apprendi* applies with equal force to facts increasing the mandatory minimum" as it does to facts increasing the statutory maximum penalty. Nor did it matter to *Alleyne's* analysis that, even without the mandatory minimum, the trial judge would have been free to impose a 7-year sentence because it fell within the statutory sentencing range authorized by the jury's findings. Both the "floor" and "ceiling" of a sentencing range "define the legally prescribed penalty." *Ibid.* And under our Constitution, when "a finding of fact alters the legally prescribed punishment so as to aggravate it" that finding must be made by a jury of the defendant's peers beyond a reasonable doubt. Along the way, the Court observed that there can be little doubt that "[e]levating the low end of a sentencing range heightens the loss of liberty associated with the crime: The defendant's expected punishment has increased as a result of the narrowed range and the prosecution is empowered, by invoking the mandatory minimum, to require the judge to impose a higher punishment than he might wish." *Id.,* at 113 (internal quotation marks omitted).

By now, the lesson for our case is clear. Based on the facts reflected in the jury's verdict, Mr. Haymond faced a lawful prison term of between zero and 10 years under § 2252(b)(2). But then a judge—acting without a jury and based only on a preponderance of the evidence—found that Mr. Haymond had engaged in additional conduct in violation of the terms of his supervised release. Under § 3583(k), that judicial factfinding triggered a new punishment in the form of a prison term of at least five years and up to life. So just like the facts the judge found at the defendant's sentencing hearing in *Alleyne*, the facts the judge found here increased "the legally prescribed range of allowable sentences" in violation of the Fifth and Sixth Amendments. In this case, that meant Mr. Haymond faced a minimum of five years in prison instead of as little as none. Nor did the absence of a jury's finding beyond a reasonable doubt only infringe the rights of the accused; it also divested the "people at large"—the men and women who make up a jury of a defendant's peers—of their constitutional authority to set the metes and bounds of judicially administered criminal punishments.

III

In reply, the government and the dissent offer many and sometimes competing arguments, but we find none persuasive.

A

The government begins by pointing out that *Alleyne* arose in a different procedural posture. There, the trial judge applied a "sentencing enhancement" based on his own factual findings at the defendant's initial sentencing hearing; meanwhile, Mr. Haymond received his new punishment from a judge at a hearing to consider the revocation of his term of supervised release. This procedural distinction makes all the difference, we are told, because the Sixth Amendment's jury trial promise applies only to "criminal prosecutions," which end with the issuance of a sentence and do not extend to "postjudgment sentence-administration proceedings."

But we have been down this road before. Our precedents * * * have repeatedly rejected efforts to dodge the demands of the Fifth and Sixth Amendments by the simple expedient of relabeling a criminal prosecution a "sentencing enhancement." Calling part of a criminal prosecution a "sentence modification" imposed at a "postjudgment sentence-administration proceeding" can fare no better. As this Court has repeatedly explained, any "increase in a defendant's authorized punishment contingent on the finding of a fact" requires a jury and proof beyond a reasonable doubt no matter what the government chooses to call the exercise.

To be sure, and as the government and dissent emphasize, founding-era prosecutions traditionally ended at final judgment. But at that time, generally, questions of guilt and punishment both were resolved in a single proceeding subject to the Fifth and Sixth Amendment's demands. Over time, procedures changed as legislatures sometimes bifurcated criminal prosecutions into separate trial and penalty phases. But none of these developments licensed judges to sentence individuals to punishments beyond the legal limits fixed by the facts found in the jury's verdict. To the contrary, we recognized in *Apprendi* and *Alleyne*, a "criminal prosecution" continues and the defendant remains an "accused" with all the rights provided by the Sixth Amendment, until a final sentence is imposed.

Today, we merely acknowledge that an accused's final sentence includes any supervised release sentence he may receive. Nor in saying that do we say anything new: This Court has already recognized that supervised release punishments arise from and are "treat[ed] . . . as part of the penalty for the initial offense." *Johnson v. United States*, 529 U. S. 694, 700 (2000). The defendant receives a term of supervised release thanks to his initial offense, and whether that release is later revoked or sustained, it constitutes a part of the final sentence for his crime. As at the initial sentencing hearing, that does not mean a jury must find every fact in a revocation hearing that may affect the judge's exercise of discretion within the range of punishments authorized by the jury's verdict. But it does mean that a jury must find any facts that trigger a new mandatory minimum prison term.

* * * If the government and dissent were correct, Congress could require anyone convicted of even a modest crime to serve a sentence of supervised release for the rest of his life. At that point, a judge could try and convict him of any violation of the terms of his release under a preponderance of the evidence standard, and then sentence him to pretty much anything. At oral argument, the government even conceded that, under its theory, a defendant on supervised release would have no Sixth Amendment right to a jury trial when charged with an infraction carrying the death penalty. * * *

B

Where it previously suggested that Mr. Haymond's supervised release revocation proceeding was entirely divorced from his criminal prosecution, the government next turns around and suggests that Mr. Haymond's sentence for violating the terms of his supervised release was actually fully authorized by the jury's verdict. After all, the government observes, on the strength of the jury's findings the judge was entitled to impose as punishment a term of supervised release; and, in turn, that term of supervised release was from the outset always subject to the possibility of judicial revocation and § 3583(k)'s mandatory prison sentence. Presto: Sixth Amendment problem solved.

But we have been down this road too. In *Apprendi* and *Alleyne*, the jury's verdict triggered a statute that authorized a judge at sentencing to increase the defendant's term of imprisonment based on judge-found facts. This Court had no difficulty rejecting that scheme as an impermissible evasion of the historic rule that a jury must find all of the facts necessary to authorize a judicial punishment. And what was true there can be no less true here: A mandatory minimum 5-year sentence that comes into play only as a result of additional judicial factual findings by a preponderance of the evidence cannot stand. This Court's observation that postrevocation sanctions are treated as part of the penalty for the initial offense only highlights the constitutional infirmity of § 3583(k): Treating Mr. Haymond's 5-year mandatory minimum prison term as part of his sentence for his original offense makes clear that it mirrors the unconstitutional sentencing enhancement in *Alleyne*.

Notice, too, that following the government down this road would lead to the same destination as the last: If the government were right, a jury's conviction on one crime would (again) permit perpetual supervised release and allow the government to evade the need for another jury trial on any other offense the defendant might commit, no matter how grave the punishment. And if there's any doubt about the incentives such a rule would create, consider this case. Instead of seeking a revocation of supervised release, the government could have chosen to prosecute Mr. Haymond under a statute mandating a term of imprisonment of 10 to 20 years for repeat child-pornography offenders. 18 U. S. C. § 2252(b)(2). But why bother with an old-fashioned jury trial for a new crime when a quick-and-easy "supervised release revocation hearing" before a judge carries a penalty of five years to life? This displacement of the jury's traditional supervisory role, under cover of a welter of new labels, exemplifies the "Framers' fears that the jury right could be lost not only by gross denial, but by erosion." *Apprendi*, 530 U. S., at 483.

C

Pivoting once more, the government and the dissent seem to accept for argument's sake that postjudgment sentence-administration proceedings can implicate the Fifth and Sixth Amendments. But, they contend, § 3583(k)'s supervised release revocation procedures are practically identical to historic parole and probation revocation procedures. See, e.g., *Gagnon v. Scarpelli*, 411 U. S. 778 (1973); *Morrissey v. Brewer*, 408 U. S. 471 (1972). And, because those other procedures have usually been understood to comport with the Fifth and Sixth Amendments, they submit, § 3583(k)'s procedures must do so as well.

But this argument, too, rests on a faulty premise, overlooking a critical difference between § 3583(k) and traditional parole and probation practices. Before the Sentencing Reform Act of 1984, a federal criminal defendant could serve as little as a third of his assigned prison term before becoming eligible for release on parole. Or he might avoid prison altogether in favor of probation. If the defendant violated the terms of his parole or probation, a judge could send him to prison. But either way and as we've seen, a judge generally could sentence the defendant to serve only the remaining prison term authorized by statute for his original crime of conviction. Thus, a judge could not imprison a defendant for any longer than the jury's factual findings allowed—a result entirely harmonious with the Fifth and Sixth Amendments.

All that changed beginning in 1984. That year, Congress overhauled federal sentencing procedures to make prison terms more determinate and abolish the practice of parole. Now, when a defendant is sentenced to prison he generally must serve the great bulk of his assigned term. In parole's place, Congress established the system of supervised release. But unlike parole, supervised release wasn't introduced to replace a portion of the defendant's prison term, only to encourage rehabilitation after the completion of his prison term.

In this case, that structural difference bears constitutional consequences. Where parole and probation violations generally exposed a defendant only to the remaining prison term authorized for his crime of conviction, as found by a unanimous jury under the reasonable doubt standard, supervised release violations subject to § 3583(k) can, at least as applied in cases like ours, expose a defendant to an additional mandatory minimum prison term well beyond that authorized by the jury's verdict— all based on facts found by a judge by a mere preponderance of the evidence. In fact, § 3583(k) differs in this critical respect not only from parole and probation; it also represents a break from the supervised release practices that Congress authorized in § 3583(e)(3) and that govern most federal criminal proceedings today. Unlike all those procedures, § 3583(k) alone requires a substantial increase in the minimum sentence to which a defendant may be exposed based only on judge-found facts under a preponderance standard. And, as we explained in *Alleyne* and reaffirm today, that offends the Fifth and Sixth Amendments' ancient protections.

D

The dissent suggests an analogy between revocation under § 3583(k) and prison disciplinary procedures that do not normally require the involvement of a jury. But the analogy is a strained one: While the Sixth Amendment surely does not require a jury to find every fact that the government relies on to adjust the terms of a prisoner's confinement (say, by reducing some of his privileges as a sanction for violating the prison rules), that does not mean the government can send a free man back to prison for years based on judge-found facts.

E

Finally, much of the dissent is consumed by what it calls the "potentially revolutionary" consequences of our opinion. But what agitates the dissent so much is an issue not presented here: whether all supervised release proceedings comport with *Apprendi*. As we have emphasized, our decision is limited to § 3583(k)—an unusual provision enacted little more than a decade ago—and the *Alleyne* problem raised by its 5-year mandatory minimum term of imprisonment. Section § 3583(e), which governs supervised release revocation proceedings generally, does not contain any similar mandatory minimum triggered by judge-found facts.

Besides, even if our opinion could be read to cast doubts on § 3583(e) and its consistency with *Apprendi*, the practical consequences of a holding to that effect would not come close to fulfilling the dissent's apocalyptic prophecy. In most cases (including this one), combining a defendant's initial and post-revocation sentences issued under § 3583(e) will not yield a term of imprisonment that exceeds the statutory maximum term of imprisonment the jury has authorized for the original crime of conviction. That's because courts rarely sentence defendants to the statutory maxima, and revocation penalties under § 3583(e)(3) are only a small fraction of those available under § 3583(k). So even if § 3583(e)(3) turns out to raise Sixth Amendment issues in a small set of cases, it hardly follows that "as a practical matter supervised-release revocation proceedings cannot be held" or that "the whole idea of supervised release must fall." Indeed, the vast majority of supervised release revocation proceedings under subsection (e)(3) would likely be unaffected.

In the end, the dissent is left only to echo an age-old criticism: Jury trials are inconvenient for the government. Yet like much else in our Constitution, the jury system isn't designed to promote efficiency but to protect liberty. * * *

IV

Having concluded that the application of § 3583(k)'s mandatory minimum in this case violated Mr. Haymond's right to trial by jury, we face the question of remedy. Recall that the Tenth Circuit declared the last two sentences of § 3583(k) "unconstitutional and unenforceable." * * *

Before us, the government suggests that the Tenth Circuit erred in declaring those two sentences "unenforceable." That remedy, the government says, sweeps too broadly. In the government's view, any constitutional infirmity can be cured simply by requiring juries acting under the reasonable doubt standard, rather than judges proceeding under the preponderance of the evidence standard, to find the facts necessary to trigger § 3583(k)'s mandatory minimum. This remedy would be consistent with the statute's terms, the government assures us, because "the court" authorized to revoke a term of supervised release in § 3583(k) can and should be construed as embracing not only judges but also juries. And, the government insists, that means we should direct the court of appeals to send this case back to the district court so a jury may be empaneled to decide whether Mr. Haymond violated § 3583(k). Unsurprisingly, Mr. Haymond contests all of this vigorously.

We decline to tangle with the parties' competing remedial arguments today. The Tenth Circuit did not address these arguments; it appears the government did not even discuss the possibility of empaneling a jury in its brief to that court * * * . [W]e believe the wiser course lies in returning the case to the court of appeals for it to have the opportunity to address the government's remedial argument in the first instance, including any question concerning whether that argument was adequately preserved in this case.

JUSTICE BREYER, concurring in the judgment.

I agree with much of the dissent, in particular that the role of the judge in a supervised-release proceeding is consistent with traditional parole. * * * I would not transplant the *Apprendi* line of cases to the supervised-release context.

Nevertheless, I agree with the plurality that this specific provision of the supervised-release statute, § 3583(k), is unconstitutional. Revocation of supervised release is typically understood as part of the penalty for the initial offense. The consequences that flow from violation of the conditions of supervised release are first and foremost considered sanctions for the defendant's "breach of trust"—his failure to follow the court-imposed conditions that followed his initial conviction—not for the particular conduct triggering the revocation as if that conduct were being sentenced as new federal criminal conduct. Consistent with that view, the consequences for violation of conditions of supervised release under § 3583(e), which governs most revocations, are limited by the severity of the original crime of conviction, not the conduct that results in revocation.

Section 3583(k) is difficult to reconcile with this understanding of supervised release. In particular, three aspects of this provision, considered in combination, lead me to think it is less like ordinary revocation and more like punishment for a new offense, to which the jury right would typically attach. First, § 3583(k) applies only when a defendant commits a discrete set of federal criminal offenses specified in the statute. Second, § 3583(k) takes away the judge's discretion to decide whether violation of a condition of supervised release should result in imprisonment and for how long. Third, § 3583(k) limits the judge's discretion in a particular manner: by imposing a mandatory minimum term of imprisonment of "not less than 5 years" upon a judge's finding that a defendant has "commit[ted] any" listed "criminal offense."

Taken together, these features of § 3583(k) more closely resemble the punishment of new criminal offenses, but without granting a defendant the rights, including the jury right, that attend a new criminal prosecution. And in an ordinary criminal prosecution, a jury must find facts that trigger a mandatory minimum prison term.

Accordingly, I would hold that § 3583(k) is unconstitutional and remand for the Court of Appeals to address the question of remedy. Because this is the course adopted by the plurality, I concur in the judgment.

JUSTICE ALITO, with whom THE CHIEF JUSTICE, JUSTICE THOMAS, and JUSTICE KAVANAUGH join, dissenting.

I do not think that there is a constitutional basis for today's holding, which is set out in JUSTICE BREYER's opinion, but it is narrow and has saved our jurisprudence from the consequences of the plurality opinion, which is not based on the original meaning of the Sixth Amendment, is irreconcilable with precedent, and sports rhetoric with potentially revolutionary implications. The plurality opinion appears to have been carefully crafted for the purpose of laying the groundwork for later decisions of much broader scope.

I

A

What do I mean by this? Many passages in the opinion suggest that the entire system of supervised release, which has been an integral part of the federal criminal justice system for the past 35 years, is fundamentally flawed in ways that cannot be fixed. * * *

Many statements and passages in the plurality opinion strongly suggest that the Sixth Amendment right to a jury trial applies to any supervised-release revocation proceeding. Take the opinion's opening line: "Only a jury, acting on proof beyond a reasonable doubt, may take a person's liberty." In a supervised-release revocation proceeding, a judge, based on the preponderance of the evidence, may make a finding that takes a person's liberty, in the sense that the defendant is sent back to prison. Later, after noting that the Sixth Amendment applies to a "criminal prosecution," the plurality gives that term a broad definition that appears to encompass any supervised-release revocation proceeding. * * *

Later statements are even more explicit. Quoting *Blakely v. Washington*, 542 U. S. 296, 304 (2004), out of context, the plurality states that "a jury must find beyond a reasonable doubt every fact which the law makes essential to a punishment that a judge might later seek to impose." If sending a defendant found to have violated supervised release back to prison is "punishment," then the thrust of the plurality's statement is that any factual finding needed to bring that about must be made by a jury, not by a judge, as is currently done.

[T]he plurality huffs that "the demands of the Fifth and Sixth Amendments" cannot be "dodge[d]" "by the simple expedient of relabeling a criminal prosecution a ... 'sentence modification' imposed at a postjudgment sentence administration proceeding." The meaning of this statement is unmistakable and cannot have been inadvertent: A supervised-release revocation proceeding is a criminal prosecution and is therefore governed by the Sixth Amendment (and the Fifth Amendment to boot). * * *

Finally, while the plurality appears to say that the Sixth Amendment does not apply to parole revocation proceedings, the plurality characterizes supervised release as "critical[ly] differen[t]." This is so, the plurality explains, because parole relieved a prisoner from serving part of the prison sentence originally imposed, whereas a term of supervised release is added to the term of imprisonment specified by the sentencing judge. As I will explain, this difference is purely formal and should have no constitutional consequences. But for now the important point is the plain implication of what the plurality says: Parole was constitutional, but supervised release ... well, that is an entirely different animal.

The intimation in all these statements is clear enough: All supervised-release revocation proceedings must be conducted in compliance with the Sixth Amendment—which means that the defendant is entitled to a jury trial, which means that as a practical matter supervised-release revocation proceedings cannot be held. In 2018, federal district courts completed 1809 criminal jury trials. During that same year, they adjudicated 16,946 revocations of supervised release, and there is simply no way that the federal courts could empanel enough juries to adjudicate all those proceedings, let alone try all those proceedings in accordance with the Sixth Amendment's Confrontation Clause. So, if every supervised-release revocation proceeding is a criminal prosecution, as the plurality suggests, the whole concept of supervised release will come crashing down.

The strategy of the plurality opinion is only thinly veiled. It provides the framework to be used in ending supervised release. It provides no clear ground for limiting the rationale of the opinion so that it does not lead to that result. And then it says: We are not doing that today.

B

Is it possible to read the plurality opinion more narrowly? Can it be understood to condemn only one narrow statutory provision, namely, § 3583(k), which required the judge to send respondent Haymond back to prison for at least five years once the judge found that he had violated a condition of his supervised release by again possessing child pornography? On this reading, the only Sixth Amendment defect would be the mandatory minimum period of additional confinement that the statute imposes. There would be no problem if the judge had been free to choose the term, if any, of additional confinement. Does the plurality mean to go no further than this?

There are passages in the opinion that hint at this narrower interpretation. * * * But the previously quoted statements pointing to a broader understanding remain, and the plurality does nothing to disavow that reading. To the contrary, the plurality doubles down, assuring us that this broader understanding would not be too disruptive.

* * *

II

This should not have been a difficult or complicated case. I start with the proposition that the old federal parole system did not implicate the Sixth Amendment's jury trial right. A parole revocation proceeding was not a "criminal prosecution" within the meaning of the Sixth Amendment, and revocation did not result in a new sentence. When a prisoner was paroled, the Executive was simply exercising the authority conferred by law to grant the defendant a conditional release from serving part of the sentence imposed after a guilty verdict.

Supervised release, for reasons already explained, is not fundamentally different and therefore should not be treated any differently for Sixth Amendment purposes. When a jury finds a federal defendant guilty of violating a particular criminal statute, the maximum period of confinement authorized is the maximum term of imprisonment plus the maximum term of supervised release. If a prisoner does not end up spending this full period in confinement, that is because service of part of the period is excused due to satisfactory conduct during the period of supervised release. Any other reading exalts form over substance in a way that has enormous consequences that cannot be justified on constitutional grounds.

Once this is understood, it follows that the procedures that must be followed at a supervised-release revocation proceeding are the same that had to be followed at a parole revocation proceeding, and these were settled long ago. At a parole revocation hearing, the fundamental requisites of due process had to be observed, but a parolee did not have a right to a jury trial. Neither the Confrontation Clause nor the formal rules of evidence had to be followed. Due process did not require proof beyond a reasonable doubt as is necessary at trial * * * .

For the past 35 years, it has been understood that the same rules apply at a supervised-release revocation proceeding. There is no good reason to depart from that understanding.

III

The plurality * * * makes no real effort to show that the Sixth Amendment was originally understood to require a jury trial in a proceeding like a supervised-release revocation proceeding. Of course, nothing like supervised release—or for that matter, parole—existed when the Sixth Amendment was ratified, so I will not attempt to make the affirmative case that the Sixth Amendment was specifically understood not to apply to such proceedings. But there is a strong case for the proposition that the terms of the Sixth Amendment and the original understanding of the scope of the jury trial right do not require the plurality's interpretation. And our prior precedents emphatically refute that interpretation.

The Sixth Amendment limits the scope of the jury trial right in three significant ways: It provides "who may assert the right ('the accused'); when the right may be asserted ('[i]n all criminal prosecutions'); and what the right guarantees" ("the right to a . . . trial, by an impartial jury"). The plurality can reach its conclusion only by ignoring these limitations.

A

I begin with who may assert the jury trial right. The text of the Sixth Amendment makes clear that this is "a right of the 'accused' and only the 'accused.'" A. Amar, The Bill of Rights 111 (1998). The "accused" is an individual "[c]harged with a crime, by a legal process." N. Webster, An American Dictionary of the English Language (1828). At the founding, "accused" described a status preceding "convicted." * * * And this understanding of the Sixth Amendment language—"accused" as distinct from "convicted"—endures today. * * *

Despite the plurality's suggestion otherwise, respondent was no longer the "accused" while he served his term of supervised release. To be sure, he was formerly the accused—at the time when he was duly indicted and tried for possession of child pornography. But after a jury convicted him and authorized the judge to sentence him to terms of imprisonment and supervised release, respondent was transformed into the convicted. And his status as such remained the same while he served his sentences, including during the proceeding to determine whether he had adhered to the conditions attached to the term of supervised release that was permitted by law and thus implicitly authorized by the jury's verdict.

This is especially so given that respondent's reimprisonment was not primarily a punishment for new criminal conduct. The principal reason for assigning a penalty to a supervised-release violation is not that the violative act is a crime (indeed, under other provisions in § 3583, the act need not even be criminal); rather, it is that the violative act is a breach of trust. In other words, it makes little sense to treat respondent as the accused—i.e., one charged with a crime—when he has been charged not with a crime, but with violating the terms of a jury-authorized sentence that flowed from his original conviction. The plurality's extension of the jury trial right to respondent's supervised-release revocation proceeding thus flounders from the start for the simple reason that respondent cannot easily be viewed as an "accused" in the conventional sense of the term.

B

It is similarly awkward to characterize a supervised-release revocation proceeding as part of the defendant's "criminal prosecution." A supervised-release revocation proceeding is not part of the criminal prosecution that landed a defendant in prison in the first place because a criminal prosecution ends when sentence has been pronounced on the convicted * * * . This follows from the early understanding that a "prosecution" concludes when a court enters final judgment. [Citing treatises and law dictionaries.]

In fact, two prior precedents—which the plurality effectively ignores—drew this exact line in stating that parole- and probation-revocation proceedings are not part of a criminal prosecution. Unless the plurality is willing to own up to attempting to overrule these precedents, its failure to engage with them is inexcusable.

The first is *Morrissey*, 408 U. S., at 472, a landmark case in which the Court held that due process requires a State to afford a parolee "some opportunity to be heard" before revoking parole. In considering that question, the Court "beg[an] with the proposition that the revocation of parole is not part of a criminal prosecution and thus the full panoply of rights due a defendant in such a proceeding does not apply in parole revocations." The Court made clear that "[p]arole arises after the end of the criminal prosecution, including imposition of sentence."

The second is *Gagnon*, 411 U. S. 778, where the Court considered whether a probationer has a right to appointed counsel prior to the revocation of probation. There, the Court reasoned that "[p]robation revocation, like parole revocation, is not a stage of a criminal prosecution." Thus, in both contexts, the Court emphasized that parole- and probation-revocation proceedings are not part of a criminal prosecution. And that understanding carried significant consequences: It denied parolees and probationers the "full panoply of rights" to which a defendant is entitled in a criminal prosecution.

Supervised-release revocation proceedings are not part of the defendant's criminal prosecution for the same reasons. As we said in *United States v. Johnson*, 529 U. S. 53, 59 (2000), which the plurality all but ignores, "[s]upervised release has no statutory function until confinement ends," which itself has no function until the criminal prosecution has ended. * * *

The fact that *Morrissey* and *Gagnon* involved parole and probation, not supervised release, does not matter for present purposes. These cases did not turn on any features of parole or probation that might distinguish them from supervised release. Rather, those decisions recognized an obvious fact: The administration of a sentence occurs after a court imposes that sentence—i.e., after the criminal prosecution has ended. That fact is equally true here. No matter what penalties flow from the revocation of parole, probation, or supervised release, the related proceedings are not part of the criminal prosecution.

* * *

C

The plurality attempts to pass off its reasoning as nothing more than the logical outgrowth of the *Apprendi* line of cases, but that is untrue. The plurality invokes these cases to support the idea that the Sixth Amendment cannot be evaded by "[r]elabeling" of a criminal prosecution as a " 'sentence modification' " imposed at a " 'postjudgment sentence-administration proceeding.' ". But nothing like that was involved in *Apprendi* or later related cases. Instead, the Court in those cases rejected what it saw as attempts to place the label "sentencing enhancement" on what, in its view, were essentially elements of charged offenses. All of the cases in the *Apprendi* line involved actual sentencing proceedings, and thus there was never any question whether they arose in a "criminal prosecution." That is not this case.

* * *

1

Since *Apprendi* itself, the Court has time and again endeavored to draw its understanding of the jury trial right from historical practices that existed at the founding and soon afterward. * * * In this case, the plurality can muster no support for the proposition that the jury trial right was extended to anything like a supervised-release or parole revocation proceeding at the time of the adoption of the Sixth Amendment. Supervised release was not instituted until 1984, and parole was unknown until the 19th century, so close historic analogues are lacking. But the nearest practices that can be found do not support the plurality.

[Justice Alito reviews historical practices such as release on bond and corporal punishment of prisoners, and parole and probation, and concludes that none of these practices triggered a jury trial right.]

From each of the foregoing examples, a clear historical fact emerges: American juries have simply played no role in the administration of previously imposed sentences. * * *

2

The plurality's extension of the jury trial right to the administration of previously imposed sentences also sidelines what has until now been the core feature of the *Apprendi* line of cases—a meaningful connection to the trial for the charged offense. * * * The Court's rationale has been that "the core crime and the fact triggering [an increased maximum or] mandatory minimum sentence together constitute a new, aggravated crime, each element of which must be submitted to the jury." *Alleyne*, 570 U. S., at 113.

And this rationale, of course, is key to the *Apprendi* line of cases, because the Sixth Amendment protects only the rights of "the accused," that is, those charged with a particular crime.

* * *

Here, the factual basis for revoking respondent's supervised release did not go * * * to what happened in the commission of the offense; it did not even relate to the commission of the offense. It had virtually nothing to do with the child-pornography offense that led to respondent's conviction, incarceration, and supervised release. The same would be true of a defendant convicted of burglary, arson, or any other crime: His failure to attend an employment class or to pass a drug test while on supervised release would have nothing to do with how he carried out those offenses. * * * Thus, no reasonable person would describe such postjudgment facts that go only to the administration of a previously imposed sentence as "ingredients" or "elements" of the charged offense. * * *

It is telling that the plurality never brings itself to acknowledge this clear departure from the *Apprendi* line of cases. For nearly two decades now, the Court has insisted that these cases turn on "a specific statutory offense," and its "ingredients" and "elements." Yet today we learn that—at least as far as the plurality is concerned—none of that really mattered.

* * *

Today's decision is based in part on an opinion that is unpardonably vague and suggestive in dangerous ways. It is not grounded on any plausible interpretation of the original meaning of the Sixth Amendment, and it is contradicted by precedents that are unceremoniously overruled. It represents one particular view about crime and punishment that is ascendant in some quarters today but is not required by the Constitution. If the Court eventually takes the trip that this opinion proposes, the consequences will be far reaching and unfortunate.

For these reasons, I respectfully dissent.

IV. TRIAL BY JURY

C. REQUISITE FEATURES OF THE JURY

2. Unanimity

Page 1284. Replacing *Apodaca v. Oregon* and "QUESTIONS ON SIZE AND UNANIMITY":

In *Apodaca v. Oregon*, 406 U.S. 404 (1972), the Court declined to impose a unanimity requirement on the states, letting stand a felony conviction based on a 10–2 vote. In the following case, the Court overrules

Apodaca, incorporating to the states the Sixth Amendment's unanimity requirement in jury trials.

RAMOS V. LOUISIANA
Supreme Court of the United States, 2020.
140 S.Ct. 1390.

JUSTICE GORSUCH delivered the opinion of the Court.

Accused of a serious crime, Evangelisto Ramos insisted on his innocence and invoked his right to a jury trial. Eventually, 10 jurors found the evidence against him persuasive. But a pair of jurors believed that the State of Louisiana had failed to prove Mr. Ramos's guilt beyond reasonable doubt; they voted to acquit.

In 48 States and federal court, a single juror's vote to acquit is enough to prevent a conviction. But not in Louisiana. Along with Oregon, Louisiana has long punished people based on 10-to-2 verdicts like the one here. So, instead of the mistrial he would have received almost anywhere else, Mr. Ramos was sentenced to life in prison without the possibility of parole.

Why do Louisiana and Oregon allow nonunanimous convictions? Though it's hard to say why these laws persist, their origins are clear. Louisiana first endorsed nonunanimous verdicts for serious crimes at a constitutional convention in 1898. According to one committee chairman, the avowed purpose of that convention was to "establish the supremacy of the white race," and the resulting document included many of the trappings of the Jim Crow era: a poll tax, a combined literacy and property ownership test, and a grandfather clause that in practice exempted white residents from the most onerous of these requirements.

Nor was it only the prospect of African-Americans voting that concerned the delegates. Just a week before the convention, the U. S. Senate passed a resolution calling for an investigation into whether Louisiana was systemically excluding African-Americans from juries. Seeking to avoid unwanted national attention, and aware that this Court would strike down any policy of overt discrimination against African-American jurors as a violation of the Fourteenth Amendment, the delegates sought to undermine African-American participation on juries in another way. With a careful eye on racial demographics, the convention delegates sculpted a "facially race-neutral" rule permitting 10-to-2 verdicts in order "to ensure that African-American juror service would be meaningless."

Adopted in the 1930s, Oregon's rule permitting nonunanimous verdicts can be similarly traced to the rise of the Ku Klux Klan and efforts to dilute "the influence of racial, ethnic, and religious minorities on Oregon juries." In fact, no one before us contests any of this; courts in both

Louisiana and Oregon have frankly acknowledged that race was a motivating factor in the adoption of their States' respective nonunanimity rules.

We took this case to decide whether the Sixth Amendment right to a jury trial—as incorporated against the States by way of the Fourteenth Amendment—requires a unanimous verdict to convict a defendant of a serious offense. Louisiana insists that this Court has never definitively passed on the question and urges us to find its practice consistent with the Sixth Amendment. By contrast, the dissent doesn't try to defend Louisiana's law on Sixth or Fourteenth Amendment grounds; tacitly, it seems to admit that the Constitution forbids States from using nonunanimous juries. Yet, unprompted by Louisiana, the dissent suggests our precedent requires us to rule for the State anyway. What explains all this? To answer the puzzle, it's necessary to say a bit more about the merits of the question presented, the relevant precedent, and, at last, the consequences that follow from saying what we know to be true.

I

The Sixth Amendment promises that "[i]n all criminal prosecutions, the accused shall enjoy the right to a speedy and public trial, by an impartial jury of the State and district wherein the crime shall have been committed, which district shall have been previously ascertained by law." The Amendment goes on to preserve other rights for criminal defendants but says nothing else about what a "trial by an impartial jury" entails.

Still, the promise of a jury trial surely meant something—otherwise, there would have been no reason to write it down. Nor would it have made any sense to spell out the places from which jurors should be drawn if their powers as jurors could be freely abridged by statute. Imagine a constitution that allowed a "jury trial" to mean nothing but a single person rubberstamping convictions without hearing any evidence—but simultaneously insisting that the lone juror come from a specific judicial district "previously ascertained by law." And if that's not enough, imagine a constitution that included the same hollow guarantee twice—not only in the Sixth Amendment, but also in Article III. No: The text and structure of the Constitution clearly suggest that the term "trial by an impartial jury" carried with it some meaning about the content and requirements of a jury trial.

One of these requirements was unanimity. Wherever we might look to determine what the term "trial by an impartial jury trial" meant at the time of the Sixth Amendment's adoption—whether it's the common law, state practices in the founding era, or opinions and treatises written soon afterward—the answer is unmistakable. A jury must reach a unanimous verdict in order to convict.

The requirement of juror unanimity emerged in 14thcentury England and was soon accepted as a vital right protected by the common law. As Blackstone explained, no person could be found guilty of a serious crime unless "the truth of every accusation . . . should . . . be confirmed by the unanimous suffrage of twelve of his equals and neighbors, indifferently chosen, and superior to all suspicion." A " 'verdict, taken from eleven, was no verdict' " at all. This same rule applied in the young American States. Six State Constitutions explicitly required unanimity. Another four preserved the right to a jury trial in more general terms. But the variations did not matter much; consistent with the common law, state courts appeared to regard unanimity as an essential feature of the jury trial.

It was against this backdrop that James Madison drafted and the States ratified the Sixth Amendment in 1791. By that time, unanimous verdicts had been required for about 400 years. If the term "trial by an impartial jury" carried any meaning at all, it surely included a requirement as long and widely accepted as unanimity.

Influential, postadoption treatises confirm this understanding. For example, in 1824, Nathan Dane reported as fact that the U. S. Constitution required unanimity in criminal jury trials for serious offenses. A few years later, Justice Story explained in his Commentaries on the Constitution that "in common cases, the law not only presumes every man innocent, until he is proved guilty; but unanimity in the verdict of the jury is indispensable." Similar statements can be found in American legal treatises throughout the 19th century.

Nor is this a case where the original public meaning was lost to time and only recently recovered. This Court has, repeatedly and over many years, recognized that the Sixth Amendment requires unanimity. As early as 1898, the Court said that a defendant enjoys a "constitutional right to demand that his liberty should not be taken from him except by the joint action of the court and the unanimous verdict of a jury of twelve persons." A few decades later, the Court elaborated that the Sixth Amendment affords a right to "a trial by jury as understood and applied at common law, . . . includ[ing] all the essential elements as they were recognized in this country and England when the Constitution was adopted." And, the Court observed, this includes a requirement "that the verdict should be unanimous." In all, this Court has commented on the Sixth Amendment's unanimity requirement no fewer than 13 times over more than 120 years.

There can be no question either that the Sixth Amendment's unanimity requirement applies to state and federal criminal trials equally. This Court has long explained that the Sixth Amendment right to a jury trial is "fundamental to the American scheme of justice" and incorporated against the States under the Fourteenth Amendment. This Court has long explained, too, that incorporated provisions of the Bill of Rights bear the same content when asserted against States as they do when asserted against the federal government. So if the Sixth Amendment's right to a jury trial requires a unanimous verdict to support a conviction in federal court, it requires no less in state court.

II

A

How, despite these seemingly straightforward principles, have Louisiana's and Oregon's laws managed to hang on for so long? It turns out that the Sixth Amendment's otherwise simple story took a strange turn in 1972. That year, the Court confronted these States' unconventional schemes for the first time—in *Apodaca v. Oregon* and a companion case, *Johnson v. Louisiana*. Ultimately, the Court could do no more than issue a badly fractured set of opinions. Four dissenting Justices would not have hesitated to strike down the States' laws, recognizing that the Sixth Amendment requires unanimity and that this guarantee is fully applicable against the States under the Fourteenth Amendment. But a four-Justice plurality took a very different view of the Sixth Amendment. These Justices declared that the real question before them was whether unanimity serves an important "function" in "contemporary society." Then, having reframed the question, the plurality wasted few words before concluding that unanimity's costs outweigh its benefits in the modern era, so the Sixth Amendment should not stand in the way of Louisiana or Oregon.

The ninth Member of the Court adopted a position that was neither here nor there. On the one hand, Justice Powell agreed that, as a matter of "history and precedent, . . . the Sixth Amendment requires a unanimous jury verdict to convict." But, on the other hand, he argued that the Fourteenth Amendment does not render this guarantee against the federal government fully applicable against the States. In this way, Justice Powell doubled down on his belief in "dual-track" incorporation—the idea that a single right can mean two different things depending on whether it is being invoked against the federal or a state government.

Justice Powell acknowledged that his argument for dual-track incorporation came "late in the day." Late it was. The Court had already, nearly a decade earlier, "rejected the notion that the Fourteenth Amendment applies to the States only a 'watered-down, subjective version of the individual guarantees of the Bill of Rights.'" It's a point we've restated many times since, too, including as recently as last year. Still, Justice Powell frankly explained, he was "unwillin[g]" to follow the Court's precedents. So he offered up the essential fifth vote to uphold Mr. Apodaca's conviction—if based only on a view of the Fourteenth Amendment that he knew was (and remains) foreclosed by precedent. * * *

III

Louisiana's approach may not be quite as tough as trying to defend Justice Powell's dual-track theory of incorporation, but it's pretty close. How does the State deal with the fact this Court has said 13 times over 120 years that the Sixth Amendment does require unanimity? Or the fact that five Justices in *Apodaca* said the same? The best the State can offer is to suggest that all these statements came in dicta. But even supposing (without granting) that Louisiana is right and it's dicta all the way down, why would the Court now walk away from many of its own statements about the Constitution's meaning? And what about the prior 400 years of English and American cases requiring unanimity—should we dismiss all those as dicta too?

Sensibly, Louisiana doesn't dispute that the common law required unanimity. Instead, it argues that the drafting history of the Sixth Amendment reveals an intent by the framers to leave this particular feature behind. The State points to the fact that Madison's proposal for the Sixth Amendment originally read: "The trial of all crimes . . . shall be by an impartial jury of freeholders of the vicinage, with the requisite of unanimity for conviction, of the right of challenge, and other accustomed requisites. . . ." Louisiana notes that the House of Representatives approved this text with minor modifications. Yet, the State stresses, the Senate replaced "impartial jury of freeholders of the vicinage" with "impartial jury of the State and district wherein the crime shall have been committed" and also removed the explicit references to unanimity, the right of challenge, and "other accustomed requisites." In light of these revisions, Louisiana would have us infer an intent to abandon the common law's traditional unanimity requirement.

But this snippet of drafting history could just as easily support the opposite inference. Maybe the Senate deleted the language about unanimity, the right of challenge, and "other accustomed prerequisites" because all this was so plainly included in the promise of a "trial by an impartial jury" that Senators considered the language surplusage. The truth is that we have little contemporaneous evidence shedding light on why the Senate acted as it did. So, rather than dwelling on text left on the cutting room floor, we are much better served by interpreting the language Congress retained and the States ratified. And, as we've seen, at the time of the Amendment's adoption, the right to a jury trial meant a trial in which the jury renders a unanimous verdict.

Further undermining Louisiana's inference about the drafting history is the fact it proves too much. If the Senate's deletion of the word "unanimity" changed the meaning of the text that remains, then the same would seemingly have to follow for the other deleted words as well. So it's not just unanimity that died in the Senate, but all the "other accustomed requisites" associated with the common law jury trial right—i.e., everything history might have taught us about what it means to have a jury trial. Taking the State's argument from drafting history to its logical conclusion would thus leave the right to a "trial by jury" devoid of meaning. A right mentioned twice in the Constitution would be reduced to an empty promise. That can't be right.

Faced with this hard fact, Louisiana's only remaining option is to invite us to distinguish between the historic features of common law jury trials that (we think) serve "important enough" functions to migrate silently into the Sixth Amendment and those that don't. And, on the State's account, we should conclude that unanimity isn't worthy enough to make the trip.

But to see the dangers of Louisiana's overwise approach, there's no need to look any further than *Apodaca* itself. There, four Justices, pursuing the functionalist approach Louisiana espouses, began by describing the " 'essential' " benefit of a jury trial as " 'the interposition . . . of the commonsense judgment of a group of laymen' " between the defendant and the possibility of an " 'overzealous prosecutor.' " And measured against that muddy yardstick, they quickly concluded that requiring 12 rather than 10 votes to convict offers no meaningful improvement. Meanwhile, these Justices argued, States have good and important reasons for dispensing with unanimity, such as seeking to reduce the rate of hung juries.

Who can profess confidence in a breezy cost-benefit analysis like that? Lost in the accounting are the racially discriminatory reasons that Louisiana and Oregon adopted their peculiar rules in the first place. What's more, the plurality never explained why the promised benefit of abandoning unanimity—reducing the rate of hung juries—always scores as a credit, not a cost. But who can say whether any particular hung jury is a waste, rather than an example of a jury doing exactly what the plurality said it should—deliberating carefully and safeguarding against overzealous prosecutions? And what about the fact, too, that some studies suggest that the elimination of unanimity has only a small effect on the rate of hung juries? Or the fact that others profess to have found that requiring unanimity may provide other possible benefits, including more openminded and more thorough deliberations? It seems the *Apodaca* plurality never even conceived of such possibilities.

Our real objection here isn't that the *Apodaca* plurality's cost-benefit analysis was too skimpy. The deeper problem is that the plurality subjected the ancient guarantee of a unanimous jury verdict to its own functionalist assessment in the first place. And Louisiana asks us to repeat the error today, just replacing *Apodaca*'s functionalist assessment with our own updated version. All this overlooks the fact that, at the time of the Sixth Amendment's adoption, the right to trial by jury included a right to a unanimous verdict. When the American people chose to enshrine that right in the Constitution, they weren't suggesting fruitful topics for future cost-benefit analyses. They were seeking to ensure that their children's children would enjoy the same hard-won liberty they enjoyed. As judges, it is not our role to reassess whether the right to a unanimous jury is "important enough" to retain. With humility, we must accept that this right may serve purposes evading our current notice. We are entrusted to preserve and protect that liberty, not balance it away aided by no more than social statistics. * * *

IV

* * *

B

1

There's another obstacle the dissent must overcome. Even if we accepted the premise that *Apodaca* established a precedent, no one on the Court today is prepared to say it was rightly decided, and *stare decisis* isn't supposed to be the art of methodically ignoring what everyone knows to be true. Of course, the precedents of this Court warrant our deep respect as embodying the considered views of those who have come before. But *stare decisis* has never been treated as "an inexorable command." And the doctrine is "at its weakest when we interpret the Constitution" because a mistaken judicial interpretation of that supreme law is often "practically impossible" to correct through other means. To balance these considerations, when it revisits a precedent this Court has traditionally considered "the quality of the decision's reasoning; its consistency with related decisions; legal developments since the decision; and reliance on the decision." In this case, each factor points in the same direction.

Start with the quality of the reasoning. Whether we look to the plurality opinion or Justice Powell's separate concurrence, *Apodaca* was gravely mistaken; again, no Member of the Court today defends either as rightly decided. Without repeating what we've already explained in detail, it's just an implacable fact that the plurality spent almost no time grappling with the historical meaning of the Sixth Amendment's jury trial right, this Court's long-repeated statements that it demands unanimity, or the racist origins of Louisiana's and Oregon's laws. Instead, the plurality subjected the Constitution's jury trial right to an incomplete functionalist analysis of its own creation for which it spared one paragraph. And, of course, five Justices expressly rejected the plurality's conclusion that the Sixth Amendment does not require unanimity. Meanwhile, Justice Powell refused to follow this Court's incorporation precedents. Nine Justices (including Justice Powell) recognized this for what it was; eight called it an error.

Looking to *Apodaca*'s consistency with related decisions and recent legal developments compounds the reasons for concern. *Apodaca* sits uneasily with 120 years of preceding case law. Given how unmoored it was from the start, it might seem unlikely that later developments could have done more to undermine the decision. Yet they have. While Justice Powell's dual-track theory of incorporation was already foreclosed in 1972, some at that time still argued that it might have a role to play outside the realm of criminal procedure. Since then, the Court has held otherwise. Until recently, dual-track incorporation attracted at least a measure of support in dissent. But this Court has now roundly rejected it. Nor has the plurality's rejection of the Sixth Amendment's historical unanimity requirement aged more gracefully. As we've seen, in the years since *Apodaca*, this Court has spoken inconsistently about its meaning—but nonetheless referred to the traditional unanimity requirement on at least eight occasions. In light of all this, calling *Apodaca* an outlier would be perhaps too suggestive of the possibility of company.

When it comes to reliance interests, it's notable that neither Louisiana nor Oregon claims anything like the prospective economic, regulatory, or social disruption litigants seeking to preserve precedent usually invoke. No one, it seems, has signed a contract, entered a marriage, purchased a home, or opened a business based on the expectation that, should a crime occur, at least the accused may be sent away by a 10-to-2 verdict. Nor does anyone suggest that nonunanimous verdicts have "become part of our national culture." It would be quite surprising if they had, given that nonunanimous verdicts are insufficient to convict in 48 States and federal court.

Instead, the only reliance interests that might be asserted here fall into two categories. The first concerns the fact Louisiana and Oregon may need to retry defendants convicted of felonies by nonunanimous verdicts whose cases are still pending on direct appeal. The dissent claims that this fact supplies the winning argument for retaining *Apodaca* because it has generated "enormous reliance interests" and overturning the case would provoke a "crushing" "tsunami" of follow-on litigation.

The overstatement may be forgiven as intended for dramatic effect, but prior convictions in only two States are potentially affected by our judgment. Those States credibly claim that the number of nonunanimous felony convictions still on direct appeal are somewhere in the hundreds, and retrying or plea bargaining these cases will surely impose a cost. But new rules of criminal procedure usually do, often affecting significant numbers of pending cases across the whole country. For example, after *Booker v. United States* held that the Federal Sentencing Guidelines must be advisory rather than mandatory, this Court vacated and remanded nearly 800 decisions to the courts of appeals. Similar consequences likely followed when *Crawford v. Washington* overturned prior interpretations of the Confrontation Clause or *Arizona v. Gant* changed the law for searches incident to arrests. Our decision here promises to cause less, and certainly nothing before us supports the dissent's surmise that it will cause wildly more, disruption than these other decisions. * * *

Reversed.

JUSTICE SOTOMAYOR, concurring

[Justice Sotomayor joined all portions of the majority opinion reproduced above. She wrote separately on the question of *stare decisis* and to make clear that she is amenable to interpretive methods other than public meaning originalism.]

JUSTICE KAVANAUGH, concurring

[Justice Kavanaugh joined all portions of the majority opinion reproduced above. He wrote separately on the question of *stare decisis*, describing a framework for its application in future cases.]

JUSTICE THOMAS, concurring

[Justice Thomas did not join the majority opinion, but concurred in the judgment based on his view that the Privileges and Immunities clause of the Fourteenth Amendment made all provisions of the Bill of Rights enforceable against the states, including the unanimity requirement of the Sixth Amendment.]

JUSTICE ALITO, dissenting

[Justice Alito dissented with Chief Justice Roberts and Justice Kagan on *stare decisis* grounds.]

Thoughts After Ramos v. Louisiana

In his majority opinion, Justice Gorsuch describes the Court's opinion in *Apodaca v. Oregon* as "badly fractured." There is some irony in that account given how fractured is the Court's decision in *Ramos* itself. Justices Sotomayor and Kavanaugh joined all parts of the majority opinion reproduced here, but declined to join another section in which Justice Gorsuch, with Justices Ginsburg and Breyer, addresses the dissenting justices' valuation of the precedential value of *Apodaca* under *Marks v. United States,* 430 U.S. 188 (1977). Another portion of Justice Gorsuch's opinion, addressing the retroactive application of *Ramos* to criminal convictions that are final, garnered support from Justices Ginsburg, Breyer, and Sotomayor, but not Justice Kavanaugh. In addition to these fractures in the majority, Justice Alito took some umbrage in his dissenting opinion, criticizing both the tone of the majority opinion and its indictment of nonunanimous jury practices in Oregon and Louisiana as grounded in racism.

Ramos is also notable for Justice Gorsuch's full-throated originalism. Although Justice Sotomayor was careful in her concurring opinion to make clear that she is open to other modes of constitutional interpretation, the fact that she, Justice Ginsburg, Justice Breyer, and Justice Kavanaugh all signed-on to an opinion that rests entirely on an analysis of the Sixth Amendment's original public meaning highlights the ascendant influence of originalism on the Court. Notably, that analysis leads the Court to a result that most would regard as liberal or progressive in the context of contemporary political discourse. Of course, this is not the first time that a purportedly conservative Justice has deployed originalism to advance individual rights in the criminal procedure context. Justice Scalia's opinion in *Crawford v. Washington*, 541 U.S. 36 (2004), provides a ready example. So, too, his opinion in *Apprendi*, which provided Justice Gorsuch with the grounding for his plurality opinion in *Haymond*. Nevertheless, *Ramos* is significant for the fact that the Court's newest members signaled not only their sympathies with originalism, but neutrality with respect to results. In *Ramos*, method seems to drive the outcome.

The Court in *Ramos* does not reach the question of retroactive application of its holding to criminal convictions that are final. On May 28, 2020, the Court granted certiorari on that question in *Edwards v. Vannoy*.

D. JURY SELECTION AND COMPOSITION

5. The Use of Peremptory Challenges

b. *Constitutional Limits on Peremptory Challenges*

Fact-Intensive Reviews of Peremptory Challenges: Snyder v. Louisiana and Foster v. Chapman

Page 1332. After the section on *Snyder* and *Foster*, add the following case:

FLOWERS V. MISSISSIPPI

Supreme Court of the United States, 2019.
139 S.Ct. 2228.

JUSTICE KAVANAUGH delivered the opinion of the Court.

In *Batson v. Kentucky*, 476 U. S. 79 (1986), this Court ruled that a State may not discriminate on the basis of race when exercising peremptory challenges against prospective jurors in a criminal trial. In

1996, Curtis Flowers allegedly murdered four people in Winona, Mississippi. Flowers is black. He has been tried six separate times before a jury for murder. The same lead prosecutor represented the State in all six trials. In the initial three trials, Flowers was convicted, but the Mississippi Supreme Court reversed each conviction. In the first trial, Flowers was convicted, but the Mississippi Supreme Court reversed the conviction due to "numerous instances of prosecutorial misconduct." In the second trial, the trial court found that the prosecutor discriminated on the basis of race in the peremptory challenge of a black juror. The trial court seated the black juror. Flowers was then convicted, but the Mississippi Supreme Court again reversed the conviction because of prosecutorial misconduct at trial. In the third trial, Flowers was convicted, but the Mississippi Supreme Court yet again reversed the conviction, this time because the court concluded that the prosecutor had again discriminated against black prospective jurors in the jury selection process. * * * The fourth and fifth trials of Flowers ended in mistrials due to hung juries. In his sixth trial, which is the one at issue here, Flowers was convicted. The State struck five of the six black prospective jurors. On appeal, Flowers argued that the State again violated *Batson* in exercising peremptory strikes against black prospective jurors. In a divided 5-to-4 decision, the Mississippi Supreme Court affirmed the conviction. We granted certiorari on the *Batson* question and now reverse.

Four critical facts, taken together, require reversal. First, in the six trials combined, the State employed its peremptory challenges to strike 41 of the 42 black prospective jurors that it could have struck * * * . Second, in the most recent trial, the sixth trial, the State exercised peremptory strikes against five of the six black prospective jurors. Third, at the sixth trial, in an apparent effort to find pretextual reasons to strike black prospective jurors, the State engaged in dramatically disparate questioning of black and white prospective jurors. Fourth, the State then struck at least one black prospective juror, Carolyn Wright, who was similarly situated to white prospective jurors who were not struck by the State.

We need not and do not decide that any one of those four facts alone would require reversal. All that we need to decide, and all that we do decide, is that all of the relevant facts and circumstances taken together establish that the trial court committed clear error in concluding that the State's peremptory strike of black prospective juror Carolyn Wright was not "motivated in substantial part by discriminatory intent." *Foster v. Chatman*, 578 U. S. ___, ___ (2016) (slip op., at 23). In reaching that conclusion, we break no new legal ground. We simply enforce and reinforce *Batson* by applying it to the extraordinary facts of this case. We reverse the judgment of the Supreme Court of Mississippi, and we remand the case for further proceedings not inconsistent with this opinion.

I

The underlying events that gave rise to this case took place in Winona, Mississippi. * * * The total population of Winona is about 5,000. The town is about 53 percent black and about 46 percent white. In 1996, Bertha Tardy, Robert Golden, Derrick Stewart, and Carmen Rigby were murdered at the Tardy Furniture store in Winona. All four victims worked at the Tardy Furniture store. Three of the four victims were white; one was black. In 1997, the State charged Curtis Flowers with murder. Flowers is black. Since then, Flowers has been tried six separate times for the murders. In each of the first two trials, Flowers was tried for one individual murder. In each subsequent trial, Flowers was tried for all four of the murders together. The same state prosecutor tried Flowers each time. The prosecutor is white.

At Flowers' first trial, 36 prospective jurors—5 black and 31 white—were presented to potentially serve on the jury. The State exercised a total of 12 peremptory strikes, and it used 5 of them to strike the five qualified black prospective jurors. Flowers objected, arguing under *Batson* that the State had exercised its peremptory strikes in a racially discriminatory manner. The trial court rejected the *Batson* challenge. Because the trial court allowed the State's peremptory strikes, Flowers was tried in front of an all-white jury. * * *

At the second trial, 30 prospective jurors—5 black and 25 white—were presented to potentially serve on the jury. As in Flowers' first trial, the State again used its strikes against all five black prospective jurors. But this time, the trial court determined that the State's asserted reason for one of the strikes was a pretext for discrimination. Specifically, the trial court determined that one of the State's proffered reasons—that the juror had been inattentive and was nodding off during jury selection—for striking that juror was false, and the trial court therefore sustained Flowers' *Batson* challenge. The trial court disallowed the strike and sat that black juror on the jury. The jury at Flowers' second trial consisted of 11 white jurors and 1 black juror. * * *

At Flowers' third trial, 45 prospective jurors—17 black and 28 white—were presented to potentially serve on the jury. One of the black prospective jurors was struck for cause, leaving 16. The State exercised a total of 15 peremptory strikes, and it used all 15 against black prospective jurors. Flowers again argued that the State had used its peremptory strikes in a racially discriminatory manner. The trial court found that the State had not discriminated on the basis of race. The jury in Flowers' third trial consisted of 11 white jurors and 1 black juror. The lone black juror who served on the jury was seated after the State ran out of peremptory strikes. * * *

At Flowers' fourth trial, 36 prospective jurors—16 black and 20 white—were presented to potentially serve on the jury. The State exercised a total of 11 peremptory strikes, and it used all 11 against black prospective jurors. But because of the relatively large number of prospective jurors who were black, the State did not have enough peremptory challenges to eliminate all of the black prospective jurors. The seated jury consisted of seven white jurors and five black jurors. That jury could not reach a verdict, and the proceeding ended in a mistrial.

As to the fifth trial, there is no available racial information about the prospective jurors, as distinct from the jurors who ultimately sat on the jury. The jury was composed of nine white jurors and three black jurors. The jury could not reach a verdict, and the trial again ended in a mistrial.

At the sixth trial, which we consider here, 26 prospective jurors—6 black and 20 white—were presented to potentially serve on the jury. The State exercised a total of six peremptory strikes, and it used five of the six against black prospective jurors, leaving one black juror to sit on the jury. Flowers again argued that the State had exercised its peremptory strikes in a racially discriminatory manner. The trial court concluded that the State had offered race-neutral reasons for each of the five peremptory strikes against the five black prospective jurors. The jury at Flowers' sixth trial consisted of 11 white jurors and 1 black juror. That jury convicted Flowers of murder and sentenced him to death. * * *

* * *

II

A

* * * Peremptory strikes have very old credentials and can be traced back to the common law. Those peremptory strikes traditionally may be used to remove any potential juror for any reason—no questions asked. That blanket discretion to peremptorily strike prospective jurors for any reason can clash with the dictates of the Equal Protection Clause of the Fourteenth Amendment to the United States Constitution. This case arises at the intersection of the peremptory challenge and the Equal Protection Clause.

[Justice Kavanaugh engages in an extensive discussion of statutes and case law that led up to *Batson*.]

Four parts of *Batson* warrant particular emphasis here.

First, the *Batson* Court rejected *Swain*'s insistence that a defendant demonstrate a history of racially discriminatory strikes in order to make out a claim of race discrimination. According to the *Batson* Court, defendants had run into "practical difficulties" in trying to prove that a State had systematically "exercised peremptory challenges to exclude blacks from the jury on account of race." * * * In addition to that practical point, the Court stressed a basic equal protection point: In the eyes of the Constitution, one racially discriminatory peremptory strike is one too many. For those reasons, the *Batson* Court held that a criminal defendant could show "purposeful discrimination in selection of the petit jury solely on evidence concerning the prosecutor's exercise of peremptory challenges at the defendant's trial."

Second, the *Batson* Court rejected *Swain's* statement that a prosecutor could strike a black juror based on an assumption or belief that the black juror would favor a black defendant. In some of the most critical sentences in the *Batson* opinion, the Court emphasized that a prosecutor may not rebut a claim of discrimination "by stating merely that he challenged jurors of the defendant's race on the assumption—or his intuitive judgment—that they would be partial to the defendant because of their shared race." * * * In his concurrence, Justice Thurgood Marshall drove the point home: "Exclusion of blacks from a jury, solely because of race, can no more be justified by a belief that blacks are less likely than whites to consider fairly or sympathetically the State's case against a black defendant than it can be justified by the notion that blacks lack the intelligence, experience, or moral integrity to be entrusted with that role."

Third, the *Batson* Court did not accept the argument that race-based peremptories should be permissible because black, white, Asian, and Hispanic defendants and jurors were all "equally" subject to race-based discrimination. The Court stated that each removal of an individual juror because of his or her race is a constitutional violation. Discrimination against one defendant or juror on account of race is not remedied or cured by discrimination against other defendants or jurors on account of race. As the Court later explained: "It is axiomatic that racial classifications do not become legitimate on the assumption that all persons suffer them in equal degree."

Fourth, the *Batson* Court did not accept the argument that race-based peremptories are permissible because both the prosecution and defense could employ them in any individual case and in essence balance things out. Under the Equal Protection Clause, the Court stressed, even a single instance of race discrimination against a prospective juror is impermissible. Moreover, in criminal cases involving black defendants, the both-sides-can-do-it argument overlooks the percentage of the United States population that is black (about 12 percent) and the cold reality of jury selection in most jurisdictions. Because blacks are a minority in most jurisdictions, prosecutors often have more peremptory strikes than there are black prospective jurors on a particular panel. In the pre-*Batson* era, therefore, allowing each side in a case involving a black defendant to strike prospective jurors on the basis of race meant that a prosecutor could eliminate all of the black jurors, but a black defendant could not eliminate all of the white jurors. So in the real world of criminal trials against black defendants, both history and math tell us that a system of race-based peremptories does not treat black defendants and black prospective jurors equally with prosecutors and white prospective jurors.

B

Equal justice under law requires a criminal trial free of racial discrimination in the jury selection process. Enforcing that constitutional principle, *Batson* ended the widespread practice in which prosecutors could (and often would) routinely strike all black prospective jurors in cases involving black defendants. * * *

Of particular relevance here, *Batson's* holding raised several important evidentiary and procedural issues, three of which we underscore.

First, what factors does the trial judge consider in evaluating whether racial discrimination occurred? Our precedents allow criminal defendants raising *Batson* challenges to present a variety of evidence to support a claim that a prosecutor's peremptory strikes were made on the basis of race. For example, defendants may present:

- statistical evidence about the prosecutor's use of peremptory strikes against black prospective jurors as compared to white prospective jurors in the case;

- evidence of a prosecutor's disparate questioning and investigation of black and white prospective jurors in the case;

- side-by-side comparisons of black prospective jurors who were struck and white prospective jurors who were not struck in the case;

- a prosecutor's misrepresentations of the record when defending the strikes during the *Batson* hearing;

- relevant history of the State's peremptory strikes in past cases; or

- other relevant circumstances that bear upon the issue of racial discrimination.

Second, who enforces *Batson*? As the *Batson* Court itself recognized, the job of enforcing *Batson* rests first and foremost with trial judges. * * * [O]nce a prima facie case of racial discrimination has been established, the prosecutor must provide race-neutral reasons for the strikes. The trial court must consider the prosecutor's race-neutral explanations in light of all of the relevant facts and circumstances, and in light of the arguments of the parties. The trial judge's assessment of the prosecutor's credibility is often important. The Court has explained that "the best evidence of discriminatory intent often will be the demeanor of the attorney who exercises the challenge." * * * The trial judge must determine whether the prosecutor's proffered reasons are the actual reasons, or whether the proffered reasons are pretextual and the prosecutor instead exercised peremptory strikes on the basis of race. The ultimate inquiry is whether the State was "motivated in substantial part by discriminatory intent."

Third, what is the role of appellate review? An appeals court looks at the same factors as the trial judge, but is necessarily doing so on a paper record. "Since the trial judge's findings in the context under consideration here largely will turn on evaluation of credibility, a reviewing court ordinarily should give those findings great deference." *Batson*, 476 U. S., at 98, n. 21. The Court has described the appellate standard of review of the trial court's factual determinations in a *Batson* hearing as "highly deferential." * * *

III

In accord with the principles set forth in *Batson*, we now address Flowers' case. * * * The question for this Court is whether the Mississippi trial court clearly erred in concluding that the State was not "motivated in substantial part by discriminatory intent" when exercising peremptory strikes at Flowers' sixth trial. Because this case arises on direct review, we owe no deference to the Mississippi Supreme Court, as distinct from deference to the Mississippi trial court.

Four categories of evidence loom large in assessing the Batson issue in Flowers' case: (1) the history from Flowers' six trials, (2) the prosecutor's striking of five of six black prospective jurors at the sixth trial, (3) the prosecutor's dramatically disparate questioning of black and white prospective jurors at the sixth trial, and (4) the prosecutor's proffered reasons for striking one black juror (Carolyn Wright) while allowing other similarly situated white jurors to serve on the jury at the sixth trial. We address each in turn.

A

First, we consider the relevant history of the case. Recall that in *Swain*, the Court held that a defendant may prove racial discrimination by establishing a historical pattern of racial exclusion of jurors in the jurisdiction in question. Indeed, under *Swain*, that was the only way that a defendant could make out a claim that the State discriminated on the basis of race in the use of peremptory challenges. * * * *Batson* lowered the evidentiary burden for defendants to contest prosecutors' use of peremptory strikes and made clear that demonstrating a history of discriminatory strikes in past cases was not necessary. In doing so, however, *Batson* did not preclude defendants from still using the same kinds of historical evidence that *Swain* had allowed defendants to use to support a claim of racial discrimination. Most importantly for present purposes, after *Batson*, the trial judge may still consider historical evidence of the State's discriminatory peremptory strikes from past trials in the jurisdiction, as *Swain* had allowed. * * *

Here, our review of the history of the prosecutor's peremptory strikes in Flowers' first four trials strongly supports the conclusion that his use of peremptory strikes in Flowers' sixth trial was motivated in substantial part by discriminatory intent. (Recall that there is no record evidence from the fifth trial regarding the race of the prospective jurors.)

The numbers speak loudly. Over the course of the first four trials, there were 36 black prospective jurors against whom the State could have exercised a peremptory strike. The State tried to strike all 36. The State used its available peremptory strikes to attempt to strike every single black prospective juror that it could have struck. * * *

* * *

* * * The State appeared to proceed as if *Batson* had never been decided. The State's relentless, determined effort to rid the jury of black individuals strongly suggests that the State wanted to try Flowers before a jury with as few black jurors as possible, and ideally before an all-white jury. The trial judge was aware of the history. But the judge did not sufficiently account for the history when considering Flowers' *Batson* claim.

The State's actions in the first four trials necessarily inform our assessment of the State's intent going into Flowers' sixth trial. We cannot ignore that history. We cannot take that history out of the case.

B

We turn now to the State's strikes of five of the six black prospective jurors at Flowers' sixth trial, the trial at issue here. As *Batson* noted, a " 'pattern' of strikes against black jurors included in the particular venire might give rise to an inference of discrimination."

* * * At trial, 26 prospective jurors were presented to potentially serve on the jury. Six of the prospective jurors were black. The State accepted one black prospective juror—Alexander Robinson. The State struck the other five black prospective jurors—Carolyn Wright, Tashia Cunningham, Edith Burnside, Flancie Jones, and Dianne Copper. The resulting jury consisted of 11 white jurors and 1 black juror.

The State's use of peremptory strikes in Flowers' sixth trial followed the same pattern as the first four trials, with one modest exception: It is true that the State accepted one black juror for Flowers' sixth trial. But especially given the history of the case, that fact alone cannot insulate the State from a *Batson* challenge. In *Miller-El II*, this Court skeptically viewed the State's decision to accept one black juror, explaining that a prosecutor might do so in an attempt "to obscure the otherwise consistent pattern of opposition to" seating black jurors. The overall record of this case suggests that the same tactic may have been employed here. In light of all of the circumstances here, the State's decision to strike five of the six black prospective jurors is further evidence suggesting that the State was motivated in substantial part by discriminatory intent.

C

We next consider the State's dramatically disparate questioning of black and white prospective jurors in the jury selection process for Flowers' sixth trial. As *Batson* explained, "the prosecutor's questions and statements during voir dire examination and in exercising his challenges may support or refute an inference of discriminatory purpose."

The questioning process occurred through an initial group voir dire and then more in-depth follow-up questioning by the prosecutor and defense counsel of individual prospective jurors. The State asked the five black prospective jurors who were struck a total of 145 questions. By contrast, the State asked the 11 seated white jurors a total of 12 questions. On average, therefore, the State asked 29 questions to each struck black prospective juror. The State asked an average of one question to each seated white juror.

One can slice and dice the statistics and come up with all sorts of ways to compare the State's questioning of excluded black jurors with the State's questioning of the accepted white jurors. But any meaningful comparison yields the same basic assessment: The State spent far more time questioning the black prospective jurors than the accepted white jurors.

The State acknowledges, as it must under our precedents, that disparate questioning can be probative of discriminatory intent. * * *

But the State here argues that it questioned black and white prospective jurors differently only because of differences in the jurors' characteristics. The record refutes that explanation.

For example, Dianne Copper was a black prospective juror who was struck. The State asked her 18 follow-up questions about her relationships with Flowers' family and with witnesses in the case. Pamela Chesteen was a white juror whom the State accepted for the jury. Although the State asked questions of Chesteen during group voir dire, the State asked her no individual follow-up questions about her relationships with Flowers' family, even though the State was aware that Chesteen knew several members of Flowers' family. Similarly, the State asked no individual follow-up questions to four other white prospective jurors who, like Dianne Copper, had relationships with defense witnesses, even though the State was aware of those relationships. * * *

Likewise, the State conducted disparate investigations of certain prospective jurors. Tashia Cunningham, who is black, stated that she worked with Flowers' sister, but that the two did not work closely together. To try to disprove that statement, the State summoned a witness to challenge Cunningham's testimony. The State apparently did not conduct similar investigations of white prospective jurors.

It is certainly reasonable for the State to ask follow-up questions or to investigate the relationships of jurors to the victims, potential witnesses, and the like. But white prospective jurors who were acquainted with the Flowers' family or defense witnesses were not questioned extensively by the State or investigated. White prospective jurors who admitted that they or a relative had been convicted of a crime were accepted without apparent further inquiry by the State. The difference in the State's approaches to black and white prospective jurors was stark.

Why did the State ask so many more questions—and conduct more vigorous inquiry—of black prospective jurors than it did of white prospective jurors? No one can know for certain. But this Court's cases explain that disparate questioning and investigation of prospective jurors on the basis of race can arm a prosecutor with seemingly race-neutral reasons to strike the prospective jurors of a particular race. In other words, by asking a lot of questions of the black prospective jurors or conducting additional inquiry into their backgrounds, a prosecutor can try to find some pretextual reason—any reason—that the prosecutor can later articulate to justify what is in reality a racially motivated strike. And by not doing the same for white prospective jurors, by not asking white prospective jurors those same questions, the prosecutor can try to distort the record so as to thereby avoid being accused of treating black and white jurors differently. Disparity in questioning and investigation can produce a record that says little about white prospective jurors and is therefore resistant to characteristic-by-characteristic comparisons of struck black prospective jurors and seated white jurors. Prosecutors can decline to seek what they do not want to find about white prospective jurors.

A court confronting that kind of pattern cannot ignore it. The lopsidedness of the prosecutor's questioning and inquiry can itself be evidence of the prosecutor's objective as much as it is of the actual qualifications of the black and white prospective jurors who are struck or seated. The prosecutor's dramatically disparate questioning of black and white prospective jurors—at least if it rises to a certain level of disparity— can supply a clue that the prosecutor may have been seeking to paper the record and disguise a discriminatory intent.

To be clear, disparate questioning or investigation alone does not constitute a *Batson* violation. The disparate questioning or investigation of black and white prospective jurors may reflect ordinary race-neutral considerations. But the disparate questioning or investigation can also, along with other evidence, inform the trial court's evaluation of whether discrimination occurred.

Here, along with the historical evidence we described above from the earlier trials, as well as the State's striking of five of six black prospective jurors at the sixth trial, the dramatically disparate questioning and investigation of black prospective jurors and white prospective jurors at the sixth trial strongly suggests that the State was motivated in substantial part by a discriminatory intent. * * *

D

Finally, in combination with the other facts and circumstances in this case, the record of jury selection at the sixth trial shows that the peremptory strike of at least one of the black prospective jurors (Carolyn Wright) was motivated in substantial part by discriminatory intent. As this Court has stated, the Constitution forbids striking even a single prospective juror for a discriminatory purpose.

Comparing prospective jurors who were struck and not struck can be an important step in determining whether a *Batson* violation occurred. The comparison can suggest that the prosecutor's proffered explanations for striking black prospective jurors were a pretext for discrimination. * * * Although a defendant ordinarily will try to identify a similar white prospective juror whom the State did not strike, a defendant is not required to identify an identical white juror for the side-by-side comparison to be suggestive of discriminatory intent.

In this case, Carolyn Wright was a black prospective juror who said she was strongly in favor of the death penalty as a general matter. And she had a family member who was a prison security guard. Yet the State exercised a peremptory strike against Wright. The State said it struck Wright in part because she knew several defense witnesses and had worked at Wal-Mart where Flowers' father also worked.

Winona is a small town. Wright had some sort of connection to 34 people involved in Flowers' case, both on the prosecution witness side and the defense witness side. But three white prospective jurors—Pamela Chesteen, Harold Waller, and Bobby Lester—also knew many individuals involved in the case. Chesteen knew 31 people, Waller knew 18 people, and Lester knew 27 people. Yet * * * the State did not ask Chesteen, Waller, and Lester individual follow-up questions about their connections to witnesses. That is a telling statistic. If the State were concerned about prospective jurors' connections to witnesses in the case, the State presumably would have used individual questioning to ask those potential white jurors whether they could remain impartial despite their relationships. A State's failure to engage in any meaningful voir dire examination on a subject the State alleges it is concerned about is evidence suggesting that the explanation is a sham and a pretext for discrimination.

Payment Type

Visa   XXXXXXXXXXXX3233

21-Aug-2020 $23.32

Total Payments   **$23.32**

Order Total $23.32

Outstanding $0.00

Questions about your order? For fastest service, refer to your Box Number (see top of page) when contacting the bookstore.
Details about our Refund and Exchange policies are on the bookstore's website. We look forward to serving you again soon.

SHOP ONLINE with your bookstore website. We are the headquarters for textbooks, college gear, school supplies and gifts. Be sure to sign up for emails to find out about special offers.

Customer Copy

114174976-2

Box No **1922-2-F20-SHP**

Order No	114174976-2
Placed On	13-Aug-2020
Invoice	21-Aug-2020

Sold To

Ann Reynolds
PO Box 97
Pitman, NJ - 08071, US
Phone: (610)908-6935
E-Mail: ar1655@georgetown.edu

Ship To

Ann Reynolds
2 M Street NE,901
Washington, DC - 20002, US
Phone: (610)908-6935
Tracking 1ZX047F4139053883

Next Business Day Saver $19.00

Ship from

Georgetown University Law Center Bookstore
550 1st St NW
Washington, DC - 20001, US
E-Mail:sm8199@bncollege.com
Website
http://georgetown.bncollege.com
Phone: **(202)662-9676**

1 Your Order

Item	Description	Price	QTY	Discount	Total
1	AMERICAN CRIM.PROC.:CS.+COMM.-20 SUPP., New	$22.00	1	$0.00	$22.00

Sub-total		$22.00
+ Shipping		$0.00
+ Tax		$1.32
Total Amount	**1 Item(s)**	**$23.32**

2 Processed Payments

Both Carolyn Wright and Archie Flowers, who is the defendant's father, had worked at the local Wal-Mart. But there was no evidence that they worked together or were close in any way. Importantly, the State did not ask individual follow-up questions to determine the nature of their relationship. And during group questioning, Wright said she did not know whether Flowers' father still worked at Wal-Mart, which supports an inference that Wright and Flowers did not have a close working relationship. And white prospective jurors also had relationships with members of Flowers' family. Indeed, white prospective juror Pamela Chesteen stated that she had provided service to Flowers' family members at the bank and that she knew several members of the Flowers family. Likewise, white prospective juror Bobby Lester worked at the same bank and also encountered Flowers' family members. Although Chesteen and Lester were questioned during group voir dire, the State did not ask Chesteen or Lester individual follow-up questions in order to explore the depth of their relationships with Flowers' family. And instead of striking those jurors, the State accepted them for the jury. To be sure, both Chesteen and Lester were later struck by the defense. But the State's acceptance of Chesteen and Lester necessarily informs our assessment of the State's intent in striking similarly situated black prospective jurors such as Wright.

The State also noted that Wright had once been sued by Tardy Furniture for collection of a debt 13 years earlier. Wright said that the debt was paid off and that it would not affect her evaluation of the case. The victims in this case worked at Tardy Furniture. But the State did not explain how Wright's 13-year-old, paid-off debt to Tardy Furniture could affect her ability to serve impartially as a juror in this quadruple murder case. * * * In any event, the State did not purport to rely on that reason alone as the basis for the Wright strike, and the State in this Court does not rely on that reason alone in defending the Wright strike.

The State also explained that it exercised a peremptory strike against Wright because she had worked with one of Flowers' sisters. That was incorrect. The trial judge immediately stated as much. But * * * [w]hen a prosecutor misstates the record in explaining a strike, that misstatement can be another clue showing discriminatory intent.

That incorrect statement was not the only one made by the prosecutor. The State made apparently incorrect statements to justify the strikes of black prospective jurors Tashia Cunningham, Edith Burnside, and Flancie Jones. The State contradicted Cunningham's earlier statement that she had only a working relationship with Flowers' sister by inaccurately asserting that Cunningham and Flowers' sister were close friends. The State asserted that Burnside had tried to cover up a Tardy Furniture suit. She had not. And the State explained that it struck Jones in part because Jones was Flowers' aunt. That, too, was not true. The State's pattern of factually inaccurate statements about black prospective jurors suggests that the State intended to keep black prospective jurors off the jury.

To be sure, the back and forth of a *Batson* hearing can be hurried, and prosecutors can make mistakes when providing explanations. That is entirely understandable, and mistaken explanations should not be confused with racial discrimination. But when considered with other evidence of discrimination, a series of factually inaccurate explanations for striking black prospective jurors can be telling. So it is here.

The side-by-side comparison of Wright to white prospective jurors whom the State accepted for the jury cannot be considered in isolation in this case. In a different context, the Wright strike might be deemed permissible. But we must examine the whole picture. Our disagreement with the Mississippi courts * * * largely comes down to whether we look at the Wright strike in isolation or instead look at the Wright strike in the context of all the facts and circumstances. Our precedents require that we do the latter. * * * As we see it, the overall context here requires skepticism of the State's strike of Carolyn Wright. We must examine the Wright strike in light of the history of the State's use of peremptory strikes in the prior trials, the State's decision to strike five out of six black prospective jurors at Flowers' sixth trial, and the State's vastly disparate questioning of black and white prospective jurors during jury selection at the sixth trial. We cannot just look away. Nor can we focus on the Wright strike in isolation. In light of all the facts and circumstances, we conclude that the trial court clearly erred in ruling that the State's peremptory strike of Wright was not motivated in substantial part by discriminatory intent.

* * *

In sum, the State's pattern of striking black prospective jurors persisted from Flowers' first trial through Flowers' sixth trial. In the six trials combined, the State struck 41 of the 42 black prospective jurors it could have struck. At the sixth trial, the State struck five of six. At the sixth trial, moreover, the State engaged in dramatically disparate questioning of black and white prospective jurors. And it engaged in disparate treatment of black and white prospective jurors, in particular by striking black prospective juror Carolyn Wright. To reiterate, we need not and do not decide that any one of those four facts alone would require reversal. All that we need to decide, and all that we do decide, is that all of the relevant facts and circumstances taken together establish that the trial court at Flowers' sixth trial committed clear error in concluding that the State's peremptory strike of black prospective juror Carolyn Wright was not motivated in substantial part by discriminatory intent. In reaching that conclusion, we break no new legal ground. We simply enforce and reinforce Batson by applying it to the extraordinary facts of this case. We reverse the judgment of the Supreme Court of Mississippi, and we remand the case for further proceedings not inconsistent with this opinion. It is so ordered.

JUSTICE ALITO, concurring.

As the Court takes pains to note, this is a highly unusual case. Indeed, it is likely one of a kind. In 1996, four defenseless victims, three white and one black, were slaughtered in a furniture store in a small town in Montgomery County, Mississippi, a jurisdiction with fewer than 11,000 inhabitants. One of the victims was the owner of the store, which was widely frequented by residents of the community. The person prosecuted for this crime, petitioner Curtis Flowers, an African-American, comes from a local family whose members make up a gospel group and have many community ties.

By the time jury selection began in the case now before us, petitioner had already been tried five times for committing that heinous and inflammatory crime. Three times, petitioner was convicted and sentenced to death, but all three convictions were reversed by the State Supreme Court. Twice, the jurors could not reach a unanimous verdict. In all of the five prior trials, the State was represented by the same prosecutor, and as the Court recounts, many of those trials were marred by racial discrimination in the selection of jurors and prosecutorial misconduct. Nevertheless, the prosecution at the sixth trial was led by the same prosecutor, and the case was tried in Montgomery County where, it appears, a high concurring percentage of the potential jurors have significant connections to either petitioner, one or more of the victims, or both.

These connections and the community's familiarity with the case were bound to complicate a trial judge's task in trying to determine whether the prosecutor's asserted reason for striking a potential juror was a pretext for racial discrimination, and that is just what occurred. Petitioner argues that the prosecution improperly struck five black jurors, but for each of the five, the prosecutor gave one or more reasons that were not only facially legitimate but were of a nature that would be of concern to a great many attorneys. If another prosecutor in another case in a larger jurisdiction gave any of these reasons for exercising a peremptory challenge and the trial judge credited that explanation, an appellate court would probably have little difficulty affirming that finding. And that result, in all likelihood, would not change based on factors that are exceedingly difficult to assess, such as the number of voir dire questions the prosecutor asked different members of the venire.

But this is not an ordinary case, and the jury selection process cannot be analyzed as if it were. In light of all that had gone before, it was risky for the case to be tried once again by the same prosecutor in Montgomery

County. Were it not for the unique combinations of circumstances present here, I would have no trouble affirming the decision of the Supreme Court of Mississippi, which conscientiously applied the legal standards applicable in less unusual cases. But viewing the totality of the circumstances present here, I agree with the Court that petitioner's capital conviction cannot stand.

JUSTICE THOMAS, with whom JUSTICE GORSUCH joins as to Parts I, II, and III, dissenting.

On a summer morning in July 1996 in Winona, Mississippi, 16-year-old Derrick "Bobo" Stewart arrived for the second day of his first job. He and Robert Golden had been hired by the Tardy Furniture store to replace petitioner Curtis Flowers, who had been fired a few days prior and had his paycheck docked for damaging store property and failing to show up for work. Another employee, Sam Jones, Jr., planned to teach Stewart and Golden how to properly load furniture.

On Jones' arrival, he found a bloodbath. Store owner Bertha Tardy and bookkeeper Carmen Rigby had each been murdered with a single gunshot to the head. Golden had been murdered with two gunshots to the head, one at very close range. And Stewart had been shot, execution style, in the back of his head. When Jones entered the store, Stewart was fighting for every breath, blood pouring over his face. He died a week later.

On the morning of the murders, a .380-caliber pistol was reported stolen from the car of Flowers' uncle, and a witness saw Flowers by that car before the shootings. Officers recovered .380-caliber bullets at Tardy Furniture and matched them to bullets fired by the stolen pistol. Gunshot residue was found on Flowers' hand a few hours after. A bloody footprint found at the scene matched both the size of Flowers' shoes and the shoe style that he was seen wearing on the morning of the murders. Multiple witnesses placed Flowers near Tardy Furniture that morning, and Flowers provided inconsistent accounts of his whereabouts. Several hundred dollars were missing from the store's cash drawer, and $235 was found hidden in Flowers' headboard after the murders.

In the 2010 trial at issue here, Flowers was convicted of four counts of murder and sentenced to death. Applying heightened scrutiny, the state courts found that the evidence was more than sufficient to convict Flowers, that he was tried by an impartial jury, and that the State did not engage in purposeful race discrimination in jury selection in violation of the Equal Protection Clause.

The Court today does not dispute that the evidence was sufficient to convict Flowers or that he was tried by an impartial jury. Instead, the Court vacates Flowers' convictions on the ground that the state courts clearly erred in finding that the State did not discriminate based on race when it struck Carolyn Wright from the jury.

The only clear errors in this case are committed by today's majority. Confirming that we never should have taken this case, the Court almost entirely ignores—and certainly does not refute—the race-neutral reasons given by the State for striking Wright and four other black prospective jurors. Two of these prospective jurors knew Flowers' family and had been sued by Tardy Furniture—the family business of one of the victims and also of one of the trial witnesses. One refused to consider the death penalty and apparently lied about working side-by-side with Flowers' sister. One was related to Flowers and lied about her opinion of the death penalty to try to get out of jury duty. And one said that because she worked with two of Flowers' family members, she might favor him and would not consider only the evidence presented. The state courts' findings that these strikes were not based on race are the opposite of clearly erroneous; they are clearly correct. The Court attempts to overcome the evident race neutrality of jury selection in this trial by pointing to a supposed history of race discrimination in previous trials. But 49 of the State's 50 peremptory strikes in Flowers' previous trials were race neutral. The remaining strike occurred 20 years ago in a trial involving only one of Flowers' crimes and was never subject to appellate review; the majority offers no plausible connection between that strike and Wright's.

Today's decision distorts the record of this case, eviscerates our standard of review, and vacates four murder convictions because the State struck a juror who would have been stricken by any competent attorney. I dissent.

I.

[Justice Thomas argues that the Court should not have taken the case because, among other reasons, it is so fact-specific.]

II.

[Justice Thomas engages in an extensive review of the record and concludes that the prosecutor's strikes were race-neutral.]

III.

[Justice Thomas disagrees with the majority's conclusion that the prosecution's strikes in the previous trials evidenced discrimination.]

IV.

Much of the Court's opinion is a paean to *Batson v. Kentucky*, which requires that a duly convicted criminal go free because a juror was arguably deprived of his right to serve on the jury. That rule was suspect when it was announced, and I am even less confident of it today. *Batson* has led the Court to disregard Article III's limitations on standing by giving a windfall to a convicted criminal who, even under *Batson's* logic, suffered no injury. It has forced equal protection principles onto a procedure designed to give parties absolute discretion in making individual strikes. And it has blinded the Court to the reality that racial prejudice exists and can affect the fairness of trials.

A

In *Batson,* this Court held that the Equal Protection Clause prohibits the State from "challeng[ing] potential jurors solely on account of their race or on the assumption that black jurors as a group will be unable impartially to consider the State's case." "[I]ndividual jurors subjected to racial exclusion have the legal right to bring suit on their own behalf." *Powers v. Ohio*, 499 U. S. 400, 414 (1991). * * * Flowers, however, was not the excluded juror. * * *

Flowers should not have standing to assert the excluded juror's claim. He does not dispute that the jury that convicted him was impartial, and as the Court has said many times, " '[d]efendants are not entitled to a jury of any particular composition.' " *Holland v. Illinois*, 493 U. S. 474, 483 (1990). He therefore suffered no legally cognizable injury. The only other plausible reason a defendant could suffer an injury from a *Batson* violation is if the Court thinks that he has a better chance of winning if more members of his race are on the jury. But that thinking relies on the very assumption that *Batson* rejects: that jurors might be partial to the defendant because of their shared race. * * *

Today, the Court holds that Carolyn Wright was denied equal protection by being excluded from jury service. But she is not the person challenging Flowers' convictions (she would lack standing to do so), and I do not understand how Flowers can have standing to assert her claim. * * *

In *Powers*, the Court relied on the doctrine of third-party standing. As an initial matter, I doubt "whether a party who has no personal constitutional right at stake in a case should ever be allowed to litigate the constitutional rights of others.

Even accepting the notion of third-party standing, it is hard to see how it could be satisfied in *Batson* cases. The Court's precedents require that a litigant asserting another's rights have suffered an " 'injury in fact' " and have "a close relation" to the third party. As shown, Flowers suffered no injury in fact under the Court's precedents. Moreover, in the ordinary case, the defendant has no relation whatsoever to the struck jurors. * * *

In *Powers*, the Court concluded that defendants and struck jurors share a "common interest." But like most defendants, Flowers' interest is in avoiding prison (or execution). A struck juror, by contrast, is unlikely to feel better about being excluded from jury service simply because a convicted criminal may go free. * * *

Our remedy for *Batson* violations proves the point. The convicted criminal, who suffered no injury, gets his conviction vacated. And even if the struck juror suffered a cognizable injury, that injury certainly is not redressed by undoing the valid conviction of another. Under Article III, Flowers should not have standing.

B

The more fundamental problem is *Batson* itself. The entire line of cases following *Batson* is a misguided effort to remedy a general societal wrong by using the Constitution to regulate the traditionally discretionary exercise of peremptory challenges. "[R]ather than helping to ensure the fairness of criminal trials," *Batson* serves only to undercut that fairness by emphasizing the rights of excluded jurors at the expense of the traditional protections accorded criminal defendants of all races." I would return to our pre-*Batson* understanding—that race matters in the courtroom—and thereby return to litigants one of the most important tools to combat prejudice in their cases.

1

In *Strauder v. West Virginia*, 100 U. S. 303 (1880), the Court invalidated a state law that prohibited blacks from serving on juries. In doing so, we recognized that the racial composition of a jury could affect the outcome of a criminal case. * * * Thus, we understood that allowing the defendant an opportunity to secure representation of the defendant's race on the jury may help to overcome racial bias and provide the defendant with a better chance of having a fair trial.

In *Swain v. Alabama*, 380 U. S. 202 (1965), the Court held that individual peremptory strikes could not give rise to an equal protection challenge. *Swain* followed *Strauder* in assuming that race—like other factors that are generally unsuitable for the government to use in making classifications—can be considered in peremptory strikes * * * . That is because the peremptory challenge is one of the most important of the rights secured to the accused. * * * The strike both eliminates extremes of partiality on both sides and assures the parties that the jurors before whom they try the case will decide on the basis of the evidence placed before them, and not otherwise. * * *

Then, in a departure from the previous century of jurisprudence, the Court moved its focus from the protections accorded the defendant to the perceptions of a hypothetical struck juror. * * *

The Court's opinion in *Batson* equated a law categorically excluding a class of people from jury service with the use of discretionary peremptory strikes to remove members of that class * * * .

* * *

Batson rejects the premise that peremptory strikes can be exercised on the basis of generalizations and demands instead an assessment of individual qualifications. The Court's *Batson* jurisprudence seems to conceive of jury selection more as a project for affirming "the dignity of persons" than as a process for providing a jury that is, including in the parties' view, fairer.

2

Batson's focus on individual jurors' rights is wholly contrary to the rationale underlying peremptory challenges. And the application of equal protection analysis to individual strikes has produced distortions in our jurisprudence that are symptomatic of its poor fit, both as a matter of common sense and the protections traditionally accorded litigants.

The Court did not apply equal protection principles to individual peremptory strikes until more than 100 years after the Fourteenth Amendment was ratified. Once it did, it quickly extended *Batson* to civil actions, strikes by criminal defendants, and strikes based on sex. But even now, we do not apply generally applicable equal protection principles to peremptory strikes. For example, our precedents do not apply "strict scrutiny" to race-based peremptory strikes. And we apply "the same protection against sex discrimination as race discrimination" in reviewing peremptory strikes, even though sex is subject to "heightened" rather than "strict" scrutiny under our precedents. Finally, we have not subjected all peremptory strikes to "rational basis" review, which normally applies absent a protected characteristic. Thus, the Court's own jurisprudence seems to recognize that its equal protection principles do not naturally apply to individual, discretionary strikes.

Now that we have followed *Batson* to its logical conclusion and applied it to race- and sex-based strikes without regard to the race or sex of the defendant, it is impossible to exercise a peremptory strike that cannot be challenged by the opposing party, thereby requiring a "neutral" explanation for the strike. But requiring an explanation is inconsistent with the very nature of peremptory strikes. * * * The strike must "be exercised with full freedom, or it fails of its full purpose." Because the strike may be exercised on as little as the "sudden impressions and unaccountable prejudices we are apt to conceive upon the bare looks and gestures of another," id., at 376, reasoned explanation is often impossible. And where scrutiny of individual strikes is permitted, the strike is no longer peremptory, each and every challenge being open to examination.

In sum, as other Members of this Court have recognized, *Batson* charted the course for eliminating peremptory strikes. See, e.g., Rice v. Collins, 546 U. S. 333, 344 (2006) (BREYER, J., concurring); *Batson*, supra, at 107–108 (Marshall, J., concurring). Although those Justices welcomed the prospect, I do not. The peremptory system "has always been held essential to the fairness of trial by jury." *Lewis*, supra, at 376. And the basic premise of *Strauder*—that a juror's racial prejudices can make a trial less fair—has not become obsolete. The racial composition of a jury matters because racial biases, sympathies, and prejudices still exist. * * * The Court knows these prejudices exist. Why else would it * * * say here that "Flowers is black" and the "prosecutor is white"? Yet the Court continues to apply a line of cases that prevents, among other things, black defendants from striking potentially hostile white jurors. I remain certain that black criminal defendants will rue the day that this Court ventured down this road that inexorably will lead to the elimination of peremptory strikes.

Instead of focusing on the possibility that a juror will misperceive a peremptory strike as threatening his dignity, I would return the Court's focus to the fairness of trials for the defendant whose liberty is at stake and to the People who seek justice under the law.

* * *

If the Court's opinion today has a redeeming quality, it is this: The State is perfectly free to convict Curtis Flowers again. Otherwise, the opinion distorts our legal standards, ignores the record, and reflects utter disrespect for the careful analysis of the Mississippi courts. Any competent prosecutor would have exercised the same strikes as the State did in this trial. And although the Court's opinion might boost its self-esteem, it also needlessly prolongs the suffering of four victims' families. I respectfully dissent.

VII. THE RIGHT TO EFFECTIVE ASSISTANCE OF COUNSEL

A. INEFFECTIVENESS AND PREJUDICE

2. Scope of the Right to Effective Assistance of Counsel

First Appeal of Right: Evitts v. Lucey and Roe v. Flores-Ortega

Page 1406. Insert at the end of the note on *Roe v. Flores-Ortega*:

Justice Sotomayor wrote for the Court in *Garza v. Idaho*, 139 S.Ct. 738 (2019), as it held "that the presumption of prejudice recognized in *Flores-Ortega* applies regardless of whether the defendant has signed an appeal waiver." Garza pleaded guilty to two counts in an Idaho state court, signed appeal waivers, and was sentenced to prison. After sentencing he told his trial counsel he wanted to appeal and repeated his request that counsel file a notice of appeal several times. Counsel failed to do so, informing Garza that an appeal was "problematic" because he had waived his right to appeal. Garza filed a post-conviction petition in state court urging ineffective assistance of counsel. Despite the fact that 8 of 10 federal courts of appeal had held that *Flores-Ortega* applies regardless of whether the defendant has signed an appeal waiver, the Idaho Supreme Court found no prejudice because of the waiver.

Justice Sotomayor explained appeal waivers as follows:

> We begin with the term "appeal waivers." While the term is useful shorthand for clauses like those in Garza's plea agreements, it can misleadingly suggest a monolithic end to all appellate rights. In fact, however, no appeal waiver serves as an absolute bar to all appellate claims. As courts widely agree, a valid and enforceable appeal waiver only precludes challenges that fall within its scope. That an appeal waiver does not bar claims outside its scope follows from the fact that, "[a]lthough the analogy may not hold in all respects, plea bargains are essentially contracts." *Puckett v. United States*, 556 U. S. 129, 137 (2009).

> As with any type of contract, the language of appeal waivers can vary widely, with some waiver clauses leaving many types of claims unwaived. Additionally, even a waived appellate claim can still go forward if the prosecution forfeits or waives the waiver. Accordingly, a defendant who has signed an appeal waiver does not, in directing counsel to file a notice of appeal, necessarily undertake a quixotic or frivolous quest.

> Separately, all jurisdictions appear to treat at least some claims as unwaiveable. Most fundamentally, courts agree that defendants retain the right to challenge whether the waiver itself is valid and enforceable—for example, on the grounds that it was unknowing or involuntary. Consequently, while signing an appeal waiver means giving up some, many, or even most appellate claims, some claims nevertheless remain.

Justice Sotomayor concluded that filing a notice of appeal is a ministerial burden on counsel given that the claims to be pursued may be vague when the notice is filed, so that great specificity is not required. She rejected Idaho's argument that Garza's counsel was entitled to make a strategic decision:

> Idaho maintains that the risk of breaching the defendant's plea agreement renders counsel's choice to override the defendant's instructions a strategic one. See *Strickland,* 466 U. S., at 690–691 ("[S]trategic choices made after thorough investigation of law and facts relevant to plausible options are virtually unchallengeable . . . "). That is not so. While we do not address what constitutes a defendant's breach of an appeal waiver or any responsibility counsel may have to discuss the potential consequences of such a breach, it should be clear from the foregoing that simply filing a notice of appeal does not

necessarily breach a plea agreement, given the possibility that the defendant will end up raising claims beyond the waiver's scope. And in any event, the bare decision whether to appeal is ultimately the defendant's, not counsel's, to make. Where, as here, a defendant has expressly requested an appeal, counsel performs deficiently by disregarding the defendant's instructions.

* * *

Flores-Ortega's reasoning shows why an appeal waiver does not complicate this straightforward application. That case, like this one, involves a lawyer who forfeited an appellate proceeding by failing to file a notice of appeal. As the Court explained, given that past precedents call for a presumption of prejudice whenever " 'the accused is denied counsel at a critical stage,' " it makes even greater sense to presume prejudice when counsel's deficiency forfeits an "appellate proceeding altogether." After all, there is no disciplined way to accord any presumption of reliability to judicial proceedings that never took place.

That rationale applies just as well here because * * * Garza retained a right to appeal at least some issues despite the waivers he signed. In other words, Garza had a right to a proceeding, and he was denied that proceeding altogether as a result of counsel's deficient performance.

That Garza surrendered many claims by signing his appeal waivers does not change things. First, this Court has made clear that when deficient counsel causes the loss of an entire proceeding, it will not bend the presumption-of-prejudice rule simply because a particular defendant seems to have had poor prospects. * * *

Second, while the defendant in *Flores-Ortega* did not sign an appeal waiver, he did plead guilty, and—as the Court pointed out—"a guilty plea reduces the scope of potentially appealable issues" on its own. In other words, with regard to the defendant's appellate prospects, *Flores-Ortega* presented at most a difference of degree, not kind, and prescribed a presumption of prejudice regardless of how many appellate claims were foreclosed. We do no different today.

Instead, we reaffirm that, when counsel's constitutionally deficient performance deprives a defendant of an appeal that he otherwise would have taken, the defendant has made out a successful ineffective assistance of counsel claim entitling him to an appeal, with no need for a further showing of his claims' merit, regardless of whether the defendant has signed an appeal waiver.

Justice Sotomayor rejected Idaho's and the United States's (as amicus) argument that the presumption of prejudice did not apply because Garza had no right to appeal at all. "Garza did retain a right to his appeal; he simply had fewer possible claims than some other appellants." She also rejected the United States's argument that Garza should have to show a non-frivolous ground to support an appeal. She explained as follows:

> The more administrable and workable rule, rather, is the one compelled by our precedent: When counsel's deficient performance forfeits an appeal that a defendant otherwise would have taken, the defendant gets a new opportunity to appeal. That is the rule already in use in 8 of the 10 Federal Circuits to have considered the question, and neither Idaho nor its *amici* have pointed us to any evidence that it has proved unmanageable there.

Justice Thomas, joined by Justice Gorsuch and in part by Justice Alito, dissented. He concluded that Garza's counsel acted reasonably:

> Petitioner Gilberto Garza avoided a potential life sentence by negotiating with the State of Idaho for reduced charges and a 10-year sentence. In exchange, Garza waived several constitutional and statutory rights, including "his right to appeal." Despite this express waiver, Garza asked his attorney to challenge on appeal the very sentence for which he had bargained. Garza's counsel quite reasonably declined to file an appeal for that purpose, recognizing that his client had waived this right and that filing an appeal would potentially jeopardize his plea bargain. Yet, the majority finds Garza's counsel constitutionally ineffective, holding that an attorney's performance is *per se* deficient and *per se* prejudicial any time the attorney declines a criminal defendant's request to appeal an issue that the defendant has waived. In effect, this results in a "defendant-always-wins" rule that has no basis in *Roe* v. *Flores-Ortega* (2000), or our other ineffective-assistance precedents, and certainly no basis in the original meaning of the Sixth Amendment.

Justice Thomas argued for a different approach, one that would place a higher burden on a defendant who had executed an appeal waiver:

> In my view, a defendant who has executed an appeal waiver cannot show prejudice arising from his counsel's decision not to appeal unless he (1) identifies claims he would have pursued that were outside the appeal waiver; (2) shows that the plea was involuntary or unknowing; or (3) establishes that the government breached the plea agreement.

He distinguished *Flores-Ortega* as follows:

> The Court purports to follow *Flores-Ortega*, but glosses over the important factual and legal differences between that case and this one. The most obvious difference is also the most crucial: There was no appellate waiver in *Flores-Ortega*. The proximate cause of the

defendant's failure to appeal in that case was his counsel's failure to file one. Not so here. Garza knowingly waived his appeal rights and never expressed a desire to withdraw his plea. It was thus Garza's agreement to waive his appeal rights, not his attorney's actions, that caused the forfeiture of his appeal. Thus, *Flores-Ortega* is inapposite.

Justice Thomas found that Garza failed to show his counsel was deficient and also could not show prejudice:

> The Constitution does not compel attorneys to take irrational means to their client's stated ends when doing so only courts disaster. Garza ultimately faults his plea-stage attorney for failing to put his plea agreements in jeopardy. But I have no doubt that if a similarly situated attorney breached a plea agreement by appealing a waived issue and subjected his client to an increased prison term, that defendant would argue that his counsel was ineffective for filing the appeal. What Garza wants—and what the majority gives him—is a *per se* deficiency rule ensuring that criminal defendants can always blame their plea-stage counsel on collateral review, even where they did not ask counsel to appeal nonwaived claims or breach the plea agreement for the sake of some further (achievable) goal. Declining to file an appeal under these circumstances is reasonable, not deficient.

> As for prejudice, Garza cannot benefit from a presumed-prejudice finding since he cannot establish that his counsel caused the forfeiture of his appeal, as *Flores-Ortega* requires. Garza knowingly and voluntarily bargained away his right to appeal in exchange for a lower sentence. If any prejudice resulted from that decision, it cannot be attributed to his counsel.

In Part III of his opinion (not joined by Justice Alito), Justice Thomas examined the history of the Sixth Amendment, the right to counsel for indigent defendants and the development of the concept of effective assistance of counsel. He examined the *Strickland* standard as well as some per se rules the Court has developed and criticized the way in which the law had developed:

> There are a few problems with these precedents that should cause us to pause before extending them. First, the ineffective-assistance standard apparently originated not in the Sixth Amendment, but in our Due Process Clause jurisprudence. Second, "[t]he Constitution, by its terms, does not mandate any particular remedy for violations of its own provisions." * * * *Strickland* does not explain how the Constitution requires a new trial for violations of any right to counsel.

> [O]ur precedents seek to use the Sixth Amendment right to counsel to achieve an end it is not designed to guarantee. The right to counsel is not an assurance of an error-free trial or even a reliable result. It ensures fairness in a single respect: permitting the accused

to employ the services of an attorney. The structural protections provided in the Sixth Amendment certainly seek to promote reliable criminal proceedings, but there is no substantive right to a particular level of reliability. In assuming otherwise, our ever-growing right-to-counsel precedents directly conflict with the government's legitimate interest in the finality of criminal judgments. I would proceed with far more caution than the Court has traditionally demonstrated in this area.

Justice Thomas then went further and questioned the holding in *Gideon v. Wainwright*. He argued that the historical basis of the Sixth Amendment was to abrogate the laws prohibiting defendants from *retaining* counsel. He argued that there was nothing in the origins of the Sixth Amendment that requires the government to *provide* counsel nor was there anything supporting the notion that there is right to *effective* assistance of counsel.

3. Assessing Counsel's Effectiveness

Page 1416. Add after *Florida v. Nixon*:

Conceding Guilt over a Defendant's Objection: McCoy v. Louisiana

MCCOY V. LOUISIANA
Supreme Court of the United States, 2018.
138 S.Ct. 1500.

JUSTICE GINSBURG delivered the opinion of the Court.

In Florida v. Nixon, 543 U. S. 175 (2004), this Court considered whether the Constitution bars defense counsel from conceding a capital defendant's guilt at trial "when [the] defendant, informed by counsel, neither consents nor objects." In that case, defense counsel had several times explained to the defendant a proposed guilt-phase concession strategy, but the defendant was unresponsive. We held that when counsel confers with the defendant and the defendant remains silent, neither approving nor protesting counsel's proposed concession strategy, "[no] blanket rule demand[s] the defendant's explicit consent" to implementation of that strategy.

In the case now before us, in contrast to *Nixon*, the defendant vociferously insisted that he did not engage in the charged acts and adamantly objected to any admission of guilt. Yet the trial court permitted counsel, at the guilt phase of a capital trial, to tell the jury the defendant "committed three murders. . . . [H]e's guilty." We hold that a defendant has the right to insist that counsel refrain from admitting guilt, even when counsel's experienced-based view is that confessing guilt offers the defendant the best chance to avoid the death penalty. Guaranteeing a defendant the right "to have the *Assistance* of Counsel for *his* defence," the Sixth Amendment so demands. With individual liberty—and, in capital cases, life—at stake, it is the defendant's prerogative, not counsel's, to decide on the objective of his defense: to admit guilt in the hope of gaining mercy at the sentencing stage, or to maintain his innocence, leaving it to the State to prove his guilt beyond a reasonable doubt.

I

On May 5, 2008, Christine and Willie Young and Gregory Colston were shot and killed in the Youngs' home in Bossier City, Louisiana. The three victims were the mother, stepfather, and son of Robert McCoy's estranged wife, Yolanda. Several days later, police arrested McCoy in Idaho. Extradited to Louisiana, McCoy was appointed counsel from the public defender's office. A Bossier Parish grand jury indicted McCoy on three counts of first-degree murder, and the prosecutor gave notice of intent to seek the death penalty. McCoy pleaded not guilty. Throughout the proceedings, he insistently maintained he was out of State at the time of the killings and that corrupt police killed the victims when a drug deal went wrong. At defense counsel's request, a court-appointed sanity commission examined McCoy and found him competent to stand trial.

In December 2009 and January 2010, McCoy told the court his relationship with assigned counsel had broken down irretrievably. He sought and gained leave to represent himself until his parents engaged new counsel for him. In March 2010, Larry English, engaged by McCoy's parents, enrolled as McCoy's counsel. English eventually concluded that the evidence against McCoy was overwhelming and that, absent a concession at the guilt stage that McCoy was the killer, a death sentence would be impossible to avoid at the penalty phase.[a] McCoy, English reported, was "furious" when told, two weeks before trial was scheduled to begin, that English would concede McCoy's commission of the triple murders.[b] McCoy told English "not to make that concession," and English knew of McCoy's complete opposition to English telling the jury that McCoy was guilty of killing the three victims; instead of any concession, McCoy pressed English to pursue acquittal.

---

[a] Part of English's strategy was to concede that McCoy committed the murders and to argue that he should be convicted only of second-degree murder, because his "mental incapacity prevented him from forming the requisite specific intent to commit first degree murder." But the second-degree strategy would have encountered a shoal, for Louisiana does not permit introduction of evidence of a defendant's diminished capacity absent the entry of a plea of not guilty by reason of insanity.

[b] The dissent states that English told McCoy his proposed trial strategy eight months before trial. English did encourage McCoy, "[a] couple of months before the trial," to plead guilty rather than proceed to trial. But English declared under oath that "the first time [he] told [McCoy] that [he] intended to concede to the jury that [McCoy] was the killer" was July 12, 2011, two weeks before trial commenced. Encouraging a guilty plea pretrial, of course, is not equivalent to imparting to a defendant counsel's strategic determination to concede guilt should trial occur.

At a July 26, 2011 hearing, McCoy sought to terminate English's representation, and English asked to be relieved if McCoy secured other counsel. With trial set to start two days later, the court refused to relieve English and directed that he remain as counsel of record. "[Y]ou are the attorney," the court told English when he expressed disagreement with McCoy's wish to put on a defense case, and "you have to make the trial decision of what you're going to proceed with."

At the beginning of his opening statement at the guilt phase of the trial, English told the jury there was "no way reasonably possible" that they could hear the prosecution's evidence and reach "any other conclusion than Robert McCoy was the cause of these individuals' death." McCoy protested; out of earshot of the jury, McCoy told the court that English was "selling [him] out" by maintaining that McCoy "murdered [his] family." The trial court reiterated that English was "representing" McCoy and told McCoy that the court would not permit "any other outbursts." Continuing his opening statement, English told the jury the evidence is "unambiguous," "my client committed three murders." McCoy testified in his own defense, maintaining his innocence and pressing an alibi difficult to fathom. In his closing argument, English reiterated that McCoy was the killer. On that issue, English told the jury that he "took [the] burden off of [the prosecutor]." The jury then returned a unanimous verdict of guilty of first-degree murder on all three counts. At the penalty phase, English again conceded "Robert McCoy committed these crimes," but urged mercy in view of McCoy's "serious mental and emotional issues." The jury returned three death verdicts.

Represented by new counsel, McCoy unsuccessfully moved for a new trial, arguing that the trial court violated his constitutional rights by allowing English to concede McCoy "committed three murders" over McCoy's objection. The Louisiana Supreme Court affirmed the trial court's ruling that defense counsel had authority so to concede guilt, despite the defendant's opposition to any admission of guilt. The concession was permissible, the court concluded, because counsel reasonably believed that admitting guilt afforded McCoy the best chance to avoid a death sentence.

We granted certiorari in view of a division of opinion among state courts of last resort on the question whether it is unconstitutional to allow defense counsel to concede guilt over the defendant's intransigent and unambiguous objection. * * *

II

A

The Sixth Amendment guarantees to each criminal defendant "the Assistance of Counsel for his defence." At common law, self-representation was the norm. See Faretta v. California, 422 U. S. 806, 823 (1975) (citing 1 F. Pollock & F. Maitland, The History of English Law 211 (2d ed. 1909)).

As the laws of England and the American Colonies developed, providing for a right to counsel in criminal cases, self-representation remained common and the right to proceed without counsel was recognized. Even now, when most defendants choose to be represented by counsel, see, e.g., Goldschmidt & Stemen, Patterns and Trends in Federal Pro Se Defense, 1996–2011: An Exploratory Study, 8 Fed. Cts. L. Rev. 81, 91 (2015) (0.2% of federal felony defendants proceeded pro se), an accused may insist upon representing herself—however counterproductive that course may be. * * *

The choice is not all or nothing: To gain assistance, a defendant need not surrender control entirely to counsel. For the Sixth Amendment, in "grant[ing] to the accused personally the right to make his defense," speaks of the "assistance" of counsel, and an assistant, however expert, is still an assistant. * * * Trial management is the lawyer's province: Counsel provides his or her assistance by making decisions such as "what arguments to pursue, what evidentiary objections to raise, and what agreements to conclude regarding the admission of evidence." Gonzalez v. United States, 553 U. S. 242, 248 (2008). Some decisions, however, are reserved for the client—notably, whether to plead guilty, waive the right to a jury trial, testify in one's own behalf, and forgo an appeal. See Jones v. Barnes, 463 U. S. 745, 751 (1983).

Autonomy to decide that the objective of the defense is to assert innocence belongs in this latter category. Just as a defendant may steadfastly refuse to plead guilty in the face of overwhelming evidence against her, or reject the assistance of legal counsel despite the defendant's own inexperience and lack of professional qualifications, so may she insist on maintaining her innocence at the guilt phase of a capital trial. These are not strategic choices about how best to achieve a client's objectives; they are choices about what the client's objectives in fact are. * * *

Counsel may reasonably assess a concession of guilt as best suited to avoiding the death penalty, as English did in this case. But the client may not share that objective. He may wish to avoid, above all else, the opprobrium that comes with admitting he killed family members. Or he may hold life in prison not worth living and prefer to risk death for any hope, however small, of exoneration. * * * When a client expressly asserts that the objective of "his defence" is to maintain innocence of the charged criminal acts, his lawyer must abide by that objective and may not override it by conceding guilt. U. S. Const., Amdt. 6 (emphasis added); see ABA Model Rule of Professional Conduct 1.2(a) (2016) (a "lawyer shall abide by a client's decisions concerning the objectives of the representation").

Preserving for the defendant the ability to decide whether to maintain his innocence should not displace counsel's, or the court's, respective trial management roles. See Gonzalez, 553 U. S., at 249 ("[n]umerous choices affecting conduct of the trial" do not require client consent, including "the objections to make, the witnesses to call, and the arguments to advance"). Counsel, in any case, must still develop a trial strategy and discuss it with her client, see *Nixon*, 543 U. S., at 178, explaining why, in her view, conceding guilt would be the best option. In this case, the court had determined that McCoy was competent to stand trial, i.e., that McCoy had sufficient present ability to consult with his lawyer with a reasonable degree of rational understanding. If, after consultations with English concerning the management of the defense, McCoy disagreed with English's proposal to concede McCoy committed three murders, it was not open to English to override McCoy's objection. English could not interfere with McCoy's telling the jury "I was not the murderer," although counsel could, if consistent with providing effective assistance, focus his own collaboration on urging that McCoy's mental state weighed against conviction.

B

[The Court distinguished Florida v. Nixon on the ground that Nixon did not make his complaint about his lawyer's strategy until after trial. The Court also rejected both the Louisiana Supreme Court's conclusion that English's refusal to maintain McCoy's innocence was necessitated by Louisiana Rule of Professional Conduct 1.2(d) (2017), which provides that "[a] lawyer shall not counsel a client to engage, or assist a client, in conduct that the lawyer knows is criminal or fraudulent," and the suggestion that the case was similar to *Nix v. Whiteside,* 475 U. S. 157, 173–176 (1986) [Text, page 1470]). It found that Nix told his lawyer that he intended to commit perjury and that there was no such avowed perjury as to McCoy. The Court reasoned that English disbelieved McCoy but this did not warrant English to admit McCoy's guilt over his objection. The Court rejected the dissent's suggestion that the case presented rare facts that were unlikely to recur.]

III

Because a client's autonomy, not counsel's competence, is in issue, we do not apply our ineffective-assistance-of-counsel jurisprudence, Strickland v. Washington, 466 U. S. 668 (1984), or United States v. Cronic, 466 U. S. 648 (1984), to McCoy's claim. To gain redress for attorney error, a defendant ordinarily must show prejudice. Here, however, the violation of McCoy's protected autonomy right was complete when the court allowed counsel to usurp control of an issue within McCoy's sole prerogative.

Violation of a defendant's Sixth Amendment-secured autonomy ranks as error of the kind our decisions have called "structural"; when present, such an error is not subject to harmless-error review. * * *

* * *

[Justice Ginsburg's explanation of why the error was "structural" is found in Chapter 13 of this Supplement.]

Larry English was placed in a difficult position; he had an unruly client and faced a strong government case. He reasonably thought the objective of his representation should be avoidance of the death penalty. But McCoy insistently maintained: "I did not murder my family." Once he communicated that to court and counsel, strenuously objecting to English's proposed strategy, a concession of guilt should have been off the table. The trial court's allowance of English's admission of McCoy's guilt despite McCoy's insistent objections was incompatible with the Sixth Amendment. Because the error was structural, a new trial is the required corrective.

For the reasons stated, the judgment of the Louisiana Supreme Court is reversed, and the case is remanded for further proceedings not inconsistent with this opinion.

JUSTICE ALITO, with whom JUSTICE THOMAS and JUSTICE GORSUCH join, dissenting.

The Constitution gives us the authority to decide real cases and controversies; we do not have the right to simplify or otherwise change the facts of a case in order to make our work easier or to achieve a desired result. But that is exactly what the Court does in this case. The Court overturns petitioner's convictions for three counts of first-degree murder by attributing to his trial attorney, Larry English, something that English never did. The Court holds that English violated petitioner's constitutional rights by "admit[ting] h[is] client's guilt of a charged crime over the client's intransigent objection." But English did not admit that petitioner was guilty of first-degree murder. Instead, faced with overwhelming evidence that petitioner shot and killed the three victims, English admitted that petitioner committed one element of that offense, *i.e.*, that he killed the victims. But English strenuously argued that petitioner was not guilty of first-degree murder because he lacked the intent (the *mens rea*) required for the offense. So the Court's newly discovered fundamental right simply does not apply to the real facts of this case.

I

The real case is far more complex. Indeed, the real situation English faced at the beginning of petitioner's trial was the result of a freakish confluence of factors that is unlikely to recur.

Retained by petitioner's family, English found himself in a predicament as the trial date approached. The evidence against his client was truly "overwhelming," as the Louisiana Supreme Court aptly noted.

Among other things, the evidence showed the following. Before the killings took place, petitioner had abused and threatened to kill his wife, and she was therefore under police protection. On the night of the killings, petitioner's mother-in-law made a 911 call and was heard screaming petitioner's first name. She yelled: " 'She ain't here, Robert . . . I don't know where she is. The detectives have her. Talk to the detectives. She ain't in there, Robert.' " Moments later, a gunshot was heard, and the 911 call was disconnected.

Officers were dispatched to the scene, and on arrival, they found three dead or dying victims—petitioner's mother-in-law, her husband, and the teenage son of petitioner's wife. The officers saw a man who fit petitioner's description fleeing in petitioner's car. They chased the suspect, but he abandoned the car along with critical evidence linking him to the crime: the cordless phone petitioner's mother-in-law had used to call 911 and a receipt for the type of ammunition used to kill the victims. Petitioner was eventually arrested while hitchhiking in Idaho, and a loaded gun found in his possession was identified as the one used to shoot the victims. In addition to all this, a witness testified that petitioner had asked to borrow money to purchase bullets shortly before the shootings, and surveillance footage showed petitioner purchasing the ammunition on the day of the killings. And two of petitioner's friends testified that he confessed to killing at least one person.

Despite all this evidence, petitioner, who had been found competent to stand trial and had refused to plead guilty by reason of insanity, insisted that he did not kill the victims. He claimed that the victims were killed by the local police and that he had been framed by a farflung conspiracy of state and federal officials, reaching from Louisiana to Idaho. Petitioner believed that even his attorney and the trial judge had joined the plot.

Unwilling to go along with this incredible and uncorroborated defense, English told petitioner "some eight months" before trial that the only viable strategy was to admit the killings and to concentrate on attempting to avoid a sentence of death. At that point—aware of English's strong views—petitioner could have discharged English and sought new counsel willing to pursue his conspiracy defense; under the Sixth Amendment, that was his right. See United States v. Gonzalez-Lopez, 548 U. S. 140, 144 (2006). But petitioner stated "several different times" that he was "confident with Mr. English."

The weekend before trial, however, petitioner changed his mind. He asked the trial court to replace English, and English asked for permission to withdraw. Petitioner stated that he had secured substitute counsel, but he was unable to provide the name of this new counsel, and no new attorney ever appeared. The court refused these requests and also denied petitioner's last-minute request to represent himself. (Petitioner does not challenge these decisions here.) So petitioner and English were stuck with each other, and petitioner availed himself of his right to take the stand to tell his wild story. Under those circumstances, what was English supposed to do?

The Louisiana Supreme Court held that English could not have put on petitioner's desired defense without violating state ethics rules, but this Court effectively overrules the state court on this issue of state law. However, even if it is assumed that the Court is correct on this ethics issue, the result of mounting petitioner's conspiracy defense almost certainly would have been disastrous. That approach stood no chance of winning an acquittal and would have severely damaged English's credibility in the eyes of the jury, thus undermining his ability to argue effectively against the imposition of a death sentence at the penalty phase of the trial. As English observed, taking that path would have only "help[ed] the District Attorney send [petitioner] to the death chamber." (In Florida v. Nixon, 543 U. S. 175, 191–192 (2004), this Court made essentially the same point.) So, again, what was English supposed to do?

When pressed at oral argument before this Court, petitioner's current counsel eventually provided an answer: English was not required to take any affirmative steps to support petitioner's bizarre defense, but instead of conceding that petitioner shot the victims, English should have ignored that element entirely. So the fundamental right supposedly violated in this case comes down to the difference between the two statements set out below.

Constitutional: "First-degree murder requires proof both that the accused killed the victim and that he acted with the intent to kill. I submit to you that my client did not have the intent required for conviction for that offense."

Unconstitutional: "First-degree murder requires proof both that the accused killed the victim and that he acted with the intent to kill. I admit that my client shot and killed the victims, but I submit to you that he did not have the intent required for conviction for that offense."

The practical difference between these two statements is negligible. If English had conspicuously refrained from endorsing petitioner's story and had based his defense solely on petitioner's dubious mental condition, the jury would surely have gotten the message that English was essentially conceding that petitioner killed the victims. But according to petitioner's current attorney, the difference is fundamental. The first formulation, he admits, is perfectly fine. The latter, on the other hand, is a violation so egregious that the defendant's conviction must be reversed even if there is no chance that the misstep caused any harm. It is no wonder that the Court declines to embrace this argument and instead turns to an issue that the case at hand does not actually present.

II

The constitutional right that the Court has now discovered—a criminal defendant's right to insist that his attorney contest his guilt with respect to all charged offenses—is like a rare plant that blooms every decade or so. Having made its first appearance today, the right is unlikely to figure in another case for many years to come. Why is this so?

First, it is hard to see how the right could come into play in any case other than a capital case in which the jury must decide both guilt and punishment. In all other cases, guilt is almost always the only issue for the jury, and therefore admitting guilt of all charged offenses will achieve nothing. It is hard to imagine a situation in which a competent attorney might take that approach. So the right that the Court has discovered is effectively confined to capital cases.

Second, few rational defendants facing a possible death sentence are likely to insist on contesting guilt where there is no real chance of acquittal and where admitting guilt may improve the chances of avoiding execution. Indeed, under such circumstances, the odds are that a rational defendant will plead guilty in exchange for a life sentence. By the same token, an attorney is unlikely to insist on admitting guilt over the defendant's objection unless the attorney believes that contesting guilt would be futile. So the right is most likely to arise in cases involving irrational capital defendants.[c]

Third, where a capital defendant and his retained attorney cannot agree on a basic trial strategy, the attorney and client will generally part ways unless, as in this case, the court is not apprised until the eve of trial. The client will then either search for another attorney or decide to represent himself. So the field of cases in which this right might arise is limited further still—to cases involving irrational capital defendants who disagree with their attorneys' proposed strategy yet continue to retain them.

Fourth, if counsel is appointed, and unreasonably insists on admitting guilt over the defendant's objection, a capable trial judge will almost certainly grant a timely request to appoint substitute counsel. And if such a request is denied, the ruling may be vulnerable on appeal.

Finally, even if all the above conditions are met, the right that the Court now discovers will not come into play unless the defendant expressly protests counsel's strategy of admitting guilt. Where the defendant is

---

[c] The Court imagines cases in which a rational defendant prefers even a minuscule chance of acquittal over either the social opprobrium that would result from an admission of guilt or the sentence of imprisonment that would be imposed upon conviction. Such cases are likely to be rare, and in any event, as explained below, the defendant will almost always be able to get his way if he acts in time.

advised of the strategy and says nothing, or is equivocal, the right is deemed to have been waived. See *Nixon*, 543 U. S., at 192.

In short, the right that the Court now discovers is likely to appear only rarely, and because the present case is so unique, it is hard to see how it meets our stated criteria for granting review. See this Court's Rules 10(b)–(c). Review would at least be understandable if the strategy that English pursued had worked an injustice, but the Court does not make that claim—and with good reason. Endorsing petitioner's bizarre defense would have been extraordinarily unwise, and dancing the fine line recommended by petitioner's current attorney would have done no good. It would have had no effect on the outcome of the trial, and it is hard to see how that approach would have respected petitioner's "autonomy," any more than the more straightforward approach that English took. If petitioner is retried, it will be interesting to see what petitioner's current counsel or any other attorney to whom the case is handed off will do. It is a safe bet that no attorney will put on petitioner's conspiracy defense.

III

While the question that the Court decides is unlikely to make another appearance for quite some time, a related—and difficult—question may arise more frequently: When guilt is the sole issue for the jury, is it ever permissible for counsel to make the unilateral decision to concede an element of the offense charged? If today's decision were understood to address that question, it would have important implications.

Under current precedent, there are some decisions on which a criminal defendant has the final say. For example, a defendant cannot be forced to enter a plea against his wishes. See Brookhart v. Janis, 384 U. S. 1, 5–7 (1966). Similarly, no matter what counsel thinks best, a defendant has the right to insist on a jury trial and to take the stand and testify in his own defense. See Harris v. New York, 401 U. S. 222, 225 (1971). And if, as in this case, a defendant and retained counsel do not see eye to eye, the client can always attempt to find another attorney who will accede to his wishes. A defendant can also choose to dispense with counsel entirely and represent himself.

While these fundamental decisions must be made by a criminal defendant, most of the decisions that arise in criminal cases are the prerogative of counsel. (Our adversarial system would break down if defense counsel were required to obtain the client's approval for every important move made during the course of the case.) Among the decisions that counsel is free to make unilaterally are the following: choosing the basic line of defense, moving to suppress evidence, delivering an opening statement and deciding what to say in the opening, objecting to the admission of evidence, cross-examining witnesses, offering evidence and calling defense witnesses, and deciding what to say in summation. See, e.g.,

New York v. Hill, 528 U. S. 110, 114–115 (2000). On which side of the line does conceding some but not all elements of the charged offense fall?

Some criminal offenses contain elements that the prosecution can easily prove beyond any shadow of a doubt. A prior felony conviction is a good example. See 18 U. S. C. § 922(g) (possession of a firearm by a convicted felon). Suppose that the prosecution is willing to stipulate that the defendant has a prior felony conviction but is prepared, if necessary, to offer certified judgments of conviction for multiple prior violent felonies. If the defendant insists on contesting the convictions on frivolous grounds, must counsel go along? Does the same rule apply to all elements? If there are elements that may not be admitted over the defendant's objection, must counsel go further and actually contest those elements? Or is it permissible if counsel refrains from expressly conceding those elements but essentially admits them by walking the fine line recommended at argument by petitioner's current attorney?

What about conceding that a defendant is guilty, not of the offense charged, but of a lesser included offense? That is what English did in this case. He admitted that petitioner was guilty of the noncapital offense of second-degree murder in an effort to prevent a death sentence.[d] Is admitting guilt of a lesser included offense over the defendant's objection always unconstitutional? Where the evidence strongly supports conviction for first-degree murder, is it unconstitutional for defense counsel to make the decision to admit guilt of any lesser included form of homicide—even manslaughter? What about simple assault?

These are not easy questions, and the fact that they have not come up in this Court for more than two centuries suggests that they will arise infrequently in the future. I would leave those questions for another day and limit our decision to the particular (and highly unusual) situation in the actual case before us. And given the situation in which English found himself when trial commenced, I would hold that he did not violate any fundamental right by expressly acknowledging that petitioner killed the victims instead of engaging in the barren exercise that petitioner's current counsel now recommends.

IV

Having discovered a new right not at issue in the real case before us, the Court compounds its error by summarily concluding that a violation of this right "ranks as error of the kind our decisions have called 'structural.'"

---

[d] The Court asserts that, under Louisiana law, English's "second-degree strategy would have encountered a shoal" and necessarily failed. But the final arbiter of Louisiana law—the Louisiana Supreme Court—disagreed. It held that "[t]he jury was left with several choices" after English's second-degree concession, "including returning a responsive verdict of second degree murder" and "not returning the death penalty."

The Court concedes that the Louisiana Supreme Court did not decide the structural-error question and that we " 'did not grant certiorari to review' that question." We have stated time and again that we are "a court of review, not of first view" and, for that reason, have refused to decide issues not addressed below. * * *

In this case, however, the court-of-review maxim does not suit the majority's purposes, so it is happy to take the first view. And the majority does so without adversarial briefing on the question. * * *

The Court ignores the question actually presented by the case before us and instead decides this case on the basis of a newly discovered constitutional right that is not implicated by what really occurred at petitioner's trial. I would base our decision on what really took place, and under the highly unusual facts of this case, I would affirm the judgment below.

I therefore respectfully dissent.

CHAPTER 11

SENTENCING

■ ■ ■

I. INTRODUCTION

E. SENTENCING ALTERNATIVES OTHER THAN INCARCERATION

1. Fines and Forfeitures

Page 1545. Insert after headnote on *Austin v. United States*:

Excessive Fines Clause Binding on the States:
Timbs v. Indiana

In *Timbs v. Indiana*, 139 S.Ct. 1682 (2019), the Court held that the Eighth Amendment prohibition on excessive fines was binding on the States, because it had been incorporated through the Fourteenth Amendment. The Court's extensive incorporation analysis—together with a different take by Justice Thomas, concurring in the judgment—is fully set forth in Chapter 1 of this Supplement.

3. Restitution

Restitution for Victims of Child Pornography:
Paroline v. United States

Page 1548. Add at the bottom of the page:

In *Lagos v. United States*, 138 S.Ct. 1684 (2018), Justice Breyer wrote for a unanimous Court rejecting lower courts' analyses of the provision of the Mandatory Victims Restitution Act of 1996 requiring defendants to "reimburse the victim for lost income and necessary child care, transportation, and other expenses incurred during participation in the investigation or prosecution of the offense or attendance at proceedings related to the Offense." Lagos pled guilty to using a company he controlled to defraud a lender of tens of millions of dollars. When the lender became aware of the scheme and Lagos's company went bankrupt, the lender spent nearly $5 million dollars to conduct a private investigation and to participate as a party in the bankruptcy proceedings. The expenditures included legal, accounting and consulting fees. At sentencing the district court required Lagos to reimburse the lender for these expenditures, and the Fifth Circuit affirmed. Justice Breyer concluded that the words "investigation" and "proceedings" in the Act are limited to government investigations and criminal proceedings and do not include private investigations and civil or bankruptcy proceedings.

II. GUIDELINES SENTENCING

D. SUPREME COURT CONSTRUCTION OF THE FEDERAL SENTENCING GUIDELINES

2. Application of Advisory Guidelines After *Booker*

Page 1589. Add after the first partial paragraph:

Guideline Reductions and Sentence Modifications: The Required Explanation

In *Chavez-Meza v. United States*, 138 S.Ct. 1959 (2018), the Court held that a district judge who originally sentenced the defendant to the bottom of his Guideline range (135–168 months) for possessing methamphetamine with intent to distribute adequately explained the reasons for imposing a revised sentence of 114 months after the Sentencing Commission lowered the relevant Guideline range to 108 to 135 months.

Justice Breyer wrote for the majority. He relied on *Rita v. United States*, 551 U. S. 338 (2007), in which the Court set forth the explanation requirement at sentencing, and concluded that "[a]t bottom, the sentencing judge need only set forth enough to satisfy the appellate court that he has considered the parties' arguments and has a reasoned basis for exercising his own legal decisionmaking authority." The government argued that this was a sentence modification and "this fact alone should secure it a virtually automatic victory." Justice Breyer found that it was unnecessary to go so far. He concluded that "[e]ven assuming (purely for argument's sake) district courts have equivalent duties when initially sentencing a defendant and when later modifying the sentence, what the District Court did here was sufficient."

Justice Breyer reasoned that "a judge's choice among points on a range will often simply reflect the judge's belief that the chosen sentence is the 'right' sentence (or as close as possible to the 'right' sentence) based on various factors, including those found in § 3553(a)," and because "that is so, it is unsurprising that changing the applicable range may lead a judge to choose a nonproportional point on the new range." He also found it appropriate to consider what the judge said at the original sentencing as well as at the resentencing.

Finally, Justice Breyer indicated that the Court was not saying that a sentence modification never requires a more detailed explanation than was provided in this case, and explained that "under different facts and a different record, the district court's use of a barebones form order in response to a motion like petitioner's would be inadequate."

Justice Kennedy, joined by Justices Kagan and Sotomayor, dissented. He explained that "[m]y disagreement with the majority is based on a serious problem—the difficulty for prisoners and appellate courts in ascertaining a district court's reasons for imposing a sentence when the court fails to state those reasons on the record; yet, in the end, my disagreement turns on a small difference, for a remedy is simple and easily attained." His remedy is "a slight expansion of the AO-247 form," "to include just a few more categories covering the factors most often bearing on a trial court's sentencing determination," so that "district judges would have a helpful form that might well reduce the time for consideration of cases—and even if not would help ensure the full consideration which tends to result in uniformity and fairness."

Sentencing Under a Guideline That Advises a Greater Sentence than the Guideline Existing When the Crime Was Committed: Peugh v. United States

Page 1590. Add after the discussion of *Peugh v. United States*:

Justice Alito wrote for a unanimous Court in *Koons v. United States*, 138 S.Ct. 1783 (2018), as it held that five defendants who were sentenced below mandatory minimums because they gave substantial assistance to the government did not qualify for sentence reductions under 18 U.S.C. § 3582(c)(2), which makes defendants eligible if they were sentenced "based on a sentencing range" that was later lowered by the United States Sentencing Commission. Justice Alito reasoned that their sentences were not "based on" their lowered Guidelines ranges but, instead, were "based on" their mandatory minimums and substantial assistance.

In another sentencing case, Justice Kennedy wrote for the Court in *Hughes v. United States*, 138 S.Ct. 1765 (2018), holding that a defendant may seek relief under § 3582(c)(2) if he entered a plea agreement under Federal Rule of Criminal Procedure 11(c)(1)(C) (Type-C agreement), which permits the defendant and the Government to "agree that a specific sentence or sentencing range is the appropriate disposition of the case," and "binds the court [to the agreed-upon sentence] once [it] accepts the plea agreement." Justice Kennedy noted that in deciding whether to approve the agreement the district court must consider the Sentencing Guidelines and may not accept the agreement unless the sentence is within the applicable Guidelines range, or it is outside that range for justifiable reasons specifically set out.

The government indicted Hughes in 2013 on drug and gun charges for his participation in a conspiracy to distribute methamphetamine. The parties negotiated a Type-C plea agreement pursuant to which Hughes agreed to plead guilty to two of the four charges (conspiracy to distribute methamphetamine and being a felon in possession of a gun) and in exchange the government agreed to dismiss the other two charges and to refrain from filing an information giving formal notification to the District Court of his prior drug felonies. Hughes would have faced a mandatory life sentence if the government had filed the information. The agreement stipulated that Hughes would receive a sentence of 180 months, but it did not refer to any particular Guidelines range. The district court calculated the guideline range as 188 to 235 months before hearing from Hughes, his mother and his daughter and approving the agreement in light of the sentencing factors set forth in 18 U.S.C. § 3553 (a).

The Sentencing Commission amended the Guidelines less than two months after Hughes' sentencing and reduced the base offense level by two levels for most drug offenses. The Commission later made the amendment retroactive for defendants who, like Hughes, already had been sentenced under the higher offense levels. Under the revised Guidelines Hughes' sentencing range is 151 to 188 months, which is approximately three to four years lower than the range in effect when he was sentenced. Hughes filed a motion for a sentence reduction. The lower courts concluded that he was ineligible, and the Supreme Court reversed.

Justice Kennedy noted that the Guidelines are only advisory and cited *Koons* as an example:

> If the Guidelines range was not "a relevant part of the analytic framework the judge used to determine the sentence or to approve the agreement," * * * then the defendant's sentence was not based on that sentencing range, and relief under § 3582(c)(2) is unavailable. And that is so regardless of whether a defendant pleaded guilty pursuant to a Type-C agreement or whether the agreement itself referred to a Guidelines range. The statutory language points to the reasons for the sentence that the district court imposed, not the reasons for the parties' plea agreement. Still, cases like *Koons* are a narrow exception to the general rule that, in most cases, a defendant's sentence will be "based on" his Guidelines range. In federal sentencing the Guidelines are a district court's starting point, so when the Commission lowers a defendant's Guidelines range the defendant will be eligible for relief under § 3582(c)(2) absent clear demonstration, based on the record as a whole, that the court would have imposed the same sentence regardless of the Guidelines.

Justice Sotomayor concurred. She noted that the Court confronted the same question in *Freeman v. United States*, 564 U. S. 522 (2011), which ended in a 4–1–4 decision that left lower courts confused as to whether the plurality [opinion by Chief Justice Roberts] or the concurring opinion [of Justice Sotomayor] controlled. She voted with the majority in *Hughes* "to ensure clarity and stability in the law and promote[ ] 'uniformity in sentencing imposed by different federal courts for similar criminal conduct.' "

Chief Justice Roberts, joined by Justices Thomas and Alito, dissented and relied upon his *Freeman* plurality opinion and Justice Sotomayor's *Freeman* concurrence:

> As the Court points out, a district court considering whether to accept a Type-C agreement must consult the Guidelines, as the District Court did here. But "when determining the sentence to impose," the district court may base its decision on "one thing and one thing only—the plea agreement." Freeman, 564 U. S., at 545 (ROBERTS, C. J., dissenting). The Court characterizes this distinction as "artificial," arguing that the district court's ultimate imposition of a sentence often has as much to do with its Guidelines calculation as anything else. But that is not so: With a Type-C agreement, the sentence is set by the parties, not by a judge applying the Guidelines. Far from being "artificial," that distinction is central to what makes a Type-C plea a Type-C plea. "In the (C) agreement context" it is "the binding plea agreement that is the foundation for the term of imprisonment." Freeman, 564 U. S., at 535 (opinion of SOTOMAYOR, J.). "To hold otherwise would be to contravene the very purpose of (C) agreements—to bind the district court and allow the Government and the defendant to determine what sentence he will receive." Id., at 536.

* * *

> The Court finds new justification for its interpretation in Peugh v. United States, 569 U. S. 530 (2013), and Molina-Martinez v. United States, 578 U. S. ___ (2016). But those cases—which do not concern the language of § 3582(c)(2) or sentencing pursuant to Type-C agreements—do not inform the distinct question at hand. * * *

The Chief Justice observed that "[t]he Government may well be able to limit the frustrating effects of today's decision in the long run * * * by adding a provision to every Type-C agreement in which the defendant agrees to waive any right to seek a sentence reduction following future Guidelines amendments."

CHAPTER 12

DOUBLE JEOPARDY

■ ■ ■

V. MULTIPLE PROSECUTIONS OF CONVICTED DEFENDANTS

Page 1666. Add the following new section:

E. WAIVER BY DEFENDANT

CURRIER V. VIRGINIA
Supreme Court of the United States, 2018.
138 S.Ct. 2144.

JUSTICE GORSUCH **announced the judgment of the Court and delivered the opinion of the Court with respect to Parts I and II, and an opinion with respect to Part III, in which** THE CHIEF JUSTICE, JUSTICE THOMAS, **and** JUSTICE ALITO **join.**

About to face trial, Michael Currier worried the prosecution would introduce prejudicial but probative evidence against him on one count that could infect the jury's deliberations on others. To address the problem, he agreed to sever the charges and hold two trials instead of one. But after the first trial finished, Mr. Currier turned around and argued that proceeding with the second would violate his right against double jeopardy. All of which raises the question: can a defendant who agrees to have the charges against him considered in two trials later successfully argue that the second trial offends the Fifth Amendment's Double Jeopardy Clause?

I

This case began when police dredged up a safe full of guns from a Virginia river. Paul Garrison, the safe's owner, had reported it stolen from his home. Before the theft, Mr. Garrison said, it contained not just the guns but also $71,000 in cash. Now, most of the money was missing. As the investigation unfolded, the police eventually found their way to Mr. Garrison's nephew. Once confronted, the nephew quickly confessed. Along the way, he pointed to Michael Currier as his accomplice. A neighbor also reported that she saw Mr. Currier leave the Garrison home around the time of the crime. On the strength of this evidence, a grand jury indicted Mr. Currier for burglary, grand larceny, and unlawful possession of a firearm by a convicted felon. The last charge followed in light of Mr. Currier's previous convictions for (as it happens) burglary and larceny.

Because the prosecution could introduce evidence of his prior convictions to prove the felon-in-possession charge, and worried that the evidence might prejudice the jury's consideration of the other charges, Mr. Currier and the government agreed to a severance. They asked the court to try the burglary and larceny charges first. Then, they said, the felon-in-possession charge could follow in a second trial. Some jurisdictions routinely refuse requests like this. Instead, they seek to address the risk of prejudice with an instruction directing the jury to consider the defendant's prior convictions only when assessing the felon-in-possession charge. Other jurisdictions allow parties to stipulate to the defendant's past convictions so the particulars of those crimes don't reach the jury's ears. Others take a more protective approach yet and view severance requests with favor. Because Virginia falls into this last group, the trial court granted the parties' joint request in this case.

The promised two trials followed. At the first, the prosecution produced the nephew and the neighbor who testified to Mr. Currier's involvement in the burglary and larceny. But Mr. Currier argued that the nephew lied and the neighbor was unreliable and, in the end, the jury acquitted. Then, before the second trial on the firearm charge could follow, Mr. Currier sought to stop it. Now, he argued, holding a second trial would amount to double jeopardy. Alternatively and at the least, he asked the court to forbid the government from relitigating in the second trial any issue resolved in his favor at the first. So, for example, he said the court should exclude from the new proceeding any evidence about the burglary and larceny. The court replied that it could find nothing in the Double Jeopardy Clause requiring either result so it allowed the second trial to proceed unfettered. In the end, the jury convicted Mr. Currier on the felon-in-possession charge.

Before the Virginia Court of Appeals, Mr. Currier repeated his double jeopardy arguments without success. The court held that the "concern that lies at the core" of the Double Jeopardy Clause—namely, "the avoidance of prosecutorial oppression and overreaching through successive trials"—had no application here because the charges were severed for Mr. Currier's benefit and at his behest. The Virginia Supreme Court summarily affirmed. Because courts have reached conflicting results on the double jeopardy arguments Mr. Currier pressed in this case, we granted certiorari to resolve them.

II

The Double Jeopardy Clause, applied to the States through the Fourteenth Amendment, provides that no person may be tried more than once "for the same offence." This guarantee recognizes the vast power of the sovereign, the ordeal of a criminal trial, and the injustice our criminal justice system would invite if prosecutors could treat trials as dress rehearsals until they secure the convictions they seek. See *Green v. United States*, 355 U. S. 187, 188 (1957). At the same time, this Court has said, the Clause was not written or originally understood to pose "an insuperable obstacle to the administration of justice" in cases where "there is no semblance of [these] type[s] of oppressive practices." *Wade v. Hunter*, 336 U. S. 684, 688–689 (1949).

On which side of the line does our case fall? Mr. Currier suggests this Court's decision in *Ashe v. Swenson*, 397 U. S. 436 (1970), requires a ruling for him. There, the government accused a defendant of robbing six poker players in a game at a private home. At the first trial, the jury acquitted the defendant of robbing one victim. Then the State sought to try the defendant for robbing a second victim. This Court held the second prosecution violated the Double Jeopardy Clause. To be sure, the Clause speaks of barring successive trials for the same offense. And, to be sure, the State sought to try the defendant for a *different* robbery. But, the Court reasoned, because the first jury necessarily found that the defendant "was not one of the robbers," a second jury could not "rationally" convict the defendant of robbing the second victim without calling into question the earlier acquittal. In these circumstances, the Court indicated, any relitigation of the issue whether the defendant participated as "one of the robbers" would be tantamount to the forbidden relitigation of the same offense resolved at the first trial.

Ashe's suggestion that the relitigation of an issue can sometimes amount to the impermissible relitigation of an offense represented a significant innovation in our jurisprudence. Some have argued that it sits uneasily with this Court's double jeopardy precedent and the Constitution's original meaning. But whatever else may be said about *Ashe*, we have emphasized that its test is a demanding one. *Ashe* forbids a second trial only if to secure a conviction the prosecution must prevail on an issue the jury necessarily resolved in the defendant's favor in the first trial. A second trial "is not precluded simply because it is unlikely—or even very unlikely—that the original jury acquitted without finding the fact in question." To say that the second trial is tantamount to a trial of the same offense as the first and thus forbidden by the Double Jeopardy Clause, we must be able to say that "it would have been *irrational* for the jury" in the first trial to acquit without finding in the defendant's favor on a fact essential to a conviction in the second.

Bearing all that in mind, a critical difference immediately emerges between our case and *Ashe*. Even assuming without deciding that Mr. Currier's second trial qualified as the retrial of the same offense under *Ashe*, he consented to it. Nor does anyone doubt that trying all three charges in one trial would have prevented any possible *Ashe* complaint Mr. Currier might have had.

How do these features affect the double jeopardy calculus? A precedent points the way. In *Jeffers v. United States*, 432 U. S. 137 (1977), the defendant sought separate trials on each of the counts against him to reduce the possibility of prejudice. The court granted his request. After the jury convicted the defendant in the first trial of a lesser-included offense, he argued that the prosecution could not later try him for a greater offense. In any other circumstance the defendant likely would have had a good argument. Historically, courts have treated greater and lesser-included offenses as the same offense for double jeopardy purposes, so a conviction on one normally precludes a later trial on the other. But, *Jeffers* concluded, it's different when the defendant consents to two trials where one could have done. If a single trial on multiple charges would suffice to avoid a double jeopardy complaint, "there is no violation of the Double Jeopardy Clause when [the defendant] elects to have the . . . offenses tried separately and persuades the trial court to honor his election." 432 U. S., at 152.

What was true in *Jeffers*, we hold, can be no less true here. If a defendant's consent to two trials can overcome concerns lying at the historic core of the Double Jeopardy Clause, so too we think it must overcome a double jeopardy complaint under *Ashe*. Nor does anything in *Jeffers* suggest that the outcome should be different if the first trial yielded an acquittal rather than a conviction when a defendant consents to severance. While we acknowledge that *Ashe*'s protections apply only to trials following acquittals, as a general rule, the Double Jeopardy Clause protects against a second prosecution for the same offense after conviction as well as against a second prosecution for the same offense after acquittal. Because the Clause applies equally in both situations, consent to a second trial should in general have equal effect in both situations.

Holding otherwise would introduce an unwarranted inconsistency not just with *Jeffers* but with other precedents too. In *United States v. Dinitz*, 424 U. S. 600 (1976), for example, this Court held that a defendant's mistrial motion implicitly invited a second trial and was enough to foreclose any double jeopardy complaint about it. In reaching this holding, the Court expressly rejected "the contention that the permissibility of a retrial depends on a knowing, voluntary, and intelligent waiver" from the defendant. Instead, it explained, none of the "prosecutorial or judicial overreaching" forbidden by the Constitution can be found when a second trial follows thanks to the defendant's motion. In United States v. Scott, 437 U. S. 82 (1978), this Court likewise held that a defendant's motion effectively invited a retrial of the same offense, and "the Double Jeopardy Clause, which guards against Government oppression, does not relieve a defendant from the consequences of [a] voluntary choice" like that. * * * While relinquishing objections sometimes turns on state or federal procedural rules, these precedents teach that consenting to two trials when one would have avoided a double jeopardy problem precludes any constitutional violation associated with holding a second trial. In these circumstances, our cases hold, the defendant wins a potential benefit and experiences none of the prosecutorial "oppression" the Double Jeopardy Clause exists to prevent. Nor, again, can we discern a good reason to treat *Ashe* double jeopardy complaints more favorably than traditional ones when a defendant consents to severance.

Against these precedents, Mr. Currier asks us to consider others, especially *Harris v. Washington*, 404 U. S. 55 (1971) (per curiam) and *Turner v. Arkansas*, 407 U. S. 366 (1972) (per curiam). But these cases merely applied *Ashe*'s test and concluded that a second trial was impermissible. They did not address the question whether double jeopardy protections apply if the defendant *consents* to a second trial. Meanwhile, as we've seen, *Jeffers*, *Dinitz*, and *Scott* focus on that question directly and make clear that a defendant's consent dispels any specter of double jeopardy abuse that holding two trials might otherwise present. This Court's teachings are consistent and plain: the "Clause, which guards against Government oppression, does not relieve a defendant from the consequences of his voluntary choice." *Scott, supra,* at 99.

Mr. Currier replies that he had no real choice but to seek two trials. Without a second trial, he says, evidence of his prior convictions would have tainted the jury's consideration of the burglary and larceny charges. And, he notes, Virginia law guarantees a severance in cases like his unless the defendant and prosecution agree to a single trial. But no one disputes that the Constitution permitted Virginia to try all three charges at once with appropriate cautionary instructions. So this simply isn't a case where the defendant had to give up one constitutional right to secure another. Instead, Mr. Currier faced a lawful choice between two courses of action that each bore potential costs and rationally attractive benefits. It might have been a hard choice. But litigants every day face difficult decisions. Whether it's the defendant who finds himself in the shoes of Jeffers, Dinitz, and Scott and forced to choose between allowing an imperfect trial to proceed or seeking a second that promises its own risks. Or whether it's the defendant who must decide between exercising his right to testify in his own defense or keeping impeachment evidence of past bad acts from the jury. See, e.g., *Brown v. United States*, 356 U. S. 148, 154–157 (1958). This Court has held repeatedly that difficult strategic choices like these are "not the same as no choice," *United States v. Martinez-Salazar*, 528 U. S. 304, 315 (2000), and the Constitution "does not . . . forbid requiring" a litigant to make them, *McGautha v. California*, 402 U. S. 183, 213 (1971).

III

Even if he voluntarily consented to holding the second trial, Mr. Currier argues, that consent did not extend to the relitigation of any issues the first jury resolved in his favor. So, Mr. Currier says, the court should have excluded evidence suggesting he possessed the guns in Mr. Garrison's home, leaving the prosecution to prove that he possessed them only later, maybe down by the river. To support this argument, Mr. Currier points to issue preclusion principles in civil cases and invites us to import them for the first time into the criminal law through the Double Jeopardy Clause. In his view, the Clause should do much more than bar the retrial of the same offense (or crimes tantamount to the same offense under *Ashe*); it should be read now to prevent the parties from retrying any issue or introducing any evidence about a previously tried issue. While the dissent today agrees with us that the trial court committed no double jeopardy violation in holding the second trial, on this alternative argument it sides with Mr. Currier.

We cannot. Even assuming for argument's sake that Mr. Currier's consent to *holding* a second trial didn't more broadly imply consent to the *manner* it was conducted, we must reject his argument on a narrower ground. Just last Term this Court warned that issue preclusion principles should have only "guarded application . . . in criminal cases." *Bravo-Fernandez v. United States*, 580 U. S. ___, ___ (2016) (slip op. at 4). We think that caution remains sound.

Mr. Currier's problems begin with the text of the Double Jeopardy Clause. As we've seen, the Clause speaks not about prohibiting the relitigation of issues or evidence but offenses. Contrast this with the language of the Reexamination Clause. There, the Seventh Amendment says that "[i]n Suits at common law . . . *no fact* tried by a jury, *shall be otherwise re-examined* in any Court of the United States, than according to the rules of the common law." (Emphasis added.) Words in one provision are, of course, often understood "by comparing them with other words and sentences in the same instrument." 1 J. Story, Commentaries on the Constitution of the United States § 400, p. 384 (1833). So it's difficult to ignore that only in the Seventh Amendment—and only for civil suits—can we find anything resembling contemporary issue preclusion doctrine.

What problems the text suggests, the original public understanding of the Fifth Amendment confirms. The Double Jeopardy Clause took its cue from English common law pleas that prevented courts from retrying a criminal defendant previously acquitted or convicted of the crime in question. * * *

* * *

This Court's contemporary double jeopardy cases confirm what the text and history suggest. Under *Blockburger v. United States*, 284 U. S. 299 (1932), the courts apply today much the same double jeopardy test they did at the founding. To prevent a second trial on a new charge, the defendant must show an identity of statutory elements between the two charges against him; it's not enough that "a substantial overlap [exists] in the proof offered to establish the crimes." *Iannelli v. United States*, 420 U. S. 770, 785, n. 17 (1975). Of course, *Ashe* later pressed *Blockburger's* boundaries by suggesting that, in narrow circumstances, the retrial of an issue can be considered tantamount to the retrial of an offense. But, as we've seen, even there a court's ultimate focus remains on the practical identity of offenses, and the only available remedy is the traditional double jeopardy bar against the retrial of the same offense—not a bar against the relitigation of issues or evidence. Even at the outer reaches of our double jeopardy jurisprudence, then, this Court has never sought to regulate the retrial of issues or evidence in the name of the Double Jeopardy Clause.

Nor in acknowledging this do we plow any new ground. In *Dowling v. United States*, 493 U. S. 342 (1990), the defendant faced charges of bank robbery. At trial, the prosecution introduced evidence of the defendant's involvement in an earlier crime, even though the jury in that case had acquitted. Like Mr. Currier, the defendant in *Dowling* argued that the trial court should have barred relitigation of an issue resolved in his favor in an earlier case and therefore excluded evidence of the acquitted offense. But the Court refused the request and in doing so expressly "decline[d] to extend *Ashe* . . . to exclude in all circumstances, as [the defendant] would have it, relevant and probative evidence that is otherwise admissible under the Rules of Evidence simply because it relates to alleged criminal conduct for which a defendant has been acquitted." If a second trial is permissible, the admission of evidence at that trial is governed by normal evidentiary rules—not by the terms of the Double Jeopardy Clause. "So far as merely evidentiary . . . facts are concerned," the Double Jeopardy Clause "is inoperative." *Yates v. United States*, 354 U. S. 298, 338 (1957).

On its own terms, too, any effort to transplant civil preclusion principles into the Double Jeopardy Clause would quickly meet trouble. While the Clause embodies a kind of "claim preclusion" rule, even this rule bears little in common with its civil counterpart. In civil cases, a claim generally may not be tried if it arises out of the same transaction or common nucleus of operative facts as another already tried. But in a criminal case, *Blockburger* precludes a trial on an offense only if a court has previously heard the same offense as measured by its statutory elements. And this Court has emphatically refused to import into criminal double jeopardy law the civil law's more generous "same transaction" or same criminal "episode" test. See *Garrett v. United States*, 471 U. S. 773, 790 (1985); see also *Ashe*, 397 U. S., at 448 (Harlan, J., concurring).

It isn't even clear that civil preclusion principles would help defendants like Mr. Currier. Issue preclusion addresses the effect in a current case of a prior adjudication in *another case*. So it doesn't often have much to say about the preclusive effects of rulings "within the framework of a continuing action." Usually, only the more flexible law of the case doctrine governs the preclusive effect of an earlier decision "within a single action." And that doctrine might counsel against affording conclusive effect to a prior jury verdict on a particular issue when the parties *agreed* to hold a second trial covering much the same terrain at a later stage of the proceedings. Besides, even if issue preclusion is the right doctrine for cases like ours, its application usually depends on an underlying confidence that the result achieved in the initial litigation was substantially correct. As a result, the doctrine does not often bar the relitigation of issues when "[t]he party against whom preclusion is sought could not, as a matter of law, have obtained review of the judgment in the initial action." Restatement (Second) of Judgments § 28. In criminal cases, of course, the government cannot obtain appellate review of acquittals. So a faithful application of civil preclusion principles in our case and others like it might actually militate *against* finding preclusion.

Neither Mr. Currier nor the dissent offers a persuasive reply to these points. They cannot dispute that the text of the Double Jeopardy Clause, which bars a prosecution for the same offense, is inconsistent with an issue preclusion rule that purports to bar a second prosecution involving a different offense. They decline to "engage" with the Clause's history, though the dissent appears to agree that the Clause was not originally understood to include an issue preclusion rule. Neither Mr. Currier nor the dissent seeks to show that, even taken on their own terms, civil issue preclusion principles would apply to cases like this one. Without text, history, or logic to stand on, the dissent leans heavily on a comparison to *Dowling*. In *Dowling*, the dissent emphasizes, the two trials involved different criminal episodes while the two trials here addressed the same set of facts. But *Dowling* did not rest its holding on this feature and the dissent does not explain its relevance. If issue preclusion really did exist in criminal law, why wouldn't it preclude the retrial of *any* previously tried issue, regardless whether that issue stems from the same or a different "criminal episode"?

In the end, Mr. Currier and the dissent must emphasize various policy reasons for adopting a new rule of issue preclusion into the criminal law. They contend that issue preclusion is "needed" to combat the "prosecutorial excesses" that could result from the proliferation of criminal offenses, though we aren't sure what to make of this given the dissent's later claim that "issue preclusion requires no showing of prosecutorial overreaching," In any event, there are risks with the approach Mr. Currier and the dissent propose. Consider, for example, the ironies that grafting civil preclusion principles onto the criminal law could invite. Issue preclusion is sometimes applied offensively against civil defendants who lost on an issue in an earlier case. *Parklane Hosiery Co.* v. *Shore*, 439 U. S. 322, 331–332 (1979). By parallel logic, could we expect the government to invoke the doctrine to bar criminal defendants from relitigating issues decided against them in a prior trial? It's an outcome few defendants would welcome but one some have already promoted. See, e.g., Kennelly, Precluding the Accused: Offensive Collateral Estoppel in Criminal Cases, 80 Va. L. Rev. 1379, 1380–1381, 1416, 1426–1427 (1994); Vestal, Issue Preclusion and Criminal Prosecutions, 65 Iowa L. Rev. 281, 297, 320–321 (1980).

Maybe worse yet, consider the possible effect on severances. Today, some state courts grant severance motions liberally to benefit defendants. But what would happen if this Court unilaterally increased the costs associated with severance in the form of allowing issue preclusion for defendants only? Granting a severance is no small thing. It means a court must expend resources for two trials where the Constitution would have permitted one. Witnesses and victims must endure a more protracted ordeal. States sometimes accept these costs to protect a defendant from potential prejudice. But 20 States appearing before us have warned that some jurisdictions might respond to any decision increasing the costs of severed trials by making them less freely available. Of course, that's only a prediction. But it's a hard if unwanted fact that "[t]oday's elaborate body of procedural rules" can contribute to making "trials expensive [and] rare." W. Stuntz, The Collapse of American Criminal Justice 39 (2011). And it would be a mistake to ignore the possibility that by making severances more costly we might wind up making them rarer too.

The fact is, civil preclusion principles and double jeopardy are different doctrines, with different histories, serving different purposes. Historically, both claim and issue preclusion have sought to "promot[e] judicial economy by preventing needless litigation." That interest may make special sense in civil cases where often only money is at stake. But the Double Jeopardy Clause and the common law principles it built upon govern *criminal* cases and concern more than efficiency. They aim instead, as we've seen, to balance vital interests against abusive prosecutorial practices with consideration to the public's safety. The Clause's terms and history simply do not contain the rights Mr. Currier seeks.

Nor are we at liberty to rewrite those terms or that history. While the growing number of criminal offenses in our statute books may be cause for concern, no one should expect (or want) judges to revise the Constitution to address every social problem they happen to perceive. The proper authorities, the States and Congress, are empowered to adopt new laws or rules experimenting with issue or claim preclusion in criminal cases if they wish. In fact, some States have already done so. On these matters, the

Constitution dictates no answers but entrusts them to a selfgoverning people to resolve.

JUSTICE KENNEDY, concurring in part.

I join Parts I and II of the Court's opinion, which, in my view, suffice to resolve this case in a full and proper way.

There is a strong public "interest in giving the prosecution one complete opportunity to convict those who have violated its laws." *Arizona v. Washington*, 434 U. S. 497, 509 (1978). The reason that single opportunity did not occur in one trial here was because both parties consented to sever the possession charge to avoid introducing evidence of petitioner's prior conviction during his trial for burglary and larceny. * * *

* * *

The end result is that when a defendant's voluntary choices lead to a second prosecution he cannot later use the Double Jeopardy Clause, whether thought of as protecting against multiple trials or the relitigation of issues, to forestall that second prosecution. The extent of the Double Jeopardy Clause protections discussed and defined in *Ashe* need not be reexamined here; for, whatever the proper formulation and implementation of those rights are, they can be lost when a defendant agrees to a second prosecution. Of course, this conclusion is premised on the defendant's having a voluntary choice, and a different result might obtain if that premise were absent. Cf. Turner v. Arkansas, 407 U. S. 366, 367 (1972) (per curiam) (applying *Ashe* to a second trial where state law prohibited a single trial of the charges at issue).

JUSTICE GINSBURG, with whom JUSTICE BREYER, JUSTICE SOTOMAYOR, and JUSTICE KAGAN join, dissenting.

* * *

I would hold that Currier's acquiescence in severance of the felon-in-possession charge does not prevent him from raising a plea of issue preclusion based on the jury acquittals of breaking and entering and grand larceny.

I

This Court's decisions "have recognized that the [Double Jeopardy] Clause embodies two vitally important interests." *Yeager v. United States*, 557 U. S. 110, 117 (2009). The first is the deeply ingrained principle that the State with all its resources and power should not be allowed to make repeated attempts to convict an individual for an alleged offense, thereby subjecting him to embarrassment, expense and ordeal and compelling him to live in a continuing state of anxiety and insecurity, as well as enhancing the possibility that even though innocent he may be found guilty. The second interest the Clause serves is preservation of the "finality of judgments," particularly acquittals * * *.

The Clause effectuates its overall guarantee through multiple protections. Historically, among those protections, the Court has safeguarded the right not to be subject to multiple trials for the "same offense." See *Brown v. Ohio*, 432 U. S. 161, 165 (1977). That claim-preclusive rule stops the government from litigating the "same offense" or criminal charge in successive prosecutions, regardless of whether the first trial ends in a conviction or an acquittal. To determine whether two offenses are the "same," this Court has held, a court must look to the offenses' elements. *Blockburger v. United States*, 284 U. S. 299, 304 (1932). If each offense "requires proof of a fact which the other does not," *Blockburger* established, the offenses are discrete and the prosecution of one does not bar later prosecution of the other. If, however, two offenses are greater and lesser included offenses, the government cannot prosecute them successively.

Also shielded by the Double Jeopardy Clause is the issue-preclusive effect of an acquittal. First articulated in *Ashe v. Swenson*, 397 U. S. 436 (1970), the issue-preclusive aspect of the Double Jeopardy Clause prohibits the government from relitigating issues necessarily resolved in a defendant's favor at an earlier trial presenting factually related offenses. *Ashe* involved the robbery of six poker players by a group of masked men. Missouri tried Ashe first for the robbery of Donald Knight. At trial, proof that Knight was the victim of a robbery was "unassailable"; the sole issue in dispute was whether Ashe was one of the robbers. A jury found Ashe not guilty. Missouri then tried Ashe for robbing a different poker player at the same table. The witnesses at the second trial "were for the most part the same," although their testimony for the prosecution was "substantially stronger" than it was at the first trial. The State also "refined its case" by declining to call a witness whose identification testimony at the first trial had been "conspicuously negative." The second time around, the State secured a conviction.

Although the second prosecution involved a different victim and thus a different "offense," this Court held that the second prosecution violated the Double Jeopardy Clause. A component of that Clause, the Court explained, rests on the principle that "when an issue of ultimate fact has once been determined by a valid and final judgment, that issue cannot again be litigated between the same parties in any future lawsuit." Consequently, "after a jury determined by its verdict that [Ashe] was not one of the robbers," the State could not "constitutionally hale him before a new jury to litigate that issue again."

In concluding that the Double Jeopardy Clause includes issue-preclusion protection for defendants, the Court acknowledged that no prior decision had "squarely held [issue preclusion] to be a constitutional requirement." "Until perhaps a century ago," the Court explained, "few situations arose calling for [issue preclusion's] application." "[A]t common law" and "under early federal criminal statutes, offense categories were relatively few and distinct," and "[a] single course of criminal conduct was likely to yield but a single offense." "[W]ith the advent of specificity in draftsmanship and the extraordinary proliferation of overlapping and related statutory offenses," however, "it became possible for prosecutors to spin out a startlingly numerous series of offenses from a single alleged criminal transaction." With this proliferation, "the potential for unfair and abusive reprosecutions became far more pronounced."

Toward the end of the 19th century, courts increasingly concluded that greater protections than those traditionally afforded under the Double Jeopardy Clause were needed to spare defendants from prosecutorial excesses. Federal courts, cognizant of the increased potential for exposing defendants to multiple charges based on the same criminal episode, borrowed issue-preclusion principles from the civil context to bar relitigation of issues necessarily resolved against the government in a criminal trial. * * * By 1970, when *Ashe* was decided, issue preclusion, "[a]lthough first developed in civil litigation," had become "an established rule of federal criminal law." The question presented in *Ashe* was whether issue preclusion is not just an established rule of federal criminal procedure, but also a rule of constitutional stature. The Court had no hesitation in concluding that it is.

Since *Ashe*, this Court has reaffirmed that issue preclusion ranks with claim preclusion as a Double Jeopardy Clause component. *Harris v. Washington*, 404 U. S. 55, 56 (1971) (per curiam). Given criminal codes of prolix character, issue preclusion both arms defendants against prosecutorial excesses and preserves the integrity of acquittals * * *.

II

* * *

The sole issue in dispute at the first trial, Currier maintains, was whether he participated in the break-in and theft. The case was submitted to the jury, which acquitted Currier of both offenses.

* * *

III

The Court holds that even if Currier could have asserted a double jeopardy issue-preclusion defense in opposition to the second trial, he relinquished that right by acquiescing in severance of the felon-in-possession charge. This holding is not sustainable. A defendant's consent to severance does not waive his right to rely on the issue-preclusive effect of an acquittal.

A

It bears clarification first that, contra to the Court's presentation, issue preclusion requires no showing of prosecutorial overreaching. * * * This Court so ruled in *Harris v. Washington*, 404 U. S. 55 (1971), and it has subsequently reinforced the point in *Turner v. Arkansas*, 407 U. S. 366 (1972) (per curiam), and *Yeager v. United States*, 557 U. S. 110 (2009).

In *Harris*, the Washington Supreme Court declined to give an acquittal issue-preclusive effect because there was "no indication of bad faith of the state in deliberately making a 'trial run' in the first prosecution." *State v. Harris*, 78 Wash. 2d 894, 901, 480 P. 2d 484, 488 (1971). The State Supreme Court further observed that "it was to the advantage of the defendant, and not the state, to separate the trials" because certain evidence was inadmissible in the first trial that would be admissible in the second. This Court reversed and explained that an acquittal has issue-preclusive effect "irrespective of the good faith of the State in bringing successive prosecutions."

In *Turner*, Arkansas prosecutors believed the defendant had robbed and murdered someone. An Arkansas statute required that murder be charged separately, with no other charges appended. After a jury acquitted Turner on the murder charge, the State sought to try him for robbery. Even though state law, not an overzealous prosecutor, dictated the sequential trials, this Court held that the defendant was entitled to assert issue preclusion and found the case "squarely controlled by *Ashe*."

In *Yeager*, the defendant stood trial on numerous factually related offenses. After a jury acquitted on some counts but hung on others, the prosecution sought to retry a number of the hung counts. The defendant argued that issue preclusion should apply in the second trial. In opposition, the prosecution stressed that a retrial "presen[ted] none of the governmental overreaching that double jeopardy is supposed to prevent." Indeed, the prosecution had "attempted to bring all the charges in a single proceeding," and it was seeking a second trial on some charges only "because the jury hung." The Court did not regard as controlling the lack of prosecutorial overreaching. Instead, it emphasized that "[a] jury's verdict of acquittal represents the community's collective judgment regarding all the evidence and arguments presented to it" and that, once rendered, an acquittal's "finality is unassailable."

B

There is in Currier's case no suggestion that he expressly waived a plea of issue preclusion at a second trial, or that he failed to timely assert the plea. Instead, the contention, urged by the prosecution and embraced by this Court, is that Currier surrendered his right to assert the issuepreclusive effect of his first-trial acquittals by consenting to two trials.

This Court "indulge[s] every reasonable presumption against waiver of fundamental constitutional rights." *Johnson v. Zerbst*, 304 U. S. 458, 464 (1938) (internal quotation marks omitted). It has found "waiver by conduct" only where a defendant has engaged in "conduct inconsistent with the assertion of [the] right." *Pierce Oil Corp. v. Phoenix Refining Co.*, 259 U. S. 125, 129 (1922). * * * Where, however, a defendant takes no action inconsistent with the assertion of a right, the defendant will not be found to have waived the right.

Currier took no action inconsistent with assertion of an issue-preclusion plea. To understand why, one must comprehend just what issue preclusion forecloses. Unlike the right against a second trial for the same offense (claim preclusion), issue preclusion prevents relitigation of a previously rejected theory of criminal liability without necessarily barring a successive trial. Take *Ashe*, for example. Issue preclusion prevented the prosecution from arguing, at a second trial, that Ashe was one of the robbers who held up the poker players at gunpoint. But if the prosecution sought to prove, instead, that Ashe waited outside during the robbery and then drove the getaway car, issue preclusion would not have barred that trial. Similarly here, the prosecution could not again attempt to prove that Currier participated in the break-in and theft of the safe at the Garrisons' residence. But a second trial could be mounted if the prosecution alleged, for instance, that Currier was present at the river's edge when others showed up to dump the safe in the river, and that Currier helped to empty out and replace the guns contained in the safe.

In short, issue preclusion does not operate, as claim preclusion does, to bar a successive trial altogether. Issue preclusion bars only a subset of possible trials—those in which the prosecution rests its case on a theory of liability a jury earlier rejected. That being so, consenting to a second trial is not inconsistent with—and therefore does not foreclose—a defendant's gaining the issue-preclusive effect of an acquittal.

The Court cites *Jeffers v. United States*, 432 U. S. 137 (1977), *United States v. Dinitz*, 424 U. S. 600 (1976), and *United States v. Scott*, 437 U. S. 82 (1978), as support for a second trial, on the ground that Currier consented to it. Those decisions do not undermine the inviolacy of an acquittal.

In *Jeffers*, the defendant was charged with two offenses, one of which was a lesser included offense of the other. He asked for, and gained, separate trials of the two charges. After *conviction* on the lesser included charge, he argued that a second trial on the remaining charge would violate his double jeopardy right "against multiple prosecutions." A plurality of this Court rejected Jeffers' argument, reasoning that he had waived the relevant right because he was "solely responsible for the successive prosecutions."

Jeffers presented a claim-preclusion question. The Court there said not one word about issue preclusion. Nor did the Court address the staying power of an acquittal. It had no occasion to do so, as Jeffers was *convicted* on the first charge. * * *

Dinitz and *Scott* are even weaker reeds. In *Dinitz*, the defendant requested, and gained, a mistrial after the trial judge expelled his lead counsel from the courtroom. In *Scott*, the defendant sought and obtained dismissal of two of three counts prior to their submission to the jury. The question in each case was whether the defendant's actions deprived him of the right to be spared from a second trial on the same offenses. Both decisions simply concluded that when a defendant voluntarily seeks to terminate a trial before a substantive ruling on guilt or innocence, the Double Jeopardy Clause is not offended by a second trial. The cases, however, said nothing about the issue-preclusive effect of a prior acquittal at a subsequent trial. * * *

IV

Venturing beyond JUSTICE KENNEDY's rationale for resolving this case, the plurality would take us back to the days before the Court recognized issue preclusion as a constitutionally grounded component of the Double Jeopardy Clause. * * * I would not engage in that endeavor to restore things past. One decision, however, should be set straight. The plurality asserts that *Dowling v. United States*, 493 U. S. 342 (1990), established that issue preclusion has no role to play in regulating the issues or evidence presented at a successive trial. *Dowling* did no such thing. The case is tied to Federal Rule of Evidence 404(b), which allows the prosecution to introduce evidence of a defendant's past criminal conduct for described purposes other than to show a defendant's bad character. See Fed. Rule Evid. 404(b)(2). The defendant in *Dowling* was prosecuted for robbing a bank. To bolster its case that Dowling was the perpetrator, the Government sought to introduce evidence that Dowling participated in a home invasion two weeks after the bank robbery. One difficulty for the prosecution: Dowling had been acquitted of the home invasion. Nevertheless, the trial court admitted the evidence, informing the jurors that Dowling had been acquitted of the home-invasion charge and instructing them on the "limited purpose" for which the evidence was introduced.

The Court in *Dowling* "decline[d] to extend *Ashe*" to forbid the prosecution from introducing evidence, under Rule 404(b), of a crime for which the defendant had been acquitted, one involving criminal conduct unrelated to the bank robbery for which Dowling stood trial. The charge for which Dowling was acquitted took place at a different time and involved different property, a different location, and different victims. * * * It surely could not be said that, in the bank robbery trial, Dowling was being tried a second time for the later-occurring home invasion offense. Here, by contrast, the two trials involved the same criminal episode. * * *

Extending *Dowling* from the Evidence Rule 404(b) context in which it was embedded to retrials involving the same course of previously acquitted conduct would undermine issue-preclusion's core tenet. That tenet was well stated by Judge Friendly in *United States* v. *Kramer*, 289 F. 2d 909 (CA2 1961):

> "A defendant who has satisfied one jury that he had no responsibility for a crime ought not be forced to convince another of this [lack of responsibility] . . . . The very nub of [issue preclusion] is to extend *res judicata* beyond those cases where the prior judgment is a complete bar. The Government is free, within limits set by the Fifth Amendment, to charge an acquitted defendant with other crimes claimed to arise from the same or related conduct; but it may not prove the new charge by asserting facts necessarily determined against it on the first trial . . . ." *Id.,* at 915–916 (citation omitted).

So here. The first trial established that Currier did not participate in breaking and entering the Garrisons' residence or in stealing their safe. The government can attempt to prove Currier possessed firearms through a means other than breaking and entering the Garrisons' residence and stealing their safe. But the government should not be permitted to show in the felon-in-possession trial what it failed to show in the first trial, *i.e.,* Currier's participation in the charged breaking and entering and grand larceny, after a full and fair opportunity to do so.

* * *

IX. DUAL SOVEREIGNS

Page 1687. Add after the runover paragraph:

Adhering to the Dual Sovereignty Doctrine:
Gamble v. United States

GAMBLE V. UNITED STATES
Supreme Court of the United States, 2019.
139 S.Ct. 1960.

JUSTICE ALITO delivered the opinion of the Court.

We consider in this case whether to overrule a longstanding interpretation of the Double Jeopardy Clause of the Fifth Amendment. That Clause provides that no person may be "twice put in jeopardy" "for the same offence." Our double jeopardy case law is complex, but at its core, the Clause means that those acquitted or convicted of a particular "offence" cannot be tried a second time for the same "offence." But what does the Clause mean by an "offence"?

We have long held that a crime under one sovereign's laws is not "the same offence" as a crime under the laws of another sovereign. Under this "dual-sovereignty" doctrine, a State may prosecute a defendant under state law even if the Federal Government has prosecuted him for the same conduct under a federal statute.

Or the reverse may happen, as it did here. Terance Gamble, convicted by Alabama for possessing a firearm as a felon, now faces prosecution by the United States under its own felon-in-possession law. Attacking this second prosecution on double jeopardy grounds, Gamble asks us to overrule the dual-sovereignty doctrine. He contends that it departs from the founding-era understanding of the right enshrined by the Double Jeopardy Clause. But the historical evidence assembled by Gamble is feeble; pointing the other way are the Clause's text, other historical evidence, and 170 years of precedent. Today we affirm that precedent, and with it the decision below.

I

In November 2015, a local police officer in Mobile, Alabama, pulled Gamble over for a damaged headlight. Smelling marijuana, the officer searched Gamble's car, where he found a loaded 9-mm handgun. Since Gamble had been convicted of second-degree robbery, his possession of the handgun violated an Alabama law providing that no one convicted of "a crime of violence" "shall own a firearm or have one in his or her possession." After Gamble pleaded guilty to this state offense, federal prosecutors indicted him for the same instance of possession under a federal law—one forbidding those convicted of "a crime punishable by imprisonment for a term exceeding one year . . . to ship or transport in interstate or foreign commerce, or possess in or affecting commerce, any firearm or ammunition." 18 U. S. C. § 922(g)(1).

Gamble moved to dismiss on one ground: The federal indictment was for "the same offence" as the one at issue in his state conviction and thus exposed him to double jeopardy. But because this Court has long held that two offenses "are *not* the 'same offence'" for double jeopardy purposes if "prosecuted by different sovereigns," *Heath* v. *Alabama*, 474 U. S. 82, 92 (1985), the District Court denied Gamble's motion to dismiss. Gamble then pleaded guilty to the federal offense while preserving his right to challenge the denial of his motion to dismiss on double jeopardy grounds. But on appeal the Eleventh Circuit affirmed, citing the dual-sovereignty doctrine. We granted certiorari to determine whether to overturn that doctrine.

II

Gamble contends that the Double Jeopardy Clause must forbid successive prosecutions by different sovereigns because that is what the founding-era common law did. But before turning to that historical claim, see Part III *infra*, we review the Clause's text and some of the cases Gamble asks us to overturn.

A

We start with the text of the Fifth Amendment. Although the dual-sovereignty rule is often dubbed an "exception" to the double jeopardy right, it is not an exception at all. On the contrary, it follows from the text that defines that right in the first place. "[T]he language of the Clause . . . protects individuals from being twice put in jeopardy 'for the same *offence*,' not for the same *conduct* or *actions*" * * *. As originally understood, then, an "offence" is defined by a law, and each law is defined by a sovereign. So where there are two sovereigns, there are two laws, and two "offences." * * *

Faced with this reading, Gamble falls back on an episode from the Double Jeopardy Clause's drafting history. The first Congress, working on an earlier draft that would have banned " 'more than one trial or one punishment for the same offence,' " voted down a proposal to add " 'by any law of the United States.' " 1 Annals of Cong. 753 (1789). In rejecting this addition, Gamble surmises, Congress must have intended to bar successive prosecutions regardless of the sovereign bringing the charge.

Even if that inference were justified—something that the Government disputes—it would count for little. The private intent behind a drafter's rejection of one version of a text is shoddy evidence of the public meaning of an altogether different text. * * *

* * *

We see no reason to abandon the sovereign-specific reading of the phrase "same offence," from which the dual-sovereignty rule immediately follows.

B

Our cases * * * reveal[ ] how fidelity to the Double Jeopardy Clause's text does more than honor the formal difference between two distinct criminal codes. It honors the substantive differences between the interests that two sovereigns can have in punishing the same act.

The question of successive federal and state prosecutions arose in three antebellum cases implying and then spelling out the dual-sovereignty doctrine. The first, *Fox* v. *Ohio*, 5 How. 410 (1847), involved an Ohio prosecution for the passing of counterfeit coins. The defendant argued that since Congress can punish counterfeiting, the States must be barred from doing so, or else a person could face two trials for the same offense, contrary to the Fifth Amendment. We rejected the defendant's premise that under the Double Jeopardy Clause "offences falling within the competency of different authorities to restrain or punish them would not properly be subjected to the consequences which those authorities might ordain and affix to their perpetration." Indeed, we observed, the nature of the crime or its effects on "public safety" might well "deman[d]" separate prosecutions. Generalizing from this point, we declared in a second case that "the same act might, as to its character and tendencies, and the consequences it involved, constitute an offence against both the State and Federal governments, and might draw to its commission the penalties denounced by either, as appropriate to its character in reference to each." *United States* v. *Marigold*, 9 How. 560, 569 (1850).

A third antebellum case, *Moore* v. *Illinois*, 14 How. 13, expanded on this concern for the different interests of separate sovereigns, after tracing it to the text in the manner set forth above. Recalling that the Fifth Amendment prohibits double jeopardy not "for the same ac[t]" but "for the same offence," and that "[a]n offence, in its legal signification, means the transgression of a law," we drew the now-familiar inference: A single act "may be an offence or transgression of the laws of " two sovereigns, and hence punishable by both. Then we gave color to this abstract principle—and to the diverse interests it might vindicate—with an example. An assault on a United States marshal, we said, would offend against the Nation and a State: the first by "hindering" the "execution of legal process," and the second by "breach[ing]" the "peace of the State." That duality of harm explains how "one act" could constitute "two offences, for each of which [the offender] is justly punishable."

This principle comes into still sharper relief when we consider a prosecution in this country for crimes committed abroad. If, as Gamble suggests, only one sovereign may prosecute for a single act, no American court—state or federal—could prosecute conduct already tried in a foreign court. Imagine, for example, that a U. S. national has been murdered in another country. That country could rightfully seek to punish the killer for committing an act of violence within its territory. The foreign country's interest lies in protecting the peace in that territory rather than protecting the American specifically. But the United States looks at the same conduct and sees an act of violence against one of its nationals, a person under the particular protection of its laws. The murder of a U. S. national is an offense to the United States as much as it is to the country where the murder occurred and to which the victim is a stranger. That is why the killing of an American abroad is a federal offense that can be prosecuted in our courts, see 18 U. S. C. § 2332(a)(1), and why customary international law allows this exercise of jurisdiction.

* * *

We cemented that foundation 70 years after the last of those antebellum cases, in a decision upholding a federal prosecution that followed one by a State. See *United States* v. *Lanza*, 260 U. S. 377, 382 (1922) ("[A]n act denounced as a crime by both national and state sovereignties is an offense against the peace and dignity of both and may be punished by each"). And for decades more, we applied our precedent without qualm or quibble. See, *e.g.*, *Screws* v. *United States*, 325 U. S. 91 (1945); *Jerome* v. *United States*, 318 U. S. 101 (1943); *Puerto Rico* v. *Shell Co. (P. R.), Ltd.*, 302 U. S. 253 (1937); *Westfall* v. *United States*, 274 U. S. 256 (1927); *Hebert* v. *Louisiana*, 272 U. S. 312 (1926). When petitioners in 1959 asked us twice to reverse course, we twice refused, finding "[n]o consideration or persuasive reason not presented to the Court in the prior cases" for disturbing our "firmly established" doctrine. *Abbate* v. *United States*, 359 U. S. 187, 195; see also *Bartkus* v. *Illinois*, 359 U. S. 121. And then we went on enforcing it, adding another six decades of cases to the doctrine's history. See, *e.g.*, *Puerto Rico* v. *Sánchez Valle*, 579 U. S. ___ 2016); *Heath* v. *Alabama*, 474 U. S. 82 (1985); *United States* v. *Wheeler*, 435 U. S. 313 (1978); *Rinaldi* v. *United States*, 434 U. S. 22 (1977) (*per curiam*).

C

We briefly address two objections to this analysis.

First, the dissents contend that our dual-sovereignty rule errs in treating the Federal and State *Governments* as two separate sovereigns when in fact sovereignty belongs to the people. See *post*, at 3 (opinion of GINSBURG, J.); *post*, at 7 (opinion of GORSUCH, J.). This argument is based on a non sequitur. Yes, our Constitution rests on the principle that the people are sovereign, but that does not mean that they have conferred all the attributes of sovereignty on a single government. Instead, the people, by adopting the Constitution, " 'split the atom of sovereignty.' " *Alden* v. *Maine*, 527 U. S. 706, 751 (1999). * * *

It is true that the Republic is " 'ONE WHOLE,' " *post*, at 3 (opinion of GINSBURG, J.) (quoting The Federalist No. 82, p. 493 (C. Rossiter ed. 1961) (A. Hamilton)). But there is a difference between the whole and a single part, and that difference underlies decisions as foundational to our legal system as *McCulloch* v. *Maryland*, 4 Wheat. 316 (1819). There, in terms so directly relevant as to seem presciently tailored to answer this very objection, Chief Justice Marshall distinguished precisely between "the people of a State" and "[t]he people of all the States"; between the "sovereignty which the people of a single state possess" and the sovereign powers "conferred by the people of the United States on the government of the Union,"; and thus between "the action of a part" and "the action of the whole." In short, *McCulloch*'s famous holding that a State may not tax the national bank rested on a recognition that the States and the Nation have different "interests" and "right[s]." One strains to imagine a clearer statement of the premises of our dual-sovereignty rule, or a more authoritative source. The United States is a *federal* republic; it is not, contrary to JUSTICE GORSUCH's suggestion, *post*, at 10–11, a unitary state like the United Kingdom.

Gamble and the dissents lodge a second objection to this line of reasoning. They suggest that because the division of federal and state power was meant to promote liberty, it cannot support a rule that exposes Gamble to a second sentence. . This argument fundamentally misunderstands the governmental structure established by our Constitution. Our federal system advances individual liberty in many ways. Among other things, it limits the powers of the Federal Government and protects certain basic liberties from infringement. But because the powers of the Federal Government and the States often overlap, allowing both to regulate often results in two layers of regulation. Taxation is an example that comes immediately to mind. It is also not at all uncommon for the Federal Government to permit activities that a State chooses to forbid or heavily restrict—for example, gambling and the sale of alcohol. And a State may choose to legalize an activity that federal law prohibits, such as the sale of marijuana. So while our system of federalism is fundamental to the protection of liberty, it does not always maximize individual liberty at the expense of other interests. * * *

III

Gamble claims that our precedent contradicts the common-law rights that the Double Jeopardy Clause was originally understood to engraft onto the Constitution * * *. Gamble argues that those who ratified the Fifth Amendment understood these common-law principles (which the Amendment constitutionalized) to bar a domestic prosecution following one by a foreign nation. For support, he appeals to early English and American cases and treatises. We have highlighted one hurdle to Gamble's reading: the sovereign-specific original meaning of "offence." But the doctrine of *stare decisis* is another obstacle.

[The Court engages in a lengthy discussion of a case involving a man named Hutchinson, whose case other than a bail decision is not reported. Gamble claimed that the case established that a prior acquittal in Portugal for homicide barred an English prosecution for the same offense. The Court relied upon *Gage* v. *Bulkeley*, Ridg. T. H. 263, 27 Eng. Rep. 824 (Ch. 1744), as rejecting Gamble's view of the Hutchinson case. The Court found that Lord Chancellor Hardwicke determined that foreign judgments are not binding in an English court of law, a judgment of one sovereign cannot bind another, and Hutchinson was spared a trial in England as a matter of discretion.]

Summing up the import of the preratification cases on which Gamble's argument rests, we have the following: (1) not a single reported case in which a foreign acquittal or conviction barred a later prosecution for the same act in either Britain or America; (2) not a single reported decision in which a foreign judgment was held to be binding in a civil case in a court of law; (3) fragmentary and not entirely consistent evidence about a 17th-century case in which a defendant named Hutchinson, having been tried and acquitted for murder someplace in the Iberian Peninsula, is said to have been spared a second trial for this crime on some ground, perhaps out of "merc[y]," not as a matter of right; (4) two cases (one criminal, one in admiralty) in which a party invoked a prior foreign judgment, but the court did not endorse or rest anything on the party's reliance on that judgment; and (5) two Court of Chancery cases actually holding that foreign judgments were *not* (or not generally) treated as barring trial at common law. This is the flimsy foundation in case law for Gamble's argument that when the Fifth Amendment was ratified, it was well understood that a foreign criminal judgment would bar retrial for the same act.

[The Court also rejects Gamble's contention that treatise writers supported his argument, finds that 19th century state cases were inconclusive, and distinguishes two earlier federal decisions.]

IV

Besides appealing to the remote past, Gamble contends that recent changes—one doctrinal, one practical—blunt the force of *stare decisis* here. They do not.

A

If historical claims form the chorus of Gamble's argument, his refrain is "incorporation." In Gamble's telling, the recognition of the Double Jeopardy Clause's incorporation against the States, see *Benton* v. *Maryland*, 395 U. S. 784, 794 (1969), washed away any theoretical foundation for the dual-sovereignty rule. But this incorporation-changes-everything argument trades on a false analogy.

The analogy Gamble draws is to the evolution of our doctrine on the Fourth Amendment right against unreasonable searches and seizures. We have long enforced this right by barring courts from relying on evidence gathered in an illegal search. Thus, in *Weeks* v. *United States*, 232 U. S. 383, 391–393 (1914), the Court held that federal prosecutors could not rely on the fruits of an unreasonable search undertaken by federal agents. But what if state or local police conducted a search that would have violated the Fourth Amendment if conducted by federal agents? Before incorporation, the state search would not have violated the Federal Constitution, so federal law would not have barred admission of the resulting evidence in a state prosecution. But by the very same token, under what was termed "the silver-platter doctrine," state authorities could hand such evidence over to *federal* prosecutors for use in a federal case.

Once the Fourth Amendment was held to apply to the States as well as the Federal Government, however, the silver-platter doctrine was scuttled. See *Elkins* v. *United States*, 364 U. S. 206 (1960); *Wolf* v. *Colorado*, 338 U. S. 25 (1949). Now the fruits of unreasonable state searches are inadmissible in federal and state courts alike.

Gamble contends that the incorporation of the Double Jeopardy Clause should likewise end the dual-sovereignty rule, but his analogy fails. The silver-platter doctrine was based on the fact that the state searches to which it applied did not at that time violate federal law. Once the Fourth Amendment was incorporated against the States, the status of those state searches changed. Now they did violate federal law, so the basis for the silver-platter doctrine was gone.

By contrast, the premises of the dual-sovereignty doctrine have survived incorporation intact. Incorporation meant that the States were now required to abide by this Court's interpretation of the Double Jeopardy Clause. But that interpretation has long included the dual-sovereignty doctrine, and there is no logical reason why incorporation should change it. After all, the doctrine rests on the fact that only same-sovereign successive prosecutions are prosecutions for the "same offense"—and that is just as true after incorporation as before.

B

If incorporation is the doctrinal shift that Gamble invokes to justify a departure from precedent, the practical change he cites is the proliferation of federal criminal law. Gamble says that the resulting overlap of federal and criminal codes heightens the risk of successive prosecutions under state and federal law for the same criminal conduct. Thus, Gamble contends, our precedent should yield to " 'far-reaching systemic and structural changes' " that make our "earlier error all the more egregious and harmful." But unlike Gamble's appeal to incorporation, this argument obviously assumes that the dual-sovereignty doctrine was legal error from the start. So the argument is only as strong as Gamble's argument about the original understanding of double jeopardy rights, an argument that we have found wanting.

Insofar as the expansion of the reach of federal criminal law has been questioned on constitutional rather than policy grounds, the argument has focused on whether Congress has overstepped its legislative powers under the Constitution. See, *e.g.*, *Gonzales* v. *Raich*, 545 U. S. 1, 57–74 (2005) (THOMAS, J., dissenting). Eliminating the dual-sovereignty rule would do little to trim the reach of federal criminal law, and it would not even prevent many successive state and federal prosecutions for the same criminal conduct unless we also overruled the long-settled rule that an "offence" for double jeopardy purposes is defined by statutory elements, not by what might be described in a looser sense as a unit of criminal conduct.

See *Blockburger* v. *United States*, 284 U. S. 299 (1932). Perhaps believing that two revolutionary assaults in the same case would be too much, Gamble has not asked us to overrule *Blockburger* along with the dual-sovereignty rule.

* * *

The judgment of the Court of Appeals for the Eleventh Circuit is affirmed.

JUSTICE THOMAS, concurring.

I agree that the historical record does not bear out my initial skepticism of the dual-sovereignty doctrine. See *Puerto Rico* v. *Sánchez Valle*, 579 U. S. ___ (2016) (GINSBURG, J., joined by THOMAS, J. concurring). The founding generation foresaw very limited potential for overlapping criminal prosecutions by the States and the Federal Government. The Founders therefore had no reason to address the double jeopardy question that the Court resolves today. Given their understanding of Congress' limited criminal jurisdiction and the absence of an analogous dual-sovereign system in England, it is difficult to conclude that the People who ratified the Fifth Amendment understood it to prohibit prosecution by a State and the Federal Government for the same offense. And, of course, we are not entitled to interpret the Constitution to align it with our personal sensibilities about "unjust" prosecutions. * * *

I write separately to address the proper role of the doctrine of *stare decisis*. In my view, the Court's typical formulation of the *stare decisis* standard does not comport with our judicial duty under Article III because it elevates demonstrably erroneous decisions—meaning decisions outside the realm of permissible interpretation—over the text of the Constitution and other duly enacted federal law. * * *

* * *

When faced with a demonstrably erroneous precedent, my rule is simple: We should not follow it. This view of *stare decisis* follows directly from the Constitution's supremacy over other sources of law—including our own precedents. * * * [B]ecause the Constitution is supreme over other sources of law, it requires us to privilege its text over our own precedents when the two are in conflict. I am aware of no legitimate reason why a court may privilege a demonstrably erroneous interpretation of the Constitution over the Constitution itself.

* * *

JUSTICE GINSBURG, dissenting.

Terance Martez Gamble pleaded guilty in Alabama state court to both possession of a firearm by a person convicted of "a crime of violence" and drug possession, and was sentenced to ten years' imprisonment, all but one year suspended. Apparently regarding Alabama's sentence as too lenient, federal prosecutors pursued a parallel charge, possession of a firearm by a convicted felon, in violation of federal law. Gamble again pleaded guilty and received nearly three more years in prison.

Had either the Federal Government or Alabama brought the successive prosecutions, the second would have violated Gamble's right not to be "twice put in jeopardy . . . for the same offence." U. S. Const., Amdt. 5, cl. 2. Yet the Federal Government was able to multiply Gamble's time in prison because of the doctrine that, for double jeopardy purposes, identical criminal laws enacted by "separate sovereigns" are different "offence[s]."

I dissent from the Court's adherence to that misguided doctrine. Instead of frittering away Gamble's liberty upon a metaphysical subtlety, two sovereignties, I would hold that the Double Jeopardy Clause bars successive prosecutions for the same offense by parts of the whole USA.

I

* * *

B

* * *

1

Justification for the separate-sovereigns doctrine centers on the word "offence": An "offence," the argument runs, is the violation of a sovereign's law, the United States and each State are separate sovereigns, ergo successive state and federal prosecutions do not place a defendant in "jeopardy . . . for the same offence."

This compact syllogism is fatally flawed. The United States and its constituent States, unlike foreign nations, are "kindred systems," "parts of ONE WHOLE." The Federalist No. 82, p. 493 (C. Rossiter ed. 1961) (A. Hamilton). They compose one people, bound by an overriding Federal Constitution. Within that "WHOLE," the Federal and State Governments should be disabled from accomplishing together "what neither government [could] do alone—prosecute an ordinary citizen twice for the same offence." Amar & Marcus, Double Jeopardy Law After Rodney King, 95 Colum. L. Rev. 1, 2 (1995).

The notion that the Federal Government and the States are separate sovereigns overlooks a basic tenet of our federal system. The doctrine treats *governments* as sovereign, with state power to prosecute carried over from years predating the Constitution. In the system established by the Federal Constitution, however, ultimate sovereignty resides in the *governed.* * * * States may be separate, but their populations are part of the people composing the United States.

In our "compound republic," the division of authority between the United States and the States was meant to operate as "a double security [for] the rights of the people." The Federalist No. 51, at 323 (J. Madison).

The separate-sovereigns doctrine, however, scarcely shores up people's rights. Instead, it invokes federalism to withhold liberty.

It is the doctrine's premise that each government has—and must be allowed to vindicate—a distinct interest in enforcing its own criminal laws. That is a peculiar way to look at the Double Jeopardy Clause, which by its terms safeguards the "person" and restrains the government. * * *

2

* * *

[T]he Court has reasoned that the separate-sovereigns doctrine is necessary to prevent either the Federal Government or a State from encroaching on the other's law enforcement prerogatives. Without this doctrine, the Court has observed, the Federal Government, by prosecuting first, could bar a State from pursuing more serious charges for the same offense; and conversely, a State, by prosecuting first, could effectively nullify federal law. This concern envisions federal and state prosecutors working at cross purposes, but cooperation between authorities is the norm. And when federal-state tension exists, successive prosecutions for the federal and state offenses may escape double-jeopardy blockage under the test prescribed in *Blockburger* v. *United States*, 284 U. S. 299 (1932). Offenses are distinct, *Blockburger* held, if "each . . . requires proof of a fact which the other does not."

* * *

II

A

* * *

Before incorporation, the separate-sovereigns doctrine had a certain logic: Without a carve-out for successive prosecutions by separate sovereigns, the Double Jeopardy Clause would have barred the Federal Government from prosecuting a defendant previously tried by a State, but would not have prevented a State from prosecuting a defendant previously tried by the Federal Government. Incorporation changed this. Operative against the States since 1969, when the Court decided *Benton* v. *Maryland*, 395 U. S. 784, the double jeopardy proscription now applies to the Federal

Government and the States alike. The remaining office of the separate-sovereigns doctrine, then, is to enable federal and state prosecutors, proceeding one after the other, to expose defendants to double jeopardy.

The separate-sovereigns doctrine's persistence contrasts with the fate of analogous dual-sovereignty doctrines following application of the rights at issue to the States. Prior to incorporation of the Fourth Amendment as a restraint on state action, federal prosecutors were free to use evidence obtained illegally by state or local officers, then served up to federal officers on a "silver platter." See *Elkins* v. *United States*, 364 U. S. 206, 208–214 (1960); *Weeks* v. *United States*, 232 U. S. 383, 398 (1914). Once the Fourth Amendment applied to the States, abandonment of this "silver platter doctrine" was impelled by "principles of logic" and the reality that, from the perspective of the victim of an unreasonable search and seizure, it mattered not at all "whether his constitutional right ha[d] been invaded by a federal agent or by a state officer." *Elkins*, 364 U. S., at 208, 215. * * *

* * *

The Court regards incorporation as immaterial because application of the Double Jeopardy Clause to the States did not affect comprehension of the word "offence" to mean the violation of one sovereign's law. But the Court attributed a separate-sovereigns meaning to "offence" at least in part because the Double Jeopardy Clause did not apply to the States. Incorporation of the Clause should prompt the Court to consider the protection against double jeopardy from the defendant's perspective and to ask why each of two governments within the United States should be permitted to try a defendant once for the same offense when neither could try him or her twice.

* * *

B

The expansion of federal criminal law has exacerbated the problems created by the separate-sovereigns doctrine. Ill effects of the doctrine might once have been tempered by the limited overlap between federal and state criminal law. * * *

* * *

Against all this, there is little to be said for keeping the separate-sovereigns doctrine. Gamble's case does not implicate the reliance interests of private parties. The closest thing to a reliance interest would be the interest Federal and State Governments have in avoiding avulsive changes that could complicate ongoing prosecutions. As the Court correctly explains, however, overruling the separate-sovereigns doctrine would not affect large numbers of cases. In prosecutions based on the same conduct, federal and state prosecutors will often charge offenses having different elements, charges that, under *Blockburger*, will not trigger double jeopardy protection. * * *

* * *

JUSTICE GORSUCH, dissenting.

A free society does not allow its government to try the same individual for the same crime until it's happy with the result. Unfortunately, the Court today endorses a colossal exception to this ancient rule against double jeopardy. My colleagues say that the federal government and each State are "separate sovereigns" entitled to try the same person for the same crime. So if all the might of one "sovereign" cannot succeed against the presumptively free individual, another may insist on the chance to try again. And if both manage to succeed, so much the better; they can add one punishment on top of the other. But this "separate sovereigns exception" to the bar against double jeopardy finds no meaningful support in the text of the Constitution, its original public meaning, structure, or history. Instead, the Constitution promises all Americans that they will never suffer double jeopardy. I would enforce that guarantee.

I

* * *

The rule against double jeopardy was firmly entrenched in both the American colonies and England at the time of our Revolution. And the Fifth Amendment, which prohibits placing a defendant "twice . . . in jeopardy of life or limb" for "the same offence" sought to carry the traditional common law rule into our Constitution. As Joseph Story put it, the Constitution's prohibition against double jeopardy grew from a "great privilege secured by the common law" and meant "that a party shall not be tried a second time for the same offence, after he has once been convicted, or acquitted of the offence charged, by the verdict of a jury, and judgment has passed thereon for or against him."

Given all this, it might seem that Mr. Gamble should win this case handily. Alabama prosecuted him for violating a state law that "prohibits a convicted felon from possessing a pistol" and sentenced him to a year in prison. But then the federal government, apparently displeased with the sentence, charged Mr. Gamble under 18 U. S. C. § 922(g)(1) with being a felon in possession of a firearm based on the same facts that gave rise to the state prosecution. Ultimately, a federal court sentenced him to 46 months in prison and three years of supervised release. Most any ordinary speaker of English would say that Mr. Gamble was tried twice for "the same offence," precisely what the Fifth Amendment prohibits. * * *

So how does the government manage to evade the Fifth Amendment's seemingly plain command? On the government's account, the fact that federal and state authorities split up the prosecution makes all the difference. Though the Double Jeopardy Clause doesn't say anything about allowing "separate sovereigns" to do sequentially what neither may do separately, the government assures us the Fifth Amendment's phrase "same offence" does this work. Adopting the government's argument, the Court supplies the following syllogism: "[A]n 'offence' is defined by a law, and each law is defined by a sovereign. So where there are two sovereigns, there are two laws, and two 'offences.' "

But the major premise of this argument—that "where there are two laws there are 'two offenses' "—is mistaken. * * * The framers understood the term "offence" to mean a "transgression." And they understood that the same transgression might be punished by two pieces of positive law: After all, constitutional protections were not meant to be flimsy things but to embody "principles that are permanent, uniform, and universal." * * * We know that the framers didn't conceive of the term "same offence" in some technical way as referring only to the same statute. And if double jeopardy prevents *one* government from prosecuting a defendant multiple times for the same offense under the banner of separate statutory labels, on what account can it make a difference when *many* governments collectively seek to do the same thing?

The government identifies no evidence suggesting that the framers understood the term "same offence" to bear such a lawyerly sovereign-specific meaning. * * *

The history of the Double Jeopardy Clause itself supplies more evidence yet. The original draft prohibited "more than one trial or one punishment for the same offence." One representative then proposed adding the words "by any law of the United States" after "same offence." That proposal clearly would have codified the government's sovereign-specific view of the Clause's operation. Yet, Congress proceeded to reject it.

Viewed from the perspective of an ordinary reader of the Fifth Amendment, whether at the time of its adoption or in our own time, none of this can come as a surprise. Imagine trying to explain the Court's separate sovereigns rule to a criminal defendant, then or now. Yes, you were sentenced to state prison for being a felon in possession of a firearm. And don't worry—the State can't prosecute you again. But a federal prosecutor *can* send you to prison again for exactly the same thing. What's more, that federal prosecutor may work hand-in-hand with the same state prosecutor who already went after you. They can share evidence and discuss what worked and what didn't the first time around. And the federal prosecutor can pursue you even if you were *acquitted* in the state case. None of that offends the Constitution's plain words protecting a person from being placed "twice . . . in jeopardy of life or limb" for "the same offence." Really?

II

Without meaningful support in the text of the Double Jeopardy Clause, the government insists that the separate sovereigns exception is at least compelled by the structure of our Constitution. On its view, adopted by the Court today, allowing the federal and state governments to punish the same defendant for the same conduct "honors the substantive differences between the interests that two sovereigns can have" in our federal system.

But this argument errs from the outset. The Court seems to assume that sovereignty in this country belongs to the state and federal governments, much as it once belonged to the King of England. But as Chief Justice Marshall explained, "[t]he government of the Union . . . is emphatically, and truly, a government of the people," and all sovereignty "emanates from them." Alexander Hamilton put the point this way: "[T]he national and State systems are to be regarded" not as different sovereigns foreign to one another but "as ONE WHOLE." Under our Constitution, the federal and state governments are but two expressions of a single and sovereign people.

* * *

From its mistaken premise, the Court continues to the flawed conclusion that the federal and state governments can successively prosecute the same person for the same offense. This turns the point of our federal experiment on its head. When the "ONE WHOLE" people of the United States assigned different aspects of their sovereign power to the federal and state governments, they sought not to *multiply* governmental power but to *limit* it. * * * Yet today's Court invokes federalism not to protect individual liberty but to threaten it, allowing two governments to achieve together an objective denied to each. The Court brushes this concern aside because "the powers of the Federal Government and the States often overlap," which "often results in two layers of regulation." But the Court's examples—taxation, alcohol, and marijuana—involve areas that the federal and state governments each may regulate separately under the Constitution as interpreted by this Court. That is miles away from the separate sovereigns exception, which allows the federal and state governments to accomplish together what *neither* may do separately consistent with the Constitution's commands. * * *

III

A

If the Constitution's text and structure do not supply persuasive support for the government's position, what about a more thorough exploration of the common law from which the Fifth Amendment was drawn? * * *

By 1791 when the Fifth Amendment was adopted, an array of common law authorities suggested that a prosecution in *any* court, so long as the court had jurisdiction over the offense, was enough to bar future reprosecution in another court. * * *

* * *

B

What we know about the common law before the Fifth Amendment's ratification in 1791 finds further confirmation in how later legal thinkers in both England and America described the rule they had inherited.

* * *

[Justice Gorsuch discusses early federal and state cases. He concludes that they endorse the rule of the Hutchinson case, discussed in the majority opinion, which he asserts established that an acquittal in one jurisdiction bars reprosecution in another.]

IV

With the text, principles of federalism, and history now arrayed against it, the government is left to suggest that we should retain the separate sovereigns exception under the doctrine of *stare decisis*. But if that's the real basis for today's result, let's at least acknowledge this: By all appearances, the Constitution as originally adopted and understood did *not* allow successive state and federal prosecutions for the same offense, yet the government wants this Court to tolerate the practice anyway.

Stare decisis has many virtues, but when it comes to enforcing the Constitution this Court must take (and always has taken) special care in the doctrine's application. After all, judges swear to protect and defend the Constitution, not to protect what it prohibits. And while we rightly pay heed to the considered views of those who have come before us, especially in close cases, *stare decisis* isn't supposed to be "the art of being methodically ignorant of what everyone knows." Indeed, blind obedience to *stare decisis* would leave this Court still abiding grotesque errors like *Dred Scott* v. *Sandford*, *Plessy* v. *Ferguson*, and *Korematsu* v. *United States*. * * *

[Justice Gorsuch suggests that the quality of the decisions establishing the separate-sovereign approach to double jeopardy was poor, the cases were decided by the narrowest of margins, the underpinnings of the approach were undermined by subsequent decisions, the world of criminal justice has changed with the expansion of federal criminal law, and the "reliance" of law enforcement on the approach does not warrant retaining it given the cooperation that exists among federal and state prosecutors and the narrow scope of the *Blockburger* definition of same offense.]

Enforcing the Constitution always bears its costs. But when the people adopted the Constitution and its Bill of Rights, they thought the liberties promised there worth the costs. It is not for this Court to reassess this judgment to make the prosecutor's job easier. Nor is there any doubt that the benefits the framers saw in prohibiting double prosecutions remain real, and maybe more vital than ever, today. When governments may unleash all their might in multiple prosecutions against an individual, exhausting themselves only when those who hold the reins of power are content with the result, it is "the poor and the weak," and the unpopular and controversial, who suffer first—and there is nothing to stop them from being the last. The separate sovereigns exception was wrong when it was invented, and it remains wrong today.

I respectfully dissent.

CHAPTER 13

POST-CONVICTION CHALLENGES

■ ■ ■

II. GROUNDS FOR DIRECT ATTACKS ON A CONVICTION

D. THE EFFECT OF AN ERROR ON THE VERDICT

1. Harmless Error

Page 1723. Add the following after the section on *Gonzalez-Lopez*:

Defense Counsel's Conceding Guilt over the Defendant's Objection Is a Structural Error: McCoy v. Louisiana

The defendant in *McCoy v. Louisiana*, 138 S.Ct. 1500 (2018), was tried for capital murder. All the evidence indicated that he committed the murders. But the defendant steadfastly denied committing the murders, and blamed it all on a far-flung conspiracy against him. He testified to that effect at trial. Trial counsel chose, as a matter of strategy—and over McCoy's strenuous objections—to concede that the defendant did the killings, but to argue that he did not have the requisite mental state to commit murder, given his serious mental and emotional issues. McCoy was convicted of murder and sentenced to death.

The Supreme Court, in an opinion by Justice Ginsburg for six Justices, held that defense counsel has no authority under the Sixth Amendment to concede guilt over the objection of the defendant. That is because the decision whether or not to contest guilt is a matter of personal autonomy and a decision to be made by the client. [The Court's discussion of this point is set out in full in this Supplement, Chapter Ten.]

The Court further found that when defense counsel does make such an argument, it constitutes a structural error, not susceptible to harmless error review. Justice Ginsburg explained the Court's ruling on structural error as follows:

> Because a client's autonomy, not counsel's competence, is in issue, we do not apply our ineffective-assistance-of-counsel jurisprudence to McCoy's claim. To gain redress for attorney error, a defendant

ordinarily must show prejudice. Here, however, the violation of McCoy's protected autonomy right was complete when the court allowed counsel to usurp control of an issue within McCoy's sole prerogative.

Violation of a defendant's Sixth Amendment-secured autonomy ranks as error of the kind our decisions have called "structural"; when present, such an error is not subject to harmless-error review. * * * An error may be ranked structural, we have explained, "if the right at issue is not designed to protect the defendant from erroneous conviction but instead protects some other interest," such as "the fundamental legal principle that a defendant must be allowed to make his own choices about the proper way to protect his own liberty." An error might also count as structural when its effects are too hard to measure, as is true of the right to counsel of choice, or where the error will inevitably signal fundamental unfairness, as we have said of a judge's failure to tell the jury that it may not convict unless it finds the defendant's guilt beyond a reasonable doubt.

Under at least the first two rationales, counsel's admission of a client's guilt over the client's express objection is error structural in kind. Such an admission blocks the defendant's right to make the fundamental choices about his own defense. And the effects of the admission would be immeasurable, because a jury would almost certainly be swayed by a lawyer's concession of his client's guilt. McCoy must therefore be accorded a new trial without any need first to show prejudice.

Justice Alito, joined by Justices Thomas and Gorsuch, dissented.

2. Plain Error

Application of the Plain Error Standard: United States v. Olano

Page 1729. Add after the discussion of *Olano*:

In *Rosales-Mireles v. United States*, 138 S.Ct. 1897 (2018), Justice Sotomayor wrote for seven justices as the Court held that a miscalculation of a Guidelines sentencing range that has been determined to be plain and to affect a defendant's substantial rights calls for a court of appeals to exercise its discretion under Rule 52(b) to vacate the defendant's sentence in the ordinary case.

Rosales-Mireles pled guilty to illegal reentry into the United States. The Probation Office mistakenly counted a state misdemeanor conviction twice in calculating the Guidelines range, and its presentence report yielded a Guidelines range of 77 to 96 months when the correctly calculated range would have been 70 to 87 months. Rosales-Mireles did not object to the error in the District Court, which relied on the miscalculated Guidelines range to sentence him to 78 months of imprisonment. He challenged the incorrect Guidelines range for the first time on appeal. The Fifth Circuit found that the error was plain and affected Rosales-Mireles' substantial rights but declined to remand the case because he had not established that the error would seriously affect the fairness, integrity, or public reputation of judicial proceedings because neither the error nor the resulting sentence "would shock the conscience."

The opinion sets forth the four prongs that must be satisfied before an error is declared to be plain: (1) the error must not have been intentionally relinquished or abandoned; (2) it must be plain (i.e., clear or obvious); (3) it must have affected the defendant's substantial rights; and (4) the error must seriously affect the fairness, integrity, or public reputation of judicial proceedings. The Court's focus was on the fourth prong.

Justice Sotomayor reasoned that (a) district judges have ultimate responsibility to apply the Guidelines correctly, but the Guidelines are sufficiently complex that judges sometimes make mistakes; (b) the Court in *Olano* rejected a rule that would have called for relief only "in those circumstances in which a miscarriage of justice would otherwise result"— i.e., where a defendant is actually innocent—so that the Fifth Circuit's rule was also unduly restrictive; (c) *Molina-Martinez* recognized that "[w]hen a defendant is sentenced under an incorrect Guidelines range—whether or not the defendant's ultimate sentence falls within the correct range—the error itself can, and most often will, be sufficient to show a reasonable probability of a different outcome absent the error"; and (d) "[t]he risk of unnecessary deprivation of liberty particularly undermines the fairness, integrity, or public reputation of judicial proceedings in the context of a plain Guidelines error because of the role the district court plays in calculating the range and the relative ease of correcting the error."

Justice Thomas, joined by Justice Alito, dissented. He agreed with the conclusion that the Fifth Circuit's rule was unduly narrow, but concluded that the Court's broad statement that Guideline errors will ordinarily satisfy the fourth prong of plain-error review contravened precedents establishing that this prong must applied on a case-specific and fact-intensive basis.

In Davis v. United States, 140 S.Ct. 1060 (2020), the Court made clear that plain-error review is available in the context of appeals based on unpreserved issues of fact. In a per curiam opinion, the Court rejected the Fifth Circuit's practice of declining to hear appeals based on unpreserved issues of fact.

Appellate Court May Not Invoke Plain Error to Increase a Sentence in the Absence of a Government Appeal: Greenlaw v. United States

Page 1735. Add after the discussion of *Greenlaw v. United States*:

In *United States v. Sineneng-Smith*, 140 S.Ct. 1575 (2020), a unanimous Supreme Court overturned a Ninth Circuit opinion holding that 8 U.S.C. § 1324(a)(1)(A)(iv) is constitutionally overbroad on grounds that the Ninth Circuit violated the principle of party presentation.

Sineneng-Smith, an attorney, was convicted on several counts relating to a scheme to defraud her immigrant clients by accepting fees to file applications for a defunct labor certification program. Among these were counts under 8 U.S.C. § 1324(a)(1)(A)(iv), which prohibits "encourage[ing] or induc[ing] an alien to come to, enter, or reside in the United States, knowing or in reckless disregard of the fact that such coming to, entry, or residence is or will be in violation of law." On appeal to the Ninth Circuit, Sineneng-Smith argued that her conduct did not constitute a violation of 8 U.S.C. § 1324(a)(1)(A)(iv) or, in the alternative, that the statute was unconstitutional as applied to her because it was vague and violated her First Amendment rights.

During oral argument, a panel of the Ninth Circuit expressed concerns that 8 U.S.C. § 1324(a)(1)(A)(iv) might be unconstitutional on its face, and assigned several amici to brief and argue the issue while also "permitting" the parties to file supplemental briefs. After a rehearing, where appointed amici played the leading role, the panel held that 8 U.S.C. § 1324(a)(1)(A)(iv) is unconstitutionally overbroad, and, accordingly, reversed Sineneng-Smith's convictions on those counts.

Writing for the Court, Justice Ginsburg held that the Ninth Circuit's hijacking of Sineneng-Smith's appeal derogated "so drastically from the principle of party presentation as to constitute an abuse of discretion." The Court therefore vacated the Ninth Circuit's opinion and remanded the case for reconsideration based on the arguments actually presented by the parties in the appeal.

The Federal Rules of Criminal Procedure

■ ■ ■

TITLE I.   APPLICABILITY

Rule 1. Scope; Definitions

(a) Scope.

(1) *In General.* These rules govern the procedure in all criminal proceedings in the United States district courts, the United States courts of appeals, and the Supreme Court of the United States.

(2) *State or Local Judicial Officer.* When a rule so states, it applies to a proceeding before a state or local judicial officer.

(3) *Territorial Courts.* These rules also govern the procedure in all criminal proceedings in the following courts:

(A)   the district court of Guam;

(B)   the district court for the Northern Mariana Islands, except as otherwise provided by law; and

(C)   the district court of the Virgin Islands, except that the prosecution of offenses in that court must be by indictment or information as otherwise provided by law.

(4) *Removed Proceedings.* Although these rules govern all proceedings after removal from a state court, state law governs a dismissal by the prosecution.

(5) *Excluded Proceedings.* Proceedings not governed by these rules include:

(A)   the extradition and rendition of a fugitive;

(B)   a civil property forfeiture for violating a federal statute;

(C)   the collection of a fine or penalty;

(D)   a proceeding under a statute governing juvenile delinquency to the extent the procedure is inconsistent with the statute, unless Rule 20(d) provides otherwise;

(E)   a dispute between seamen under 22 U.S.C. §§ 256–258; and

(F) a proceeding against a witness in a foreign country under 28 U.S.C. § 1784.

(b) Definitions. The following definitions apply to these rules:

(1) "Attorney for the government" means:

(A) the Attorney General or an authorized assistant;

(B) a United States attorney or an authorized assistant;

(C) when applicable to cases arising under Guam law, the Guam Attorney General or other person whom Guam law authorizes to act in the matter; and

(D) any other attorney authorized by law to conduct proceedings under these rules as a prosecutor.

(2) "Court" means a federal judge performing functions authorized by law.

(3) "Federal judge" means:

(A) a justice or judge of the United States as these terms are defined in 28 U.S.C. § 451;

(B) a magistrate judge; and

(C) a judge confirmed by the United States Senate and empowered by statute in any commonwealth, territory, or possession to perform a function to which a particular rule relates.

(4) "Judge" means a federal judge or a state or local judicial officer.

(5) "Magistrate judge" means a United States magistrate judge as defined in 28 U.S.C. §§ 631–639.

(6) "Oath" includes an affirmation.

(7) "Organization" is defined in 18 U.S.C. § 18.

(8) "Petty offense" is defined in 18 U.S.C. § 19.

(9) "State" includes the District of Columbia, and any commonwealth, territory, or possession of the United States.

(10) "State or local judicial officer" means:

(A) a state or local officer authorized to act under 18 U.S.C. § 3041; and

(B) a judicial officer empowered by statute in the District of Columbia or in any commonwealth, territory, or possession to perform a function to which a particular rule relates.

(11) "Telephone" means any technology for transmitting live electronic voice communication.

(12) "Victim" means a "crime victim" as defined in 18 U.S.C. § 3771(e).

(c) Authority of a Justice or Judge of the United States. When these rules authorize a magistrate judge to act, any other federal judge may also act.

Rule 2. Interpretation

These rules are to be interpreted to provide for the just determination of every criminal proceeding, to secure simplicity in procedure and fairness in administration, and to eliminate unjustifiable expense and delay.

TITLE II. PRELIMINARY PROCEEDINGS

Rule 3. The Complaint

The complaint is a written statement of the essential facts constituting the offense charged. Except as provided in Rule 4.1, it must be made under oath before a magistrate judge or, if none is reasonably available, before a state or local judicial officer.

Rule 4. Arrest Warrant or Summons on a Complaint

(a) Issuance. If the complaint or one or more affidavits filed with the complaint establish probable cause to believe that an offense has been committed and that the defendant committed it, the judge must issue an arrest warrant to an officer authorized to execute it. At the request of an attorney for the government, the judge must issue a summons, instead of a warrant, to a person authorized to serve it. A judge may issue more than one warrant or summons on the same complaint. If an individual fails to appear in response to a summons, a judge may, and upon request of an attorney for the government must, issue a warrant. If an organizational defendant fails to appear in response to a summons, a judge may take any action authorized by United States law.

(b) Form.

(1) *Warrant.* A warrant must:

(A) contain the defendant's name or, if it is unknown, a name or description by which the defendant can be identified with reasonable certainty;

(B) describe the offense charged in the complaint;

(C) command that the defendant be arrested and brought without unnecessary delay before a magistrate judge or, if none is reasonably available, before a state or local judicial officer; and

(D) be signed by a judge.

(2) *Summons.* A summons must be in the same form as a warrant except that it must require the defendant to appear before a magistrate judge at a stated time and place.

(c) Execution or Service, and Return.

(1) *By Whom.* Only a marshal or other authorized officer may execute a warrant. Any person authorized to serve a summons in a federal civil action may serve a summons.

(2) *Location.* A warrant may be executed, or a summons served, within the jurisdiction of the United States or anywhere else a federal statute authorizes an arrest. A summons to an organization under Rule 4(c)(3)(D) may also be served at a place not within a judicial district of the United States.

(3) *Manner.*

(A) A warrant is executed by arresting the defendant. Upon arrest, an officer possessing the original or a duplicate original warrant must show it to the defendant. If the officer does not possess the warrant, the officer must inform the defendant of the warrant's existence and of the offense charged and, at the defendant's request, must show the original or a duplicate original warrant to the defendant as soon as possible.

(B) A summons is served on an individual defendant:

(i)   by delivering a copy to the defendant personally; or

(ii) by leaving a copy at the defendant's residence or usual place of abode with a person of suitable age and discretion residing at that location and by mailing a copy to the defendant's last known address.

(C) A summons is served on an organization in a judicial district of the United States by delivering a copy to an officer, to a managing or general agent, or to another agent appointed or legally authorized to receive service of process. If the agent is one authorized by statute and the statute so requires, a copy must also be mailed to the organization.

(D) A summons is served on an organization not within a judicial district of the United States:

(i)   by delivering a copy, in a manner authorized by the foreign jurisdiction's law, to a managing or general agent, or to an agent appointed or legally authorized to receive service of process; or

(ii) by any other means that gives notice, including one that is:

(a) stipulated by the parties;

(b) undertaken by a foreign authority in response to a letter rogatory, a letter of request, or a request submitted under an applicable international agreement; or

(c) permitted by an international agreement.

(4) *Return.*

(A) After executing a warrant, the officer must return it to the judge before whom the defendant is brought in accordance with Rule 5. The officer may do so by reliable electronic means. At the request of an attorney for the government, an unexecuted warrant must be brought back to and canceled by a magistrate judge or, if none is reasonably available, by a state or local judicial officer.

(B) The person to whom a summons was delivered for service must return it on or before the return day.

(C) At the request of an attorney for the government, a judge may deliver an unexecuted warrant, an unserved summons, or a copy of the warrant or summons to the marshal or other authorized person for execution or service.

(d) Warrant by Telephone or Other Reliable Electronic Means. In accordance with Rule 4.1, a magistrate judge may issue a warrant or summons based on information communicated by telephone or other reliable electronic means.

Rule 4.1. Complaint, Warrant, or Summons by Telephone or Other Reliable Electronic Means

(a) In General. A magistrate judge may consider information communicated by telephone or other reliable electronic means when reviewing a complaint or deciding whether to issue a warrant or summons.

(b) Procedures. If a magistrate judge decides to proceed under this rule, the following procedures apply:

(1) *Taking Testimony Under Oath.* The judge must place under oath—and may examine—the applicant and any person on whose testimony the application is based.

(2) *Creating a Record of the Testimony and Exhibits.*

(A) *Testimony Limited to Attestation.* If the applicant does no more than attest to the contents of a written affidavit submitted by reliable electronic means, the judge must acknowledge the attestation in writing on the affidavit.

(B) *Additional Testimony or Exhibits.* If the judge considers additional testimony or exhibits, the judge must:

(i) have the testimony recorded verbatim by an electronic recording device, by a court reporter, or in writing;

(ii) have any recording or reporter's notes transcribed, have the transcription certified as accurate, and file it;

(iii) sign any other written record, certify its accuracy, and file it; and

(iv) make sure that the exhibits are filed.

(3) *Preparing a Proposed Duplicate Original of a Complaint, Warrant, or Summons.* The applicant must prepare a proposed duplicate original of a complaint, warrant, or summons, and must read or otherwise transmit its contents verbatim to the judge.

(4) *Preparing an Original Complaint, Warrant, or Summons.* If the applicant reads the contents of the proposed duplicate original, the judge must enter those contents into an original complaint, warrant, or summons. If the applicant transmits the contents by reliable electronic means, the transmission received by the judge may serve as the original.

(5) *Modification.* The judge may modify the complaint, warrant, or summons. The judge must then:

(A) transmit the modified version to the applicant by reliable electronic means; or

(B) file the modified original and direct the applicant to modify the proposed duplicate original accordingly.

(6) *Issuance.* To issue the warrant or summons, the judge must:

(A) sign the original documents;

(B) enter the date and time of issuance on the warrant or summons; and

(C) transmit the warrant or summons by reliable electronic means to the applicant or direct the applicant to sign the judge's name and enter the date and time on the duplicate original.

(c) Suppression Limited. Absent a finding of bad faith, evidence obtained from a warrant issued under this rule is not subject to suppression on the ground that issuing the warrant in this manner was unreasonable under the circumstances.

Rule 5. Initial Appearance

(a) In General.

(1) *Appearance Upon an Arrest.*

(A) A person making an arrest within the United States must take the defendant without unnecessary delay before a magistrate judge, or before a state or local judicial officer as Rule 5(c) provides, unless a statute provides otherwise.

(B) A person making an arrest outside the United States must take the defendant without unnecessary delay before a magistrate judge, unless a statute provides otherwise.

(2) *Exceptions.*

(A) An officer making an arrest under a warrant issued upon a complaint charging solely a violation of 18 U.S.C. § 1073 need not comply with this rule if:

(i) the person arrested is transferred without unnecessary delay to the custody of appropriate state or local authorities in the district of arrest; and

(ii) an attorney for the government moves promptly, in the district where the warrant was issued, to dismiss the complaint.

(B) If a defendant is arrested for violating probation or supervised release, Rule 32.1 applies.

(C) If a defendant is arrested for failing to appear in another district, Rule 40 applies.

(3) *Appearance Upon a Summons.* When a defendant appears in response to a summons under Rule 4, a magistrate judge must proceed under Rule 5(d) or (e), as applicable.

(b) Arrest Without a Warrant. If a defendant is arrested without a warrant, a complaint meeting Rule 4(a)'s requirement of probable cause must be promptly filed in the district where the offense was allegedly committed.

(c) Place of Initial Appearance; Transfer to Another District.

(1) *Arrest in the District Where the Offense Was Allegedly Committed.* If the defendant is arrested in the district where the offense was allegedly committed:

(A) the initial appearance must be in that district; and

(B) if a magistrate judge is not reasonably available, the initial appearance may be before a state or local judicial officer.

(2) *Arrest in a District Other Than Where the Offense Was Allegedly Committed.* If the defendant was arrested in a district other than where the offense was allegedly committed, the initial appearance must be:

(A) in the district of arrest; or

(B) in an adjacent district if:

(i) the appearance can occur more promptly there; or

(ii) the offense was allegedly committed there and the initial appearance will occur on the day of arrest.

(3) *Procedures in a District Other Than Where the Offense Was Allegedly Committed.* If the initial appearance occurs in a district other than where the offense was allegedly committed, the following procedures apply:

(A) the magistrate judge must inform the defendant about the provisions of Rule 20;

(B) if the defendant was arrested without a warrant, the district court where the offense was allegedly committed must first issue a warrant before the magistrate judge transfers the defendant to that district;

(C) the magistrate judge must conduct a preliminary hearing if required by Rule 5.1;

(D) the magistrate judge must transfer the defendant to the district where the offense was allegedly committed if:

(i) the government produces the warrant, a certified copy of the warrant, or a reliable electronic form of either; and

(ii) the judge finds that the defendant is the same person named in the indictment, information, or warrant; and

(E) when a defendant is transferred and discharged, the clerk must promptly transmit the papers and any bail to the clerk in the district where the offense was allegedly committed.

(4) *Procedure for Persons Extradited to the United States.* If the defendant is surrendered to the United States in accordance with a request for the defendant's extradition, the initial appearance must be in the district (or one of the districts) where the offense is charged.

(d) Procedure in a Felony Case.

(1) *Advice.* If the defendant is charged with a felony, the judge must inform the defendant of the following:

(A) the complaint against the defendant, and any affidavit filed with it;

(B) the defendant's right to retain counsel or to request that counsel be appointed if the defendant cannot obtain counsel;

(C) the circumstances, if any, under which the defendant may secure pretrial release;

(D) any right to a preliminary hearing;

(E) the defendant's right not to make a statement, and that any statement made may be used against the defendant; and

(F) that a defendant who is not a United States citizen may request that an attorney for the government or a federal law enforcement official notify a consular officer from the defendant's country of nationality that the defendant has been arrested—but that even without the defendant's request, a treaty or other international agreement may require consular notification.

(2) *Consulting with Counsel.* The judge must allow the defendant reasonable opportunity to consult with counsel.

(3) *Detention or Release.* The judge must detain or release the defendant as provided by statute or these rules.

(4) *Plea.* A defendant may be asked to plead only under Rule 10.

(e) Procedure in a Misdemeanor Case. If the defendant is charged with a misdemeanor only, the judge must inform the defendant in accordance with Rule 58(b)(2).

(f) Video Teleconferencing. Video teleconferencing may be used to conduct an appearance under this rule if the defendant consents.

Rule 5.1. Preliminary Hearing

(a) In General. If a defendant is charged with an offense other than a petty offense, a magistrate judge must conduct a preliminary hearing unless:

(1) the defendant waives the hearing;

(2) the defendant is indicted;

(3) the government files an information under Rule 7(b) charging the defendant with a felony;

(4) the government files an information charging the defendant with a misdemeanor; or

(5) the defendant is charged with a misdemeanor and consents to trial before a magistrate judge.

(b) Selecting a District. A defendant arrested in a district other than where the offense was allegedly committed may elect to have the preliminary hearing conducted in the district where the prosecution is pending.

(c) Scheduling. The magistrate judge must hold the preliminary hearing within a reasonable time, but no later than 14 days after the initial appearance if the defendant is in custody and no later than 21 days if not in custody.

(d) Extending the Time. With the defendant's consent and upon a showing of good cause—taking into account the public interest in the prompt disposition of criminal cases—a magistrate judge may extend the time limits in Rule 5.1(c) one or more times. If the defendant does not consent, the magistrate judge may extend the time limits only on a showing that extraordinary circumstances exist and justice requires the delay.

(e) Hearing and Finding. At the preliminary hearing, the defendant may cross-examine adverse witnesses and may introduce evidence but may not object to evidence on the ground that it was unlawfully acquired. If the magistrate judge finds probable cause to believe an offense has been committed and the defendant committed it, the magistrate judge must promptly require the defendant to appear for further proceedings.

(f) Discharging the Defendant. If the magistrate judge finds no probable cause to believe an offense has been committed or the defendant committed it, the magistrate judge must dismiss the complaint and discharge the defendant. A discharge does not preclude the government from later prosecuting the defendant for the same offense.

(g) Recording the Proceedings. The preliminary hearing must be recorded by a court reporter or by a suitable recording device. A recording of the proceeding may be made available to any party upon request. A copy of the recording and a transcript may be provided to any party upon request and upon any payment required by applicable Judicial Conference regulations.

(h) Producing a Statement.

(1) *In General.* Rule 26.2(a)–(d) and (f) applies at any hearing under this rule, unless the magistrate judge for good cause rules otherwise in a particular case.

(2) *Sanctions for Not Producing a Statement.* If a party disobeys a Rule 26.2 order to deliver a statement to the moving party, the magistrate judge must not consider the testimony of a witness whose statement is withheld.

TITLE III. THE GRAND JURY, THE INDICTMENT, AND THE INFORMATION

Rule 6. The Grand Jury

(a) Summoning a Grand Jury.

(1) *In General.* When the public interest so requires, the court must order that one or more grand juries be summoned. A grand jury must have 16 to 23 members, and the court must order that enough legally qualified persons be summoned to meet this requirement.

(2) *Alternate Jurors.* When a grand jury is selected, the court may also select alternate jurors. Alternate jurors must have the same qualifications and be selected in the same manner as any other juror. Alternate jurors replace jurors in the same sequence in which the alternates were selected. An alternate juror who replaces a juror is subject to the same challenges, takes the same oath, and has the same authority as the other jurors.

(b) Objection to the Grand Jury or to a Grand Juror.

(1) *Challenges.* Either the government or a defendant may challenge the grand jury on the ground that it was not lawfully drawn, summoned, or selected, and may challenge an individual juror on the ground that the juror is not legally qualified.

(2) *Motion to Dismiss an Indictment.* A party may move to dismiss the indictment based on an objection to the grand jury or on an individual juror's lack of legal qualification, unless the court has previously ruled on the same objection under Rule 6(b)(1). The motion to dismiss is governed by 28 U.S.C. § 1867(e). The court must not dismiss the indictment on the ground that a grand juror was not legally qualified if the record shows that at least 12 qualified jurors concurred in the indictment.

(c) Foreperson and Deputy Foreperson. The court will appoint one juror as the foreperson and another as the deputy foreperson. In the foreperson's absence, the deputy foreperson will act as the foreperson. The foreperson may administer oaths and affirmations and will sign all indictments. The foreperson—or another juror designated by the foreperson—will record the number of jurors concurring in every indictment and will file the record with the clerk, but the record may not be made public unless the court so orders.

(d) Who May Be Present.

(1) *While the Grand Jury Is in Session.* The following persons may be present while the grand jury is in session: attorneys for the government, the witness being questioned, interpreters when needed, and a court reporter or an operator of a recording device.

(2) *During Deliberations and Voting.* No person other than the jurors, and any interpreter needed to assist a hearing-impaired or speech-impaired juror, may be present while the grand jury is deliberating or voting.

(e) Recording and Disclosing the Proceedings.

(1) *Recording the Proceedings.* Except while the grand jury is deliberating or voting, all proceedings must be recorded by a court reporter or by a suitable recording device. But the validity of a prosecution is not affected by the unintentional failure to make a recording. Unless the court orders otherwise, an attorney for the government will retain control of the recording, the reporter's notes, and any transcript prepared from those notes.

(2) *Secrecy.*

(A) No obligation of secrecy may be imposed on any person except in accordance with Rule 6(e)(2)(B).

(B) Unless these rules provide otherwise, the following persons must not disclose a matter occurring before the grand jury:

    (i)   a grand juror;

    (ii) an interpreter;

    (iii) a court reporter;

    (iv) an operator of a recording device;

    (v)   a person who transcribes recorded testimony;

    (vi) an attorney for the government; or

    (vii) a person to whom disclosure is made under Rule 6(e)(3)(A)(ii) or (iii).

(3) *Exceptions.*

(A) Disclosure of a grand-jury matter—other than the grand jury's deliberations or any grand juror's vote—may be made to:

    (i)   an attorney for the government for use in performing that attorney's duty;

    (ii) any government personnel—including those of a state, state subdivision, Indian tribe, or foreign government—that an attorney for the government considers necessary to assist in performing that attorney's duty to enforce federal criminal law; or

(iii) a person authorized by 18 U.S.C. § 3322.

(B) A person to whom information is disclosed under Rule 6(e)(3)(A)(ii) may use that information only to assist an attorney for the government in performing that attorney's duty to enforce federal criminal law. An attorney for the government must promptly provide the court that impaneled the grand jury with the names of all persons to whom a disclosure has been made, and must certify that the attorney has advised those persons of their obligation of secrecy under this rule.

(C) An attorney for the government may disclose any grand-jury matter to another federal grand jury.

(D) An attorney for the government may disclose any grand-jury matter involving foreign intelligence, counterintelligence (as defined in 50 U.S.C. § 3003), or foreign intelligence information (as defined in Rule 6(e)(3)(D)(iii)) to any federal law enforcement, intelligence, protective, immigration, national defense, or national security official to assist the official receiving the information in the performance of that official's duties. An attorney for the government may also disclose any grand-jury matter involving, within the United States or elsewhere, a threat of attack or other grave hostile acts of a foreign power or its agent, a threat of domestic or international sabotage or terrorism, or clandestine intelligence gathering activities by an intelligence service or network of a foreign power or by its agent, to any appropriate federal, state, state subdivision, Indian tribal, or foreign government official, for the purpose of preventing or responding to such threat or activities.

(i) Any official who receives information under Rule 6(e)(3)(D) may use the information only as necessary in the conduct of that person's official duties subject to any limitations on the unauthorized disclosure of such information. Any state, state subdivision, Indian tribal, or foreign government official who receives information under Rule 6(e)(3)(D) may use the information only in a manner consistent with any guidelines issued by the Attorney General and the Director of National Intelligence.

(ii) Within a reasonable time after disclosure is made under Rule 6(e)(3)(D), an attorney for the government must file, under seal, a notice with the court in the district where the grand jury convened stating that such information was disclosed and the departments, agencies, or entities to which the disclosure was made.

(iii) As used in Rule 6(e)(3)(D), the term "foreign intelligence information" means:

(a) information, whether or not it concerns a United States person, that relates to the ability of the United States to protect against—

- actual or potential attack or other grave hostile acts of a foreign power or its agent;

- sabotage or international terrorism by a foreign power or its agent; or

- clandestine intelligence activities by an intelligence service or network of a foreign power or by its agent; or

(b) information, whether or not it concerns a United States person, with respect to a foreign power or foreign territory that relates to—

- the national defense or the security of the United States; or

- the conduct of the foreign affairs of the United States.

(E) The court may authorize disclosure—at a time, in a manner, and subject to any other conditions that it directs—of a grand-jury matter:

(i) preliminarily to or in connection with a judicial proceeding;

(ii) at the request of a defendant who shows that a ground may exist to dismiss the indictment because of a matter that occurred before the grand jury;

(iii) at the request of the government, when sought by a foreign court or prosecutor for use in an official criminal investigation;

(iv) at the request of the government if it shows that the matter may disclose a violation of State, Indian tribal, or foreign criminal law, as long as the disclosure is to an appropriate state, state-subdivision, Indian tribal, or foreign government official for the purpose of enforcing that law; or

(v) at the request of the government if it shows that the matter may disclose a violation of military criminal law under the Uniform Code of Military Justice, as long as the disclosure is to an appropriate military official for the purpose of enforcing that law.

(F) A petition to disclose a grand-jury matter under Rule 6(e)(3)(E)(i) must be filed in the district where the grand jury convened. Unless the hearing is ex parte—as it may be when the government is the petitioner—the petitioner must serve the petition on, and the court must afford a reasonable opportunity to appear and be heard to:

(i) an attorney for the government;

(ii) the parties to the judicial proceeding; and

(iii) any other person whom the court may designate.

(G) If the petition to disclose arises out of a judicial proceeding in another district, the petitioned court must transfer the petition to the other court unless the petitioned court can reasonably determine whether disclosure is proper. If the petitioned court decides to transfer, it must send to the transferee court the material sought to be disclosed, if feasible, and a written evaluation of the need for continued grand-jury secrecy. The transferee court must afford those persons identified in Rule 6(e)(3)(F) a reasonable opportunity to appear and be heard.

(4) *Sealed Indictment.* The magistrate judge to whom an indictment is returned may direct that the indictment be kept secret until the defendant is in custody or has been released pending trial. The clerk must then seal the indictment, and no person may disclose the indictment's existence except as necessary to issue or execute a warrant or summons.

(5) *Closed Hearing.* Subject to any right to an open hearing in a contempt proceeding, the court must close any hearing to the extent necessary to prevent disclosure of a matter occurring before a grand jury.

(6) *Sealed Records.* Records, orders, and subpoenas relating to grand-jury proceedings must be kept under seal to the extent and as long as necessary to prevent the unauthorized disclosure of a matter occurring before a grand jury.

(7) *Contempt.* A knowing violation of Rule 6, or of any guidelines jointly issued by the Attorney General and the Director of National Intelligence under Rule 6, may be punished as a contempt of court.

(f) **Indictment and Return.** A grand jury may indict only if at least 12 jurors concur. The grand jury—or its foreperson or deputy foreperson—must return the indictment to a magistrate judge in open court. To avoid unnecessary cost or delay, the magistrate judge may take the return by video teleconference from the court where the grand jury sits. If a complaint or information is pending against the defendant and 12 jurors do not concur in the indictment, the foreperson must promptly and in writing report the lack of concurrence to the magistrate judge.

(g) Discharging the Grand Jury. A grand jury must serve until the court discharges it, but it may serve more than 18 months only if the court, having determined that an extension is in the public interest, extends the grand jury's service. An extension may be granted for no more than 6 months, except as otherwise provided by statute.

(h) Excusing a Juror. At any time, for good cause, the court may excuse a juror either temporarily or permanently, and if permanently, the court may impanel an alternate juror in place of the excused juror.

(i) "Indian Tribe" Defined. "Indian tribe" means an Indian tribe recognized by the Secretary of the Interior on a list published in the Federal Register under 25 U.S.C. § 479a–1.

Rule 7. The Indictment and the Information

(a) When Used.

(1) *Felony.* An offense (other than criminal contempt) must be prosecuted by an indictment if it is punishable:

(A) by death; or

(B) by imprisonment for more than one year.

(2) *Misdemeanor.* An offense punishable by imprisonment for one year or less may be prosecuted in accordance with Rule 58(b)(1).

(b) Waiving Indictment. An offense punishable by imprisonment for more than one year may be prosecuted by information if the defendant—in open court and after being advised of the nature of the charge and of the defendant's rights—waives prosecution by indictment.

(c) Nature and Contents.

(1) *In General.* The indictment or information must be a plain, concise, and definite written statement of the essential facts constituting the offense charged and must be signed by an attorney for the government. It need not contain a formal introduction or conclusion. A count may incorporate by reference an allegation made in another count. A count may allege that the means by which the defendant committed the offense are unknown or that the defendant committed it by one or more specified means. For each count, the indictment or information must give the official or customary citation of the statute, rule, regulation, or other provision of law that the defendant is alleged to have violated. For purposes of an indictment referred to in section 3282 of title 18, United States Code, for which the identity of the defendant is unknown, it shall be sufficient for the indictment to describe the defendant as an individual whose name is unknown, but who has a particular DNA profile, as that term is defined in section 3282.

(2) *Citation Error.* Unless the defendant was misled and thereby prejudiced, neither an error in a citation nor a citation's omission is a ground to dismiss the indictment or information or to reverse a conviction.

(d) Surplusage. Upon the defendant's motion, the court may strike surplusage from the indictment or information.

(e) Amending an Information. Unless an additional or different offense is charged or a substantial right of the defendant is prejudiced, the court may permit an information to be amended at any time before the verdict or finding.

(f) Bill of Particulars. The court may direct the government to file a bill of particulars. The defendant may move for a bill of particulars before or within 14 days after arraignment or at a later time if the court permits. The government may amend a bill of particulars subject to such conditions as justice requires.

Rule 8. Joinder of Offenses or Defendants

(a) Joinder of Offenses. The indictment or information may charge a defendant in separate counts with 2 or more offenses if the offenses charged—whether felonies or misdemeanors or both—are of the same or similar character, or are based on the same act or transaction, or are connected with or constitute parts of a common scheme or plan.

(b) Joinder of Defendants. The indictment or information may charge 2 or more defendants if they are alleged to have participated in the same act or transaction, or in the same series of acts or transactions, constituting an offense or offenses. The defendants may be charged in one or more counts together or separately. All defendants need not be charged in each count.

Rule 9. Arrest Warrant or Summons on an Indictment or Information

(a) Issuance. The court must issue a warrant—or at the government's request, a summons—for each defendant named in an indictment or named in an information if one or more affidavits accompanying the information establish probable cause to believe that an offense has been committed and that the defendant committed it. The court may issue more than one warrant or summons for the same defendant. If a defendant fails to appear in response to a summons, the court may, and upon request of an attorney for the government must, issue a warrant. The court must issue the arrest warrant to an officer authorized to execute it or the summons to a person authorized to serve it.

(b) Form.

(1) *Warrant.* The warrant must conform to Rule 4(b)(1) except that it must be signed by the clerk and must describe the offense charged in the indictment or information.

(2) *Summons.* The summons must be in the same form as a warrant except that it must require the defendant to appear before the court at a stated time and place.

(c) Execution or Service; Return; Initial Appearance.

(1) *Execution or Service.*

(A) The warrant must be executed or the summons served as provided in Rule 4(c)(1), (2), and (3).

(B) The officer executing the warrant must proceed in accordance with Rule 5(a)(1).

(2) *Return.* A warrant or summons must be returned in accordance with Rule 4(c)(4).

(3) *Initial Appearance.* When an arrested or summoned defendant first appears before the court, the judge must proceed under Rule 5.

(d) Warrant by Telephone or Other Means. In accordance with Rule 4.1, a magistrate judge may issue an arrest warrant or summons based on information communicated by telephone or other reliable electronic means.

TITLE IV. ARRAIGNMENT AND PREPARATION FOR TRIAL

Rule 10. Arraignment

(a) In General. An arraignment must be conducted in open court and must consist of:

(1) ensuring that the defendant has a copy of the indictment or information;

(2) reading the indictment or information to the defendant or stating to the defendant the substance of the charge; and then

(3) asking the defendant to plead to the indictment or information.

(b) Waiving Appearance. A defendant need not be present for the arraignment if:

(1) the defendant has been charged by indictment or misdemeanor information;

(2) the defendant, in a written waiver signed by both the defendant and defense counsel, has waived appearance and has affirmed that the defendant received a copy of the indictment or information and that the plea is not guilty; and

(3) the court accepts the waiver.

(c) Video Teleconferencing. Video teleconferencing may be used to arraign a defendant if the defendant consents.

Rule 11. Pleas

(a) Entering a Plea.

(1) *In General.* A defendant may plead not guilty, guilty, or (with the court's consent) nolo contendere.

(2) *Conditional Plea.* With the consent of the court and the government, a defendant may enter a conditional plea of guilty or nolo contendere, reserving in writing the right to have an appellate court review an adverse determination of a specified pretrial motion. A defendant who prevails on appeal may then withdraw the plea.

(3) *Nolo Contendere Plea.* Before accepting a plea of nolo contendere, the court must consider the parties' views and the public interest in the effective administration of justice.

(4) *Failure to Enter a Plea.* If a defendant refuses to enter a plea or if a defendant organization fails to appear, the court must enter a plea of not guilty.

(b) Considering and Accepting a Guilty or Nolo Contendere Plea.

(1) *Advising and Questioning the Defendant.* Before the court accepts a plea of guilty or nolo contendere, the defendant may be placed under oath, and the court must address the defendant personally in open court. During this address, the court must inform the defendant of, and determine that the defendant understands, the following:

(A) the government's right, in a prosecution for perjury or false statement, to use against the defendant any statement that the defendant gives under oath;

(B) the right to plead not guilty, or having already so pleaded, to persist in that plea;

(C) the right to a jury trial;

(D) the right to be represented by counsel—and if necessary have the court appoint counsel—at trial and at every other stage of the proceeding;

(E) the right at trial to confront and cross-examine adverse witnesses, to be protected from compelled self-incrimination, to testify and present evidence, and to compel the attendance of witnesses;

(F) the defendant's waiver of these trial rights if the court accepts a plea of guilty or nolo contendere;

(G) the nature of each charge to which the defendant is pleading;

(H) any maximum possible penalty, including imprisonment, fine, and term of supervised release;

(I) any mandatory minimum penalty;

(J) any applicable forfeiture;

(K) the court's authority to order restitution;

(L) the court's obligation to impose a special assessment;

(M) in determining a sentence, the court's obligation to calculate the applicable sentencing-guideline range and to consider that range, possible departures under the Sentencing Guidelines, and other sentencing factors under 18 U.S.C. § 3553(a);

(N) the terms of any plea-agreement provision waiving the right to appeal or to collaterally attack the sentence; and

(O) that, if convicted, a defendant who is not a United States citizen may be removed from the United States, denied citizenship, and denied admission to the United States in the future.

(2) *Ensuring That a Plea Is Voluntary.* Before accepting a plea of guilty or nolo contendere, the court must address the defendant personally in open court and determine that the plea is voluntary and did not result from force, threats, or promises (other than promises in a plea agreement).

(3) *Determining the Factual Basis for a Plea.* Before entering judgment on a guilty plea, the court must determine that there is a factual basis for the plea.

(c) Plea Agreement Procedure.

(1) *In General.* An attorney for the government and the defendant's attorney, or the defendant when proceeding pro se, may discuss and reach a plea agreement. The court must not participate in these discussions. If the defendant pleads guilty or nolo contendere to either a charged offense or a lesser or related offense, the plea agreement may specify that an attorney for the government will:

(A) not bring, or will move to dismiss, other charges;

(B) recommend, or agree not to oppose the defendant's request, that a particular sentence or sentencing range is appropriate or that a particular provision of the Sentencing Guidelines, or policy statement, or sentencing factor does or does not apply (such a recommendation or request does not bind the court); or

(C) agree that a specific sentence or sentencing range is the appropriate disposition of the case, or that a particular provision of the Sentencing Guidelines, or policy statement, or sentencing factor does or does not apply (such a recommendation or request binds the court once the court accepts the plea agreement).

(2) *Disclosing a Plea Agreement.* The parties must disclose the plea agreement in open court when the plea is offered, unless the court for good cause allows the parties to disclose the plea agreement in camera.

(3) *Judicial Consideration of a Plea Agreement.*

(A) To the extent the plea agreement is of the type specified in Rule 11(c)(1)(A) or (C), the court may accept the agreement, reject it, or defer a decision until the court has reviewed the presentence report.

(B) To the extent the plea agreement is of the type specified in Rule 11(c)(1)(B), the court must advise the defendant that the defendant has no right to withdraw the plea if the court does not follow the recommendation or request.

(4) *Accepting a Plea Agreement.* If the court accepts the plea agreement, it must inform the defendant that to the extent the plea agreement is of the type specified in Rule 11(c)(1)(A) or (C), the agreed disposition will be included in the judgment.

(5) *Rejecting a Plea Agreement.* If the court rejects a plea agreement containing provisions of the type specified in Rule 11(c)(1)(A) or (C), the court must do the following on the record and in open court (or, for good cause, in camera):

(A) inform the parties that the court rejects the plea agreement;

(B) advise the defendant personally that the court is not required to follow the plea agreement and give the defendant an opportunity to withdraw the plea; and

(C) advise the defendant personally that if the plea is not withdrawn, the court may dispose of the case less favorably toward the defendant than the plea agreement contemplated.

(d) Withdrawing a Guilty or Nolo Contendere Plea. A defendant may withdraw a plea of guilty or nolo contendere:

(1) before the court accepts the plea, for any reason or no reason; or

(2) after the court accepts the plea, but before it imposes sentence if:

(A) the court rejects a plea agreement under Rule 11(c)(5); or

(B) the defendant can show a fair and just reason for requesting the withdrawal.

(e) Finality of a Guilty or Nolo Contendere Plea. After the court imposes sentence, the defendant may not withdraw a plea of guilty or nolo contendere, and the plea may be set aside only on direct appeal or collateral attack.

(f) Admissibility or Inadmissibility of a Plea, Plea Discussions, and Related Statements. The admissibility or inadmissibility of a plea, a plea discussion, and any related statement is governed by Federal Rule of Evidence 410.

(g) Recording the Proceedings. The proceedings during which the defendant enters a plea must be recorded by a court reporter or by a suitable recording device. If there is a guilty plea or a nolo contendere plea, the record must include the inquiries and advice to the defendant required under Rule 11(b) and (c).

(h) Harmless Error. A variance from the requirements of this rule is harmless error if it does not affect substantial rights.

Rule 12. Pleadings and Pretrial Motions

(a) Pleadings. The pleadings in a criminal proceeding are the indictment, the information, and the pleas of not guilty, guilty, and nolo contendere.

(b) Pretrial Motions.

(1) *In General.* A party may raise by pretrial motion any defense, objection, or request that the court can determine without a trial on the merits. Rule 47 applies to a pretrial motion.

(2) *Motions That May Be Made at Any Time.* A motion that the court lacks jurisdiction may be made at any time while the case is pending.

(3) *Motions That Must Be Made Before Trial.* The following defenses, objections, and requests must be raised by pretrial motion if the basis for the motion is then reasonably available and the motion can be determined without a trial on the merits:

(A) a defect in instituting the prosecution, including

(i) improper venue;

(ii) preindictment delay;

(iii) a violation of the constitutional right to a speedy trial;

(iv) selective or vindictive prosecution; and

(v) an error in the grand-jury proceeding or preliminary hearing;

(B) a defect in the indictment or information, including;

(i) joining two or more offense in the same count (duplicity);

(ii) charging the same offense in more than one count (multiplicity);

(iii) lack of specificity;

(iv) improper joinder; and

(v) failure to state an offense;

(C) suppression of evidence;

(D) severance of charges or defendants under Rule 14; and

(E) discovery under Rule 16.

(4) *Notice of the Government's Intent to Use Evidence.*

(A) *At the Government's Discretion.* At the arraignment or as soon afterward as practicable, the government may notify the defendant of its intent to use specified evidence at trial in order to afford the defendant an opportunity to object before trial under Rule 12(b)(3)(C).

(B) *At the Defendant's Request.* At the arraignment or as soon afterward as practicable, the defendant may, in order to have an opportunity to move to suppress evidence under Rule 12(b)(3)(C), request notice of the government's intent to use (in its evidence-in-chief at trial) any evidence that the defendant may be entitled to discover under Rule 16.

(c) Deadline for a Pretrial Motion; Consequences of Not Making a Timely Motion.

(1) *Setting the Deadline.* The court may, at the arraignment or as soon afterward as practicable, set a deadline for the parties to make pretrial motions and may also schedule a motion hearing. If the court does not set one, the deadline is the start of trial.

(2) *Extending or Resetting the Deadline.* At any time before trial, the court may extend or reset the deadline for pretrial motions.

(3) *Consequences of Not Making a Timely Motion Under Rule 12(b)(3).* If a party does not meet the deadline for making a Rule 12(b)(3) motion, the motion is untimely. But a court may consider the defense, objection, or request if the party shows good cause.

(d) Ruling on a Motion. The court must decide every pretrial motion before trial unless it finds good cause to defer a ruling. The court must not defer ruling on a pretrial motion if the deferral will adversely affect a party's right to appeal. When factual issues are involved in deciding a motion, the court must state its essential findings on the record.

(e) [Reserved.]

(f) Recording the Proceedings. All proceedings at a motion hearing, including any findings of fact and conclusions of law made orally by the court, must be recorded by a court reporter or a suitable recording device.

(g) Defendant's Continued Custody or Release Status. If the court grants a motion to dismiss based on a defect in instituting the prosecution, in the indictment, or in the information, it may order the defendant to be released or detained under 18 U.S.C. § 3142 for a specified time until a new indictment or information is filed. This rule does not affect any federal statutory period of limitations.

(h) Producing Statements at a Suppression Hearing. Rule 26.2 applies at a suppression hearing under Rule 12(b)(3)(C). At a suppression hearing, a law enforcement officer is considered a government witness.

Rule 12.1. Notice of an Alibi Defense

(a) Government's Request for Notice and Defendant's Response.

(1) *Government's Request.* An attorney for the government may request in writing that the defendant notify an attorney for the government of any intended alibi defense. The request must state the time, date, and place of the alleged offense.

(2) *Defendant's Response.* Within 14 days after the request, or at some other time the court sets, the defendant must serve written notice on an attorney for the government of any intended alibi defense. The defendant's notice must state:

(A) each specific place where the defendant claims to have been at the time of the alleged offense; and

(B) the name, address, and telephone number of each alibi witness on whom the defendant intends to rely.

(b) Disclosing Government Witnesses.

(1) *Disclosure.*

(A) *In General.* If the defendant serves a Rule 12.1(a)(2) notice, an attorney for the government must disclose in writing to the defendant or the defendant's attorney:

(i) the name of each witness—and the address and telephone number of each witness other than a victim—that the government intends to rely on to establish that the defendant was present at the scene of the alleged offense; and

(ii) each government rebuttal witness to the defendant's alibi defense.

(B) *Victim's Address and Telephone Number.* If the government intends to rely on a victim's testimony to establish that the defendant was present at the scene of the alleged offense and the defendant establishes a need for the victim's address and telephone number, the court may:

(i) order the government to provide the information in writing to the defendant or the defendant's attorney; or

(ii) fashion a reasonable procedure that allows preparation of the defense and also protects the victim's interests.

(2) *Time to Disclose.* Unless the court directs otherwise, an attorney for the government must give its Rule 12.1(b)(1) disclosure within 14 days after the defendant serves notice of an intended alibi defense under Rule 12.1(a)(2), but no later than 14 days before trial.

(c) Continuing Duty to Disclose.

(1) *In General.* Both an attorney for the government and the defendant must promptly disclose in writing to the other party the name of each additional witness—and the address and telephone number of each additional witness other than a victim—if:

    (A) the disclosing party learns of the witness before or during trial; and

    (B) the witness should have been disclosed under Rule 12.1(a) or (b) if the disclosing party had known of the witness earlier.

(2) *Address and Telephone Number of an Additional Victim Witness.* The address and telephone number of an additional victim witness must not be disclosed except as provided in Rule 12.1(b)(1)(B).

(d) Exceptions. For good cause, the court may grant an exception to any requirement of Rule 12.1(a)–(c).

(e) Failure to Comply. If a party fails to comply with this rule, the court may exclude the testimony of any undisclosed witness regarding the defendant's alibi. This rule does not limit the defendant's right to testify.

(f) Inadmissibility of Withdrawn Intention. Evidence of an intention to rely on an alibi defense, later withdrawn, or of a statement made in connection with that intention, is not, in any civil or criminal proceeding, admissible against the person who gave notice of the intention.

Rule 12.2. Notice of an Insanity Defense; Mental Examination

(a) Notice of an Insanity Defense. A defendant who intends to assert a defense of insanity at the time of the alleged offense must so notify an attorney for the government in writing within the time provided for filing a pretrial motion, or at any later time the court sets, and file a copy of the notice with the clerk. A defendant who fails to do so cannot rely on an insanity defense. The court may, for good cause, allow the defendant to file the notice late, grant additional trial-preparation time, or make other appropriate orders.

(b) Notice of Expert Evidence of a Mental Condition. If a defendant intends to introduce expert evidence relating to a mental disease or defect or any other mental condition of the defendant bearing on either (1) the issue of guilt or (2) the issue of punishment in a capital case, the defendant must—within the time provided for filing a pretrial motion or at any later time the court sets—notify an attorney for the government in writing of this intention and file a copy of the notice with the clerk. The court may, for good cause, allow the defendant to file the notice late, grant the parties additional trial-preparation time, or make other appropriate orders.

(c) Mental Examination.

(1) *Authority to Order an Examination; Procedures.*

(A) The court may order the defendant to submit to a competency examination under 18 U.S.C. § 4241.

(B) If the defendant provides notice under Rule 12.2(a), the court must, upon the government's motion, order the defendant to be examined under 18 U.S.C. § 4242. If the defendant provides notice under Rule 12.2(b) the court may, upon the government's motion, order the defendant to be examined under procedures ordered by the court.

(2) *Disclosing Results and Reports of Capital Sentencing Examination.* The results and reports of any examination conducted solely under Rule 12.2(c)(1) after notice under Rule 12.2(b)(2) must be sealed and must not be disclosed to any attorney for the government or the defendant unless the defendant is found guilty of one or more capital crimes and the defendant confirms an intent to offer during sentencing proceedings expert evidence on mental condition.

(3) *Disclosing Results and Reports of the Defendant's Expert Examination.* After disclosure under Rule 12.2(c)(2) of the results and reports of the government's examination, the defendant must disclose to the government the results and reports of any examination on mental condition conducted by the defendant's expert about which the defendant intends to introduce expert evidence.

(4) *Inadmissibility of a Defendant's Statements.* No statement made by a defendant in the course of any examination conducted under this rule (whether conducted with or without the defendant's consent), no testimony by the expert based on the statement, and no other fruits of the statement may be admitted into evidence against the defendant in any criminal proceeding except on an issue regarding mental condition on which the defendant:

(A) has introduced evidence of incompetency or evidence requiring notice under Rule 12.2(a) or (b)(1), or

(B) has introduced expert evidence in a capital sentencing proceeding requiring notice under Rule 12.2(b)(2).

(d) Failure to Comply.

(1) *Failure to Give Notice or to Submit to Examination.* The court may exclude any expert evidence from the defendant on the issue

of the defendant's mental disease, mental defect, or any other mental condition bearing on the defendant's guilt or the issue of punishment in a capital case if the defendant fails to:

> (A) give notice under Rule 12.2(b); or

> (B) submit to an examination when ordered under Rule 12.2(c).

(2) *Failure to Disclose.* The court may exclude any expert evidence for which the defendant has failed to comply with the disclosure requirement of Rule 12.2(c)(3).

(e) Inadmissibility of Withdrawn Intention. Evidence of an intention as to which notice was given under Rule 12.2(a) or (b), later withdrawn, is not, in any civil or criminal proceeding, admissible against the person who gave notice of the intention.

Rule 12.3. Notice of a Public-Authority Defense

(a) Notice of the Defense and Disclosure of Witnesses.

(1) *Notice in General.* If a defendant intends to assert a defense of actual or believed exercise of public authority on behalf of a law enforcement agency or federal intelligence agency at the time of the alleged offense, the defendant must so notify an attorney for the government in writing and must file a copy of the notice with the clerk within the time provided for filing a pretrial motion, or at any later time the court sets. The notice filed with the clerk must be under seal if the notice identifies a federal intelligence agency as the source of public authority.

(2) *Contents of Notice.* The notice must contain the following information:

> (A) the law enforcement agency or federal intelligence agency involved;

> (B) the agency member on whose behalf the defendant claims to have acted; and

> (C) the time during which the defendant claims to have acted with public authority.

(3) *Response to the Notice.* An attorney for the government must serve a written response on the defendant or the defendant's attorney within 14 days after receiving the defendant's notice, but no later than 21 days before trial. The response must admit or deny that the defendant exercised the public authority identified in the defendant's notice.

(4) Disclosing Witnesses.

(A) *Government's Request.* An attorney for the government may request in writing that the defendant disclose the name, address, and telephone number of each witness the defendant intends to rely on to establish a public-authority defense. An attorney for the government may serve the request when the government serves its response to the defendant's notice under Rule 12.3(a)(3), or later, but must serve the request no later than 21 days before trial.

(B) *Defendant's Response.* Within 14 days after receiving the government's request, the defendant must serve on an attorney for the government a written statement of the name, address, and telephone number of each witness.

(C) *Government's Reply.* Within 14 days after receiving the defendant's statement, an attorney for the government must serve on the defendant or the defendant's attorney a written statement of the name of each witness—and the address and telephone number of each witness other than a victim—that the government intends to rely on to oppose the defendant's public-authority defense.

(D) *Victim's Address and Telephone Number.* If the government intends to rely on a victim's testimony to oppose the defendant's public-authority defense and the defendant establishes a need for the victim's address and telephone number, the court may:

(i) order the government to provide the information in writing to the defendant or the defendant's attorney; or

(ii) fashion a reasonable procedure that allows for preparing the defense and also protects the victim's interests.

(5) Additional Time. The court may, for good cause, allow a party additional time to comply with this rule.

(b) Continuing Duty to Disclose.

(1) In General. Both an attorney for the government and the defendant must promptly disclose in writing to the other party the name of any additional witness—and the address, and telephone number of any additional witness other than a victim—if:

(A) the disclosing party learns of the witness before or during trial; and

(B) the witness should have been disclosed under Rule 12.3(a)(4) if the disclosing party had known of the witness earlier.

(2) *Address and Telephone Number of an Additional Victim-Witness.* The address and telephone number of an additional victim-witness must not be disclosed except as provided in Rule 12.3(a)(4)(D).

(c) **Failure to Comply.** If a party fails to comply with this rule, the court may exclude the testimony of any undisclosed witness regarding the public-authority defense. This rule does not limit the defendant's right to testify.

(d) **Protective Procedures Unaffected.** This rule does not limit the court's authority to issue appropriate protective orders or to order that any filings be under seal.

(e) **Inadmissibility of Withdrawn Intention.** Evidence of an intention as to which notice was given under Rule 12.3(a), later withdrawn, is not, in any civil or criminal proceeding, admissible against the person who gave notice of the intention.

Rule 12.4. Disclosure Statement

(a) **Who Must File.**

(1) *Nongovernmental Corporate Party.* Any nongovernmental corporate party to a proceeding in a district court must file a statement that identifies any parent corporation and any publicly held corporation that owns 10% or more of its stock or states that there is no such corporation.

(2) *Organizational Victim.* Unless the government shows good cause, it must file a statement identifying any organizational victim of the criminal activity. If the organizational victim is a corporation, the statement must also disclose the information required by Rule 12.4(a)(1) to the extent it can be obtained through due diligence.

(b) **Time to File; Later Filing.** A party must:

(1) file the Rule 12.4(a) statement within 28 days after the defendant's initial appearance; and

(2) promptly file a later statement if any required information changes.

Rule 13. Joint Trial of Separate Cases

The court may order that separate cases be tried together as though brought in a single indictment or information if all offenses and all defendants could have been joined in a single indictment or information.

Rule 14. Relief from Prejudicial Joinder

(a) **Relief.** If the joinder of offenses or defendants in an indictment, an information, or a consolidation for trial appears to prejudice a defendant or the government, the court may order separate trials of counts, sever the defendants' trials, or provide any other relief that justice requires.

(b) **Defendant's Statements.** Before ruling on a defendant's motion to sever, the court may order an attorney for the government to deliver to the court for in camera inspection any defendant's statement that the government intends to use as evidence.

Rule 15. Depositions

(a) **When Taken.**

(1) *In General.* A party may move that a prospective witness be deposed in order to preserve testimony for trial. The court may grant the motion because of exceptional circumstances and in the interest of justice. If the court orders the deposition to be taken, it may also require the deponent to produce at the deposition any designated material that is not privileged, including any book, paper, document, record, recording, or data.

(2) *Detained Material Witness.* A witness who is detained under 18 U.S.C. § 3144 may request to be deposed by filing a written motion and giving notice to the parties. The court may then order that the deposition be taken and may discharge the witness after the witness has signed under oath the deposition transcript.

(b) **Notice.**

(1) *In General.* A party seeking to take a deposition must give every other party reasonable written notice of the deposition's date and location. The notice must state the name and address of each deponent. If requested by a party receiving the notice, the court may, for good cause, change the deposition's date or location.

(2) *To the Custodial Officer.* A party seeking to take the deposition must also notify the officer who has custody of the defendant of the scheduled date and location.

(c) **Defendant's Presence.**

(1) *Defendant in Custody.* Except as authorized by Rule 15(c)(3), the officer who has custody of the defendant must produce the defendant at the deposition and keep the defendant in the witness's presence during the examination, unless the defendant:

(A) waives in writing the right to be present; or

(B) persists in disruptive conduct justifying exclusion after being warned by the court that disruptive conduct will result in the defendant's exclusion.

(2) *Defendant Not in Custody.* Except as authorized by Rule 15(c)(3), a defendant who is not in custody has the right upon request to be present at the deposition, subject to any conditions imposed by the court. If the government tenders the defendant's expenses as provided in Rule 15(d) but the defendant still fails to appear, the defendant—absent good cause—waives both the right to appear and any objection to the taking and use of the deposition based on that right.

(3) *Taking Depositions Outside the United States Without the Defendant's Presence.* The deposition of a witness who is outside the United States may be taken without the defendant's presence if the court makes case-specific findings of all the following:

(A) the witness's testimony could provide substantial proof of a material fact in a felony prosecution;

(B) there is a substantial likelihood that the witness's attendance at trial cannot be obtained;

(C) the witness's presence for a deposition in the United States cannot be obtained;

(D) the defendant cannot be present because:

(i) the country where the witness is located will not permit the defendant to attend the deposition;

(ii) for an in-custody defendant, secure transportation and continuing custody cannot be assured at the witness's location; or

(iii) for an out-of-custody defendant, no reasonable conditions will assure an appearance at the deposition or at trial or sentencing; and

(E) the defendant can meaningfully participate in the deposition through reasonable means.

(d) Expenses. If the deposition was requested by the government, the court may—or if the defendant is unable to bear the deposition expenses, the court must—order the government to pay:

(1) any reasonable travel and subsistence expenses of the defendant and the defendant's attorney to attend the deposition; and

(2) the costs of the deposition transcript.

(e) Manner of Taking. Unless these rules or a court order provides otherwise, a deposition must be taken and filed in the same manner as a deposition in a civil action, except that:

(1) A defendant may not be deposed without that defendant's consent.

(2) The scope and manner of the deposition examination and cross-examination must be the same as would be allowed during trial.

(3) The government must provide to the defendant or the defendant's attorney, for use at the deposition, any statement of the deponent in the government's possession to which the defendant would be entitled at trial.

(f) Admissibility and Use as Evidence. An order authorizing a deposition to be taken under this rule does not determine its admissibility. A party may use all or part of a deposition as provided by the Federal Rules of Evidence.

(g) Objections. A party objecting to deposition testimony or evidence must state the grounds for the objection during the deposition.

(h) Depositions by Agreement Permitted. The parties may by agreement take and use a deposition with the court's consent.

Rule 16. Discovery and Inspection

(a) Government's Disclosure.

(1) *Information Subject to Disclosure.*

(A) *Defendant's Oral Statement.* Upon a defendant's request, the government must disclose to the defendant the substance of any relevant oral statement made by the defendant, before or after arrest, in response to interrogation by a person the defendant knew was a government agent if the government intends to use the statement at trial.

(B) *Defendant's Written or Recorded Statement.* Upon a defendant's request, the government must disclose to the defendant, and make available for inspection, copying, or photographing, all of the following:

(i) any relevant written or recorded statement by the defendant if:

- the statement is within the government's possession, custody, or control; and

- the attorney for the government knows—or through due diligence could know—that the statement exists;

(ii) the portion of any written record containing the substance of any relevant oral statement made before or after arrest if the defendant made the statement in response to interrogation by a person the defendant knew was a government agent; and

(iii) the defendant's recorded testimony before a grand jury relating to the charged offense.

(C) *Organizational Defendant.* Upon a defendant's request, if the defendant is an organization, the government must disclose to the defendant any statement described in Rule 16(a)(1)(A) and (B) if the government contends that the person making the statement:

(i)   was legally able to bind the defendant regarding the subject of the statement because of that person's position as the defendant's director, officer, employee, or agent; or

(ii) was personally involved in the alleged conduct constituting the offense and was legally able to bind the defendant regarding that conduct because of that person's position as the defendant's director, officer, employee, or agent.

(D) *Defendant's Prior Record.* Upon a defendant's request, the government must furnish the defendant with a copy of the defendant's prior criminal record that is within the government's possession, custody, or control if the attorney for the government knows—or through due diligence could know—that the record exists.

(E) *Documents and Objects.* Upon a defendant's request, the government must permit the defendant to inspect and to copy or photograph books, papers, documents, data, photographs, tangible objects, buildings or places, or copies or portions of any of these items, if the item is within the government's possession, custody, or control and:

(i)   the item is material to preparing the defense;

(ii) the government intends to use the item in its case-in-chief at trial; or

(iii) the item was obtained from or belongs to the defendant.

(F) *Reports of Examinations and Tests.* Upon a defendant's request, the government must permit a defendant to inspect and to copy or photograph the results or reports of any physical or mental examination and of any scientific test or experiment if:

(i) the item is within the government's possession, custody, or control;

(ii) the attorney for the government knows—or through due diligence could know—that the item exists; and

(iii) the item is material to preparing the defense or the government intends to use the item in its case-in-chief at trial.

(G) *Expert Witnesses.* At the defendant's request, the government must give to the defendant a written summary of any testimony that the government intends to use under Rules 702, 703, or 705 of the Federal Rules of Evidence during its case-in-chief at trial. If the government requests discovery under subdivision (b)(1)(C)(ii) and the defendant complies, the government must, at the defendant's request, give to the defendant a written summary of testimony that the government intends to use under Rules 702, 703, or 705 of the Federal Rules of Evidence as evidence at trial on the issue of the defendant's mental condition. The summary provided under this subparagraph must describe the witness's opinions, the bases and reasons for those opinions, and the witness's qualifications.

(2) *Information Not Subject to Disclosure.* Except as permitted by Rule 16(a)(1)(A)–(D), (F), and (G), this rule does not authorize the discovery or inspection of reports, memoranda, or other internal government documents made by an attorney for the government or other government agent in connection with investigating or prosecuting the case. Nor does this rule authorize the discovery or inspection of statements made by prospective government witnesses except as provided in 18 U.S.C. § 3500.

(3) *Grand Jury Transcripts.* This rule does not apply to the discovery or inspection of a grand jury's recorded proceedings, except as provided in Rules 6, 12(h), 16(a)(1), and 26.2.

(b) Defendant's Disclosure.

(1) *Information Subject to Disclosure.*

(A) *Documents and Objects.* If a defendant requests disclosure under Rule 16(a)(1)(E) and the government complies, then the defendant must permit the government, upon request, to inspect and to copy or photograph books, papers, documents, data, photographs, tangible objects, buildings or places, or copies or portions of any of these items if:

(i) the item is within the defendant's possession, custody, or control; and

(ii) the defendant intends to use the item in the defendant's case-in-chief at trial.

(B) *Reports of Examinations and Tests.* If a defendant requests disclosure under Rule 16(a)(1)(F) and the government complies, the defendant must permit the government, upon request, to inspect and to copy or photograph the results or reports of any physical or mental examination and of any scientific test or experiment if:

(i) the item is within the defendant's possession, custody, or control; and

(ii) the defendant intends to use the item in the defendant's case-in-chief at trial, or intends to call the witness who prepared the report and the report relates to the witness's testimony.

(C) *Expert Witnesses.* The defendant must, at the government's request, give to the government a written summary of any testimony that the defendant intends to use under Rules 702, 703, or 705 of the Federal Rules of Evidence as evidence at trial, if—

(i) the defendant requests disclosure under subdivision (a)(1)(G) and the government complies; or

(ii) the defendant has given notice under Rule 12.2(b) of an intent to present expert testimony on the defendant's mental condition.

This summary must describe the witness's opinions, the bases and reasons for those opinions, and the witness's qualifications.

(2) *Information Not Subject to Disclosure.* Except for scientific or medical reports, Rule 16(b)(1) does not authorize discovery or inspection of:

(A) reports, memoranda, or other documents made by the defendant, or the defendant's attorney or agent, during the case's investigation or defense; or

(B) a statement made to the defendant, or the defendant's attorney or agent, by:

(i) the defendant;

(ii) a government or defense witness; or

(iii) a prospective government or defense witness.

(c) Continuing Duty to Disclose. A party who discovers additional evidence or material before or during trial must promptly disclose its existence to the other party or the court if:

(1) the evidence or material is subject to discovery or inspection under this rule; and

(2) the other party previously requested, or the court ordered, its production.

(d) Regulating Discovery.

(1) *Protective and Modifying Orders.* At any time the court may, for good cause, deny, restrict, or defer discovery or inspection, or grant other appropriate relief. The court may permit a party to show good cause by a written statement that the court will inspect ex parte. If relief is granted, the court must preserve the entire text of the party's statement under seal.

(2) *Failure to Comply.* If a party fails to comply with this rule, the court may:

(A) order that party to permit the discovery or inspection; specify its time, place, and manner; and prescribe other just terms and conditions;

(B) grant a continuance;

(C) prohibit that party from introducing the undisclosed evidence; or

(D) enter any other order that is just under the circumstances.

Rule 16.1. Pretrial Discovery Conference; Request for Court Action

(a) Discovery Conference. No later than 14 days after the arraignment, the attorney for the government and the defendant's attorney must confer and try to agree on a timetable and procedures for pretrial disclosure under Rule 16.

(b) Request for Court Action. After the discovery conference, one or both parties may ask the court to determine or modify the time, place, manner, or other aspects of disclosure to facilitate preparation for trial.

Rule 17. Subpoena

(a) Content. A subpoena must state the court's name and the title of the proceeding, include the seal of the court, and command the witness to attend and testify at the time and place the subpoena specifies. The clerk must issue a blank subpoena—signed and sealed—to the party requesting it, and that party must fill in the blanks before the subpoena is served.

(b) Defendant Unable to Pay. Upon a defendant's ex parte application, the court must order that a subpoena be issued for a named witness if the defendant shows an inability to pay the witness's fees and the necessity of the witness's presence for an adequate defense. If the court orders a subpoena to be issued, the process costs and witness fees will be paid in the same manner as those paid for witnesses the government subpoenas.

(c) Producing Documents and Objects.

(1) *In General.* A subpoena may order the witness to produce any books, papers, documents, data, or other objects the subpoena designates. The court may direct the witness to produce the designated items in court before trial or before they are to be offered in evidence. When the items arrive, the court may permit the parties and their attorneys to inspect all or part of them.

(2) *Quashing or Modifying the Subpoena.* On motion made promptly, the court may quash or modify the subpoena if compliance would be unreasonable or oppressive.

(3) *Subpoena for Personal or Confidential Information About a Victim.* After a complaint, indictment, or information is filed, a subpoena requiring the production of personal or confidential information about a victim may be served on a third party only by court order. Before entering the order and unless there are exceptional circumstances, the court must require giving notice to the victim so that the victim can move to quash or modify the subpoena or otherwise object.

(d) Service. A marshal, a deputy marshal, or any nonparty who is at least 18 years old may serve a subpoena. The server must deliver a copy of the subpoena to the witness and must tender to the witness one day's witness-attendance fee and the legal mileage allowance. The server need not tender the attendance fee or mileage allowance when the United States, a federal officer, or a federal agency has requested the subpoena.

(e) Place of Service.

(1) *In the United States.* A subpoena requiring a witness to attend a hearing or trial may be served at any place within the United States.

(2) *In a Foreign Country.* If the witness is in a foreign country, 28 U.S.C. § 1783 governs the subpoena's service.

(f) Issuing a Deposition Subpoena.

(1) *Issuance.* A court order to take a deposition authorizes the clerk in the district where the deposition is to be taken to issue a subpoena for any witness named or described in the order.

(2) *Place.* After considering the convenience of the witness and the parties, the court may order—and the subpoena may require—the witness to appear anywhere the court designates.

(g) Contempt. The court (other than a magistrate judge) may hold in contempt a witness who, without adequate excuse, disobeys a subpoena issued by a federal court in that district. A magistrate judge may hold in contempt a witness who, without adequate excuse, disobeys a subpoena issued by that magistrate judge as provided in 28 U.S.C. § 636(e).

(h) Information Not Subject to a Subpoena. No party may subpoena a statement of a witness or of a prospective witness under this rule. Rule 26.2 governs the production of the statement.

Rule 17.1. Pretrial Conference

On its own, or on a party's motion, the court may hold one or more pretrial conferences to promote a fair and expeditious trial. When a conference ends, the court must prepare and file a memorandum of any matters agreed to during the conference. The government may not use any statement made during the conference by the defendant or the defendant's attorney unless it is in writing and is signed by the defendant and the defendant's attorney.

TITLE V.   VENUE

Rule 18. Place of Prosecution and Trial

Unless a statute or these rules permit otherwise, the government must prosecute an offense in a district where the offense was committed. The court must set the place of trial within the district with due regard for the convenience of the defendant, any victim, and the witnesses, and the prompt administration of justice.

Rule 19. [Reserved]

Rule 20. Transfer for Plea and Sentence

(a) Consent to Transfer. A prosecution may be transferred from the district where the indictment or information is pending, or from which a warrant on a complaint has been issued, to the district where the defendant is arrested, held, or present if:

(1) the defendant states in writing a wish to plead guilty or nolo contendere and to waive trial in the district where the indictment, information, or complaint is pending, consents in writing to the court's disposing of the case in the transferee district, and files the statement in the transferee district; and

(2) the United States attorneys in both districts approve the transfer in writing.

(b) Clerk's Duties. After receiving the defendant's statement and the required approvals, the clerk where the indictment, information, or complaint is pending must send the file, or a certified copy, to the clerk in the transferee district.

(c) Effect of a Not Guilty Plea. If the defendant pleads not guilty after the case has been transferred under Rule 20(a), the clerk must return the papers to the court where the prosecution began, and that court must restore the proceeding to its docket. The defendant's statement that the defendant wished to plead guilty or nolo contendere is not, in any civil or criminal proceeding, admissible against the defendant.

(d) Juveniles.

(1) *Consent to Transfer.* A juvenile, as defined in 18 U.S.C. § 5031, may be proceeded against as a juvenile delinquent in the district where the juvenile is arrested, held, or present if:

(A) the alleged offense that occurred in the other district is not punishable by death or life imprisonment;

(B) an attorney has advised the juvenile;

(C) the court has informed the juvenile of the juvenile's rights—including the right to be returned to the district where the offense allegedly occurred—and the consequences of waiving those rights;

(D) the juvenile, after receiving the court's information about rights, consents in writing to be proceeded against in the transferee district, and files the consent in the transferee district;

(E) the United States attorneys for both districts approve the transfer in writing; and

(F) the transferee court approves the transfer.

(2) *Clerk's Duties.* After receiving the juvenile's written consent and the required approvals, the clerk where the indictment, information, or complaint is pending or where the alleged offense occurred must send the file, or a certified copy, to the clerk in the transferee district.

Rule 21. Transfer for Trial

(a) For Prejudice. Upon the defendant's motion, the court must transfer the proceeding against that defendant to another district if the court is satisfied that so great a prejudice against the defendant exists in the transferring district that the defendant cannot obtain a fair and impartial trial there.

(b) For Convenience. Upon the defendant's motion, the court may transfer the proceeding, or one or more counts, against that defendant to another district for the convenience of the parties, any victim, and the witnesses, and in the interest of justice.

(c) Proceedings on Transfer. When the court orders a transfer, the clerk must send to the transferee district the file, or a certified copy, and any bail taken. The prosecution will then continue in the transferee district.

(d) Time to File a Motion to Transfer. A motion to transfer may be made at or before arraignment or at any other time the court or these rules prescribe.

Rule 22. [Transferred]

TITLE VI. TRIAL

Rule 23. Jury or Nonjury Trial

(a) Jury Trial. If the defendant is entitled to a jury trial, the trial must be by jury unless:

(1) the defendant waives a jury trial in writing;

(2) the government consents; and

(3) the court approves.

(b) Jury Size.

(1) *In General.* A jury consists of 12 persons unless this rule provides otherwise.

(2) *Stipulation for a Smaller Jury.* At any time before the verdict, the parties may, with the court's approval, stipulate in writing that:

(A) the jury may consist of fewer than 12 persons; or

(B) a jury of fewer than 12 persons may return a verdict if the court finds it necessary to excuse a juror for good cause after the trial begins.

(3) *Court Order for a Jury of 11.* After the jury has retired to deliberate, the court may permit a jury of 11 persons to return a verdict, even without a stipulation by the parties, if the court finds good cause to excuse a juror.

(c) Nonjury Trial. In a case tried without a jury, the court must find the defendant guilty or not guilty. If a party requests before the finding of guilty or not guilty, the court must state its specific findings of fact in open court or in a written decision or opinion.

Rule 24. Trial Jurors

(a) Examination.

(1) *In General.* The court may examine prospective jurors or may permit the attorneys for the parties to do so.

(2) *Court Examination.* If the court examines the jurors, it must permit the attorneys for the parties to:

(A) ask further questions that the court considers proper; or

(B) submit further questions that the court may ask if it considers them proper.

(b) Peremptory Challenges. Each side is entitled to the number of peremptory challenges to prospective jurors specified below. The court may allow additional peremptory challenges to multiple defendants, and may allow the defendants to exercise those challenges separately or jointly.

(1) *Capital Case.* Each side has 20 peremptory challenges when the government seeks the death penalty.

(2) *Other Felony Case.* The government has 6 peremptory challenges and the defendant or defendants jointly have 10 peremptory challenges when the defendant is charged with a crime punishable by imprisonment of more than one year.

(3) *Misdemeanor Case.* Each side has 3 peremptory challenges when the defendant is charged with a crime punishable by fine, imprisonment of one year or less, or both.

(c) Alternate Jurors.

(1) *In General.* The court may impanel up to 6 alternate jurors to replace any jurors who are unable to perform or who are disqualified from performing their duties.

(2) *Procedure.*

(A) Alternate jurors must have the same qualifications and be selected and sworn in the same manner as any other juror.

(B) Alternate jurors replace jurors in the same sequence in which the alternates were selected. An alternate juror who replaces a juror has the same authority as the other jurors.

(3) *Retaining Alternate Jurors.* The court may retain alternate jurors after the jury retires to deliberate. The court must ensure that a retained alternate does not discuss the case with anyone until that alternate replaces a juror or is discharged. If an alternate replaces a juror after deliberations have begun, the court must instruct the jury to begin its deliberations anew.

(4) *Peremptory Challenges.* Each side is entitled to the number of additional peremptory challenges to prospective alternate jurors specified below. These additional challenges may be used only to remove alternate jurors.

(A) *One or Two Alternates.* One additional peremptory challenge is permitted when one or two alternates are impaneled.

(B) *Three or Four Alternates.* Two additional peremptory challenges are permitted when three or four alternates are impaneled.

(C) *Five or Six Alternates.* Three additional peremptory challenges are permitted when five or six alternates are impaneled.

Rule 25. Judge's Disability

(a) During Trial. Any judge regularly sitting in or assigned to the court may complete a jury trial if:

(1) the judge before whom the trial began cannot proceed because of death, sickness, or other disability; and

(2) the judge completing the trial certifies familiarity with the trial record.

(b) After a Verdict or Finding of Guilty.

(1) *In General.* After a verdict or finding of guilty, any judge regularly sitting in or assigned to a court may complete the court's duties if the judge who presided at trial cannot perform those duties because of absence, death, sickness, or other disability.

(2) *Granting a New Trial.* The successor judge may grant a new trial if satisfied that:

(A) a judge other than the one who presided at the trial cannot perform the post-trial duties; or

(B) a new trial is necessary for some other reason.

Rule 26. Taking Testimony

In every trial the testimony of witnesses must be taken in open court, unless otherwise provided by a statute or by rules adopted under 28 U.S.C. §§ 2072–2077.

Rule 26.1. Foreign Law Determination

A party intending to raise an issue of foreign law must provide the court and all parties with reasonable written notice. Issues of foreign law are questions of law, but in deciding such issues a court may consider any relevant material or source—including testimony—without regard to the Federal Rules of Evidence.

Rule 26.2. Producing a Witness's Statement

(a) Motion to Produce. After a witness other than the defendant has testified on direct examination, the court, on motion of a party who did not call the witness, must order an attorney for the government or the defendant and the defendant's attorney to produce, for the examination and use of the moving party, any statement of the witness that is in their possession and that relates to the subject matter of the witness's testimony.

(b) Producing the Entire Statement. If the entire statement relates to the subject matter of the witness's testimony, the court must order that the statement be delivered to the moving party.

(c) Producing a Redacted Statement. If the party who called the witness claims that the statement contains information that is privileged or does not relate to the subject matter of the witness's testimony, the court must inspect the statement in camera. After excising any privileged or unrelated portions, the court must order delivery of the redacted statement to the moving party. If the defendant objects to an excision, the court must preserve the entire statement with the excised portion indicated, under seal, as part of the record.

(d) Recess to Examine a Statement. The court may recess the proceedings to allow time for a party to examine the statement and prepare for its use.

(e) Sanction for Failure to Produce or Deliver a Statement. If the party who called the witness disobeys an order to produce or deliver a statement, the court must strike the witness's testimony from the record. If an attorney for the government disobeys the order, the court must declare a mistrial if justice so requires.

(f) "Statement" Defined. As used in this rule, a witness's "statement" means:

(1) a written statement that the witness makes and signs, or otherwise adopts or approves;

(2) a substantially verbatim, contemporaneously recorded recital of the witness's oral statement that is contained in any recording or any transcription of a recording; or

(3) the witness's statement to a grand jury, however taken or recorded, or a transcription of such a statement.

(g) Scope. This rule applies at trial, at a suppression hearing under Rule 12, and to the extent specified in the following rules:

(1) Rule 5.1(h) (preliminary hearing);

(2) Rule 32(i)(2) (sentencing);

(3) Rule 32.1(e) (hearing to revoke or modify probation or supervised release);

(4) Rule 46(j) (detention hearing); and

(5) Rule 8 of the Rules Governing Proceedings under 28 U.S.C. § 2255.

Rule 26.3. Mistrial

Before ordering a mistrial, the court must give each defendant and the government an opportunity to comment on the propriety of the order, to state whether that party consents or objects, and to suggest alternatives.

Rule 27. Proving an Official Record

A party may prove an official record, an entry in such a record, or the lack of a record or entry in the same manner as in a civil action.

Rule 28. Interpreters

The court may select, appoint, and set the reasonable compensation for an interpreter, including an interpreter for the victim. The compensation must be paid from funds provided by law or by the government, as the court may direct.

Rule 29. Motion for a Judgment of Acquittal

(a) Before Submission to the Jury. After the government closes its evidence or after the close of all the evidence, the court on the defendant's motion must enter a judgment of acquittal of any offense for which the evidence is insufficient to sustain a conviction. The court may on its own consider whether the evidence is insufficient to sustain a conviction. If the court denies a motion for a judgment of acquittal at the close of the government's evidence, the defendant may offer evidence without having reserved the right to do so.

(b) Reserving Decision. The court may reserve decision on the motion, proceed with the trial (where the motion is made before the close of all the evidence), submit the case to the jury, and decide the motion either before the jury returns a verdict or after it returns a verdict of guilty or is discharged without having returned a verdict. If the court reserves decision, it must decide the motion on the basis of the evidence at the time the ruling was reserved.

(c) After Jury Verdict or Discharge.

(1) *Time for a Motion.* A defendant may move for a judgment of acquittal, or renew such a motion, within 14 days after a guilty verdict or after the court discharges the jury, whichever is later.

(2) *Ruling on the Motion.* If the jury has returned a guilty verdict, the court may set aside the verdict and enter an acquittal. If the jury has failed to return a verdict, the court may enter a judgment of acquittal.

(3) *No Prior Motion Required.* A defendant is not required to move for a judgment of acquittal before the court submits the case to the jury as a prerequisite for making such a motion after jury discharge.

(d) Conditional Ruling on a Motion for a New Trial.

(1) *Motion for a New Trial.* If the court enters a judgment of acquittal after a guilty verdict, the court must also conditionally determine whether any motion for a new trial should be granted if the judgment of acquittal is later vacated or reversed. The court must specify the reasons for that determination.

(2) *Finality.* The court's order conditionally granting a motion for a new trial does not affect the finality of the judgment of acquittal.

(3) *Appeal.*

(A) *Grant of a Motion for a New Trial.* If the court conditionally grants a motion for a new trial and an appellate court later reverses the judgment of acquittal, the trial court must proceed with the new trial unless the appellate court orders otherwise.

(B) *Denial of a Motion for a New* Trial. If the court conditionally denies a motion for a new trial, an appellee may assert that the denial was erroneous. If the appellate court later reverses the judgment of acquittal, the trial court must proceed as the appellate court directs.

Rule 29.1. Closing Argument

Closing arguments proceed in the following order:

(a) the government argues;

(b) the defense argues; and

(c) the government rebuts.

Rule 30. Jury Instructions

(a) In General. Any party may request in writing that the court instruct the jury on the law as specified in the request. The request must be made at the close of the evidence or at any earlier time that the court reasonably sets. When the request is made, the requesting party must furnish a copy to every other party.

(b) Ruling on a Request. The court must inform the parties before closing arguments how it intends to rule on the requested instructions.

(c) Time for Giving Instructions. The court may instruct the jury before or after the arguments are completed, or at both times.

(d) Objections to Instructions. A party who objects to any portion of the instructions or to a failure to give a requested instruction must inform the court of the specific objection and the grounds for the objection before the jury retires to deliberate. An opportunity must be given to object out of the jury's hearing and, on request, out of the jury's presence. Failure to object in accordance with this rule precludes appellate review, except as permitted under Rule 52(b).

Rule 31. Jury Verdict

(a) Return. The jury must return its verdict to a judge in open court. The verdict must be unanimous.

(b) Partial Verdicts, Mistrial, and Retrial.

(1) *Multiple Defendants.* If there are multiple defendants, the jury may return a verdict at any time during its deliberations as to any defendant about whom it has agreed.

(2) *Multiple Counts.* If the jury cannot agree on all counts as to any defendant, the jury may return a verdict on those counts on which it has agreed.

(3) *Mistrial and Retrial.* If the jury cannot agree on a verdict on one or more counts, the court may declare a mistrial on those counts. The government may retry any defendant on any count on which the jury could not agree.

(c) Lesser Offense or Attempt. A defendant may be found guilty of any of the following:

(1) an offense necessarily included in the offense charged;

(2) an attempt to commit the offense charged; or

(3) an attempt to commit an offense necessarily included in the offense charged, if the attempt is an offense in its own right.

(d) Jury Poll. After a verdict is returned but before the jury is discharged, the court must on a party's request, or may on its own, poll the jurors individually. If the poll reveals a lack of unanimity, the court may direct the jury to deliberate further or may declare a mistrial and discharge the jury.

TITLE VII. POST-CONVICTION PROCEDURES

Rule 32. Sentencing and Judgment

(a) [Reserved.]

(b) Time of Sentencing.

(1) *In General.* The court must impose sentence without unnecessary delay.

(2) *Changing Time Limits.* The court may, for good cause, change any time limits prescribed in this rule.

(c) Presentence Investigation.

(1) *Required Investigation.*

(A) *In General.* The probation officer must conduct a presentence investigation and submit a report to the court before it imposes sentence unless:

(i) 18 U.S.C. § 3593(c) or another statute requires otherwise; or

(ii) the court finds that the information in the record enables it to meaningfully exercise its sentencing authority under 18 U.S.C. § 3553, and the court explains its finding on the record.

(B) *Restitution.* If the law permits restitution, the probation officer must conduct an investigation and submit a report that contains sufficient information for the court to order restitution.

(2) *Interviewing the Defendant.* The probation officer who interviews a defendant as part of a presentence investigation must, on request, give the defendant's attorney notice and a reasonable opportunity to attend the interview.

(d) Presentence Report.

(1) *Applying the Advisory Sentencing Guidelines.* The presentence report must:

(A) identify all applicable guidelines and policy statements of the Sentencing Commission;

(B) calculate the defendant's offense level and criminal history category;

(C) state the resulting sentencing range and kinds of sentences available;

(D) identify any factor relevant to:

(i) the appropriate kind of sentence, or

(ii) the appropriate sentence within the applicable sentencing range; and

(E) identify any basis for departing from the applicable sentencing range.

(2) *Additional Information.* The presentence report must also contain the following:

(A) the defendant's history and characteristics, including:

(i) any prior criminal record;

(ii) the defendant's financial condition; and

(iii) any circumstances affecting the defendant's behavior that may be helpful in imposing sentence or in correctional treatment;

(B) information that assesses any financial, social, psychological, and medical impact on any victim;

(C) when appropriate, the nature and extent of nonprison programs and resources available to the defendant;

(D) when the law provides for restitution, information sufficient for a restitution order;

(E) if the court orders a study under 18 U.S.C. § 3552(b), any resulting report and recommendation;

(F) a statement of whether the government seeks forfeiture under Rule 32.2 and any other law; and

(G) any other information that the court requires, including information relevant to the factors under 18 U.S.C. § 3553(a).

(3) *Exclusions.* The presentence report must exclude the following:

(A) any diagnoses that, if disclosed, might seriously disrupt a rehabilitation program;

(B) any sources of information obtained upon a promise of confidentiality; and

(C) any other information that, if disclosed, might result in physical or other harm to the defendant or others.

(e) Disclosing the Report and Recommendation.

(1) *Time to Disclose.* Unless the defendant has consented in writing, the probation officer must not submit a presentence report to the court or disclose its contents to anyone until the defendant has pleaded guilty or nolo contendere, or has been found guilty.

(2) *Minimum Required Notice.* The probation officer must give the presentence report to the defendant, the defendant's attorney, and an attorney for the government at least 35 days before sentencing unless the defendant waives this minimum period.

(3) *Sentence Recommendation.* By local rule or by order in a case, the court may direct the probation officer not to disclose to anyone other than the court the officer's recommendation on the sentence.

(f) Objecting to the Report.

(1) *Time to Object.* Within 14 days after receiving the presentence report, the parties must state in writing any objections, including objections to material information, sentencing guideline ranges, and policy statements contained in or omitted from the report.

(2) *Serving Objections.* An objecting party must provide a copy of its objections to the opposing party and to the probation officer.

(3) *Action on Objections.* After receiving objections, the probation officer may meet with the parties to discuss the objections. The probation officer may then investigate further and revise the presentence report as appropriate.

(g) Submitting the Report. At least 7 days before sentencing, the probation officer must submit to the court and to the parties the presentence report and an addendum containing any unresolved objections, the grounds for those objections, and the probation officer's comments on them.

(h) Notice of Possible Departure from Sentencing Guidelines. Before the court may depart from the applicable sentencing range on a ground not identified for departure either in the presentence report or in a party's prehearing submission, the court must give the parties reasonable notice that it is contemplating such a departure. The notice must specify any ground on which the court is contemplating a departure.

(i) Sentencing.

(1) *In General.* At sentencing, the court:

(A) must verify that the defendant and the defendant's attorney have read and discussed the presentence report and any addendum to the report;

(B) must give to the defendant and an attorney for the government a written summary of—or summarize in camera— any information excluded from the presentence report under Rule 32(d)(3) on which the court will rely in sentencing, and give them a reasonable opportunity to comment on that information;

(C) must allow the parties' attorneys to comment on the probation officer's determinations and other matters relating to an appropriate sentence; and

(D) may, for good cause, allow a party to make a new objection at any time before sentence is imposed.

(2) *Introducing Evidence; Producing a Statement.* The court may permit the parties to introduce evidence on the objections. If a witness testifies at sentencing, Rule 26.2(a)–(d) and (f) applies. If a party fails to comply with a Rule 26.2 order to produce a witness's statement, the court must not consider that witness's testimony.

(3) *Court Determinations.* At sentencing, the court:

(A) may accept any undisputed portion of the presentence report as a finding of fact;

(B) must—for any disputed portion of the presentence report or other controverted matter—rule on the dispute or determine that a ruling is unnecessary either because the matter will not affect sentencing, or because the court will not consider the matter in sentencing; and

(C) must append a copy of the court's determinations under this rule to any copy of the presentence report made available to the Bureau of Prisons.

(4) *Opportunity to Speak.*

(A) *By a Party.* Before imposing sentence, the court must:

(i) provide the defendant's attorney an opportunity to speak on the defendant's behalf;

(ii) address the defendant personally in order to permit the defendant to speak or present any information to mitigate the sentence; and

(iii) provide an attorney for the government an opportunity to speak equivalent to that of the defendant's attorney.

(B) *By a Victim.* Before imposing sentence, the court must address any victim of the crime who is present at sentencing and must permit the victim to be reasonably heard.

(C) *In Camera Proceedings.* Upon a party's motion and for good cause, the court may hear in camera any statement made under Rule 32(i)(4).

(j) **Defendant's Right to Appeal.**

(1) *Advice of a Right to Appeal.*

(A) *Appealing a Conviction.* If the defendant pleaded not guilty and was convicted, after sentencing the court must advise the defendant of the right to appeal the conviction.

(B) *Appealing a Sentence.* After sentencing—regardless of the defendant's plea—the court must advise the defendant of any right to appeal the sentence.

(C) *Appeal Costs.* The court must advise a defendant who is unable to pay appeal costs of the right to ask for permission to appeal in forma pauperis.

(2) *Clerk's Filing of Notice.* If the defendant so requests, the clerk must immediately prepare and file a notice of appeal on the defendant's behalf.

(k) **Judgment.**

(1) *In General.* In the judgment of conviction, the court must set forth the plea, the jury verdict or the court's findings, the adjudication, and the sentence. If the defendant is found not guilty or is otherwise entitled to be discharged, the court must so order. The judge must sign the judgment, and the clerk must enter it.

(2) *Criminal Forfeiture.* Forfeiture procedures are governed by Rule 32.2.

Rule 32.1. Revoking or Modifying Probation or Supervised Release

(a) Initial Appearance.

(1) *Person In Custody.* A person held in custody for violating probation or supervised release must be taken without unnecessary delay before a magistrate judge.

(A) If the person is held in custody in the district where an alleged violation occurred, the initial appearance must be in that district.

(B) If the person is held in custody in a district other than where an alleged violation occurred, the initial appearance must be in that district, or in an adjacent district if the appearance can occur more promptly there.

(2) *Upon a Summons.* When a person appears in response to a summons for violating probation or supervised release, a magistrate judge must proceed under this rule.

(3) *Advice.* The judge must inform the person of the following:

(A) the alleged violation of probation or supervised release;

(B) the person's right to retain counsel or to request that counsel be appointed if the person cannot obtain counsel; and

(C) the person's right, if held in custody, to a preliminary hearing under Rule 32.1(b)(1).

(4) *Appearance in the District With Jurisdiction.* If the person is arrested or appears in the district that has jurisdiction to conduct a revocation hearing—either originally or by transfer of jurisdiction—the court must proceed under Rule 32.1(b)–(e).

(5) *Appearance in a District Lacking Jurisdiction.* If the person is arrested or appears in a district that does not have jurisdiction to conduct a revocation hearing, the magistrate judge must:

(A) if the alleged violation occurred in the district of arrest, conduct a preliminary hearing under Rule 32.1(b) and either:

(i) transfer the person to the district that has jurisdiction, if the judge finds probable cause to believe that a violation occurred; or

(ii) dismiss the proceedings and so notify the court that has jurisdiction, if the judge finds no probable cause to believe that a violation occurred; or

(B) if the alleged violation did not occur in the district of arrest, transfer the person to the district that has jurisdiction if:

(i) the government produces certified copies of the judgment, warrant, and warrant application, or produces copies of those certified documents by reliable electronic means; and

(ii) the judge finds that the person is the same person named in the warrant.

(6) *Release or Detention.* The magistrate judge may release or detain the person under 18 U.S.C. § 3143(a)(1) pending further proceedings. The burden of establishing by clear and convincing evidence that the person will not flee or pose a danger to any other person or to the community rests with the person.

(b) Revocation.

(1) *Preliminary Hearing.*

(A) *In General.* If a person is in custody for violating a condition of probation or supervised release, a magistrate judge must promptly conduct a hearing to determine whether there is probable cause to believe that a violation occurred. The person may waive the hearing.

(B) *Requirements.* The hearing must be recorded by a court reporter or by a suitable recording device. The judge must give the person:

(i) notice of the hearing and its purpose, the alleged violation, and the person's right to retain counsel or to request that counsel be appointed if the person cannot obtain counsel;

(ii) an opportunity to appear at the hearing and present evidence; and

(iii) upon request, an opportunity to question any adverse witness, unless the judge determines that the interest of justice does not require the witness to appear.

(C) *Referral.* If the judge finds probable cause, the judge must conduct a revocation hearing. If the judge does not find probable cause, the judge must dismiss the proceeding.

(2) *Revocation Hearing.* Unless waived by the person, the court must hold the revocation hearing within a reasonable time in the district having jurisdiction. The person is entitled to:

(A) written notice of the alleged violation;

(B) disclosure of the evidence against the person;

(C) an opportunity to appear, present evidence, and question any adverse witness unless the court determines that the interest of justice does not require the witness to appear;

(D) notice of the person's right to retain counsel or to request that counsel be appointed if the person cannot obtain counsel; and

(E) an opportunity to make a statement and present any information in mitigation.

(c) Modification.

(1) *In General.* Before modifying the conditions of probation or supervised release, the court must hold a hearing, at which the person has the right to counsel and an opportunity to make a statement and present any information in mitigation.

(2) *Exceptions.* A hearing is not required if:

(A) the person waives the hearing; or

(B) the relief sought is favorable to the person and does not extend the term of probation or of supervised release; and

(C) an attorney for the government has received notice of the relief sought, has had a reasonable opportunity to object, and has not done so.

(d) Disposition of the Case. The court's disposition of the case is governed by 18 U.S.C. § 3563 and § 3565 (probation) and § 3583 (supervised release).

(e) Producing a Statement. Rule 26.2(a)–(d) and (f) applies at a hearing under this rule. If a party fails to comply with a Rule 26.2 order to produce a witness's statement, the court must not consider that witness's testimony.

Rule 32.2. Criminal Forfeiture

(a) Notice to the Defendant. A court must not enter a judgment of forfeiture in a criminal proceeding unless the indictment or information contains notice to the defendant that the government will seek the forfeiture of property as part of any sentence in accordance with the applicable statute. The notice should not be designated as a count of the indictment or information. The indictment or information need not identify the property subject to forfeiture or specify the amount of any forfeiture money judgment that the government seeks.

(b) Entering a Preliminary Order of Forfeiture.

(1) *Forfeiture Phase of the Trial.*

(A) *Forfeiture Determinations.* As soon as practical after a verdict or finding of guilty, or after a plea of guilty or nolo contendere is accepted, on any count in an indictment or information regarding which criminal forfeiture is sought, the court must determine what property is subject to forfeiture under the applicable statute. If the government seeks forfeiture of specific property, the court must determine whether the government has established the requisite nexus between the property and the offense. If the government seeks a personal money judgment, the court must determine the amount of money that the defendant will be ordered to pay.

(B) *Evidence and Hearing.* The court's determination may be based on evidence already in the record, including any written plea agreement, and on any additional evidence or information submitted by the parties and accepted by the court as relevant and reliable. If the forfeiture is contested, on either party's request the court must conduct a hearing after the verdict or finding of guilty.

(2) *Preliminary Order.*

(A) *Contents of a Specific Order.* If the court finds that property is subject to forfeiture, it must promptly enter a preliminary order of forfeiture setting forth the amount of any money judgment, directing the forfeiture of specific property, and directing the forfeiture of any substitute property if the government has met the statutory criteria. The court must enter the order without regard to any third party's interest in the property. Determining whether a third party has such an interest must be deferred until any third party files a claim in an ancillary proceeding under Rule 32.2(c).

(B) *Timing.* Unless doing so is impractical, the court must enter the preliminary order sufficiently in advance of sentencing to allow the parties to suggest revisions or modifications before the order becomes final as to the defendant under Rule 32.2(b)(4).

(C) *General Order.* If, before sentencing, the court cannot identify all the specific property subject to forfeiture or calculate the total amount of the money judgment, the court may enter a forfeiture order that:

(i) lists any identified property;

(ii) describes other property in general terms; and

(iii) states that the order will be amended under Rule 32.2(e)(1) when additional specific property is identified or the amount of the money judgment has been calculated.

(3) *Seizing Property.* The entry of a preliminary order of forfeiture authorizes the Attorney General (or a designee) to seize the specific property subject to forfeiture; to conduct any discovery the court considers proper in identifying, locating, or disposing of the property; and to commence proceedings that comply with any statutes governing third-party rights. The court may include in the order of forfeiture conditions reasonably necessary to preserve the property's value pending any appeal.

(4) *Sentence and Judgment.*

(A) *When Final.* At sentencing—or at any time before sentencing if the defendant consents—the preliminary forfeiture order becomes final as to the defendant. If the order directs the defendant to forfeit specific property, it remains preliminary as to third parties until the ancillary proceeding is concluded under Rule 32.2(c).

(B) *Notice and Inclusion in the Judgment.* The court must include the forfeiture when orally announcing the sentence or must otherwise ensure that the defendant knows of the forfeiture at sentencing. The court must also include the forfeiture order, directly or by reference, in the judgment, but the court's failure to do so may be corrected at any time under Rule 36.

(C) *Time to Appeal.* The time for the defendant or the government to file an appeal from the forfeiture order, or from the court's failure to enter an order, begins to run when judgment is entered. If the court later amends or declines to amend a forfeiture order to include additional property under Rule 32.2(e), the defendant or the government may file an appeal regarding that property under Federal Rule of Appellate Procedure 4(b). The time for that appeal runs from the date when the order granting or denying the amendment becomes final.

(5) *Jury Determination.*

(A) *Retaining the Jury.* In any case tried before a jury, if the indictment or information states that the government is seeking forfeiture, the court must determine before the jury begins deliberating whether either party requests that the jury be retained to determine the forfeitability of specific property if it returns a guilty verdict.

(B) *Special Verdict Form.* If a party timely requests to have the jury determine forfeiture, the government must submit a proposed Special Verdict Form listing each property subject to forfeiture and asking the jury to determine whether the government has established the requisite nexus between the property and the offense committed by the defendant.

(6) *Notice of the Forfeiture Order.*

(A) *Publishing and Sending Notice.* If the court orders the forfeiture of specific property, the government must publish notice of the order and send notice to any person who reasonably appears to be a potential claimant with standing to contest the forfeiture in the ancillary proceeding.

(B) *Content of the Notice.* The notice must describe the forfeited property, state the times under the applicable statute when a petition contesting the forfeiture must be filed, and state the name and contact information for the government attorney to be served with the petition.

(C) *Means of Publication; Exceptions to Publication Requirement.* Publication must take place as described in Supplemental Rule G(4)(a)(iii) of the Federal Rules of Civil Procedure, and may be by any means described in Supplemental Rule G(4)(a)(iv). Publication is unnecessary if any exception in Supplemental Rule G(4)(a)(i) applies.

(D) *Means of Sending the Notice.* The notice may be sent in accordance with Supplemental Rules G(4)(b)(iii)–(v) of the Federal Rules of Civil Procedure.

(7) *Interlocutory Sale.* At any time before entry of a final forfeiture order, the court, in accordance with Supplemental Rule G(7) of the Federal Rules of Civil Procedure, may order the interlocutory sale of property alleged to be forfeitable.

(c) Ancillary Proceeding; Entering a Final Order of Forfeiture.

(1) *In General.* If, as prescribed by statute, a third party files a petition asserting an interest in the property to be forfeited, the court must conduct an ancillary proceeding, but no ancillary proceeding is required to the extent that the forfeiture consists of a money judgment.

(A) In the ancillary proceeding, the court may, on motion, dismiss the petition for lack of standing, for failure to state a claim, or for any other lawful reason. For purposes of the motion, the facts set forth in the petition are assumed to be true.

(B) After disposing of any motion filed under Rule 32.2(c)(1)(A) and before conducting a hearing on the petition, the court may permit the parties to conduct discovery in accordance with the Federal Rules of Civil Procedure if the court determines that discovery is necessary or desirable to resolve factual issues. When discovery ends, a party may move for summary judgment under Federal Rule of Civil Procedure 56.

(2) *Entering a Final Order.* When the ancillary proceeding ends, the court must enter a final order of forfeiture by amending the preliminary order as necessary to account for any third-party rights. If no third party files a timely petition, the preliminary order becomes the final order of forfeiture if the court finds that the defendant (or any combination of defendants convicted in the case) had an interest in the property that is forfeitable under the applicable statute. The defendant may not object to the entry of the final order on the ground that the property belongs, in whole or in part, to a codefendant or third party; nor may a third party object to the final order on the ground that the third party had an interest in the property.

(3) *Multiple Petitions.* If multiple third-party petitions are filed in the same case, an order dismissing or granting one petition is not appealable until rulings are made on all the petitions, unless the court determines that there is no just reason for delay.

(4) *Ancillary Proceeding Not Part of Sentencing.* An ancillary proceeding is not part of sentencing.

(d) Stay Pending Appeal. If a defendant appeals from a conviction or an order of forfeiture, the court may stay the order of forfeiture on terms appropriate to ensure that the property remains available pending appellate review. A stay does not delay the ancillary proceeding or the determination of a third party's rights or interests. If the court rules in favor of any third party while an appeal is pending, the court may amend the order of forfeiture but must not transfer any property interest to a third party until the decision on appeal becomes final, unless the defendant consents in writing or on the record.

(e) Subsequently Located Property; Substitute Property.

(1) *In General.* On the government's motion, the court may at any time enter an order of forfeiture or amend an existing order of forfeiture to include property that:

> **(A)** is subject to forfeiture under an existing order of forfeiture but was located and identified after that order was entered; or

> **(B)** is substitute property that qualifies for forfeiture under an applicable statute.

(2) *Procedure.* If the government shows that the property is subject to forfeiture under Rule 32.2(e)(1), the court must:

(A) enter an order forfeiting that property, or amend an existing preliminary or final order to include it; and

(B) if a third party files a petition claiming an interest in the property, conduct an ancillary proceeding under Rule 32.2(c).

(3) *Jury Trial Limited.* There is no right to a jury trial under Rule 32.2(e).

Rule 33. New Trial

(a) Defendant's Motion. Upon the defendant's motion, the court may vacate any judgment and grant a new trial if the interest of justice so requires. If the case was tried without a jury, the court may take additional testimony and enter a new judgment.

(b) Time to File.

(1) *Newly Discovered Evidence.* Any motion for a new trial grounded on newly discovered evidence must be filed within 3 years after the verdict or finding of guilty. If an appeal is pending, the court may not grant a motion for a new trial until the appellate court remands the case.

(2) *Other Grounds.* Any motion for a new trial grounded on any reason other than newly discovered evidence must be filed within 14 days after the verdict or finding of guilty.

Rule 34. Arresting Judgment

(a) In General. Upon the defendant's motion or on its own, the court must arrest judgment if the court does not have jurisdiction of the charged offense.

(b) Time to File. The defendant must move to arrest judgment within 14 days after the court accepts a verdict or finding of guilty, or after a plea of guilty or nolo contendere.

Rule 35. Correcting or Reducing a Sentence

(a) Correcting Clear Error. Within 14 days after sentencing, the court may correct a sentence that resulted from arithmetical, technical, or other clear error.

(b) Reducing a Sentence for Substantial Assistance.

(1) *In General.* Upon the government's motion made within one year of sentencing, the court may reduce a sentence if the defendant, after sentencing, provided substantial assistance in investigating or prosecuting another person.

(2) *Later Motion.* Upon the government's motion made more than one year after sentencing, the court may reduce a sentence if the defendant's substantial assistance involved:

(A) information not known to the defendant until one year or more after sentencing;

(B) information provided by the defendant to the government within one year of sentencing, but which did not become useful to the government until more than one year after sentencing; or

(C) information the usefulness of which could not reasonably have been anticipated by the defendant until more than one year after sentencing and which was promptly provided to the government after its usefulness was reasonably apparent to the defendant.

(3) *Evaluating Substantial Assistance.* In evaluating whether the defendant has provided substantial assistance, the court may consider the defendant's presentence assistance.

(4) *Below Statutory Minimum.* When acting under Rule 35(b), the court may reduce the sentence to a level below the minimum sentence established by statute.

(c) "Sentencing" Defined. As used in this rule, "sentencing" means the oral announcement of the sentence.

Rule 36. Clerical Error

After giving any notice it considers appropriate, the court may at any time correct a clerical error in a judgment, order, or other part of the record, or correct an error in the record arising from oversight or omission.

Rule 37. Ruling on a Motion for Relief That Is Barred by a Pending Appeal

(a) Relief Pending Appeal. If a timely motion is made for relief that the court lacks authority to grant because of an appeal that has been docketed and is pending, the court may:

(1) defer considering the motion;

(2) deny the motion; or

(3) state either that it would grant the motion if the court of appeals remands for that purpose or that the motion raises a substantial issue.

(b) Notice to the Court of Appeals. The movant must promptly notify the circuit clerk under Federal Rule of Appellate Procedure 12.1 if the district court states that it would grant the motion or that the motion raises a substantial issue.

(c) Remand. The district court may decide the motion if the court of appeals remands for that purpose.

Rule 38. Staying a Sentence or a Disability

(a) Death Sentence. The court must stay a death sentence if the defendant appeals the conviction or sentence.

(b) Imprisonment.

(1) *Stay Granted.* If the defendant is released pending appeal, the court must stay a sentence of imprisonment.

(2) *Stay Denied; Place of Confinement.* If the defendant is not released pending appeal, the court may recommend to the Attorney General that the defendant be confined near the place of the trial or appeal for a period reasonably necessary to permit the defendant to assist in preparing the appeal.

(c) Fine. If the defendant appeals, the district court, or the court of appeals under Federal Rule of Appellate Procedure 8, may stay a sentence to pay a fine or a fine and costs. The court may stay the sentence on any terms considered appropriate and may require the defendant to:

(1) deposit all or part of the fine and costs into the district court's registry pending appeal;

(2) post a bond to pay the fine and costs; or

(3) submit to an examination concerning the defendant's assets and, if appropriate, order the defendant to refrain from dissipating assets.

(d) Probation. If the defendant appeals, the court may stay a sentence of probation. The court must set the terms of any stay.

(e) Restitution and Notice to Victims.

(1) *In General.* If the defendant appeals, the district court, or the court of appeals under Federal Rule of Appellate Procedure 8, may stay—on any terms considered appropriate—any sentence providing for restitution under 18 U.S.C. § 3556 or notice under 18 U.S.C. § 3555.

(2) *Ensuring Compliance.* The court may issue any order reasonably necessary to ensure compliance with a restitution order or a notice order after disposition of an appeal, including:

    (A) a restraining order;

    (B) an injunction;

    (C) an order requiring the defendant to deposit all or part of any monetary restitution into the district court's registry; or

    (D) an order requiring the defendant to post a bond.

(f) **Forfeiture.** A stay of a forfeiture order is governed by Rule 32.2(d).

(g) **Disability.** If the defendant's conviction or sentence creates a civil or employment disability under federal law, the district court, or the court of appeals under Federal Rule of Appellate Procedure 8, may stay the disability pending appeal on any terms considered appropriate. The court may issue any order reasonably necessary to protect the interest represented by the disability pending appeal, including a restraining order or an injunction.

Rule 39. [Reserved]

TITLE VIII. SUPPLEMENTARY AND SPECIAL PROCEEDINGS

Rule 40. Arrest for Failing to Appear in Another District or for Violating Conditions of Release Set in Another District

(a) **In General.** A person must be taken without unnecessary delay before a magistrate judge in the district of arrest if the person has been arrested under a warrant issued in another district for:

    (i) failing to appear as required by the terms of that person's release under 18 U.S.C. §§ 3141–3156 or by a subpoena; or

    (ii) violating conditions of release set in another district.

(b) **Proceedings.** The judge must proceed under Rule 5(c)(3) as applicable.

(c) **Release or Detention Order.** The judge may modify any previous release or detention order issued in another district, but must state in writing the reasons for doing so.

(d) **Video Teleconferencing.** Video teleconferencing may be used to conduct an appearance under this rule if the defendant consents.

Rule 41. Search and Seizure

(a) Scope and Definitions.

(1) *Scope.* This rule does not modify any statute regulating search or seizure, or the issuance and execution of a search warrant in special circumstances.

(2) *Definitions.* The following definitions apply under this rule:

(A) "Property" includes documents, books, papers, any other tangible objects, and information.

(B) "Daytime" means the hours between 6:00 a.m. and 10:00 p.m. according to local time.

(C) "Federal law enforcement officer" means a government agent (other than an attorney for the government) who is engaged in enforcing the criminal laws and is within any category of officers authorized by the Attorney General to request a search warrant.

(D) "Domestic terrorism" and "international terrorism" have the meanings set out in 18 U.S.C. § 2331.

(E) "Tracking device" has the meaning set out in 18 U.S.C. § 3117(b).

(b) Venue for a Warrant Application. At the request of a federal law enforcement officer or an attorney for the government:

(1) a magistrate judge with authority in the district—or if none is reasonably available, a judge of a state court of record in the district—has authority to issue a warrant to search for and seize a person or property located within the district;

(2) a magistrate judge with authority in the district has authority to issue a warrant for a person or property outside the district if the person or property is located within the district when the warrant is issued but might move or be moved outside the district before the warrant is executed;

(3) a magistrate judge—in an investigation of domestic terrorism or international terrorism—with authority in any district in which activities related to the terrorism may have occurred has authority to issue a warrant for a person or property within or outside that district;

(4) a magistrate judge with authority in the district has authority to issue a warrant to install within the district a tracking device; the warrant may authorize use of the device to track the movement of a person or property located within the district, outside the district, or both; and

(5) a magistrate judge having authority in any district where activities related to the crime may have occurred, or in the District of Columbia, may issue a warrant for property that is located outside the jurisdiction of any state or district, but within any of the following:

(A) a United States territory, possession, or commonwealth;

(B) the premises—no matter who owns them—of a United States diplomatic or consular mission in a foreign state, including any appurtenant building, part of a building, or land used for the mission's purposes; or

(C) a residence and any appurtenant land owned or leased by the United States and used by United States personnel assigned to a United States diplomatic or consular mission in a foreign state.

(6) a magistrate judge with authority in any district where activities related to a crime may have occurred has authority to issue a warrant to use remote access to search electronic storage media and to seize or copy electronically stored information located within or outside that district if:

(A) the district where the media or information is located has been concealed through technological means; or

(B) in an investigation of a violation of 18 U.S.C. § 1030(a)(5), the media are protected computers that have been damaged without authorization and are located in five or more districts.

(c) Persons or Property Subject to Search or Seizure. A warrant may be issued for any of the following:

(1) evidence of a crime;

(2) contraband, fruits of crime, or other items illegally possessed;

(3) property designed for use, intended for use, or used in committing a crime; or

(4) a person to be arrested or a person who is unlawfully restrained.

(d) Obtaining a Warrant.

(1) *In General.* After receiving an affidavit or other information, a magistrate judge—or if authorized by Rule 41(b), a judge of a state court of record—must issue the warrant if there is probable cause to search for and seize a person or property or to install and use a tracking device.

(2) *Requesting a Warrant in the Presence of a Judge.*

(A) *Warrant on an Affidavit.* When a federal law enforcement officer or an attorney for the government presents an affidavit in support of a warrant, the judge may require the affiant to appear personally and may examine under oath the affiant and any witness the affiant produces.

(B) *Warrant on Sworn Testimony.* The judge may wholly or partially dispense with a written affidavit and base a warrant on sworn testimony if doing so is reasonable under the circumstances.

(C) *Recording Testimony.* Testimony taken in support of a warrant must be recorded by a court reporter or by a suitable recording device, and the judge must file the transcript or recording with the clerk, along with any affidavit.

(3) *Requesting a Warrant by Telephonic or Other Reliable Electronic Means.* In accordance with Rule 4.1, a magistrate judge may issue a warrant based on information communicated by telephone or other reliable electronic means.

(e) Issuing the Warrant.

(1) *In General.* The magistrate judge or a judge of a state court of record must issue the warrant to an officer authorized to execute it.

(2) *Contents of the Warrant.*

(A) *Warrant to Search for and Seize a Person or Property.* Except for a tracking-device warrant, the warrant must identify the person or property to be searched, identify any person or property to be seized, and designate the magistrate judge to whom it must be returned. The warrant must command the officer to:

(i) execute the warrant within a specified time no longer than 14 days;

(ii) execute the warrant during the daytime, unless the judge for good cause expressly authorizes execution at another time; and

(iii) return the warrant to the magistrate judge designated in the warrant.

(B) *Warrant Seeking Electronically Stored Information.* A warrant under Rule 41(e)(2)(A) may authorize the seizure of electronic storage media or the seizure or copying of electronically stored information. Unless otherwise specified, the warrant authorizes a later review of the media or information consistent with the warrant. The time for executing the warrant in Rule

41(e)(2)(A) and (f)(1)(A) refers to the seizure or on-site copying of the media or information, and not to any later off-site copying or review.

(C) *Warrant for a Tracking Device.* A tracking-device warrant must identify the person or property to be tracked, designate the magistrate judge to whom it must be returned, and specify a reasonable length of time that the device may be used. The time must not exceed 45 days from the date the warrant was issued. The court may, for good cause, grant one or more extensions for a reasonable period not to exceed 45 days each. The warrant must command the officer to:

(i)   complete any installation authorized by the warrant within a specified time no longer than 10 days;

(ii)   perform any installation authorized by the warrant during the daytime, unless the judge for good cause expressly authorizes installation at another time; and

(iii) return the warrant to the judge designated in the warrant.

(f)   Executing and Returning the Warrant.

(1) *Warrant to Search for and Seize a Person or Property.*

(A) *Noting the Time.* The officer executing the warrant must enter on it the exact date and time it was executed.

(B) *Inventory.* An officer present during the execution of the warrant must prepare and verify an inventory of any property seized. The officer must do so in the presence of another officer and the person from whom, or from whose premises, the property was taken. If either one is not present, the officer must prepare and verify the inventory in the presence of at least one other credible person. In a case involving the seizure of electronic storage media or the seizure or copying of electronically stored information, the inventory may be limited to describing the physical storage media that were seized or copied. The officer may retain a copy of the electronically stored information that was seized or copied.

(C) *Receipt.* The officer executing the warrant must give a copy of the warrant and a receipt for the property taken to the person from whom, or from whose premises, the property was taken or leave a copy of the warrant and receipt at the place where the officer took the property. For a warrant to use remote access to search electronic storage media and seize or copy electronically stored information, the officer must make reasonable efforts to serve a copy of the warrant and receipt on the person whose property was searched or who possessed the information that was seized or copied. Service may be accomplished by any means, including electronic means, reasonably calculated to reach that person.

(D) *Return.* The officer executing the warrant must promptly return it—together with a copy of the inventory—to the magistrate judge designated on the warrant. The officer may do so by reliable electronic means. The judge must, on request, give a copy of the inventory to the person from whom, or from whose premises, the property was taken and to the applicant for the warrant.

(2) *Warrant for a Tracking Device.*

(A) *Noting the Time.* The officer executing a tracking-device warrant must enter on it the exact date and time the device was installed and the period during which it was used.

(B) *Return.* Within 10 days after the use of the tracking device has ended, the officer executing the warrant must return it to the judge designated in the warrant. The officer may do so by reliable electronic means.

(C) *Service.* Within 10 days after the use of the tracking device has ended, the officer executing a tracking-device warrant must serve a copy of the warrant on the person who was tracked or whose property was tracked. Service may be accomplished by delivering a copy to the person who, or whose property, was tracked; or by leaving a copy at the person's residence or usual place of abode with an individual of suitable age and discretion who resides at that location and by mailing a copy to the person's last known address. Upon request of the government, the judge may delay notice as provided in Rule 41(f)(3).

(3) *Delayed Notice.* Upon the government's request, a magistrate judge—or if authorized by Rule 41(b), a judge of a state court of record—may delay any notice required by this rule if the delay is authorized by statute.

(g) Motion to Return Property. A person aggrieved by an unlawful search and seizure of property or by the deprivation of property may move for the property's return. The motion must be filed in the district where the property was seized. The court must receive evidence on any factual issue necessary to decide the motion. If it grants the motion, the court must return the property to the movant, but may impose reasonable conditions to protect access to the property and its use in later proceedings.

(h) Motion to Suppress. A defendant may move to suppress evidence in the court where the trial will occur, as Rule 12 provides.

(i) Forwarding Papers to the Clerk. The magistrate judge to whom the warrant is returned must attach to the warrant a copy of the return, of the inventory, and of all other related papers and must deliver them to the clerk in the district where the property was seized.

Rule 42. Criminal Contempt

(a) Disposition After Notice. Any person who commits criminal contempt may be punished for that contempt after prosecution on notice.

(1) *Notice.* The court must give the person notice in open court, in an order to show cause, or in an arrest order. The notice must:

(A) state the time and place of the trial;

(B) allow the defendant a reasonable time to prepare a defense; and

(C) state the essential facts constituting the charged criminal contempt and describe it as such.

(2) *Appointing a Prosecutor.* The court must request that the contempt be prosecuted by an attorney for the government, unless the interest of justice requires the appointment of another attorney. If the government declines the request, the court must appoint another attorney to prosecute the contempt.

(3) *Trial and Disposition.* A person being prosecuted for criminal contempt is entitled to a jury trial in any case in which federal law so provides and must be released or detained as Rule 46 provides. If the criminal contempt involves disrespect toward or criticism of a judge, that judge is disqualified from presiding at the contempt trial or hearing unless the defendant consents. Upon a finding or verdict of guilty, the court must impose the punishment.

(b) Summary Disposition. Notwithstanding any other provision of these rules, the court (other than a magistrate judge) may summarily punish a person who commits criminal contempt in its presence if the judge saw or heard the contemptuous conduct and so certifies; a magistrate judge may summarily punish a person as provided in 28 U.S.C. § 636(e). The contempt order must recite the facts, be signed by the judge, and be filed with the clerk.

TITLE IX.   GENERAL PROVISIONS

Rule 43. Defendant's Presence

(a) When Required. Unless this rule, Rule 5, or Rule 10 provides otherwise, the defendant must be present at:

    (1) the initial appearance, the initial arraignment, and the plea;

    (2) every trial stage, including jury impanelment and the return of the verdict; and

    (3) sentencing.

(b) When Not Required. A defendant need not be present under any of the following circumstances:

    (1) *Organizational Defendant.* The defendant is an organization represented by counsel who is present.

    (2) *Misdemeanor Offense.* The offense is punishable by fine or by imprisonment for not more than one year, or both, and with the defendant's written consent, the court permits arraignment, plea, trial, and sentencing to occur by video teleconferencing or in the defendant's absence.

    (3) *Conference or Hearing on a Legal Question.* The proceeding involves only a conference or hearing on a question of law.

    (4) *Sentence Correction.* The proceeding involves the correction or reduction of sentence under Rule 35 or 18 U.S.C. § 3582(c).

(c) Waiving Continued Presence.

    (1) *In General.* A defendant who was initially present at trial, or who had pleaded guilty or nolo contendere, waives the right to be present under the following circumstances:

        (A) when the defendant is voluntarily absent after the trial has begun, regardless of whether the court informed the defendant of an obligation to remain during trial;

        (B) in a noncapital case, when the defendant is voluntarily absent during sentencing; or

        (C) when the court warns the defendant that it will remove the defendant from the courtroom for disruptive behavior, but the defendant persists in conduct that justifies removal from the courtroom.

    (2) *Waiver's Effect.* If the defendant waives the right to be present, the trial may proceed to completion, including the verdict's return and sentencing, during the defendant's absence.

Rule 44. Right to and Appointment of Counsel

(a) Right to Appointed Counsel. A defendant who is unable to obtain counsel is entitled to have counsel appointed to represent the defendant at every stage of the proceeding from initial appearance through appeal, unless the defendant waives this right.

(b) Appointment Procedure. Federal law and local court rules govern the procedure for implementing the right to counsel.

(c) Inquiry Into Joint Representation.

(1) *Joint Representation.* Joint representation occurs when:

(A) two or more defendants have been charged jointly under Rule 8(b) or have been joined for trial under Rule 13; and

(B) the defendants are represented by the same counsel, or counsel who are associated in law practice.

(2) *Court's Responsibilities in Cases of Joint Representation.* The court must promptly inquire about the propriety of joint representation and must personally advise each defendant of the right to the effective assistance of counsel, including separate representation. Unless there is good cause to believe that no conflict of interest is likely to arise, the court must take appropriate measures to protect each defendant's right to counsel.

Rule 45. Computing and Extending Time

(a) Computing Time. The following rules apply in computing any time period specified in these rules, in any local rule or court order, or in any statute that does not specify a method of computing time.

(1) *Period Stated in Days or a Longer Unit.* When the period is stated in days or a longer unit of time:

(A) exclude the day of the event that triggers the period;

(B) count every day, including intermediate Saturdays, Sundays, and legal holidays; and

(C) include the last day of the period, but if the last day is a Saturday, Sunday, or legal holiday, the period continues to run until the end of the next day that is not a Saturday, Sunday, or legal holiday.

(2) *Period Stated in Hours.* When the period is stated in hours:

(A) begin counting immediately on the occurrence of the event that triggers the period;

(B) count every hour, including hours during intermediate Saturdays, Sundays, and legal holidays; and

(C) if the period would end on a Saturday, Sunday, or legal holiday, the period continues to run until the same time on the next day that is not a Saturday, Sunday, or legal holiday.

(3) *Inaccessibility of the Clerk's Office.* Unless the court orders otherwise, if the clerk's office is inaccessible:

(A) on the last day for filing under Rule 45(a)(1), then the time for filing is extended to the first accessible day that is not a Saturday, Sunday, or legal holiday; or

(B) during the last hour for filing under Rule 45(a)(2), then the time for filing is extended to the same time on the first accessible day that is not a Saturday, Sunday, or legal holiday.

(4) *"Last Day" Defined.* Unless a different time is set by a statute, local rule, or court order, the last day ends:

(A) for electronic filing, at midnight in the court's time zone; and

(B) for filing by other means, when the clerk's office is scheduled to close.

(5) *"Next Day" Defined.* The "next day" is determined by continuing to count forward when the period is measured after an event and backward when measured before an event.

(6) *"Legal Holiday" Defined.* "Legal holiday" means:

(A) the day set aside by statute for observing New Year's Day, Martin Luther King Jr.'s Birthday, Washington's Birthday, Memorial Day, Independence Day, Labor Day, Columbus Day, Veterans' Day, Thanksgiving Day, or Christmas Day;

(B) any day declared a holiday by the President or Congress; and

(C) for periods that are measured after an event, any other day declared a holiday by the state where the district court is located.

(b) Extending Time.

(1) *In General.* When an act must or may be done within a specified period, the court on its own may extend the time, or for good cause may do so on a party's motion made:

(A) before the originally prescribed or previously extended time expires; or

(B) after the time expires if the party failed to act because of excusable neglect.

(2) *Exception.* The court may not extend the time to take any action under Rule 35, except as stated in that rule.

(c) **Additional Time After Certain Kinds of Service.** Whenever a party must or may act within a specified time after being served and service is made under Rule 49(a)(4)(C), (D), and (E), 3 days are added after the period would otherwise expire under subdivision (a).

Rule 46. Release from Custody; Supervising Detention

(a) **Before Trial.** The provisions of 18 U.S.C. §§ 3142 and 3144 govern pretrial release.

(b) **During Trial.** A person released before trial continues on release during trial under the same terms and conditions. But the court may order different terms and conditions or terminate the release if necessary to ensure that the person will be present during trial or that the person's conduct will not obstruct the orderly and expeditious progress of the trial.

(c) **Pending Sentencing or Appeal.** The provisions of 18 U.S.C. § 3143 govern release pending sentencing or appeal. The burden of establishing that the defendant will not flee or pose a danger to any other person or to the community rests with the defendant.

(d) **Pending Hearing on a Violation of Probation or Supervised Release.** Rule 32.1(a)(6) governs release pending a hearing on a violation of probation or supervised release.

(e) **Surety.** The court must not approve a bond unless any surety appears to be qualified. Every surety, except a legally approved corporate surety, must demonstrate by affidavit that its assets are adequate. The court may require the affidavit to describe the following:

(1) the property that the surety proposes to use as security;

(2) any encumbrance on that property;

(3) the number and amount of any other undischarged bonds and bail undertakings the surety has issued; and

(4) any other liability of the surety.

(f) **Bail Forfeiture.**

(1) *Declaration.* The court must declare the bail forfeited if a condition of the bond is breached.

(2) *Setting Aside.* The court may set aside in whole or in part a bail forfeiture upon any condition the court may impose if:

(A) the surety later surrenders into custody the person released on the surety's appearance bond; or

(B) it appears that justice does not require bail forfeiture.

(3) *Enforcement.*

(A) *Default Judgment and Execution.* If it does not set aside a bail forfeiture, the court must, upon the government's motion, enter a default judgment.

(B) *Jurisdiction and Service.* By entering into a bond, each surety submits to the district court's jurisdiction and irrevocably appoints the district clerk as its agent to receive service of any filings affecting its liability.

(C) *Motion to Enforce.* The court may, upon the government's motion, enforce the surety's liability without an independent action. The government must serve any motion, and notice as the court prescribes, on the district clerk. If so served, the clerk must promptly mail a copy to the surety at its last known address.

(4) *Remission.* After entering a judgment under Rule 46(f)(3), the court may remit in whole or in part the judgment under the same conditions specified in Rule 46(f)(2).

(g) Exoneration. The court must exonerate the surety and release any bail when a bond condition has been satisfied or when the court has set aside or remitted the forfeiture. The court must exonerate a surety who deposits cash in the amount of the bond or timely surrenders the defendant into custody.

(h) Supervising Detention Pending Trial.

(1) *In General.* To eliminate unnecessary detention, the court must supervise the detention within the district of any defendants awaiting trial and of any persons held as material witnesses.

(2) *Reports.* An attorney for the government must report biweekly to the court, listing each material witness held in custody for more than 10 days pending indictment, arraignment, or trial. For each material witness listed in the report, an attorney for the government must state why the witness should not be released with or without a deposition being taken under Rule 15(a).

(i) Forfeiture of Property. The court may dispose of a charged offense by ordering the forfeiture of 18 U.S.C. § 3142(c)(1)(B)(xi) property under 18 U.S.C. § 3146(d), if a fine in the amount of the property's value would be an appropriate sentence for the charged offense.

(j) Producing a Statement.

(1) *In General.* Rule 26.2(a)–(d) and (f) applies at a detention hearing under 18 U.S.C. § 3142, unless the court for good cause rules otherwise.

(2) *Sanctions for Not Producing a Statement.* If a party disobeys a Rule 26.2 order to produce a witness's statement, the court must not consider that witness's testimony at the detention hearing.

Rule 47. Motions and Supporting Affidavits

(a) In General. A party applying to the court for an order must do so by motion.

(b) Form and Content of a Motion. A motion—except when made during a trial or hearing—must be in writing, unless the court permits the party to make the motion by other means. A motion must state the grounds on which it is based and the relief or order sought. A motion may be supported by affidavit.

(c) Timing of a Motion. A party must serve a written motion—other than one that the court may hear ex parte—and any hearing notice at least 7 days before the hearing date, unless a rule or court order sets a different period. For good cause, the court may set a different period upon ex parte application.

(d) Affidavit Supporting a Motion. The moving party must serve any supporting affidavit with the motion. A responding party must serve any opposing affidavit at least one day before the hearing, unless the court permits later service.

Rule 48. Dismissal

(a) By the Government. The government may, with leave of court, dismiss an indictment, information, or complaint. The government may not dismiss the prosecution during trial without the defendant's consent.

(b) By the Court. The court may dismiss an indictment, information, or complaint if unnecessary delay occurs in:

(1) presenting a charge to a grand jury;

(2) filing an information against a defendant; or

(3) bringing a defendant to trial.

Rule 49. Serving and Filing Papers

(a) Service on a Party.

(1) *What is Required.* Each of the following must be served on every party: any written motion (other than one to be heard ex parte), written notice, designation of the record on appeal, or similar paper.

(2) *Serving a Party's Attorney.* Unless the court orders otherwise, when these rules or a court order requires or permits service on a party represented by an attorney, service must be made on the attorney instead of the party.

(3) *Service by Electronic Means.*

(A) *Using the Court's Electronic-Filing System.* A party represented by an attorney may serve a paper on a registered user by filing it with the court's electronic-filing system. A party not represented by an attorney may do so only if allowed by court order or local rule. Service is complete upon filing, but is not effective if the serving party learns that it did not reach the person to be served.

(B) *Using Other Electronic Means.* A paper may be served by any other electronic means that the person consented to in writing. Service is complete upon transmission, but is not effective if the serving party learns that it did not reach the person to be served.

(4) *Service by Nonelectronic Means.* A paper may be served by:

(A) handing it to the person;

(B) leaving it:

(i)   at the person's office with a clerk or other person in charge or, if no one is in charge, in a conspicuous place in the office; or

(ii) if the person has no office or the office is closed, at the person's dwelling or usual place of abode with someone of suitable age and discretion who resides there;

(C) mailing it to the person's last known address—in which event service is complete upon mailing;

(D) leaving it with the court clerk if the person has no known address; or

(E) delivering it by any other means that the person consented to in writing—in which event service is complete when the person making service delivers it to the agency designated to make delivery.

(b) Filing.

(1) *When Required; Certificate of Service.* Any paper that is required to be served must be filed no later than a reasonable time after service. No certificate of service is required when a paper is served by filing it with the court's electronic-filing system. When a paper is served by other means, a certificate of service must be filed with it or within a reasonable time after service or filing.

(2) *Means of Filing.*

(A) *Electronically.* A paper is filed electronically by filing it with the court's electronic-filing system. A filing made through a person's electronic-filing account and authorized by that person, together with the person's name on a signature block, constitutes the person's signature. A paper filed electronically is written or in writing under these rules.

(B) *Nonelectronically.* A paper not filed electronically is filed by delivering it:

(i)   to the clerk; or

(ii)   to a judge who agrees to accept it for filing, and who must then note the filing date on the paper and promptly send it to the clerk.

(3) *Means Used by Represented and Unrepresented Parties.*

(A) *Represented Party.* A party represented by an attorney must file electronically, unless nonelectronic filing is allowed by the court for good cause or is allowed or required by local rule.

(B) *Unrepresented Party.* A party not represented by an attorney must file nonelectronically, unless allowed to file electronically by court order or local rule.

(4) *Signature.* Every written motion and other paper must be signed by at least one attorney of record in the attorney's name—or by a person filing a paper if the person is not represented by an attorney. The paper must state the signer's address, e-mail address, and telephone number. Unless a rule or statute specifically states otherwise, a pleading need not be verified or accompanied by an affidavit. The court must strike an unsigned paper unless the omission is promptly corrected after being called to the attorney's or person's attention.

(5) *Acceptance by the Clerk.* The clerk must not refuse to file a paper solely because it is not in the form prescribed by these rules or by a local rule or practice.

(c) Service and Filing by Nonparties. A nonparty may serve and file a paper only if doing so is required or permitted by law. A nonparty must serve every party as required by Rule 49(a), but may use the court's electronic-filing system only if allowed by court order or local rule.

(d) Notice of a Court Order. When the court issues an order on any post-arraignment motion, the clerk must serve notice of the entry on each party as required by Rule 49(a). A party may also serve notice of the entry by the same means. Except as Federal Rule of Appellate Procedure 4(b) provides otherwise, the clerk's failure to give notice does not affect the time to appeal, or relieve—or authorize the court to relieve—a party's failure to appeal within the allowed time.

Rule 49.1. Privacy Protection for Filings Made with the Court

(a) Redacted Filings. Unless the court orders otherwise, in an electronic or paper filing with the court that contains an individual's social-security number, taxpayer-identification number, or birth date, the name of an individual known to be a minor, a financial-account number, or the home address of an individual, a party or nonparty making the filing may include only:

(1) the last four digits of the social-security number and taxpayer-identification number;

(2) the year of the individual's birth;

(3) the minor's initials;

(4) the last four digits of the financial-account number; and

(5) the city and state of the home address.

(b) Exemptions from the Redaction Requirement. The redaction requirement does not apply to the following:

(1) a financial-account number or real property address that identifies the property allegedly subject to forfeiture in a forfeiture proceeding;

(2) the record of an administrative or agency proceeding;

(3) the official record of a state-court proceeding;

(4) the record of a court or tribunal, if that record was not subject to the redaction requirement when originally filed;

(5) a filing covered by Rule 49.1(d);

(6) a pro se filing in an action brought under 28 U.S.C. §§ 2241, 2254, or 2255;

(7) a court filing that is related to a criminal matter or investigation and that is prepared before the filing of a criminal charge or is not filed as part of any docketed criminal case;

(8) an arrest or search warrant; and

(9) a charging document and an affidavit filed in support of any charging document.

(c) Immigration Cases. A filing in an action brought under 28 U.S.C. § 2241 that relates to the petitioner's immigration rights is governed by Federal Rule of Civil Procedure 5.2.

(d) Filings Made Under Seal. The court may order that a filing be made under seal without redaction. The court may later unseal the filing or order the person who made the filing to file a redacted version for the public record.

(e) Protective Orders. For good cause, the court may by order in a case:

(1) require redaction of additional information; or

(2) limit or prohibit a nonparty's remote electronic access to a document filed with the court.

(f) Option for Additional Unredacted Filing Under Seal. A person making a redacted filing may also file an unredacted copy under seal. The court must retain the unredacted copy as part of the record.

(g) Option for Filing a Reference List. A filing that contains redacted information may be filed together with a reference list that identifies each item of redacted information and specifies an appropriate identifier that uniquely corresponds to each item listed. The list must be filed under seal and may be amended as of right. Any reference in the case to a listed identifier will be construed to refer to the corresponding item of information.

(h) Waiver of Protection of Identifiers. A person waives the protection of Rule 49.1(a) as to the person's own information by filing it without redaction and not under seal.

Rule 50. Prompt Disposition

Scheduling preference must be given to criminal proceedings as far as practicable.

Rule 51. Preserving Claimed Error

(a) Exceptions Unnecessary. Exceptions to rulings or orders of the court are unnecessary.

(b) Preserving a Claim of Error. A party may preserve a claim of error by informing the court—when the court ruling or order is made or sought—of the action the party wishes the court to take, or the party's objection to the court's action and the grounds for that objection. If a party does not have an opportunity to object to a ruling or order, the absence of an objection does not later prejudice that party. A ruling or order that admits or excludes evidence is governed by Federal Rule of Evidence 103.

Rule 52. Harmless and Plain Error

(a) Harmless Error. Any error, defect, irregularity, or variance that does not affect substantial rights must be disregarded.

(b) Plain Error. A plain error that affects substantial rights may be considered even though it was not brought to the court's attention.

Rule 53. Courtroom Photographing and Broadcasting Prohibited

Except as otherwise provided by a statute or these rules, the court must not permit the taking of photographs in the courtroom during judicial proceedings or the broadcasting of judicial proceedings from the courtroom.

Rule 54. [Transferred]

[Editor's Note: In the 2002 restyling of the Criminal Rules, all of Rule 54 was transferred to Rule 1.]

Rule 55. Records

The clerk of the district court must keep records of criminal proceedings in the form prescribed by the Director of the Administrative Office of the United States courts. The clerk must enter in the records every court order or judgment and the date of entry.

Rule 56. When Court is Open

(a) In General. A district court is considered always open for any filing, and for issuing and returning process, making a motion, or entering an order.

(b) Office Hours. The clerk's office—with the clerk or a deputy in attendance—must be open during business hours on all days except Saturdays, Sundays, and legal holidays.

(c) Special Hours. A court may provide by local rule or order that its clerk's office will be open for specified hours on Saturdays or legal holidays other than those set aside by statute for observing New Year's Day, Martin Luther King, Jr.'s Birthday, Washington's Birthday, Memorial Day, Independence Day, Labor Day, Columbus Day, Veterans' Day, Thanksgiving Day, and Christmas Day.

Rule 57. District Court Rules

(a) In General.

(1) *Adopting Local Rules.* Each district court acting by a majority of its district judges may, after giving appropriate public notice and an opportunity to comment, make and amend rules governing its practice. A local rule must be consistent with—but not duplicative of—federal statutes and rules adopted under 28 U.S.C. § 2072 and must conform to any uniform numbering system prescribed by the Judicial Conference of the United States.

(2) *Limiting Enforcement.* A local rule imposing a requirement of form must not be enforced in a manner that causes a party to lose rights because of an unintentional failure to comply with the requirement.

(b) Procedure When There Is No Controlling Law. A judge may regulate practice in any manner consistent with federal law, these rules, and the local rules of the district. No sanction or other disadvantage may be imposed for noncompliance with any requirement not in federal law, federal rules, or the local district rules unless the alleged violator was furnished with actual notice of the requirement before the noncompliance.

(c) Effective Date and Notice. A local rule adopted under this rule takes effect on the date specified by the district court and remains in effect unless amended by the district court or abrogated by the judicial council of the circuit in which the district is located. Copies of local rules and their amendments, when promulgated, must be furnished to the judicial council and the Administrative Office of the United States Courts and must be made available to the public.

Rule 58. Petty Offenses and Other Misdemeanors

(a) Scope.

(1) *In General.* These rules apply in petty offense and other misdemeanor cases and on appeal to a district judge in a case tried by a magistrate judge, unless this rule provides otherwise.

(2) *Petty Offense Case Without Imprisonment.* In a case involving a petty offense for which no sentence of imprisonment will be imposed, the court may follow any provision of these rules that is not inconsistent with this rule and that the court considers appropriate.

(3) *Definition.* As used in this rule, the term "petty offense for which no sentence of imprisonment will be imposed" means a petty offense for which the court determines that, in the event of conviction, no sentence of imprisonment will be imposed.

(b) Pretrial Procedure.

(1) *Charging Document.* The trial of a misdemeanor may proceed on an indictment, information, or complaint. The trial of a petty offense may also proceed on a citation or violation notice.

(2) *Initial Appearance.* At the defendant's initial appearance on a petty offense or other misdemeanor charge, the magistrate judge must inform the defendant of the following:

(A) the charge, and the minimum and maximum penalties, including imprisonment, fines, any special assessment under 18 U.S.C. § 3013, and restitution under 18 U.S.C. § 3556;

(B) the right to retain counsel;

(C) the right to request the appointment of counsel if the defendant is unable to retain counsel—unless the charge is a petty offense for which the appointment of counsel is not required;

(D) the defendant's right not to make a statement, and that any statement made may be used against the defendant;

(E) the right to trial, judgment, and sentencing before a district judge—unless:

(i)   the charge is a petty offense; or

(ii) the defendant consents to trial, judgment, and sentencing before a magistrate judge;

(F) the right to a jury trial before either a magistrate judge or a district judge—unless the charge is a petty offense;

(G) any right to a preliminary hearing under Rule 5.1, and the general circumstances, if any, under which the defendant may secure pretrial release; and

(H) that a defendant who is not a United States citizen may request that an attorney for the government or a federal law enforcement official notify a consular officer from the defendant's country of nationality that the defendant has been arrested—but that even without the defendant's request, a treaty or other international agreement may require consular notification.

(3) *Arraignment.*

(A) *Plea Before a Magistrate Judge.* A magistrate judge may take the defendant's plea in a petty offense case. In every other misdemeanor case, a magistrate judge may take the plea only if the defendant consents either in writing or on the record to be tried before a magistrate judge and specifically waives trial before a district judge. The defendant may plead not guilty, guilty, or (with the consent of the magistrate judge) nolo contendere.

(B) *Failure to Consent.* Except in a petty offense case, the magistrate judge must order a defendant who does not consent to trial before a magistrate judge to appear before a district judge for further proceedings.

(c) Additional Procedures in Certain Petty Offense Cases. The following procedures also apply in a case involving a petty offense for which no sentence of imprisonment will be imposed:

(1) *Guilty or Nolo Contendere Plea.* The court must not accept a guilty or nolo contendere plea unless satisfied that the defendant understands the nature of the charge and the maximum possible penalty.

(2) *Waiving Venue.*

(A) *Conditions of Waiving Venue.* If a defendant is arrested, held, or present in a district different from the one where the indictment, information, complaint, citation, or violation notice is pending, the defendant may state in writing a desire to plead guilty or nolo contendere; to waive venue and trial in the district where the proceeding is pending; and to consent to the court's disposing of the case in the district where the defendant was arrested, is held, or is present.

(B) *Effect of Waiving Venue.* Unless the defendant later pleads not guilty, the prosecution will proceed in the district where the defendant was arrested, is held, or is present. The district clerk must notify the clerk in the original district of the defendant's waiver of venue. The defendant's statement of a desire to plead guilty or nolo contendere is not admissible against the defendant.

(3) *Sentencing.* The court must give the defendant an opportunity to be heard in mitigation and then proceed immediately to sentencing. The court may, however, postpone sentencing to allow the probation service to investigate or to permit either party to submit additional information.

(4) *Notice of a Right to Appeal.* After imposing sentence in a case tried on a not-guilty plea, the court must advise the defendant of a right to appeal the conviction and of any right to appeal the sentence. If the defendant was convicted on a plea of guilty or nolo contendere, the court must advise the defendant of any right to appeal the sentence.

(d) Paying a Fixed Sum in Lieu of Appearance.

(1) *In General.* If the court has a local rule governing forfeiture of collateral, the court may accept a fixed-sum payment in lieu of the defendant's appearance and end the case, but the fixed sum may not exceed the maximum fine allowed by law.

(2) *Notice to Appear.* If the defendant fails to pay a fixed sum, request a hearing, or appear in response to a citation or violation notice, the district clerk or a magistrate judge may issue a notice for the defendant to appear before the court on a date certain. The notice may give the defendant an additional opportunity to pay a fixed sum in lieu of appearance. The district clerk must serve the notice on the defendant by mailing a copy to the defendant's last known address.

(3) ***Summons or Warrant.*** Upon an indictment, or upon a showing by one of the other charging documents specified in Rule 58(b)(1) of probable cause to believe that an offense has been committed and that the defendant has committed it, the court may issue an arrest warrant or, if no warrant is requested by an attorney for the government, a summons. The showing of probable cause must be made under oath or under penalty of perjury, but the affiant need not appear before the court. If the defendant fails to appear before the court in response to a summons, the court may summarily issue a warrant for the defendant's arrest.

(e) Recording the Proceedings. The court must record any proceedings under this rule by using a court reporter or a suitable recording device.

(f) New Trial. Rule 33 applies to a motion for a new trial.

(g) Appeal.

(1) ***From a District Judge's Order or Judgment.*** The Federal Rules of Appellate Procedure govern an appeal from a district judge's order or a judgment of conviction or sentence.

(2) ***From a Magistrate Judge's Order or Judgment.***

(A) *Interlocutory Appeal.* Either party may appeal an order of a magistrate judge to a district judge within 14 days of its entry if a district judge's order could similarly be appealed. The party appealing must file a notice with the clerk specifying the order being appealed and must serve a copy on the adverse party.

(B) *Appeal from a Conviction or Sentence.* A defendant may appeal a magistrate judge's judgment of conviction or sentence to a district judge within 14 days of its entry. To appeal, the defendant must file a notice with the clerk specifying the judgment being appealed and must serve a copy on an attorney for the government.

(C) *Record.* The record consists of the original papers and exhibits in the case; any transcript, tape, or other recording of the proceedings; and a certified copy of the docket entries. For purposes of the appeal, a copy of the record of the proceedings must be made available to a defendant who establishes by affidavit an inability to pay or give security for the record. The

Director of the Administrative Office of the United States Courts must pay for those copies.

(D) *Scope of Appeal.* The defendant is not entitled to a trial de novo by a district judge. The scope of the appeal is the same as in an appeal to the court of appeals from a judgment entered by a district judge.

(3) *Stay of Execution and Release Pending Appeal.* Rule 38 applies to a stay of a judgment of conviction or sentence. The court may release the defendant pending appeal under the law relating to release pending appeal from a district court to a court of appeals.

Rule 59. Matters Before a Magistrate Judge

(a) Nondispositive Matters. A district judge may refer to a magistrate judge for determination any matter that does not dispose of a charge or defense. The magistrate judge must promptly conduct the required proceedings and, when appropriate, enter on the record an oral or written order stating the determination. A party may serve and file objections to the order within 14 days after being served with a copy of a written order or after the oral order is stated on the record, or at some other time the court sets. The district judge must consider timely objections and modify or set aside any part of the order that is contrary to law or clearly erroneous. Failure to object in accordance with this rule waives a party's right to review.

(b) Dispositive Matters.

(1) *Referral to Magistrate Judge.* A district judge may refer to a magistrate judge for recommendation a defendant's motion to dismiss or quash an indictment or information, a motion to suppress evidence, or any matter that may dispose of a charge or defense. The magistrate judge must promptly conduct the required proceedings. A record must be made of any evidentiary proceeding and of any other proceeding if the magistrate judge considers it necessary. The magistrate judge must enter on the record a recommendation for disposing of the matter, including any proposed findings of fact. The clerk must immediately serve copies on all parties.

(2) *Objections to Findings and Recommendations.* Within 14 days after being served with a copy of the recommended disposition, or at some other time the court sets, a party may serve and file specific written objections to the proposed findings and recommendations. Unless the district judge directs otherwise, the objecting party must promptly arrange for transcribing the record, or whatever portions of it the parties agree to or the magistrate judge considers sufficient.

Failure to object in accordance with this rule waives a party's right to review.

(3) *De Novo Review of Recommendations.* The district judge must consider de novo any objection to the magistrate judge's recommendation. The district judge may accept, reject, or modify the recommendation, receive further evidence, or resubmit the matter to the magistrate judge with instructions.

Rule 60. Victim's Rights

(a) In General.

(1) *Notice of a Proceeding.* The government must use its best efforts to give the victim reasonable, accurate, and timely notice of any public court proceeding involving the crime.

(2) *Attending the Proceeding.* The court must not exclude a victim from a public court proceeding involving the crime, unless the court determines by clear and convincing evidence that the victim's testimony would be materially altered if the victim heard other testimony at that proceeding. In determining whether to exclude a victim, the court must make every effort to permit the fullest attendance possible by the victim and must consider reasonable alternatives to exclusion. The reasons for any exclusion must be clearly stated on the record.

(3) *Right to Be Heard on Release, a Plea, or Sentencing.* The court must permit a victim to be reasonably heard at any public proceeding in the district court concerning release, plea, or sentencing involving the crime.

(b) Enforcement and Limitations.

(1) *Time for Deciding a Motion.* The court must promptly decide any motion asserting a victim's rights described in these rules.

(2) *Who May Assert the Rights.* A victim's rights described in these rules may be asserted by the victim, the victim's lawful representative, the attorney for the government, or any other person as authorized by 18 U.S.C. § 3771(d) and (e).

(3) *Multiple Victims.* If the court finds that the number of victims makes it impracticable to accord all of them their rights described in these rules, the court must fashion a reasonable procedure that gives effect to these rights without unduly complicating or prolonging the proceedings.

(4) *Where Rights May Be Asserted.* A victim's rights described in these rules must be asserted in the district where a defendant is being prosecuted for the crime.

(5) *Limitations on Relief.* A victim may move to reopen a plea or sentence only if:

(A) the victim asked to be heard before or during the proceeding at issue, and the request was denied;

(B) the victim petitions the court of appeals for a writ of mandamus within 10 days after the denial, and the writ is granted; and

(C) in the case of a plea, the accused has not pleaded to the highest offense charged.

(6) *No New Trial.* A failure to afford a victim any right described in these rules is not grounds for a new trial.

Rule 61. Title

These rules may be known and cited as the Federal Rules of Criminal Procedure.